Lecture Notes in Economics and Mathematical Systems

Managing Editors: M. Beckmann and W. Krelle

356

P. Korhonen   A. Lewandowski
J. Wallenius (Eds.)

Multiple Criteria Decision Support

Proceedings of the International Workshop
Held in Helsinki, Finland, August 7–11, 1989

Springer-Verlag
Berlin Heidelberg New York London Paris
Tokyo Hong Kong Barcelona Budapest

ISBN 3-540-53895-X Springer-Verlag Berlin Heidelberg New York
ISBN 0-387-53895-X Springer-Verlag New York Berlin Heidelberg

Printing and binding: Druckhaus Beltz, Hemsbach/Bergstr.
2142/3140-543210 − Printed on acid-free paper

TP

Preface

Multiple Criteria Decision Making has been an important and active research area for some 20 years. In the 1970's, research focused on the theory of multiple objective mathematical programming and on procedures for solving multiple objective mathematical programming problems. During the 1980's, we observed a shift in emphasis towards multiple criteria decision support. Accordingly, much research has focused on the user interface, the behavioral foundations of decision making, and on supporting the entire decision-making process from problem structuring to solution implementation. Because of the shift in research emphasis we decided to make "Multiple Criteria Decision Support" the theme for our International Workshop, which was held at Suomen Säästöpankkiopisto in Espoo, Finland (10 miles west of Helsinki), August 7-11, 1989. We wanted to discuss "Decision Support" in the broad sense, and therefore preferred "Multiple Criteria Decision Support" to "Multiple Criteria Decision Support Systems" as the theme for the Workshop.

The Workshop was organized by the Helsinki School of Economics, and sponsored by the Helsinki School of Economics and the International Institute for Applied Systems Analysis (I.I.A.S.A.), Austria.

In total, 79 scholars from 20 countries attended the Workshop. Fifty eight papers were presented. The Workshop was opened by Dr. Jaakko Honko, former Chancellor of the Helsinki School of Economics, and the Welcoming Address was delivered by Mr. Pertti Salolainen, Minister for Foreign Trade for Finland. The Workshop emphasized the development, design, and application of decision support mechanisms in structuring and solving real-world decision problems. The Workshop consisted of three plenary lectures, a series of parallel sessions, four discussion groups, and a panel discussion regarding the state–of–the–art and future directions of multiple criteria decision support. The plenary lectures were delivered by Professor Stanley Zionts ("Negotiations and MCDM: Their Interrelationships"), Professor H. Nakayama ("Tradeoff Analysis Based Upon Parametric Optimization"), and Professor Ralph Steuer ("The History of MCDM in Pictures"). The lectures by Zionts and Nakayama have been reproduced in these Proceedings. Steuer's lecture was unique, but due to the nature of the presentation, we were unable to reproduce it in print.

The following discussion groups were organized:

- How to Get Managers Interested in MCDS? (chaired by Professor J. Spronk),

- Should We Pay More Attention to the Behavioral Aspects of MCDM? (chaired by Professor H. Moskowitz),

- How to Get More Out of Computer Graphics? (chaired by Professor A. Lewandowski),

- Why is Groupware not Widely Used in Practice? (chaired by Professor G. Kersten).

This Proceedings volume consists of most of the papers presented at the Workshop, the Welcoming Address by Mr. Pertti Salolainen, and the list of participants. The discussion groups and the panel discussion were very active, but no reports have been produced based on these discussions. In future Workshops one should document such discussions for the benefit of the research community.

The papers have been classified into six groups:

Part 1: Theory and Methodology of Multiple Criteria Decision Support (9 papers)

Part 2: Methods and Procedures for Multiple Criteria Decision Support (7 papers)

Part 3: Multiple Criteria Decision Support Systems (8 papers)

Part 4: Design of Multiple Criteria Decision Support (7 papers)

Part 5: Applications of Multiple Criteria Decision Support (6 papers)

Part 6: Decision Support for Negotiations (6 papers)

This volume provides an up-to-date coverage of the theory and practice of multiple criteria decision support. We trust that it will serve the research community as well as the previously published Conference Proceedings based on I.I.A.S.A. Workshops.

We wish to express our thanks to all organizations and individuals who helped us in organizing this Workshop. We also thank the participants and, in particular, the contributors to this volume.

A special thanks is due to Dr. Jaakko Honko, former Chancellor of the Helsinki School of Economics, and chairman of the International Advisory Committee of the Workshop, without whose help this Workshop could not have been organized.

We wish to thank Prof. Alexander Kurzhanski, System and Decision Sciences Program at I.I.A.S.A., and I.I.A.S.A. as an organization, for sponsoring this Workshop, and for arranging the publishing and printing of these Proceedings.

We would also like to thank the staff of the Local Organizing committee, consisting of Ms. Merja Halme, Mr. Markku Kuula, Ms. Johanna Pajunen, and Ms. Leena Tanner, all Ph.D. students at the Helsinki School of Economics, for its valuable help. Special thanks are due to Ms. Susanne Nyyssölä (the Helsinki School of Economics), who was our Workshop secretary.

The contributions of the following individuals to the social program of the Workshop are gratefully acknowledged: Ms. Kaiju Haanpää, Mr. Olavi Haanpää, Mr. Pekka Korpinen, Mr. Erkki Saarinen, Mr. Viljo Taipalvesi, Mr. Antti Valonen, and Mrs. Hannele Wallenius.

Mr. Tadeusz Rogowski, Institute of Automatic Control, Warsaw University of Technology, organized typing the Proceedings in a professional manner. Dr. Marek Makowski, I.I.A.S.A., coordinated the processing of this Proceedings volume.

Financial support from the following organizations is gratefully acknowledged: Foundation of Economic Education (Finland), the Ministry of Education (Finland), the Jahnsson Foundation (Finland), the Helsinki School of Economics, Foundation of the Helsinki School of Economics, Kansallis-Osake-Pankki (Finland), Finnair, Suomen Säästöpankkiopisto (Finland), and City of Karkkila (Finland).

Pekka J. Korhonen
Helsinki School
of Economics
Workshop Organizer

Andrzej Lewandowski
Wayne State University
Secretary of the International Advisory Committee

Jyrki Wallenius
Helsinki School
of Economics
Workshop Organizer

Helsinki, October 23, 1990

Welcoming Address
Pertti Salolainen, Minister for Foreign Trade, Finland

Ladies and Gentlemen:

The motivation for the establishment of the International Institute for Applied Systems Analysis in Laxenburg, Austria, 17 years ago was to make it possible for scientists from East and West to work together on significant problems of common concern. This, I believe, is still a primary goal of the Institute. Other objectives include:

- to increase international collaboration in general;

- to contribute to the advancement of systems analysis;

- to achieve application to problems of international importance.

At IIASA research is conducted in several programs, such as energy, food and agriculture, environment, human services, management and technology, and last but not least system and decision sciences program. Over the years, significant accomplishments have been made. An impressive number of scientific papers have been published. However, as always, even greater challenges lie ahead of us. Examples of such challenges are the advancement of systems analysis and its use in policy–making and international conflict resolution.

Finland joined IIASA as a member country several years ago. At the time Finland saw it important to advance the international scientific collaboration between East and West. This is very true still today. I believe that IIASA's objectives are as worthwhile today as they were 17 years ago. The Finnish IIASA Committee was founded to coordinate the involvement and participation of Finnish systems scientists in the activities of IIASA. Over the years, numerous Finnish scientists have conducted research in IIASA's different programs. In addition, annually approximately 100 Finnish scholars attend conferences and meetings organized by IIASA in different countries. Also, several Finnish graduate students have participated or are participating in IIASA's Young Scientists Summer Programs. However, this meeting that falls under the auspieces of the Systems and Decision Sciences program is one of the first IIASA workshops organized in Finland. It pleases me that a meeting is organized at the Helsinki School of Economics in such a modern and important research field as Multiple Criteria Decision Support. I believe that the desire to organize this meeting in Finland reflects the fact that the research conducted by Finnish scholars in this field is internationally highly regarded.

All of us who work in the Government or the business sector make decisions that involve tradeoffs between multiple objectives or criteria. Some better, some worse. The problem is old, but it pleases me that serious efforts are under way to provide analytical support for decision and policy making. However, in conducting scientific research one should bear in mind what the economist, Professor Tobin stated, namely that applications are the ultimate raison d'etre of our science.

Incidentally, the Finnish Government has applied multiple objective models and decision support systems in the past to help improve efficiency of operations or obtain a better understanding of complex decision processes. An example of such an application is a study performed in cooperation with the National Board of Economic Defense to help prepare contingency plans for various emergency management situations, such as nuclear power plant accidents, trade embargoes, and international conflicts. Another important application concerns the problem of stockpiling critical materials in case of an emergency situation. With the help of these models Finland is now better prepared to face various emergency management situations. The use of microcomputers, with all their modern enhancements, has become an essential component of such systems.

In general, it is my opinion that the public sector in Finland has maintained a belief in the usefulness of applying analytical decision tools in problem solving in one form or the other. For example, during the 1970's the Ministry of Finance systematically trained government employees in the use of quantitative models in problem oriented sessions. Naturally, even greater challenges lie ahead of us in improving the efficiency of government operations.

It pleases me to see such a distinguished group of scientists gathered in Finland. I would like to welcome all of you to this annual IIASA workshop. I trust that you will have a fruitful and worthwhile meeting. Those of you who are in Finland for the first time, please take the time to explore our beautiful capital. You will realize that Finland is much more than an exotic land of midnight sun and innumerable lakes. The world may recognize the Finnish origin of "sauna" and "sisu" and pay respect to Jean Sibelius as a composer of truly international stature, but these symbols cannot as such portray an image of Finland that would do justice to the diversity of the nation's cultural and economic life.

Table of Contents

Part 1
Theory and Methodology of Multiple Criteria Decision Support

Part 2

Methods and Procedures for Multiple Criteria Decision Support

Part 3

Multiple Criteria Decision Support Systems

Part 4

Design of Multiple Criteria Decision Support

Part 5

Applications of Multiple Criteria Decision Support

Part 6

Decision Support for Negotiations

Part 1

Theory and Methodology of Multiple Criteria Decision Support

Constraints and Uncertainty

Willem-Max van den Bergh, Winfried Hallerbach
Jaap Spronk
Department of Finance
Erasmus University
POBox 1738, NL–3000 DR Rotterdam
The Netherlands

1 Introduction

In the ideal world underlying standard financial theory, financial planning is not much of a problem. That is because mutually independent projects are assumed, of which the cash flows (or probability distributions of cash flows) are given, possibly together with a series of contingent claims (roughly: rights and duties connected with the project which can be exercised depending on the future state of the cash flows). In such a world, the main task of financial theory is to value the cash flows and the contingent claims associated with the project. The decision to either accept or reject the project thus depends on criteria such as the Net Present Value (NPV):

$$\sum_t \frac{CF_t}{(1+R_t)^t} \underset{<}{\overset{>}{=}} 0 \tag{1}$$

or the NPV adjusted for the value of the contingent claims:

$$\sum_t \frac{CF_t}{(1+R_t)^t} + V(\text{ContingentClaims}) \underset{<}{\overset{>}{=}} 0, \tag{2}$$

where CF_t stands for the cash flow at time t, R_t is the corresponding discount rate, reflecting the risk of the cash flow, and $V(\cdot)$ denotes the current market value of the expression between brackets.

However, the operationalization of the above decision criteria is troublesome. Notably, cash flow distributions can generally **not** be assumed to be given and fixed, contingent claims are often hard to recognize and projects are generally **not** independent of each other. Moreover, the risk premium — and thus the discount rate R_t — to be applied in the discounting of future cash flows will often be dependent on the contingent claims given to the suppliers of capital and other parties. Financial theory still has no complete solution for the problem of pricing cash flows and contingent claims.

In this paper, we discuss two practical aspects of financial planning, viz. (1) the problem of project interdependencies, to be discussed in the second section and (2) the problem that real decision makers have a far from complete picture of the uncertainties involved in undertaking projects (section 3). We will hypothesize that decision makers solve these problems among others by imposing constraints on projects and combinations of projects, possibly creating other interdependencies between projects. Two major classes of risk reduction instruments are discussed in section 3 whereas in section 4 we adress the question how to value the use of indicated risk reductions. Section 5 summarizes our conclusions.

2 Interdependencies between projects

Investment projects may depend **directly** or **indirectly** on each other and/or on the existing firm (which may be viewed as an interdependent bundle of projects). Projects **A** and **B** are said to be **directly dependent**, if the acceptance of project **A** leads to a change in the cash flows and/or the contingent claims connected with project **B** and/or vice versa. The solution of this interdependency problem is straightforward: For each cluster of interrelated projects, write down all possible combinations of projects. Treat these combinations as mutually exclusive alternatives and choose the alternative with the highest value, for instance on basis of the NPV-rule (1). Alternatively, discounting future cash flows of each project combination can take place under the assumption that no claims of third parties exist; next the net value of these claims should be taken into account in order to arrive at the Adjusted Present Value (2).

Projects are said to be **indirectly interdependent** if there are constraints on combinations of projects. We distinguish between three kinds of constraints:

(a) **hard** constraints,

(b) **self-imposed** constraints

(c) **game-type** constraints (cf. Spronk, 1985).

The solution of the problem of hard constraints (e.g. logical constraints or legal constraints) is again straightforward: as with directly dependent projects, write down the list of all combinations of projects. Check which of these combinations do and which do not meet the hard constraints and reject the latter. Treat the remaining combinations as mutually exclusive alternatives and select the one with the highest market value. In contrast to hard constraints, self-imposed constraints are by definition determined by the decision-maker himself, either to safeguard the qualities of the decision alternatives under consideration or to enlarge the chance that the alternative selected will indeed materialize. Game-type constraints are a particular kind of self-imposed constraints. That is, in game-type decision situations, decision-makers often limit their space of action (i.e. use self-imposed constraints) in order to 'take account of the other parties', either to limit the risk of 'backfiring' (which is clearly a risk consideration) or as an end in itself (which is a preference consideration: the preferences of the other player are partly included in the decision maker's own preferences).

As shown in (Spronk, 1981, 1985), both self-imposed and game-type constraints can be handled by using interactive multiple objective programming procedures using flexible constraints.

3 Uncertainty

Because the limited human capacity of understanding the complexities of the real world, the modelling of uncertainty is **always incomplete**. There are at least two ways to attack this problem, which certainly do not exclude each other:

a. Try to find a description of the projects which is as good as possible. The support which can be offered to the decision-maker consists essentially of collecting and structuring information.

b. Try to find ways to 'change the chances' which is often also possible in cases in which the chances are not known. One way to achieve this is to exclude certain investment possibilities. For instance, one may choose not to invest in certain countries to limit the political risk of the investment. Another way is to sell or acquire contingent claims on certain outcomes of the projects involved.

One way to structure the description of capital investment projects is to use **'project profiles'** (cf. Hallerbach and Spronk, 1986, and Spronk, 1989). A project profile ideally includes the following elements:

– **expectations** with respect to the cash flows of the project

– **sensitivities** of these cash flows for **unexpected changes** in factors which are known to influence the project's outcomes. For example, the level of the cash flows may decrease with 0.7% for each percent increase in the dollar price, ceteris paribus.

– **contingent claims** connected with the project, roughly speaking the 'rights and duties' available when a certain condition will materialize in the uncertain future. For instance, the 'right' to expand (or abandon) the project when demand is higher (or lower) than the levels on basis of which the project's capacity has been calculated allow. Or the 'duty' to deliver a given volume of products even if the market price would fall below a limit where production ends to be profitable.

– a **disturbance term** giving at least some idea about the part of the potential cash flow movements which are not explained by the rest of the project profile.

In this type of multi-factor approach, all dependencies between projects are normally assumed to be structured via the dependence on the common factors.

Given the profiles of the projects, one may want to change the chances, not only of the individual projects but also of the **portfolio** of projects (i.e. the firm), which can be achieved along two different avenues:

A – by **combining** probability distributions. The consequences of this portfolio effect are twofold. First, as the disturbance terms of the individual projects in general will be independent, the variability of the firm's cash flows attributable to the disturbance term will diminish as more and more projects are undertaken. Second, further risk reduction can take place by selecting specific projects in order to average the sensitivity to unexpected changes in some factor(s). The firm can for example restrict the aggregate (i.e. for the total project portfolio) sensitivity for unexpected changes in the oil price. A reduction in the firm's oil sensitivity reduces the variability of the firm's cash flows attributable to the variability of the oil factor (i.e. unexpected changes in the oil price). The 'narrowing' impact of the portfolio effect on the probability distribution of the firm's cash flows is shown in panel A of exhibit 1. Although the firm's shareholders are in a much better position to exploit this portfolio effect, this type of risk reduction can be relevant if the firm has good reasons to diversify for other parties than the shareholders (cf. the risk of backfiring in the preceding section).

B – by **truncating** probability distributions. One way is by transferring part of the risk to others (or vice versa), for instance by buying an insurance contract through which a part of the probability distribution of the firm's cash flows is 'chopped off'. The effect on the probability distribution of the firm's cash flows is shown in panel B of exhibit 1.

Also, management may want to exclude certain projects or combinations of projects because of (potential) negative effects on other parties which increase the already mentioned risk of backfiring. As a last example, management may require minimum levels for the availability of resources (varying from raw materials to cash), in order to reduce the risk of running out of these resources.

These examples show that management can choose from a variety of instruments to influence the probability function of the firm's cash flows and thus its risk. Obviously, most if not all of these **hedge instruments** have their price. Clearly, management should have an idea of these prices and of the value of the benefits to be able to decide on individual instruments to alter the risk of the firm. This holds even more if the firm wants to manage the risks associated with the resource allocation process in an integrated way.

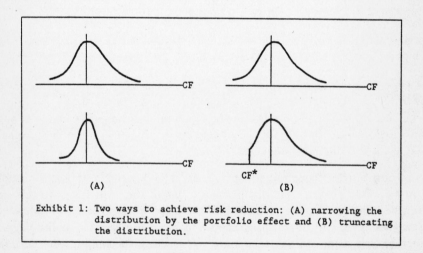

Exhibit 1: Two ways to achieve risk reduction: (A) narrowing the distribution by the portfolio effect and (B) truncating the distribution.

4 How to value risk reductions

In this section the discussion is focussed on the costs and benefits of using individual instruments to alter the risk of the firm. An integrated framework to deal with the risks of resource allocation is described in (Van den Bergh, Hallerbach and Spronk, 1990).

In this paper, we focus on two instruments to alter the firm's risk. One is (a) the limitation of the firm's sensitivity for unexpected changes in exogenous factors and the other is (b) truncating a probability distribution's tails (see exhibit 1). The general rule is: reduce risk (i.e. hedge) as long as the marginal cost of hedging is smaller than the marginal benefits. Obviously, what can be said about costs and benefits of these hedge instruments depends on the amount and kind of information available. Sometimes, the cost of using a hedge instrument is given by the market, for example in the case of an insurance contract or a currency future. In the absence of such a market price, a proxy should be found. For both cases, we assume as before that the decision maker has no complete picture of the uncertain events to come. Clearly, if the decision maker could specify the future correctly in probabilistic terms and define a preference function (e.g. a loss function), then the whole problem would boil down to a single criterion optimization problem.

Ad (a). Starting from the project profiles mentioned in the preceding section, the sensitivity of the firm as a whole for unexpected changes in the firm's environment can be defined as goal variables. As the factor sensitivities generally will be linear operators, the firm's sensitivity for any of the factors can be computed as a weighted average of the sensitivities of the individual projects for the factor; the fractions of the firm's capital invested in the respective projects serve as weights. For each of these goal variables, the decision maker may define whether it is to be maximized, to be minimized or to be set at some target level.

Normally, not all goals thus set by the decision maker can be reached simultaneously. Thus the problem is to find the **combination** of projects which has the best goal values. A procedure to achieve this is IMGP (see Spronk, 1981, 1985), in which the decision maker has the possibility to condition the set of possible project combinations by setting and systematically changing a series of constraints on the values of the goal variables. For example, the decision maker may choose to limit the firm's sensitivity for unexpected changes in the oil price by selecting some specific combination of projects. Assuming that an increasing oil price leads to lower cash flows (in real terms), the choice of the decision maker in this case 'protects' the firm against unexpected oil price changes. The price for this protection is twofold. First, with a limited (negative) sensitivity for unexpected oil price changes, the firm does not benefit from a decreasing oil price. Second, by limiting the sensitivity for oil price changes, a set of project combinations becomes infeasible. This may have consequences in terms of the attainability of the other goal varaibles. The IMGP procedure shows the decision maker what these consequences are, such that the limits set may be changed if the consequences are considered to be too serious.

Ad (b). The above mentioned risk reduction technique is two-sided: not only bad outcomes are avoided, also profitable outcomes will be missed. In some cases, the firm's management may require critical (minimum) levels for the availability of resources. In other cases (for example when the firm is partly financed with debt) the firm may be confronted with claims of third parties, that imply critical (minimum) levels for the value of the firm. In either of these cases, there are contingent claims connected with individual projects and the firm (the aggregate of projects). These contingent claims affect the cash flows of the projects and the firm when some critical level of resources is reached. When risk entails the danger of running out of resources, some minimum level of resources will be relevant as a constraint in choosing the project portfolio. In evaluating alternative projects, it is therefore important to know the cost of imposing suchlike constraints on the downside risk. Taking the view that the resource balance can adequately described as a stochastic process evolving over time, we want to know the price of chopping of a particular part of the probability distribution. For a critical minimum level CF^*, this situation is depicted in exhibit 1 panel B. Knowing the transgression probability, some type of loss function could be assumed to evaluate the downside risk. A less arbitrary solution to this valuation problem would be the availability of a fairly priced insurance contract that secures the minimum resource or cash flow level CF^*. The price of the contract indicates the cost of imposing the constraint. By comparing the marginal costs and benefits of tightening or relaxing the constraint, an optimal hedge position can be established. In many cases, however, this kind of insurance contracts are absent. As we then cannot observe the market value of the contract, we would like to know its theoretical value. As argued in (Van den Bergh and Hallerbach, 1990), (who illustrate the application to the optimal cash balance problem) a put option on the resources can serve as a synthetic insurance contract. The exercise price of this option equals the critical minimum value of the resources. The theoretical value of the option gives the value of the downside risk and, hence, the value of the constraint. On the firm level, altering the current and/or critical level of the resources by choosing a specific combination of projects influences the value of the imposed constraints. On the level of the individual projects, the implications of the choice for a specific 'overall' current and/or critical level of resources can be evaluated per project.

Clearly, the instruments suggested in the current and in the preceding section to alter the distribution of future cash flows may be combined. This is shown in detail in (Van den Bergh et al., 1990), in which an integrated framework for managing the firm's risk through financial planning is presented.

5 Summary

In this paper we discussed the problem that financial decision makers have an incomplete picture of the uncertainties connected to the portfolio of possible projects. We hypothesized that a natural way for the decision maker to solve these problems is to 'change the chances', ie. to impose constraints on certain unfavourable outcomes of the project combination selected. Two major hedge strategies have been discussed: (a) the limitation of the firm's sensitivity to unexpected changes in exogenious factors and (b) truncating relevant parts of the probability distribution of outcomes by acquiring 'stop loss insurances', ie. contingent claims on exogenious factors. It is argued that both hedging strategies could be combined in an integrated framework for managing the risk involved in financial decision making.

References

Bergh, W. M. van den, and Hallerbach, W. G. (1990). A Stochastic Cash Model with Deterministic Elements. Rivista di Matematica per le Scienze Economich e Sociali.

Bergh, W. M. van den, Hallerbach, W. G. and Spronk, J. (1990). An Integrated Approach to Manage the Risk in Financial Planning. Erasmus University, Centre for Research in Business Economics, Rotterdam (forthcoming).

Hallerbach, W. en Spronk, J. (1986). An Interactive Multi-Factor Portfolio Model. Report 8610/F, Centre for Research in Business Economics, Erasmus University, Rotterdam.

Spronk, J. (1981). Interactive Multiple Goal Programming: Applications to Financial Planning, Kluwer Nijhoff, Boston.

Spronk, J. (1985). Financial Planning with Conflicting Objectives. In: G. Fandel and J. Spronk (eds), Multiple Criteria Decision Methods and Applications, Springer, Berlin, pp. 269–288.

Spronk, J. (1989). Multi-Factorial Financial Planning. In: Lockett, A. G. and G. Islei (eds), Improving Decision Making in Organisations, Springer, Heidelberg.

Interactive Multiobjective Optimization Method in the Space of Model Variables

Grzegorz Dobrowolski *
Joint System Research Department
of the Institute for Control and Systems Engineering,
Academy of Mining and Metallurgy, Cracow,
and the Industrial Chemistry Research Institute, Warsaw.
Al. Mickiewicza 30, 31-503 Krakow, Poland.

Abstract

The prototype decision situation called the *centralized single-actor situation* is analyzed. It involves: a user and a *decision support system* with a computerized *multiobjective optimization* model. As solution to the multiobjective optimization problem is not generally unique some additional information is required to get a final selection. According to the assumption that there exists a preference structure with respect to objectives the additional information has a form of trade-off information.

An existence of another independent *preference structure with respect to model variables* is assumed and considered. A scheme of what—if experimenting is proposed to support investigation of the preference together with some elements of its implementation in the DSS.

As an illustration the *order-approximating achievement function* for the linear problem is chosen. The proposed scheme of experimenting is implemented in the MIDA system — Multiobjective Interactive Decision Aid in the programming of the chemical industry.

1   Decision situation. Introduction

A key feature of the multiobjective optimization is that a solution is not generally unique and some additional information is required to get a final selection. Important questions are: where the additional information comes from , how it is created and in what form it is involved in the solution process?

According to a hidden assumption that there exists a preference structure with respect to objectives, the additional information has a form of trade-off information given in either explicit or implicit form. If we deal with an explicit utility function, the multiobjective problem can be transformed immediately to a single-objective one. Otherwise the

---

*This study was partly sponsored by the Ministry of Education, Program RP.I.02.

additional information approximates an implicit utility function or other measure of satisfaction and an interactive scheme of a progressive manner has to be arranged to extract it.

The following prototype decision situation is assumed for the latter case that is called by Wierzbicki and Lewandowski (1988) the centralized single-actor (decision maker) situation. It involves: a user and a Decision Support System **DSS**. The user personifies a whole staff with a decision maker itself, it means: experts, analysts. The decision maker has the authority and experience to reach the decision; experts and analysts are responsible for the analysis of the decision situation. The DSS is a computer tool that computerizes a model (multiobjective optimization) based on the user's perception of the decision problem. Moreover, if the user can work with the model in an interactive fashion the DSS has some utilities to support a dialog with him.

Such an arrangement has some advantages:

- Validation of the model becomes easier as performed according to the scheme: development — execution of falsification tests.

- DSS enables the user to learn about the model behavior.

- DSS assists the user in generation of several alternatives.

The phase of choice from among the alternatives goes beyond the scope of the paper because it passively uses information obtained from a dialog with the DSS.

Many of multiobjective optimization methods gathered in papers (Hwang and Yoon, 1981, Hwang and Masud 1979, Ho, 1979) can be computerized, and probably were, in this way.

2   Objectives versus model variables

Three main items define the model (problem) that is computerized within the DSS in the form of multiobjective optimization problem:

- structure of the model,

- parameters of the model,

- variety of objectives and their ordering (completion of an objective space).

All the elements are more or less unstable during the validation phase. The structure can change as long as some phenomena are taken into consideration or neglected in consecutive steps of the analysis. Calibration of the parameters can occur not only as a consequence of identification but as a result of some trials with the model as well.

Completion of the objective space is carried out to gain controllability of the model with objectives. Therefore existence of the preference structure in the objective space is assumed, the objectives in their functional form must fully express the relative contribution of the model variables. The better it is fulfilled, the more adequate the model is.

In the above aspect the model refinement can be done only when the user is conscious about a preference structure in the model variables space. A closer observation of the user's behavior allows to appreciate the role of preference structure *vis-à-vis* the model variables even in later phases of problem solving.

The above can be summarized in the form of the observation: User's preferences refer directly to:

- either the model variables, mainly because of their strong real-life interpretation,

- or aggregates of the model variables that are eagerly accepted by the user as *true* objectives.

Because from the formal point of view the above dichotomy is meaningless (a single variable is enough to form a criterion) an approach exploring the preference in the variable space is seldom present in bibliography.

Zionts and Wallenius (1976) describe an interactive algorithm in which they measure attractiveness of the nonbasic variables of linear multiobjective problem. Gass and Dror (1983) propose a method that exploits the partial order defined for the model variables. The user selects a solution not only from the nondominated set but also with the best composition of variables.

Appreciating an important role of a man in our prototype decision situation, in the course of the paper, an existence of the preference structure with respect to the model variables is assumed and will be considered in different way than in the publications cited above.

Three different strategies can be taken into account while completion of the objective space. Distinctive (chosen by the user) model variables and the true objectives (aggregates of the model variables) are treated:

1. Jointly

2. Separately, but both groups have a status of objectives.

3. Only the true objectives constitute the objective space and a mechanism is added to deal with the distinctive variables.

The first case, a fruit of the formal approach, has serious disadvantages. The user can hardly provide any trade-off information regarding objectives taken from these two groups. As we add that the dimension of objective space is expected to be big for the case, it is easy to reach the conclusion that the user is left helpless facing, maybe, an unresolved problem. The same optimization problem pondered all the time does not make the situation better.

At least two subcases may be pointed at for the second strategy. The separate single-objective optimization problem is arranged to follow the partial order in the variables space as in (Gass and Dror, 1983). If maximization of the composite preference value would be explicitly introduced in the multiobjective problem formulation, it may result in new efficient solutions that have not to be efficient in the original formulation.

Another possible approach is to organize the hierarchical multiobjective optimization problem as it is proposed by Dobrowolski and Zebrowski (1989). The open question is how the decomposition can be done; what is more important the preferences in the objective or variables space? Assuming a scheme of coordination, it seems possible to automate the process what is especially desired for the DSS application.

User's problems with dimensionality and articulation of trade-off information are, in this case, replaced with uncomfortable necessity to deal with two or more different multiobjective problems (different objective spaces and orderings).

The third strategy is an answer to the question whether some simplifications are applicable to the problem. Let us observe that only few variables (distinctive) are of the user's interest. In fact, how do they attain their limits? A proposition is to organize a *what—if* scheme of experiments possibly based on changes of a single variable of the model each time. It suits well the *regimé* of interaction with the DSS, is easy to understand and produces an unexpected side-effect. The same scheme may be used in the sensitivity analysis with respect to parameters of the model (desirable antidote to uncertainty).

In the paper the scheme of what—if experimenting is presented together with some elements of its implementation in the DSS.

3   Schema of experiments

The user fully governs the course of the process. He choses the preferred variables and an order of their trials. A trial is arranged: *If* a preferred variable is forced in a preferred direction *what* will happen with the solution. And for the sensitivity analysis: *if* a parameter changes *what* will be the influence of it. The proposed scheme of experiments, because of its simplicity, can be used for almost all optimization models in the field of decision support. For the single-objective problem it can be applied directly, for the multiobjective one a scalarization method has to be applied.

As an illustration the order-approximating achievement function proposed by Wierzbicki (1982) and used in the construction of DSS family called DIDAS (Lewandowski et al., 1989) is chosen:

$$s(q, \overline{q}) = \min \left[\min_i z_i , \; \frac{1}{\rho p} \sum_i z_i + \frac{\epsilon}{p} \sum_i z_i \right] \tag{1}$$

$$z_i = \begin{cases} (q_i - \overline{q}_i)/s_i & \text{if } 1 \leq i \leq p_1 \text{ for maximization} \\ (\overline{q}_i - q_i)/s_i & \text{if } p_1 < i \leq p_2 \text{ for minimization} \\ \min\left[(q_i - \overline{q}_i)/s_i , (\overline{q}_i - q_i)/s_i \right] & \text{if } p_2 < i \leq p \text{ for stabilization} \end{cases}$$

$$\text{where: } q, \overline{q}, s \in R^p ; \; \rho, \epsilon \in R$$

The general formula for the experimenting scheme written for the case of scalarizing via the order-approximating function is as follows.

Let $\xi \in R$ be a preferred variable or a parameter of the model. Then its influence can be determined by solving the optimization problem:

$$\max_{\underline{\xi} \leq \xi \leq \overline{\xi}} s(q, \overline{q}, \xi) \tag{2}$$

and comparing the results with the assumed pattern solution. It is obtained by varying the function (1) with the parameter ξ. Some details are shown for the linear case:

$$q = Cx \tag{3}$$

$$x \in X = \left\{ x \in R^n \ : \ \underline{x} \le x \le \overline{x} \ ; \ \underline{y} \le Ax \le \overline{y} \right\} \tag{4}$$

where: $x, \overline{x} \in R^n$; $y, \overline{y} \in R^m$; $A \in R^{m \times n}$; $C \in R^{p \times n}$

Influence of a preferred variable can be calculated for the linear case in the following way:

$$\max \ s(q, \overline{q}, x_j) = \max \left[s(q, \overline{q}, \inf_X x_j) \ , \ s(q, \overline{q}, \sup_X x_j) \right] \tag{5}$$

and, similarly, the influence of an objective coefficient:

$$\max_{\underline{c}_{ij} \le c_{ij} \le \overline{c}_{ij}} s(q, \overline{q}, c_{ij}) = \max \left[s(q, \overline{q}, \underline{c}_{ij}) \ ; \ s(q, \overline{q}, \overline{c}_{ij}) \right] \tag{6}$$

The scheme engages a great computational effort. At least one optimization problem must be solved to model the preference with respect to a single variable. Analysis of mutual relations calls for a sequence of single trials. Fortunately, because of a strong real-life interpretation, a number of sequences cannot increase to the theoretical number of permutations.

4 An option in the DSS

The described scheme of experimenting can be manifoldly used during the decision problem solving:

- During the initial analysis stage as a means for model validation, tunning parameters, etc.

- During the exploration of efficient alternatives stage to model the user's preferences with respect to the model variables.

- To enable the sensitivity analysis of finally chosen alternatives.

Each single trial consists of several simple actions:

- modification of the model,

- activation of optimization calculations,

- exploration of results,

- comparison with previous results,

- storage of the results.

Let us discuss implementation cost of the proposed experimenting scheme. Some actions can be covered by obligatory options of the DSS. A specialized model editor, internal to the solver for the sake of efficiency, is usually present. Options for reviewing single results as well as previously performed experiments are implemented in any DSS.

New options induced by the proposed scheme deal with comparing the results and tracing experiments already done in the sequence. Comparison of experiments (alternatives) is usually implemented in a tabular form. The only problem is to support the comparison process by some specialized graphics. It is how to visualize a solution to the multiobjective optimization problem?

To create good conditions for evaluation of differences between experiments visualization by a polygon is recommended. Two or more q^* (solutions in the objective space) are overlaid each other on a single figure and presented to the user. It is done by the mapping into the polar coordinates:

$$v \; : \; R^p \ni q^* \longrightarrow \left(\gamma_i(q_i^* - q_i^0) \, , \; \frac{2\pi i}{p} \right) \in R^2 \tag{7}$$

where: q^0 is an assumed pole, γ_i are scaling coefficients.

Such a method maps well the values of objectives while the trade-off information is almost completely lost.

5 Summary

The presented above scheme of experimenting is implemented in the MIDA system — Multiobjective Interactive Decision Aid in the programming of the chemical industry. Several options are based on the scheme improving user's try and see capabilities. The options were developed as a consequence of extensive experiments and numerous applications as described in (Kopytowski and Zebrowski, 1989).

The architecture of the MIDA system and details of its implementation is described in (Dobrowolski and Rys, 1989).

6 References

Dobrowolski, G. and Zebrowski, M. (1989) Hierarchical Multiobjective Approach to a Programming Problem. In A. P. Wierzbicki and A. Lewandowski (eds.): Aspiration Based Decision Support Systems, *Lect. Notes in Econ. and Math. Syst.* 331, pp. 310–321, Springer-Verlag, New York-Heidelberg-Berlin, ISBN 3-540-51213-6.

Dobrowolski, G. and Rys, T. (1989) Architecture and Functionality of MIDA. In A. P. Wierzbicki and A. Lewandowski (eds.): Aspiration Based Decision Support Systems, *Lect. Notes in Econ. and Math. Syst.* 331, pp. 339–370, Springer-Verlag, New York-Heidelberg-Berlin, ISBN 3-540-51213-6.

Gass, S. I. and Dror, M. (1983) An interactive approach to multiple objective linear programming involving key decision variables. *Large Scale Systems* 5, pp. 95–103.

Ho, J. K. (1979) Multiple criteria optimization: A unified framework. Working Paper AMD-820, Applied Mathematics Dept., Brookhaven National Laboratory.

Hwang, C. L. and Masud, A. S. M. (1979) Multiobjective Decision Making: Methods and Applications. *Lect. Notes in Econ. and Math. Syst.*, Springer-Verlag, New York-Heidelberg-Berlin.

Hwang, C. L. and Yoon, K. (1981) Multiple Attribute Decision Making: Methods and Applications, State-of-the-Art Survey. *Lect. Notes in Econ. and Math. Syst.* 186, Springer-Verlag, New York-Heidelberg-Berlin.

Kopytowski, J. and Zebrowski, M. (1989) Experience in Theory, Software and Application of DSS in the Chemical Industry. In A. P. Wierzbicki and A. Lewandowski (eds.): Aspiration Based Decision Support Systems, *Lect. Notes in Econ. and Math. Syst.* 331, pp. 271–286, Springer-Verlag, New York-Heidelberg-Berlin, ISBN 3-540-51213-6.

Lewandowski, A., Kreglewski, T., Rogowski,T. and Wierzbicki, A. (1989) Decision Support Systems of DIDAS Family. In Aspiration Based Decision Support Systems, *Lect. Notes in Econ. and Math. Syst.* 331, pp. 21–47, Springer-Verlag, New York-Heidelberg-Berlin, ISBN 3-540-51213-6.

Lewandowski, A. and Wierzbicki, A. (1988) Aspiration Based Decision Analysis and Support. Theoretical and Methodological Backgrounds. *IIASA Working Paper* WP-88-03, International Institute for Applied System Analysis, Laxenburg, Austria.

Wierzbicki, A. (1982) A mathematical basis for satisficing decision making. *Mathematical Modelling* 3, pp. 391–405.

Zionts, S. and Wallenius, J. (1976) An interactive programming method for solving the multiple criteria problem. *Management Sci.* 22(6), pp. 652–663.

On the Metric-Invariant Set for Multicriterion Optimization

Henryk Górecki, Stanisław Fuksa
Academy of Mining and Metallurgy
Institute of Automatics
30–059 Kraków, al. Mickiewicza 30, Poland

Abstract

In the paper we give a construction of the choice of the optimal set, average with respect to metrics of the l^p-type, in the R^n criterion space. In every case, this set contains the set optimal with respect to the l^1 metric and in some cases is exactly equal to it. The concept of construction is partially based on the generalization of utopia point and displaced ideal methods.

1 Introduction

Many problems of multicriterial optimization are connected with the choice of the point (or set) from the optimal-compromise set in the criteria space. But optimality of this (or set) depends on the chosen metric. In order to overcome this we make use of the notion of the utopia point (Yu, 1973; Freimer and Yu, 1976), and introduce the notion of a limit set, which is constructed on the basis of the l^p, $p \in [1, \infty]$ metrics in R^n.

The basic properties of the utopia point and the sets $G_p(A, x_A)$, like its compactness, one can find in many papers, (Yu, 1973; Freimer and Yu, 1976; Zeleny, 1974; Nykowski, 1980) and we concern them here in part 2, and partially in part 3.

The idea of the sequence of optimal subsets with respect to the metrics of l^p-type and moving utopia point was sharply outlined in (Zeleny, 1974) in context of linearly constrained compromise set. It was named there the "displaced ideal method" and left in non-developed stadium.

For the reachable set $A \subset R^n$ in the criteria space we have the utopia point x_A. We define a set $G(A, x_A) \subset A$ which contains all the nearest points from x_A to A in every metric l^p. For the set $G(A, x_A)$ we define the next utopia point $x_{G(A, x_A)}$ and we repeat the construction. The procedure of repeating this construction may be stopped on each step by Decision Maker if it is only convenient for him. The limit set defined by this recursive sequence is optimal in some averaged sense. In what follows we show, that the limit set always contains the set $G_1(A, x_A)$ of the nearest points of A to x_A in the metric l^1. We show also that in the case of the two-dimensional criterion space the limit set is a one-point set if the set $G_1(A, x_A)$ is also represented by one point.

2 Notation and some basic relations for the p-norms in R^n

Let $\| \cdot \|_p$ be a norm in R^n

$$\|y\|_p = \left(\sum_{i=1}^{n} |y^i|^p \right)^{\frac{1}{p}}, \qquad p \in [1, \infty) \tag{1}$$

and

$$\|y\|_p = \max_{i=1,\ldots,n} |y^i|, \qquad p = \infty$$

where y^i denotes the i-th component of the vector $y \in R^n$. We denote by $\mathrm{dist}_p(A, x)$, where $A \in R^n$, $x \in R^n$, the distance between the set A and element x in the sense of the norm $\| \cdot \|_p$, i.e.:

$$\mathrm{dist}_p(A, x) = \inf_{y \in A} \|y - x\|_p.$$

By $K_p(x, r)$ we mean the ball with centre at $x \in R^n$ and radius r with respect to the norm $\| \cdot \|_p$. We have the standard inequalities and relations:

$$\left.\begin{aligned}
\|y\|_\infty &\le \|y\|_p, & p &\in [1, \infty], & y &\in R^n \\[4pt]
\|y\|_{p_2} &\le \|y\|_{p_1}, & p_2 &\ge p_1, & y &\in R^n \\[4pt]
\|y\|_\infty \le \|y\|_p &\le n^{\frac{1}{p}} \cdot \|p\|_\infty, & p &\in [1, \infty], & y &\in R^n \\[4pt]
\|y\|_1 \le n^{\frac{1}{q}} \cdot \|y\|_p &\le n \cdot \|y\|_\infty, & \frac{1}{q} &= 1 - \frac{1}{p} &&
\end{aligned}\right\} \tag{2}$$

and

$$\left.\begin{aligned}
K_{p_1}(x, r) &\subset K_{p_2}(x, r), & p_1 &\le p_2 \\[4pt]
K_p\left(x, \frac{r}{n^{1/q}}\right) \subset K_1(x, r) &\subset K_\infty(x, r), & p &\in [1, \infty]
\end{aligned}\right\} \tag{3}$$

For any set $A \subset R^n$ and the point $x \in R^n$ we define a set $G_p(A, x) \subset A \subset R^n$,

$$G_p(A, x) = \{ y \in A : \mathrm{dist}_p(A, x) = \|y - x\|_p \} \tag{4}$$

and the set $G(A, x) \subset A \subset R^n$,

$$G(A, x) = \bigcup_{p \in [1, \infty]} G_p(A, x). \tag{5}$$

One can state simple relations

$$\begin{aligned}
G_p(A, x) &\subset \overline{K_p(x, \mathrm{dist}_p(A, x))} \subset \overline{K_\infty(x, \mathrm{dist}_p(A, x))}, & 1 < p \le \infty \\[4pt]
G_1(A, x) &\subset \overline{K_\infty(x, \mathrm{dist}_1(A, x))} \subset \overline{K_1(x, n \cdot \mathrm{dist}_1(A, x))}
\end{aligned} \tag{6}$$

and
$$G(A, x) \subset \overline{K_1(x, n \cdot \text{dist}(A, x))}. \tag{7}$$

Let $A \subset R^n$ be an arbitrary set. By $x_A \subset R^n$ we denote (if it exists) the so called "utopia point" of the set A:

$$x_A = \inf \{ x \in R^n : x \geq A \} \tag{8}$$

where the relation of order $x \geq A$ denotes that each component of x is greater than or equal to the corresponding component of every vector of A.

3 Properties of the sequences of utopia points and optimal sets

Let $A \subset R^n$ be a nonvoid closed set and x_A a utopia point for A.

The idea given in introduction can be formulated in the terms of the recurrently defined sequence of sets $\{B_i\}$:

$$\begin{aligned} B_{i+1} &= G(B_i, x_{B_i}) \\ B_0 = A \subset R^n, \qquad x_B &= x_A \in R^n \end{aligned} \tag{9}$$

The set-valued function G is as in (4), (5) and x_{B_i} denotes the utopia point for B_i.

The sequences $\{x_{B_i}\}$, $\{B_i\}$ have the properties:

- they are well-defined
- $B_{i+1} \subset B_i \subset B_0 = A$
- $x_{B_{i+1}} \leq x_{B_i} \leq x_A$

$$\left.\begin{aligned} & \\ & \\ & \end{aligned}\right\} \tag{10}$$

We have the following lemmas describing the properties of the sequence under consideration.

Lemma 1. The sequence $\{x_{B_i}\}$ converges.

Proof. Observe that the sequence of comments of x_{B_i} is decreasing. On the other hand it is bounded:

$$G(B_i, x_{B_i}) \subset G(A, x_a) \subset \overline{K_1(x_A, n \cdot \text{dist}_1(A, x_A))}$$

and

$$x_{B_i} \in \overline{K_1(x_A, n \cdot \text{dist}_1(A, x_A))}.$$

Hence there exists a limit $x_{B_\infty} = \lim_i x_{B_i}$.

Lemma 2. The set $G_1(A, x_A)$ is non-empty and

$$G_1(A, x_A) = \arg\left(\max_{x \in A} \sum_{i=1}^{n} x^i\right). \tag{11}$$

Proof. Firstly, we show that the right-hand side of (11) is well defined. We always have

$$\sum_{i=1}^{n} x^i \leq \sum_{i=1}^{n} x_A^i, \qquad x \in A,$$

hence there exists the finite upper bound:

$$\sup_{x \in A} \sum_{i=1}^{n} x^i.$$

This upper bound is attained on A, because A is closed and

$$\max_{x \in H} \sum_{i=1}^{n} x^i = \max_{x \in A} \sum_{i=1}^{n} x^i,$$

where

$$H = A \cap \left\{ y \leq x_A : \sum_{i=1}^{n} y^i \geq \sum_{i=1}^{n} x_0^i, \ x_0 \in A \right\}$$

and the set H is compact as an intersection of A with a simplex.

For finishing the proof, we simply observe that

$$\{y \in R^n, \ y \leq x_A\} \cap \left\{ y : \sum_{i=1}^{n} (x_A^i - y^i) \leq r \right\} = K_1(x_A, r) \cap \{y \in R^n, \ y \leq x_A\}. \qquad (12)$$

Thus, the set of arguments of maximum in (11) is equal to the set

$$A \cap K_1\left(x_A, \overline{\left(\max_{x \in A} \sum_{i=1}^{n} x^i \right)} \right) \qquad (13)$$

which ends the proof.

As a conclusion we state:

Corollary 3. For any $y \in R^n$, $A \leq y$ we have

$$G_1(A, y) = \arg\left(\max_{x \in A} \sum_{i=1}^{n} x^i \right). \qquad (14)$$

The proof is the same as for Lemma 2. It is sufficient to observe that the relations (12), (13), are valid for x_A substituted by $y \geq x_A$.

We pass to the description of other properties of the sequence $\{B_i\}$.

Lemma 4. For any $i = 1, \ldots, \infty$ we have

$$G_1(A, x_A) \subset B_i.$$

Proof. We always have

$$G_1(A, x_A) \subset G(A, x_A) = B_1.$$

We make use of induction. Let us suppose that for some i_0 one has $G_1(A, x_A) \subset B_{i_0}$.

Applying corollary 3. to the set B_{i_0} we get

$$G_1(A, x_A) \subset G_1(B_{i_0}, x_{B_{i_0}}) = G_1(B_{i_0}, x_A). \tag{15}$$

Let us remark that $x_A \geq x_{B_{i_0}}$. But

$$G_1(B_{i_0}, x_{B_{i_0}}) \subset G(B_{i_0}, x_{B_{i_0}}) = B_{i_0+1},$$

which end the proof.

Let us observe that by (15) we also have

$$G_1(A, x_A) \subset G_1(B_i, x_{B_i}) \subset G_1(A, x_A)$$

because $B_i \subset A$ and $x_{B_i} \leq x_A$.

This means that the set $G_1(A, x_A)$ is a component of every set from the sequence $\{B_i\}_{i=1}^{\infty}$.

Other properties of the sequence $\{B_i\}$.

Lemma 5. The sets B_i are compact sets.

Proof. B_i are bounded by virtue of (7). It is sufficient to prove their closedness.

Let us consider the function g:

$$g : [1, \infty] \times R^n \times R^n \ni (p, y, x_0) \to \|y - x_0\|_p \in R^1.$$

The function g is continuous and the map d

$$d : [1, \infty] \times R^n \ni (p, x_0) \to \text{dist}_p(A, x_0) = d(p, x_0) \in R^1$$

is continuous for any closed fixed set $A \subset R^n$.

Hence, the set H

$$H = \{\, p, y \in [1, \infty] \times R^n : \|y - x_0\|_p = d(p, x_0) \,\}$$

is closed, and as a bounded set, compact.

The set F

$$F = [1, \infty] \times A \cap H \subset [1, \infty] \times R^n$$

is also compact. The projection of F on the second component of the product $[1, \infty] \times R^n$ is also compact. But the projection mentioned above is equal to

$$\bigcup_{p=1}^{\infty} G_p(A, x_0).$$

Replacing A by B_i and x_0 by x_{B_i} we get the lemma. Finally we have:

Lemma 6. The sequence of the sets $\{B_i\}$ converges to a compact set B_∞

$$B_\infty = \bigcap_i B_i, \qquad (B_{i+1} \subseteq B_i)$$

each set B_i contains the set $G_1(A, x_A)$, and the sequence of the utopia points $\{x_{B_i}\}$ also converges to the point x_{B_∞}.

In the case of the space R^2 (two-dimensional criterion space) we can state an interesting result.

Theorem 7. Let $A \subset R^2$ be a closed set with utopia point x_A. Let, in addition, the set $G_1(A, x_A)$ be a one-point set, i.e. $G_1(A, x_A) = \{x_0\}$. Then one has the relation

$$B_\infty = x_{B_\infty} = x_0$$

Proof. By lemma 6 we have the existence of x_{B_∞} and B_∞, and the compactness of B_∞. The limit set B_∞ fulfills

$$B_\infty = G(B_\infty, x_{B_\infty}).$$

Obviously, by compactness of B there exist $p_1, p_2 \in [1, \infty]$ and points

$$x_{p_1} = \begin{bmatrix} x_{p_1}^1 \\ x_{p_1}^2 \end{bmatrix}, \quad x_{p_2} = \begin{bmatrix} x_{p_2}^1 \\ x_{p_2}^2 \end{bmatrix} \in B_\infty \subset R^2,$$

such that

$$x_{B_\infty} = \begin{bmatrix} \max\limits_{i=1,2}(x_{p_i}^1) \\ \max\limits_{i=1,2}(x_{p_i}^2) \end{bmatrix}.$$

By the symmetry of the balls we have

$$\max_{i=1,2}(x_{p_i}^1) - \min_{i=1,2}(x_{p_i}^1) = a = \max_{i=1,2}(x_{p_i}^2) - \min_{i=1,2}(x_{p_i}^2),$$

as showed in Fig. 1.

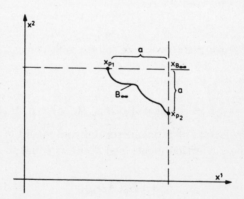

Figure 1

Thus, we conclude that

$$\text{dist}_1(B_\infty, x_{B_\infty}) \leq a,$$

and by (3)

$$\mathrm{dist}_1(B_\infty, x_{B_\infty}) \geq a = \mathrm{dist}_{p_i}(B_\infty, x_{B_\infty}) = \mathrm{dist}_1(x_{p_i}, x_{B_\infty}), \qquad i = 1, 2.$$

Hence

$$\mathrm{dist}_1(B_\infty, x_B) = a = \mathrm{dist}_1(x_{p_i}, x_{B_\infty}), \qquad i = 1, 2,$$

which gives, together with the relation $G_1(A, x_A) \subset B_\infty$ (Lemma 4) that

$$\{x_{p_1}, x_{p_2}\} \subset G_1(A, x_A) \subset B_\infty.$$

This leads to contradiction with the assumption of the theorem. This in turn means that

$$x_{p_1} = x_{p_2} = G_1(A, x_A) = x_{B_\infty}$$

and ends the proof.

The assumption that the set $G_1(A, x_A)$ is a one-point set is essential. If we omit it then the set B_∞ can be a multipoint set, as shown in Fig. 2.

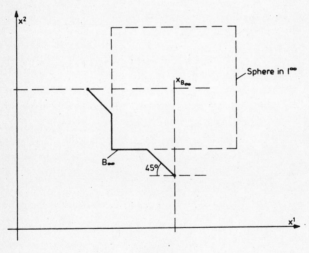

Figure 2

4   Conclusion

In this paper we study the fundamental properties of the optimal subsets and corresponding utopia points related to the basic set A of compromises without practically any assumptions on A (only closedness and existence of utopia point is needed).

Lemma 6 shows the existence and compactness of the limit set B_∞, existence of the limit utopia point together with the relation $G_1(A, x_A) \subset B_\infty$.

Theorem 7 gives an interesting relation in the case of the compromise subset A in R^2: if the $G_1(A, x_A)$ is the one-point set, then it is equal to B_∞. The result shows that the application of the idea of "displaced ideal method" with respect to family of l^p, $p \in [1, \infty]$ metrics could produce a simple solution of a decision problem. Evidently, this solution is, in described sense, invariant with respect to the metrics of l^p-type.

References

Freimer, M. and Yu, P.L. (1976). Some new results on compromise solutions.... *Management Science*, Vol. 22, No. 6.

Nykowski, I. (1980). Programowanie liniowe. PWE, (in Polish).

Yu, P.L. (1973). A class of solutions for group decision problems. *Management Science*, Vol. 19, No. 8.

Zeleny, M. (1974). A Concept of Compromise Solutions and the Method of the Displaced Ideal. *Comput. and Operational Research*, Pergamon Press, Vol. 1, pp. 479.

Structured Modelling of Multicriterion Problems

Tom Hemming
Department of Business Administration
University of Stockholm
S–106 91 Stockholm, Sweden

1   Introduction

The purpose of this paper is to discuss the possibility to use a meso language (Greek, meso means in the middle, between) as a means for graphically representing a decision problem in order to bridge the gap between the natural representation of the problem as perceived by the decision maker and the mathematical representation as perceived by the analyst. Thus the meso language has to be simple enough to be accepted by the decision maker yet it should be possible to represent decision situations in a way which is meaningful both to the analyst and the decision maker. The decision maker should be able to get an understanding of the structure of the model directly related to the system under consideration. The analyst is provided with a means to help him structure the problem in terms of a meso model expressed in the meso language. Note that the meso model is also a means for delegating data collection. Further, the meso language allows for rule-based model manipulation. In short the advantages of the meso language are that it is a means for communication, it allows for speedy structured model development and delegation of data collection.

This presentation is restricted to the class of multicriterion problems which is characterized by linear restrictions and criteria and a not explicitly known non-linear utility function that is supposed to be optimized. The meso language discussed here is largely based on a taxonomy suggested by Müller-Merbach (1978, 1981) and applied by Holvid (1977). The main contribution of this paper is to extend the use of graphics beyond the modelling of physical flows as encountered in industrial manufacturing and distribution processes to the modelling of criterion relationships. For a less structured way of using graphics as a means for analyst client communication see (Hemming, Holvid and Högberg, 1989).

2   The modelling process

The following steps can be distinguished in model building: 1) problem recognition, 2) problem formulation, 3) model building, 4) data collection, 5) model solution, and 6) choice of action.

In order to facilitate the interaction between decision maker and analyst more steps will be added between steps 2 and 3. It is striking to note how readily students accept network flow models when being taught OR. The reason is that such models are nicely supported by graphical representations. Now the idea is to represent a wider class of problems as network flow problems, which may be graphically represented. Thus the model building process will be considered as consisting of the following steps.

1. Problem recognition
2. Problem formulation
3. Survey graphs
4. Meso graphs
5. Model building
6. Data collection
7. Model solution
8. Choice of action

The steps should not be considered as executed sequentially although the meso language will be discussed in terms of a simple example basically following these steps. The example is a simplified and somewhat altered version of a well-known case called Red Brand Canners, with which students frequently have problems. For a description of the original case see (Wilson, 1980).

Red Brand Canners: The company produces three different canned good products: whole tomatoes, tomato juice, and paste. For that purpose tomatoes are needed. Tomatoes are graded as A or B tomatoes. The lower limit for the content of A tomatoes is higher for whole tomatoes than for juice. Paste can be produced using any tomato quality.

It is suggested that a model of the production of canned goods should be made. Initially, the purpose of the model is to determine which product mix maximizes total contribution (henceforth denoted profit). At a later stage it is found that there are several other criteria, such as waste tomatoes, market shares, and quality of output. The waste criterion has been brought up because of recent complaints from the EPA that the company has dumped excess tomatoes in the river.

3   Survey graphs

The purpose of survey graphs is to describe the objects and the relationships between objects for the purpose of attaining a client-analyst agreement regarding the basic properties of the system. Two types of survey graphs are needed in this stage of the decision process. One for the production flow, and one for the criterion relationships.

The production flow in this example is simple as is evident from figure 1.

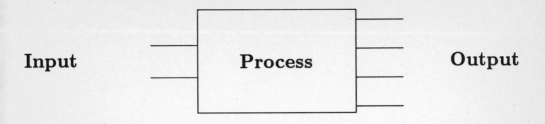

Figure 1: A simple overview of the Red Brand Canners production process.

Figure 1 can be interpreted in the following way. Tomatoes are input into the production process and various types of canned products are output. For more realistic problems it is necessary to use more complicated flow models.

Restrictions imposed by management are often arbitrary. Particularly those related to marketing and economic policy. They are often motivated by the desire to achieve profit on a long term base. Interaction with executive decision makers often reveal that trade-offs are considered between various goals like short term profit and market shares. In the case of Red Brand Canners the following criteria have been considered important and trade-offs are being discussed, in particular with respect to the first three criteria.

* Profit
* Sales
* Quality
* Waste

Many companies are experiencing an increasing pressure to consider environmental goals seriously and voluntarily trade profit for environmental improvements in order to maintain good relations with the public and local authorities. Environmental goals are no longer merely treated as restrictions imposed because of legal actions taken by parliament. In case of Red Brand Canners there is no law against dumping tomatoes in the river; still good relations with the authorities and the public (customers) dictate the goal to limit waste.

Experience from large-scale problems (Hemming, 1975b) suggest that tree structures are useful when dealing with such problems. In this particular case an appropriate tree structure is displayed in figure 2. Note that the concept of utility may as well be replaced by long-term profit or long-term growth or whatever the particular client may experience appropriate.

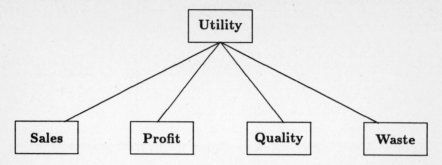

Figure 2: The criteria that have to be balanced against each other by Red Brand Canners.

4 Meso graphs

The two types of survey graphs are assumed to have been approved as appropriate by the clients. The purpose of this step is to refine the graphs to such an extent that they are directly useful for the generation of the mathematical model. The mathematical model is assumed to consist of two parts which are linked together. First, the description of the physical flows and second, a structure relating the criteria to each other. To achieve this purpose a few symbols will be used as shown in figure 3 and figure 5. The symbols in figure 3 refer to the physical flows outside and inside the company and are used as illustrated in figure 4. The symbols of figure 5 refer to the criterion relationships and their use is illustrated in figure 6.

Partitioning processes

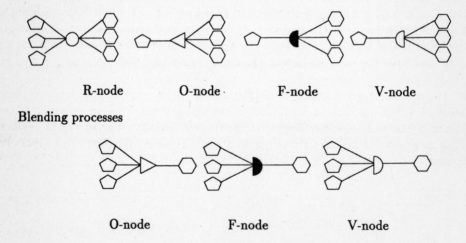

Blending processes

Figure 3: Node symbols used to model generalized network flow problems. The pentagons represent input and the hexagons output.

Using only O, F, and V type of nodes most industrial production and distribution processes may be graphically represented (Müller–Merbach, 1978, 1981). Considering industrial production and distribution processes as generalized network flow problems means that for each node in the network, balance equations have to be satisfied. For *partitioning* processes the following interpretations of the different nodes have to be made, assuming flows from left to right.

R-node: Several inputs can be partitioned into parts in an arbitrary way. (R for regular)

O-node: One input can be partitioned into parts in an arbitrary way. (O for open)

F-node: One input can be partitioned into parts in fixed proportions. (F for fixed)

V-node: One input can be partitioned into parts which may vary within certain limits. (V for variable)

For *blending* processes resulting in one output, nodes will be similarly interpreted.

O-node: Several inputs can be blended in arbitrary proportions.

F-node: Several inputs can be blended in fixed proportions.

V-node: Several inputs can be blended in proportions which may vary within certain limits.

Although criteria are difficult to handle and the individual criteria have to be aggregated to supercriteria, often in a complicated fashion, this is not the main obstacle for using OR-models in decision making, rather interactive optimization facilities imply that models will be experienced more relevant. More serious is the productivity of the OR analyst in modelling the environment of the decision situation. Modelling by means of meso graphs makes it easier to anchor the model not only with the client but also within the analyst himself.

The main physical flows of Red Brand Canners are illustrated in figure 4.

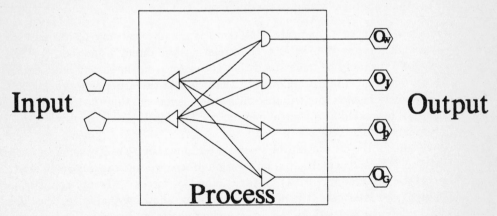

Figure 4: A meso graph of the physical flows in the Red Brand Canners production process. Output of whole tomatoes, juice, paste, and waste are denoted O_W, O_J, O_P, and O_G respectively.

The node types in figure 5 will be used to illustrate criterion relationships.

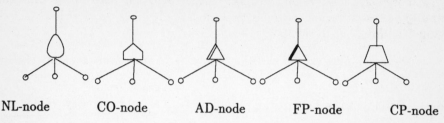

NL-node   CO-node   AD-node   FP-node   CP-node

Figure 5: Nodes used to model criterion relationships.

Five types of nodes are being used for modelling criterion relationships.

NL-node: Meaning that the criteria on the next lower level may relate in any fashion as long as it may be expressed as a functional relationship. (NL for non-linear)

CO-node: Meaning that there is a functional relationship to the next lower level such that a corresponding function is concave and increasing in each argument. (CO for concave)

AD-node: Meaning that criterion values on a lower level are naturally added to a compund measure. For example sales of 14" and 24" inch televisions may be added to total sales. (AD for additive)

FP-node: Meaning that criterion values relate to each other in fixed proportions. As long as the proportions are fixed, relations are satisfactory, else unsatisfactory. R&D may for instance always be 10% of Sales. (FP for fixed proportions)

CP-node: Control parameters may as well be input as criteria. For example, when blending gasoline, one maker may choose to have a higher energy content than another, without charging more. (CP for control parameter)

Dotted lines are used to indicate that there is no physical flow from one node to another, but that there is some other type of relationship, direct or indirect.

From figure 6 it should be understood that the criteria on the second level relate in a compensatory way concerning overall utility, that the first two criteria on the second level relate in an additive fashion to attributes on the third level, and that the third criterion on the second level is treated as a control parameter. The fourth criterion waste is denoted G and represents excess tomatoes.

The balancing of the criteria on the second level to maximize utility could be achieved by the use of an interactive multicriterion decision procedure, such as the Boundary Point Ranking method (Hemming, 1975a) or the method of forces [1] (Troutt and Hemming, 1985). In this particular case it is not that easy since allowing quality to be a variable would imply nonlinear restrictions. To avoid such unnecessary complications, conditional optimization subject to different quality levels will be assumed satisfactory.

---

[1]Program diskette and manual can be requested from Hemming.

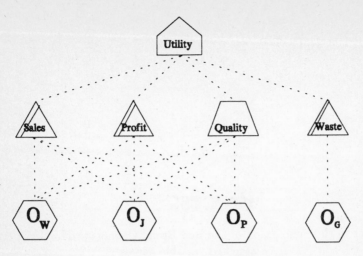

Figure 6: A meso graph illustrating the relationship between criteria for Red Brand Canners. Output of whole tomatoes, juice, paste and waste are denoted O_W, O_J, O_P, and O_G respectively.

5   Model building

Meso graphs constitute a means for modelling the criterion relationships and the production process. Industrial production and distribution processes are traditionally modelled subject to two classes of restrictions: 1) balance restrictions, 2) other restrictions, such as policy, legal, economic, and technical restrictions. Here, some policy type restrictions have been considered explicitly as criteria. How to choose those to be considered criteria and those to be considered restrictions is a problem not treated here, but rather left to the decision maker's discretion. Several types of nodes which are useful are exhibited in figure 3 and 5. Only a few are used in figures 4 and 6 displaying the production process and criterion relationships of Red Brand Canners.

The transformation of meso graphs into a mathematical model is illustrated on the Red Brand Canners multicriterion problem.

For simplicity each arc will correspond to one variable, other node denotations have been omitted, since they are not used in the mathematical model. The variable names are indicated in figure 7.

The production process is now readily modeled. Starting with output and working backwards the model is obtained. The four first balance equations are

$$W = AW + BW \tag{1}$$
$$J = AJ + BJ \tag{2}$$
$$P = AP + BP \tag{3}$$
$$G = AG + BG \tag{4}$$

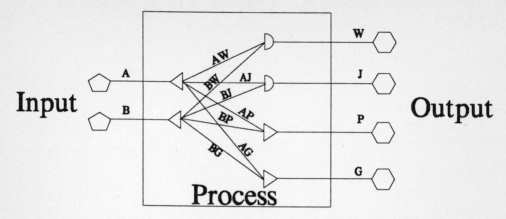

Figure 7: All arcs in the meso graph of the Red Brand Canners production process have been assigned variable names.

However, the first two nodes are V-nodes, meaning that blending conditions have to be satisfied, say, whole tomatoes have to consist of at least 75% A tomatoes and juice of at least 25% A tomatoes. Thus associated with the V-nodes are the following blending conditions.

$$AW \geq .75\,(AW + BW) \tag{5}$$
$$AJ \geq .25\,(AJ + BJ) \tag{6}$$

Continuing backwards there are two o-nodes associated with the following balance equations

$$A = AW + AJ + AP + AG \tag{7}$$
$$B = BW + BJ + BP + BG \tag{8}$$

Additional constraints that have to be considered are associated with the input and output nodes, i.e.

$$A \leq AA \tag{9}$$
$$B \leq BB \tag{10}$$

where AA and BB correspond to the availability of A and B respectively.

In addition there may be output restrictions concerning amounts that can sold. Thus correspondingly

$$W \leq WW \tag{11}$$
$$J \leq JJ \tag{12}$$
$$P \leq PP \tag{13}$$

The personnel concerned easily understand meso graphs of the type illustrated in figure 7. Thus data collection normally carried out by the analyst may be delegated to technical personnel. This would speed up the model building process, considering the huge amount of data needed for integrated production planning models savings in time will be considerable.

Next criteria will be discussed. In Figure 8 the arcs have been assigned variable names.

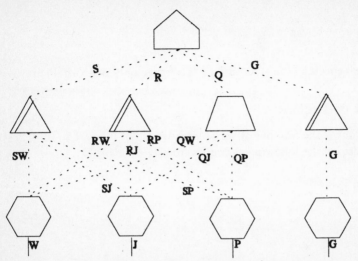

Figure 8: A meso graph of the criteria relationships for Red Brand Canners with variable names assigned to the arcs.

The criteria S, P, Q are supposed to be maximization criteria and G a minimization criterion. The following balance equations have to be satisfied

$$S = SW + SP + SJ \tag{14}$$
$$R = RW + RP + RJ \tag{15}$$

The variable quality is decided by management to be of importance only concerning juice since they got such information that they anyhow will be forced out of the market for whole tomatoes. Thus conditional optimization will be carried out for just a few values of the quality of juice expressed as percentage of A content. Thus the interactive multicriterion optimization will be carried out in terms of optimizing an implicit utility function of three variables, subject to conditional juice quality.

5.1 Choice of variables

It appears that this method for building models requires excess variables. In order to keep the number of variables down, certain rules may be applied. Consider the following structure as being part of a meso graph.

In figure 9 there are six arcs. Each arc can be expressed as a fraction of x. Thus only x has to be introduced.

In the case of Red Brand Canners the number of variables introduced could also be restricted. Balance equations (1)–(4) show that the introduction of W, J, P, and G need not necessarily be made explicit.

Balance equations (14) and (15) suggest that it is not necessary to introduce variables S and R explicitly.

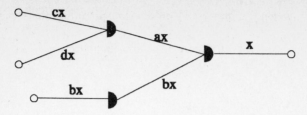

Figure 9. To represent the structure in this figure only one variable is necessary.

5.2 Model reduction

Besides keeping down the number of variables it is also of interest to limit the number of restrictions. Consider the following examples from (Holvid, 1977).

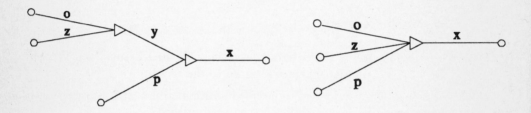

Figure 10: Elimination of unnecessary balance equations and variables. The structure to the left can be reduced to the one to the right.

Starting backwards in the network to the left, the two balance equations are

$$x = p + y$$
$$y = z + o$$

expressed in five variables. The reduced network will require just one balance equation and four variables. Care has to be taken when eliminating variables that may occur in criterion functions or other restrictions.

Other structures that may be reduced in order to reduce the corresponding model size can be found in figure 11.

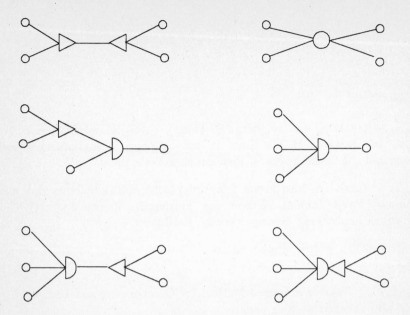

Figure 11: Structures to the left may be reduced to those to the right.

6   Conclusions

Since the meso graphs are a means of communication they also facilitate the delegation of data collection as discussed previously. Besides the pure physical collection of data, problems occur because of the sheer size of the task of collecting and coding data. For the coding and structured registration of data so-called matrix generators can be used. The advantage of using a matrix generator is that the whole LP-matrix is not coded at once but partitioned into subproblems. Matrix generators are designed to allow for easier changes of the mathematical model and data than if data are arranged directly as in the mathematical model.

An important characteristic of the meso language is that the use of graphics makes it easier to carry out a dialogue concerning relevant criteria that have to be used since long term goals are not operational. Trade-off considerations can be made interactively. Interaction is supposed to be man-machine interaction for the purpose of maximizing an implicit utility function. In case of the Red Brand Canners the model is entirely linear except for the functional relationship between utility and criteria, which is assumed to be appropriately described by a concave function which is increasing in each criterion. In such a case the boundary point ranking method (Hemming, 1975a) or the method of forces (Troutt and Hemming, 1985) would be an appropriate choice for the interactive procedure.

It is the intention of the author to further extend and formalize the meso language and to consider the possibility of allowing for computer aided design of survey and meso graphs. Any changes would be easy to make if automatic redrawing can be performed.

Besides computer aided design of meso graphs, model building would also be more efficient if matrix generators are used in a way allowing for the collection of data directly from data bases.

References

Hemming, T., Holvid, A. and Högberg, O. (1989). Models and Executive Decision Makers. In: Jackson, M. C., Keys, P. and Cropper, S. A. (eds.): Operational Research and the Social Sciences. Plenum, New York, pp. 647–652.

Hemming, T. (1975a). A New Method for Interactive Multiobjective Optimization: A Boundary Point Ranking Method. In: Thiriez, H., Zionts, S. (eds.): Multiple Criteria Decision Making. Springer-Verlag, Berlin, pp. 333–340.

Hemming, T. (1975b). Försörjningsstandard. ÖEF OA rapport, No. 2, Stockholm. (In Swedish).

Holvid, A. (1977). Towards a Unified Method for Constructing and Implementing LP Models. Unpublished working paper.

Müller-Merbach, H. (1978). Entwurf von Input-Output-Modellen. In: Proceedings in Operations Research, 7 (DGOR-Jahrestagung 1977), hrsg. von K. Brockhoff et al. Würtzburg, Physica-Verlag, Wien, pp. 521–532.

Müller-Merbach, H. (1981). Die Konstruktion von Input-Output-Modellen. In: Planung und Rechnungswesen in der Betriebswirtschaftslehre (Festagabe für Gert v.Kortzfleisch), hrsg. von Heinz Berner. Berlin: Duncker & Humblot, pp. 19–113.

Troutt, M. D. and Hemming, T. (1985). The Method of Abstract Forces for Direction Finding in Interactive Multicriterion Optimization. Working Paper, Department of Management, Southern Illinois University, Carbondale, Illinois.

Wilson, R. B. (1980). Red Brand Canners. In: Newson, E.F.P. (ed): Management Science and the Manager. Prentice-Hall, Englewood Cliffs, NJ, pp. 105–108 and pp. 179–182.

Parametric and Inverse Analysis of Multiple Criteria Optimization Problems

Gregory G. Kotkin

Computing Center of the U.S.S.R. Academy of Sciences

Vavilova 40, Moscow, U.S.S.R.

Abstract

A new approach for multiple criteria optimization problem is considered. It is based on the reduction of the multiple criteria optimization problem to the inverse optimization problem. Inverse nonlinear programming problems are a new class of optimization problems which are erased in game theory, system optimization, multicriteria optimization, etc.

We are concerned with problem definition, numerical methods and applications in multicriteria optimization of the inverse nonlinear programming problem.

Introduction to parametric analysis

Inverse nonlinear programming (i.n.p.) problems may be formulated as follows. We have to find out the pair x_* and u_* which satisfy the following system:

$$\begin{cases} \text{a)} & x_* \in \underset{x \in X(u_*)}{\text{Argmin}}\, f(x, u_*); \\[2mm] \text{b)} & G(x_*, u_*) \leq 0, \qquad H(x_*, u_*) = 0, \end{cases} \qquad (1)$$

where

$$X(u) = \{\, x \in R^n : g(x, u) \leq 0,\ h(x, u) = 0 \,\};$$

$$u \in R^m;$$

$$f(x, u), g(x, u), h(x, u), G(x, u), H(x, u) - \text{are continuous functions,}$$

$$f : R^{n+m} \to R^1, \quad g : R^{n+m} \to R^p, \quad h : R^{n+m} \to R^S,$$

$$G : R^{n+m} \to R^l, \quad H : R^{n+m} \to R^d.$$

In other words, we have to find out the solution x_* of the parametric nonlinear programming (p.n.p.) problem (1a) with given parameter u_* and the pair x_*, u_* have to satisfy additional constraints (1b).

Similar problems were studied in game theory, system optimization and multicriteria optimization, see Kurzhanski, 1986 and Antipin, 1989.

The multicriteria nonlinear programming (m.n.p.) problem may be formulated as an i.n.p. problem. Let us consider the following m.n.p. problem:

$$\min_{x \in X(0,0)} \bar{f}(x), \tag{2}$$

where $X(y, v) = \{ x \in Q \subset R^n : \bar{g}(x) \leq y, \bar{h}(x) = v \}$; $Q = \{ x \in R^n : a \leq x \leq b \}$ is rectangular constrained set, $a \in R^n$, $b \in R^n$, $a < b$, are given vectors; $\bar{f}(x), \bar{g}(x), \bar{h}(x)$ are continuous vector-functions $\bar{f} : Q \to R^{m+1}$, $\bar{g} : Q \to R^p$, $\bar{h} : Q \to R^s$.

Usually we have to find out the Pareto optimal solution $x_* \in P_x$ of the problem (2) using some additional knowledge about the solution.

In order to write this additional information in the form of the equality and inequality constraints let us consider the following parametrization of the Pareto optimal solution set:

1) $\quad S_1 = \Big\{ \underset{x \in X(0,0)}{\mathrm{Argmin}} \langle u, \bar{f}(x) \rangle, \ u \in R^{m+1}, \ u \geq 0, \ \exists i \, (u^i \neq 0) \Big\}.$

2) $\quad S_x = \Big\{ \underset{\substack{\bar{f}^i(x) \leq u^i, \ i=1,\ldots,m \\ x \in X(0,0)}}{\mathrm{Argmin}} \bar{f}^0(x), \ u \in R^m \Big\}.$ $\tag{3}$

Let us consider so-called generalized sensitivity functions $F^j : Y^j \to R^1$:

$$F^j(u, y, v) = \min_{x \in X(u,y,v)} \bar{f}^j(x),$$

where

$X(u, y, v) = \{ x \in Q : \bar{f}^i(x) \leq u^i, \ i = 0, \ldots, j-1, j+1, \ldots, m, \ \bar{g}(x) \leq y, \ \bar{h}(x) = v \},$

$j = 0, \ldots, m;$

$Y = \{ (u, y, v) : X(u, y, v) \neq \emptyset \}.$

The following theorem can be proved, see (Kotkin, 1988) and (Golikov and Kotkin, 1986)

Theorem 1.

Let us suppose that $F^j(u, y, v)$, $j = 0, \ldots, m$, are continuous functions at any $(u, 0, 0) \in Y^j$. Then

1) S_x is a weakly efficient solution set of problem (2).

2) Weakly efficient estimation set $S(0, 0)$ is an intersection of the graph of the function $\hat{F}(u) = F(u, 0, 0)$ and the image $\bar{f}(X(0, 0))$.

3) If $X(0, 0)$ is a connected (linear-wise connected) set, then $S(0, 0)$ is a connected (linear-wise connected) set.

4) If the following regularity condition holds: for any sequence $(y_k, v_k) \to (y_0, v_0)$ and any u_0 $((u_0, y_0, v_0) \in Y^0)$ there exists a $u_k \to u_0$ such that $(u_k, y_k, v_k) \in Y^0$. Then the point-to-set mapping $S(y, v)$ is continuous at $(0, 0)$, therefore the m.n.p. (2) problem is stable.

Let us assume that we can write the decision maker's additional information about the solution $x_* \in S_x$ in the form of equality and inequality constraints.

For example, if the reference point z is given, the additional constraints are

$$\bar{f}^0(x_*) - z_*^0 = \bar{f}^1(x_*) - z_*^1 = \cdots = \bar{f}^m(x_*) - z_*^m.$$

If the reservation level z_* is given, the additional constraints are $\bar{f}(x_*) \le z_*$.

In common cases, these constraints link the solution x_* and the parameter u_*:

$$G(x_*, u_*) \le 0; \qquad H(x_*, u_*) = 0,$$

where $G(x, u)$, $H(x, u)$ are continuous vector-functions.

In this case the m.n.p. problem (2) is reduced to the following inverse problem:

$$
\begin{cases}
\text{a)} \quad x_* \in \underset{\substack{\bar{f}^i(x) \le u_*^i,\ i=1,\ldots,m \\ x \in X(0,0)}}{\text{Argmin}} \ \bar{f}^0(x); \\[2ex]
\text{b)} \quad G(x_*, u_*) \le 0, \qquad H(x_*, u_*) = 0,
\end{cases}
\tag{5}
$$

In this paper we will consider a Generalized Newton method to solve the following inverse nonlinear programming problem:

$$
\begin{cases}
\text{a)} \quad x_* \in \underset{x \in R^n}{\text{Argmin}} \, f(x, u_*); \\[2ex]
\text{b)} \quad x_* = Au_* + B,
\end{cases}
\tag{6}
$$

where $f : R^{n+m} \to R^1$ is a sufficiently smooth strong convex function, A and B are given matrices. It is based on the idea that we can calculate the derivatives $x_u(u)$ of a so-called solution function

$$x(u) = \underset{x \in R^n}{\text{argmin}} \ f(x, u),$$

if we consider the second order derivatives $f_{xx}(x, u)$ and $f_{xu}(x, u)$ of the function $f(x, u)$.

Inverse problem technique

We will call the dual algorithms the numerical methods to solve the i.n.p. problem (1) which consist from two steps: calculating of the minimum of the p.n.p. problem (1a) with respect to the fixed value of the parameter u and calculating of new value of the parameter u using the constraints (1b).

Under the assumption that the functions $f(x, u)$, $g(x, u)$, $h(x, u)$, are strongly convex with respect to x functions, we have the unique solution of the p.n.p. problem (1a):

$$x(u) = \underset{x \in X(u)}{\text{argmin}} \ f(x, u), \tag{7}$$

We will call the function $x(u) : R^m \to R^n$ a solution function.

Let us use the solution function $x(u)$ in the constraints (1b): $\tilde{G}(u) = g(x(u), u)$; $\tilde{H}(u) = H(x(u), u)$.

We have to solve the following system with respect to u:

$$\tilde{G}(u) \leq 0; \qquad \tilde{H}(u) = 0. \tag{8}$$

Let us consider the solution function $x(u)$ of the i.n.p. problem (6) under the assumption that $f(x, u)$ is a sufficiently smooth and strong convex with respect to x function. Characteristic property of the solution function $x(u)$ is the gradient $f_x(x, u)$ equal to zero on the "surface" $x(u)$:

$$f_x(x(u), u) = 0. \tag{9}$$

We will use the equation (9) to calculate the derivatives of the solution function $x(u)$.

Let us consider the function $f_x(x, u)$ at the neighborhood of the point $(x_0, u_0) = (x(u_0), u_0)$:

$$f_x(x, u) = f_x(x_0, u_0) + \langle [f_{xx}, f_{xu}], [x - x_0, u - u_0] \rangle + o([x - x_0, u - u_0]). \tag{10}$$

Let us assume that the solution function $x(u)$ is a sufficiently smooth function and

$$x(u) = x(u_0) + \langle x_u(u_0), u - u_0 \rangle + o(u - u_0). \tag{11}$$

Using (9)–(11), we can derive the following equation

$$\left\langle \left[f_{xx}(x(u_0), u_0), f_{xu}(x(u_0), u_0) \right], \left[\langle x_u(u_0), u - u_0 \rangle, u - u_0 \right] \right\rangle = 0. \tag{12}$$

We have the following system of n linear equations

$$\sum_{k=1}^{n} \frac{\partial^2 f}{\partial x^i \partial x^k} w_j^k + \frac{\partial^2 f}{\partial x^i \partial u^j} = 0, \qquad i = 1, \ldots, n;$$

which have a unique solution $\frac{\partial x}{\partial u^j}(u_0) = (w_j^1, \ldots, w_j^n)$, where $j = 1, \ldots, m$.

Therefore we can calculate derivatives $x_u(u_0)$ using the system (12).

Let us show that the solution $x(u)$ is locally sufficiently smooth function in the case $u \in R^1$ under the assumption that function $f(x, u)$ is a sufficiently smooth and strong convex function with respect to x function. Let us consider the system (12) with respect to unknown function $\tilde{x}(u)$:

$$\begin{cases} \left\langle \left[f_{xx}(\tilde{x}(u), u), f_{xu}(\tilde{x}(u), u) \right], \left[\langle \tilde{x}_u(u), u - u_0 \rangle, u - u_0 \right] \right\rangle = 0; \\ \tilde{x}(u_0) = x(u_0). \end{cases} \tag{13}$$

We have the system of differential equations (13) with initial conditions that unknown function $\tilde{x}(u)$ equal to the solution $x(u)$ at some point u_0. System (13) has unique and sufficiently smooth solution $x(u)$ which equal to solution function at some neighborhood of $u_0 : \tilde{x}(u) = x(u)$.

In order to find out the solution of i.n.p. problem (6), we have to find out the root of the following vector-function $q(u) = x(u) - (Au + B)$. We can solve the system

$$q(u) = 0, \qquad u \in R^m \tag{14}$$

using the usual Newton method.

Let us rewrite the system (12) using the notation

$$v_x = x_u(u_k), \qquad v_u = u - u_k : \big\langle [f_{xx}, f_{xu}], [\langle v_x, v_u \rangle, v_u] \big\rangle = 0.$$

We have the dual method which consist of two steps: 1) solving of the p.n.p. problem (6a) with a fixed value of the parameter u; 2) usual Newton step to solve the system (14):

1) $x_{k+1} \in \underset{x \in R^n}{\text{Argmin}} \, f(x, u_k)$

2) $(v_x, v_u) \in \underset{V_x, V_u}{\text{Argmin}} \big\{ \big| \big\langle [f_{xx}, f_{xu}], [\langle v_x, v_u \rangle, v_u] \big\rangle \big|^2 + \big| x_{k+1} - (Au_k + B) - \langle v_x - A, v_u \rangle \big|^2 +$

$+ \alpha \big| [\langle v_x, v_u \rangle, v_u] \big|^2 \big\}$, where $\alpha > 0$;

$u_{k+1} = u_k + v_u.$

This method converges to the solution $u_* : a(u_*) = 0$, under the assumption that $f(x, u)$ is sufficiently smooth and strong convex function ($x(u)$ is sufficiently smooth in the case $u \in R^m$, $m > 1$) and function $q(u)$ satisfy the usual assumption of the Newton method. So we have the local convergence of this method.

References

Antipin, A. S. (1989). Some class of the inverse optimization problem. Mathematical programming method and software. Sverdlovsk (in Russian).

Evtushenko, Yu.G. (1985). Numerical Optimization Technique. Springer Verlag, New York.

Golikov, A.I. and Kotkin, G.G. (1986). Application of Sensitivity Function in Multicriteria Optimization (in Russian). Computer Center of the U.S.S.R. Academy of Sciences, Moscow.

Kotkin, G.G. (1988). Topological Properties of Perturber Pareto Set (in Russian). Computer Center of the U.S.S.R. Academy of Sciences, Moscow.

Kotkin, G.G. (1989a). Inverse Nonlinear Programming and its Applications. IIASA Working Paper, International Institute for Applied System Analysis, Laxenburg, Austria, to appear.

Kotkin, G.G. (1989b). Geometric Ideas in Nonlinear and Multicriteria Optimization. IIASA Working Paper, International Institute for Applied System Analysis, Laxenburg, Austria, to appear.

Kurzhanski, A.B. (1986). Inverse Problems in Multiobjective Dynamic Optimization. Lecture Notes in Economics and Mathematical Systems. Toward Interactive and Intelligent Decision Support Systems. Volume 1. Springer Verlag, New York.

Trade-off Analysis Based upon Parametric Optimization

Hirotaka Nakayama
Department of Applied Mathematics
Konan University
8-9-1 Okamoto, Higshinada, Kobe 658, Japan

Abstract

In multi-objective programming problems, one of most difficult tasks is 'balancing among multiple objectives', i.e. 'trade-off'. This difficulty originates from the value-judgment of decision makers. For the past decade, several methods have been developed to overcome this difficulty in multi-objective programming problems. Among them, from a practical viewpoint, the aspiration level approach is very attractive, since it does not require any consistency of the decision maker's judgment, and it makes the trade-off (or equivalently balancing) among the objectives very easy.

On the other hand, some of practical problems have very many objective functions, say, about one hundred. For this kind of problems, DM tends to be tired with answering his/her aspiration levels for all objective functions. Usually, the feeling that DM wants to improve some of criteria is much stronger than the one that he/her compromises with some compensatory relaxation of other criteria. Therefore, it is more practical in problems with very many objective functions for DM to answer only his/her improvement rather than both improvement and relaxation. To this end, parametric optimization techniques in traditional mathematical programming can be effectively used. In particular, as can be seen in Korhonen and Wallenius' paper (1988), we can trace the Pareto surface very quickly in LP type problems without solving additional auxiliary scalar optimization. This fact implies that parametric optimization techniques enable decision makers' trade-off very easy and quick, and therefore to apply the interactive multi-objective programming methods to many real problems even though they have many objective functions. In this paper, some techniques for the automatic trade-off based on parametric optimization techniques will be reported in a wider class of problems including QP cases.

1   Introduction

We consider the following multi-objective programming

[MOP]   Maximize $F(x) = (f_1(x), f_2(x), \ldots, f_r(x))$
             subject to $f_i(x) \geq \bar{f}_i, \qquad i = r+1, \ldots, s$
             $g_j(x) \geq \bar{g}_j, \qquad j = 1, \ldots, m$
             $x \in X \subset R^n.$

Here, $f_1, \ldots, f_r$ are objective functions, $f_{r+1}, \ldots, f_s$ soft constraints and g_j $(j = 1, \ldots, m)$ hard constraints. $\bar{f}_i$ and $\bar{g}_j$ are called the aspiration level of f_i and g_j, respectively. The difference between objective functions and soft constraint functions is as follows: The larger the value of objective functions are, the more desirable they are. But it is not necessary for them to meet their aspiration levels. On the other hand, soft constraint functions must attain at their aspiration levels, but do not necessarily require increase as much as possible. In developing a software for decision support, it is very important to make objective functions and soft constraint functions interchangeable depending on the situation.

We call it 'tradeoff analysis' to consider how much we have to relax some criteria for compensating for the improvement of other criteria. The aim of this paper is to present some method for making the tradeoff easy and speedy in practical problems.

One of good examples in multiobjective problems is camera lens design. A camera lens is composed of several kinds of lenses. In the lens design, the decision variables are interval of lenses, curvature of lenses, kinds of glasses, etc. The objective functions are cost, weight, length, focus, caliber, aberration, etc. In particular, there are very many kinds of aberration, e.g., aperture, spherical, astigmatism, lateral, color and so on. Therefore, it is remarkable that we often have more than 100 objective functions in camera lens design. Moreover, as is seen in design of zoom lens, it is a very important and difficult task to balance over these many conflicting criteria. This task is up to the value judgment of designers. At present, this problem is solved by the least square method with a scalarized objective function by combining all squared criteria with appropriate weights. However, it is very difficult to decide an appropriate weight, because even if the designer increase some weight so that the corresponding criteria may improve, other criteria often get too worse. It usually takes very much time for the designer to obtain a finally satisfactory weights. In developing a support system of lens design, therefore, it is important to help designers tradeoff easily and quickly.

Another good example is seen in the erection management of cablestayed bridge (Ishido et al., 1987). The decision variables in this example are the amount of shim-adjustment for each cable. The objective functions are the cost, the deviation of each cable-tension, the deviation of each camber (i.e., the shape of bridge floor), etc. In a case of bridge with 30 cables, we have about 100 objective functions, and encounter the same difficulty as in camera lens design.

In the following we present a method for making the tradeoff very easy and speedy even if the problem has many objective functions. To begin with, we shall review some technique for multiobjective programming.

2 Aspiration level techniques for interactive multi-objective programming

For simplicity for a while, suppose that X stands for all constraints including f_i $(r + 1 \leq i \leq s)$ and g_j $(1 \leq j \leq m)$ in the previous section. The aspiration level approach to multiobjective programming is now widely recognized to give an effective tool in practical problems. In this kind of methods, the aspiration level at the k-th iteration $\bar{f}^k$ is modified as follows:

$$\bar{f}^{k+1} = \mathrm{T} \circ \mathrm{P}(\bar{f}^k) \tag{2.1}$$

Here, the operator P selects the Pareto solution nearest in some sense to the given aspiration level $\bar{f}^k$. The operator T is the trade-off operator which changes the k-th aspiration level $\bar{f}^k$ if the decision maker does not compromise with the shown solution $\mathrm{P}(\bar{f}^k)$. Of course, since $\mathrm{P}(\bar{f}^k)$ is a Pareto solution, there exists no feasible solution which makes all criteria better than $\mathrm{P}(\bar{f}^k)$, and thus the decision maker has to trade-off among criteria if he wants to improve some of criteria. Based on this trade-off, a new aspiration level is decided as $\mathrm{T} \circ \mathrm{P}(\bar{f}^k)$. Similar process is continued until the decision maker obtain an agreeable solution. This idea is implemented in the satisficing trade-off method (Nakayama, 1984) and DIDASS (Grauer et al., 1984).

The operation which gives $\mathrm{P}(\bar{f}^k)$ from $\bar{f}^k$ is performed by some auxiliary scalar optimization. The objective function in this auxiliary optimization is called an achievement function in some literature (Wierzbicki, 1986). Let f_i^* be an ideal value which is usually given in such a way that $f_i^* > \max\{ f_i(x) \mid x \in X \}$, and let f_{*i} be a nadir value which is usually given by $f_{*i} = \min_{1 \leq j \leq r} f_i(x_j^*)$ where $x_j^* = \arg \max_{x \in X} f_j(x)$.

Then, typical examples of achievement function based on Tchebyshev norm are given in the following:

$$p_1 = \max_{1 \leq i \leq r} w_i(f_i^* - f_i(x)) \to \min$$

where

$$w_i = \frac{1}{f_i^* - \bar{f}_i}$$

or

$$p_2 = \max_{1 \leq i \leq r} w_i(\bar{f}_i - f_i(x)) \to \min$$

where

$$w_i = \frac{1}{f_i^* - f_{*i}} .$$

p_1 is used in the satisficing tradeoff method (Nakayama, 1984), while p_2 is used in DIDASS (Grauer et al., 1984). The desirable properties of achievement functions were discussed in the author's previous paper (Nakayama, 1985). Both of these two functions have almost the same characteristics from this point of view. However, there is a slight difference between Pareto solutions obtained by optimizing these functions. This is illustrated in Fig. 2.1.

Remark 2.1. It should be noted that the solution obtained by optimizing the functions p_1 or p_2 is just a weak Pareto solution. As is well known, if we want to get a strong Pareto

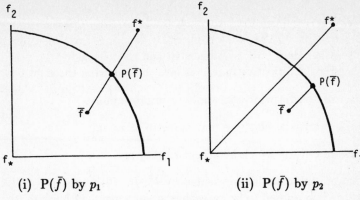

$$(i) \ P(\bar{f}) \text{ by } p_1 \qquad\qquad (ii) \ P(\bar{f}) \text{ by } p_2$$

$$\text{Figure 2.1}$$

optimal solution rather than a merely weak Pareto solution, we can use the following augmented achievement functions:

$$q_1 = \max_{1 \le i \le r} w_i(f_i^* - f_i(x)) - \varepsilon \sum_{i=1}^{r} w_i f_i(x)$$

or

$$q_2 = \max_{1 \le i \le r} w_i(\bar{f}_i - f_i(x)) - \varepsilon \sum_{i=1}^{r} w_i f_i(x).$$

Since the above achievement functions are not smooth, the minimization for them is usually performed by solving the equivalently transformed problem. Instead of minimizing p_2, for example, we solve the following:

(Q)

$$\text{Minimize} \quad z$$

$$\text{subject to} \quad w_i(\bar{f}_i - f_i(x)) \le z$$

$$x \in X.$$

From a standpoint of parametric optimization, p_2 is more convenient than p_1, because it changes only the values of right hand side according to the change of aspiration levels. In the following section, we shall discuss a method for the automatic trade-off.

3 Automatic trade-off using parametric analysis

3.1 General nonlinear cases

In practical problems, we often encounter cases with very many objective functions as was stated in the previous section. Under this circumstance, the decision maker tend to get tired with answering new aspiration levels for all objective functions. Usually, the feeling that DM wants to improve some of criteria is much stronger than the one that he/her compromises with some compensatory relaxation of other criteria. Therefore, it is more practical in problems with very many objective functions for DM to answer only his/her improvement rather than both improvement and relaxation.

Let us classify the objective functions into the following three groups:

(i) the class of criteria which he wants to improve more,

(ii) the class of criteria which he may agree to relaxing,

(iii) the class of criteria which he accept as they are.

The index set of each class is represented by I_I^k, I_R^k, I_A^k, respectively. If $I_I^k = \emptyset$, then the present solution is supposed to be agreeable to implement. Otherwise, the decision maker is asked his new acceptable level of criteria $\bar{f}_i^{k+1}$ for the class of I_I^k and I_R^k. For $i \in I_A^k$, set $\bar{f}_i^{k+1} = f_i(x^k)$. At this stage, we can use the assignment of sacrifice for f_j $(j \in I_R)$ which is automatically set in the equal proportion to $\tilde{\lambda}_i w_i$, namely, by

$$\Delta f_j = \frac{-1}{N\tilde{\lambda}_j w_j} \sum_{i \in I_I} \tilde{\lambda}_i w_i \Delta f_i \tag{3.1}$$

where N is the number of elements of the set I_R, and $\tilde{\lambda}$ is the Lagrange multiplier associated with the constraints in Problem (Q). The reason why (3.1) is available is that $(\tilde{\lambda}_1 w_1, \ldots, \tilde{\lambda}_r w_r)$ is the normal vector of the tangent hyperplane of the Pareto surface under appropriate conditions. (See Appendix).

By doing this, in cases where there are a large number of criteria, the burden of the decision maker can be decreased so much. Of course, if the decision maker does not agree with this quota Δf_j laid down automatically, he can modify them in a manual way.

3.2   LP cases

In cases where all functions in (P) are linear and X is a polyhedral set in an n-dimensional Euclidean space, the above technique can give more precise information about trade-off among the criteria. In other words, we can get the exact amount of relaxation by using parametric optimization technique so that the new aspiration level may be on the Pareto surface.

Recall that every strong Pareto solution is proper in linear cases. Therefore, we use the following augmented objective function with $\varepsilon > 0$ in the auxiliary min-max problem:

[ALP]   Minimize $z - \varepsilon \sum w_i f_i(x)$

subject to $\bar{f}_i^k - f_i(x) \leq (1/w_i)z$, $i = 1, \ldots, r$

$x \in X$

In this formulation, it is very easy to change the i-th objective function into a constraint function by replacing $1/w_i$ with 0, and vice vera. One way to decrease the burden of decision makers in tradeoff is the following:

Step 1. Ask decision makers the new aspiration level $\bar{f}_i^{k+1}$ for the objective function to be improved, f_i $(i \in I_I)$.

Step 2. Let r be the index of the objective function to be relaxed most.

Step 3. Let $f^k := f(x^k)$ where x^k is the solution to [ALP]. Decide the new aspiration level $\bar{f}_j^{k+1} := f^k - \Delta f_j^k$ $(j \in I_R)$ for the the objective function to be relaxed by solving the following linear parametric problem:

[PLP]   Minimize z

   subject to $f_i^k + t\Delta f_i^k - f_i(x) \leq 0,$ $i \in I_I$

   $f_j^k - t\Delta f_j^k - f_j(x) \leq 0,$ $j \in I_R \setminus \{r\}$

   $f_r^k - f_r(x) \leq (1/w_i)z$

   $x \in X$

where

$$\Delta f_i^k = \bar{f}_i^{k+1} - f_i^k, \qquad\qquad\qquad\qquad i \in I_I$$

$$\Delta f_j^k = \sum (\lambda_i + \varepsilon w_i)\Delta f_i/(N(\lambda_j + \varepsilon w_j)), \qquad j \in I_R \setminus \{r\}.$$

In the parametric linear programming [PLP], at first, the new base is obtained by the sensitivity analysis from the final tableau of [ALP] in which the coefficient vector of objective function is changed from $(1, -\varepsilon w_1 c_1, \ldots, -\varepsilon w_n c_n)$ into $(1, 0, \ldots, 0)$, and then the column vector associated with z in the coefficient matrix of the constraint is changed from $(1/w_1, \ldots, 1/w_{r-1}, 1/w_r)$ into $(0, \ldots, 0, 1/w_r)$. In many practical cases, the base is unchangeable for a sufficiently small $\varepsilon > 0$ for the change of the coefficient vector of objective function. Secondly, the solution of [PLP] with $t = 1$ is obtained by the right hand side sensitivity analysis. At corner points of the Pareto surface with kink, the solutions are degenerate. As in the usual parametric optimization, the dual simplex method is used for getting the new base at such degenerate solutions. Note that the obtained new aspiration level is already Pareto optimal. Therefore, since only a few pivoting are usually needed in these techniques, we can obtain the new Pareto solution associated with a new aspiration level very quickly. Moreover, we can make a microjustification around the obtained Pareto solution along the direction $(\Delta f_1^k, \ldots, \Delta f_{r-1}^k)$ by modifying the value of t. This operation can be made in some dynamic way, because each solution to [PLP] with a given t is obtained very quickly. Using some computer graphics, this enables us to develop an effective man-machine interface as a decision support system. This idea was originally realized by Korhonen-Wallenius (1987) in a slightly different way.

Remark 3.1. In (Korhonen and Wallenius, 1987), the decision maker is asked to answer his/her new acceptable value for all criteria. Of course, the new acceptable level of criteria which the decision maker does not answer can be set to be the same as before. In any case in their approach, Problem ALP (rather than PLP) for the new value of right hand side is solved by some parametric optimization technique. Therefore, the level of improvement can not be neccessarily guaranteed in some cases (in particular, where the relaxation amount is not sufficient). However, this problem can be easily overcome by moving forward or backward along the direction Δf by modification of the value of t, in other words, by seeing the trade-off along this direction. The main point in their method is that the decision maker can see the tradeoff among criteria in a visual and dynamic way. On the other hand, the point in this paper is to see quickly the exact tradeoff by inputting only the new aspiration level of criteria to be improved, $\bar{f}_i^{k+1}$ ($i \in I_I$) even though the problem has very many objective functions.

3.3 QP cases

The above technique can be used in a similar way in QP cases. However, it should be noted that the quadratic objective function can not be treated as a constraint in the auxiliary min-max problem, because otherwise the usual complementary pivoting method for QP can not be used.

We consider the following multiobjective quadratic programming problem:

[MQP]
$$f_1(x) = \frac{1}{2}x^T D x + p^T x \rightarrow \min$$
$$f_2(x) = s_2^T x \rightarrow \min$$
$$\cdots$$
$$f_r(x) = s_r^T x \rightarrow \min$$

subject to
$$Ax \geq b$$
$$x \geq 0$$

Given the ideal point f^* and the nadir point f_*, set the weight
$$w_i = \frac{1}{f_{*i} - f_i^*} .$$

Let $\bar{f}$ be an aspiration level. Then we solve the following pseudo Min-Max problem:

[AQP]
$$F(x) = w_1 f_1(x) + z^+ - z^- \rightarrow \min$$

subject to
$$-f_2(x) + (1/w_2)(z^+ - z^-) \geq -\bar{f}_2$$
$$\cdots$$
$$-f_r(x) + (1/w_r)(z^+ - z^-) \geq -\bar{f}_r$$
$$Ax \geq b$$
$$x \geq 0, \qquad z^+, z^- \geq 0.$$

We can get a Pareto solution by solving the above pseudo Min-Max problem. If the decision maker is not satisfied with the Pareto solution, he is required to answer his trade-off. For $i = 2, \ldots, r$, he is asked which criteria and what amount he wants to improve. Given the improvement of Δf_i $(i \in I_I)$, the amount Δf_j $(j \in I_R)$ may be decided automatically by (3.1) using the sensitivity analysis. Once decided the change Δf_i $(i = 2, \ldots, r)$, we get a new Pareto solution by solving the following QP with $t = 1$

[PQP]
$$F(x) = f_1(x) \to \min$$

subject to

$$f_i(x) \leq f_i^k - t\Delta f_i^k, \qquad i \in I_I$$
$$f_j(x) \leq f_j^k + t\Delta f_j^k, \qquad j \in I_R$$
$$Ax \geq b$$
$$x \geq 0, \qquad z^+, z^- \geq 0,$$

where $f^k := f(x^k)$ is the previous Pareto level. We can make a microjustification around the obtained Pareto solution along the direction $(\Delta f_2^k, \ldots, \Delta f_r^k)$ by modifying the value of t. This can be done in some dynamic way using a parametric optimization technique for [PQP].

After 2nd trade-off, we can proceed in the same way as above for [PQP]. However, we do not need to solve [PQP] from the beginning; instead we can utilize the sensitivity (or parametric) analysis in a usual manner. This enables the decision maker to see quickly the exact tradeoff by inputting only the new aspiration level of criteria to be improved, $\bar{f}_i^{k+1}$ $(i \in I_I)$ even though the problem has very many objective functions.

The reason why we do not use the auxiliary QP (i.e. [PQP] with $\bar{f}_i$ $(i = 2, \ldots, r)$ as the value of the right hand side) from the initial stage is that it may be infeasible for the given aspiration level. The above pseudo Min-Max problem can provide a Pareto solution even if the given aspiration level is infeasible.

References

Fiacco, A.V. (1983). Introduction to Sensitivity and Stability Analysis in Nonlinear Programming. Academic Press, New York.

Grauer, M., Lewandowski, A. and Wierzbicki, A.P. (1984). DIDASS — Theory, Implementation and Experiences. In M. Grauer and A.P. Wierzbicki (eds.): Interactive Decision Analysis, Proceeding of an International Workshop on Interactive Decision Analysis and Interpretative Computer Intelligence. Springer, pp. 22–30.

Ishido, K., Nakayama, H., Furukawa, K., Inoue, K. and Tanikawa, K. (1987). Multiobjective Management of Erection for Cablestayed Bridge Using Satisficing Trade-off Method. In Y. Sawaragi, K. Inoue and H. Nakayama (eds.): Toward Interactive and Intelligent Decision Support Systems. Springer, pp. 304–312.

Korhonen, P. and Laakso, J. (1986). Solving Generalized Goal Programming Problems using a Visual Interactive Approach. *European J. of Operational Res.*, 26, pp. 355–363.

Korhonen, P. and Wallenius, J. (1987). A Pareto Race. Working Paper F–180, Helsinki School of Economics, also Naval Research Logistics (1988).

Nakayama, H. (1984). Proposal of Satisficing Trade-off Method for Multiobjective Programming. *Transact. SICE*, 20, pp. 29–35 (in Japanese).

Nakayama, H. and Sawaragi, Y. (1984). Satisficing Trade-off Method for Interactive Multiobjective Programming Methods. In M. Grauer and A.P. Wierzbicki (eds.): Interactive Decision Analysis, Proceeding of an International Workshop on Interactive Decision Analysis and Interpretative Computer Intelligence. Springer, pp. 113–122.

Nakayama, H. (1989). Sensitivity and Trade-off Analysis in Linear Multiobjective Programming. In A. Lewandowski and I. Stanchev (eds.): Methodology and Software for Interactive Decision Support. Springer, pp. 86–93.

Sawaragi, Y., Nakayama, H. and Tanino, T. (1985). Theory of Multiobjective Optimization. Academic Press, New York.

Smale, S. (1975). Sufficient Conditions for an Optimum, Warwick Dynamical Systems. *Lecture Notes in Mathematics*, 468, Springer.

Wierzbicki, A.P. (1981). A Mathematical Basis for Satisficing Decision Making. In J. Morse (ed.): Organizations: Multiple Agents with Multiple Criteria. Springer, pp. 465–485.

Wierzbicki, A.P. (1986). On the Completeness and Constructiveness of Parametric, Characterization to Vector Optimization Problems. *OR spectrum*, 8, pp. 73–87.

Appendix: Tradeoff Analysis for Nonlinear Cases

Consider the following problem:

[VP]   Maximize $F(x) = (f_1(x), f_2(x), \ldots, f_r(x))$

subject to $g_j(x) \geq 0$ $j = 1, \ldots, m$

$x \in R^n.$

Theorem A1 (second order sufficient condition for Pareto optimum)
The following conditions are sufficient for x^* to be weakly Pareto optimal for [VP]:

(i) There exist $\lambda_i^* \geq 0$ $(i = 1, \ldots, r)$ with $\sum \lambda_i^* = 1$ and $\mu_j^* \geq 0$ such that

$$\nabla_x L(x^*; \lambda^*, \mu^*) := \sum \lambda_i^* \nabla f_i(x^*) + \sum \mu_j^* \nabla g_j(x^*) = 0 \tag{A1}$$

and

$$\mu_j^* g_j(x^*) = 0, \qquad g_j(x^*) \geq 0, \qquad j = 1, \ldots, m. \tag{A2}$$

(ii) For any nonzero vector h such that

$$\lambda_i^* \nabla f_i(x^*) h = 0 \qquad (i = 1, \ldots, r) \tag{A3}$$

and

$$\mu_j^* \nabla g_j(x^*) h = 0 \qquad (j = 1, \ldots, m), \tag{A4}$$

we have

$$h^T \nabla_x^2 L(x^*; \lambda^*, \mu^*) h > 0. \tag{A5}$$

Remark
The above theorem was originally given by Smale in a slightly different style (Smale, 1975). However, we can obtain the same result in an easier way via the following lemma:

Lemma A1
x^* is a weak Pareto solution to [VP] if and only if x^* is a solution to

[AP]   Minimize z

subject to $f_i(x^*) - f_i(x) \leq z,$ $i = 1, \ldots, r$ $\qquad$ (A6)

$g_j(x) \geq 0,$ $j = 1, \ldots, m$ $\qquad$ (A7)

$x \in R^n.$

Theorem A1 is also obtained from the sufficient condition for [AP]. If we want to get a second order sufficient condition for a properly strong Pareto optimal solution, it suffices to use an augmented objective function

$$z - \varepsilon \sum w_i f_i(x) \tag{A8}$$

in place of z itself. Then Theorem A1 is modified by replacing λ_i^* by $\lambda_i^* + \varepsilon$ in (A1).

Now we have a fundamental theorem for tradeoff analysis to [VP], which is a straight result from (Fiacco, 1983).

Theorem A2

Suppose that the second order sufficient condition of Theorem A1 holds. Suppose also that the vectors $(\nabla f_1(x^*), -1)$, ..., $(\nabla f_r(x^*), -1)$, $(\nabla g_{k_1}(x^*), 0)$, ..., $(\nabla g_{k_s}(x^*), 0)$ are linearly independent, where $(k_1, \ldots, k_s)$ is the index set of active constraints of (A7). In addition, suppose that the following strict complementary slackness condition holds:

$$
\begin{aligned}
\lambda_i^* > 0 \quad &\text{for any} \quad i \in \{1, \ldots, r\} \\
\mu_j^* > 0 \quad &\text{for any} \quad j \in J := \{\, j \mid g_j(x^*) = 0 \,\}.
\end{aligned}
$$

Then we have

$$
0 = \sum \lambda_i^* \Delta f_i + o(\|\Delta f\|).
$$

Remark

Theorem A2 implies that $(\lambda_1, \ldots, \lambda_r)$ is a normal vector to the Pareto surface, and therefore gives an information on tradeoff among objective functions. This gives a basis to using automatic tradeoff in the satisficing tradeoff (3.1). It is readily seen that a part of strict complementary slackness condition $\lambda_i^* > 0$ $(i = 1, \ldots, r)$ implies the solution x^* is a proper Pareto solution to [VP]. Therefore, if we use an augmented Tchebyshev norm q_1 or q_2 in auxiliary min-max problem (in practice, the augmented objective function (A8) for the problem (Q) in section 2 in order to obtain the Pareto solution x^*, this condition is automatically satisfied. Under this circumstance, $\lambda_i^* + \varepsilon$ $(i = 1, \ldots, r)$ gives tradeoff information among objectives instead of λ_i^* $(i = 1, \ldots, r)$.

Why the Analytic Hierarchy Process Is Not Like Multiattribute Utility Theory

Luis G. Vargas
Joseph M. Katz Graduate School of Business
314 Mervis Hall
University of Pittsburgh
Pittsburgh, PA 15260, U.S.A.

1   Introduction

Until not long ago, Multiattribute Utility Theory (MAUT) dominated the field of decision making despite the fact that a number of researchers have point out a variety of problems encountered when attempting to implement it. Colson and De Bruyn (1989, p. 1202) write:

> "The main criticisms of this theory and of its practice are well-known:
>
> (i) the Von Neumann-Morgenstern expected utility approach is neither validated by evidence, nor similar to actual decision processes;
>
> (ii) the construction of the multiattribute utility function requires a heavy questioning process;
>
> (iii) at the end of this process, one cannot be sure whether the preference structure discovered is assumed, reveled or constructed when starting from a true underlying vague preference;
>
> (iv) all the prescriptive implications of the model are strongly founded upon the hypothesis that, even if the decision maker has not been forced during the interview process, he is rational in the sense that he is supposed to obey a set of rather intuitively convincing axioms of behavior."

The most significant drawback of the theory is that the existence of a utility function is based on the transitivity of the preferences of decision makers because this condition is not always satisfied.

On the other hand, there is a theory that has been developed independently from MAUT that does not require transitivity — The Analytic Hierarchy Process (AHP). Both theories have been compared in applied settings. The results have almost always been favorable to the AHP. Nonetheless, practitioners of MAUT fail to recognize the validity of the AHP. Some of them believe that one cannot compare two alternatives with respect to a criterion unless one knows the range of values of the criterion on the alternatives.

Others think that because utilities are unique to within linear transformations, and under the assumption that criteria are utility independent the resulting multiattribute function is additive, that any other method yielding an additive function must satisfy the axioms of MAUT or the results it yields are arbitrary. The basic flaw in the first argument is that people make decisions without quantifying criteria, thus the range of values of the criteria are not necessary to make comparisons of alternatives. The second argument asserts that the axioms of MAUT are necessary and sufficient for the resulting function to be additive. This is false because (a) additive functions based on ratio scales do not satisfy the axioms of MAUT, and (b) utility functions are interval scales.

The objective of this work is to develop a common theoretical framework to address the point of departure of both theories. The framework is based on the classical approach to measurement: *primitives* → *axioms* → *representation and uniqueness*. We first establish the primitives of both theories, then develop the axioms for a single attribute and multiple attributes, and finally, give representation and uniqueness theorems.

We observe that when the axiom of transitivity is eliminated, MAUT must also use paired comparisons to establish preferences. The basic difference are (a) the meaning of the paired comparisons, and (b) how comparisons are synthesized from level to level of the structure developed to deal with the decision problem. To show these differences we introduce some basic notation and known results of both the AHP and MAUT.

2 Primitives

Primitives are the elements of a theory on which the axioms are based. The AHP and MAUT have some common primitive elements. Let C be a set of *properties* or *attributes*. We usually refer to them as criteria; let A be a set of n *alternatives*; let O be the space of outcomes or consequences from the alternatives; and let L be the set of lotteries built on the space of outcomes O, $O \subset L$. Let $\succsim_c$ be *a binary relation* representing "more preferred than or indifferent to" according to $C \in C$. Finally, let $U \equiv \{ u \mid u : L \to R \}$, $W \equiv \{ w \mid w : A \to [0,1] \}$, $\Omega \equiv \{ \varphi \mid \varphi : A \times A \to R \}$ and $\Theta \equiv \{ \psi \mid \psi : L \times L \to R \}$. Let $\pi : C \to \Omega$ and $\phi : C \to \Theta$ be mappings from the set of criteria C to the sets of a pairwise comparison functions. Thus, for all $C \in C$ there is a $\varphi_c \in \Omega$ and $\psi_c \in \Theta$ such that

$$A_i >_c A_j \quad \text{if and only if} \quad \varphi_c(A_i, A_j) > 1,$$
$$A_i \sim_c A_j \quad \text{if and only if} \quad \varphi_c(A_i, A_j) = 1$$

or

$$A_i >_c A_j \quad \text{if and only if} \quad \psi_c(A_i, A_j) > 0,$$
$$A_i \sim_c A_j \quad \text{if and only if} \quad \psi_c(A_i, A_j) = 0.$$

The problem is the same in both theories:

- **Utility Theory:** *Find a function $u \in U$ which captures the preferences of the decision maker(s) through the use of ψ_c.*

- **The Analytic Hierarchy Process:** *Find a function $w \in W$ which captures preferences of the decision maker(s) through the use of φ_c.*

Although the problem is almost identical, the assumptions are quite different. In UT one deals with the outcomes of the actions. Thus the probability distributions of the outcomes play a significant role in the evaluation of alternatives. In the AHP, the likelihood of occurrence of the outcomes may change from attribute to attribute. Hence we deal with the alternatives rather than with the probability distribution of their outcomes.

3 The single attribute case: Axioms and representation theorem

Utility Theory	Analytic Hierarchy Process
(U1): $>_c$ on $\mathcal{L}$ is a weak order.	
(U2): $\forall x, y \in \mathcal{L}$, if $x >_c y$ and $0 < \lambda < 1$ then $\lambda x + (1 - \lambda)z >_c \lambda y + (1 - \lambda)z$, $\forall z \in \mathcal{L}$.	(H1): (Reciprocity) $\forall A_i, A_j \in \mathcal{A}$, $\varphi_c(A_i, A_j) \cdot \varphi_c(A_j, A_i) = 1$
(U3): $\forall x, y, z \in \mathcal{L}$, if $x >_c y$ and $y >_c z$, then $\exists \alpha, \beta$, $0 < \alpha$, $\beta < 1$ for which $\alpha x + (1 - \alpha)z >_c y >_c \beta x + (1 - \beta)z$	(H2): (Boundedness) $\exists \rho > 0$ for which $1/\rho < \varphi_c(A_i, A_j) < \rho$.

UT does not use pairwise comparisons, i.e., $\psi_c(x, y)$, to construct the utility function. Instead, the utility function $u(x)$ is built directly using some of the available methods and $\psi_c(x, y) = u(x) - u(y)$ (Fishburn, 1988).

On the other hand, the AHP is built on the concept of pairwise comparison and does not make any assumptions on the type of order implied by the paired comparisons. Instead, emphasis is put on the strength of preferences and the inconsistency that they create. A function $\varphi_c \in \pi(\mathcal{C})$ is said to be consistent if and only if $\varphi_c(A_i, A_j) \varphi_c(A_j, A_k) = \varphi_c(A_i, A_k)$, $\forall A_i, A_j, A_k \in \mathcal{A}$.

The result of the representation theorem of the AHP is a ratio scale given by the principal eigenvector of a reciprocal matrix whose entries are the paired comparisons defined by φ_c. There is no such mathematical model that yields utility functions from paired comparisons.

Representation and uniqueness

The axioms U1–U3 hold if, and only if there is a real value function $u \in \mathcal{U}$ on $\mathcal{L}$ that is:

(1) *Order-preserving:*
$\forall x, y \in \mathcal{L}$:
$x >_c y$ if and only if $u(x) > u(y)$,

(2) *Linear:*
$\forall x, y \in \mathcal{L}, \ \forall \lambda \in [0,1]$:
$u[\lambda x + (1 - \lambda)y] =$
$= \lambda u(x) + (1 - \lambda)u(y)$

and

(3) *Unique* up to a positive affine transformation.

The axioms H1–H2 hold if, and only if there is a real value function $w \in \mathcal{W}$ on $\mathcal{A}$ that:

(1) *Captures dominance:*
$A_i >_c A_j$ iff
$$\frac{1}{m} \sum_{k=1}^{m} \sum_{h=1}^{n} a_{ih}^{(k)} > \frac{1}{m} \sum_{k=1}^{m} \sum_{h=1}^{n} a_{jh}^{(k)}$$
$a_{ih}^{(k)} \equiv (i, h)$ entry of the k-th power of the matrix (a_{ij}), $i, j = 1, 2, \ldots, n$ and $\varphi_c(A_i, A_j) = a_{ij}$.

and

(2) Is *unique* up to a similarity transformation.

4 The multiattribute case: Axioms and representation theorem

A Multiattribute linear utility theory (Keeney and Raiffa, 1976)

A multiattribute utility function exists if the following axiom obtains:

(U4): All attributes are mutually utility independent.

An attribute A is *utility independent* (U.I.) of another attribute B if, and only if the conditional preferences for lotteries on A given a level of B do not depend on the particular level of B. If A is U.I. of B, and B is U.I. of A, then A and B are mutually utility independent (m.u.i.).

The representation theorem that results is as follows:

Theorem 1: The axioms U1–U4 hold if, and only if there is a real value function $u \in \mathcal{U}$ on $\mathcal{L}$ given by:

$$u(x_1,\ldots,x_n) = \sum_{i=1}^{n} k_i u_i(x_i) + \sum_{i=1}^{n}\sum_{j>i} k_{ij} u_i(x_i) u_j(x_j) +$$

$$+ \sum_{i=1}^{n}\sum_{j>i}\sum_{s>j} k_{ijs} u_i(x_i) u_j(x_j) u_s(x_s) +$$

$$+ \cdots +$$

$$+ k_{123\ldots n} \prod_{i=1}^{n} u_i(x_i).$$

B Multiattribute nonlinear utility theory (Fishburn, 1988)

To introduce this theory we first assume that the alternatives are equivalent to probability distributions on the space of outcomes $\mathcal{O}$. Thus, x now denotes the probability distribution of the outcomes that may be the consequence of an alternative or course of action.

For every $C \in \mathcal{C}$, the axioms of the theory are as follows:

(F1): (Continuity)
 If $x >_c y$ and $y >_c z$ then $\exists \lambda$, $0 < \lambda < 1$, for which $y \sim \lambda x + (1 - \lambda)z$.

(F2): (Dominance)
 If $x >_c y$ and $x \gtrsim_c z$ then $x >_c \lambda y + (1 - \lambda)z$, for all λ, $0 < \lambda < 1$.
 If $y >_c x$ and $z \gtrsim_c x$ then $\lambda y + (1 - \lambda)z >_c x$, for all λ, $0 < \lambda < 1$.
 If $x \sim_c y$ and $x \sim_c z$ then $x \sim_c \lambda y + (1 - \lambda)z$, for all λ, $0 < \lambda < 1$.

(F3): (Symmetry)
 If $x >_c y$, $y >_c z$, $x >_c z$ and $y \sim_c \frac{1}{2}x + \frac{1}{2}z$ then $\exists \lambda$, $0 < \lambda < 1$, such that

$$\lambda x + (1 - \lambda)z \sim_c \frac{1}{2}x + \frac{1}{2}y.$$

Since we are dealing with multiattributes x is an n-dimensional probability distribution. Thus we write: $x = (x_1,\ldots,x_n)$, where x_i is the marginal distribution of x according to the i-th attribute.

(F4): (Marginal Indifference)
 $\forall x, y \in \mathcal{L}$, if x and y have the same marginal distributions $(x_1,\ldots,x_n)$, then x and y are indifferent according to all the attributes.

(F5): (Marginal Preference)
 $\forall x, y, z \in \mathcal{L}$, if

$$\begin{array}{lll} x & \text{has marginals} & (x_1, x_2, \ldots, x_n), \\ y & \text{has marginals} & (x_1, y_2, \ldots, x_n), \\ z & \text{has marginals} & (z_1, x_2, \ldots, x_n), \\ v & \text{has marginals} & (z_1, y_2, \ldots, x_n), \end{array}$$

then $x > z$ implies $y > v$ and $x > y$ implies $z > v$.

Theorem 2: The axioms **F1–F3** hold if, and only if there is a skew-symmetric bilinear functional ψ_c on $\mathcal{L} \times \mathcal{L}$ such that:

(1) For all $x, y \in \mathcal{L}$, $x >_c y$ if and only if $\psi_c(x, y) > 0$.

(2) It is unique up to a similarity transformation.

Theorem 3: The axioms **F1–F4** hold if, and only if there are bilinear functionals ψ_{c_i} and $\psi_{c_i c_j}$, $C_i, C_j \in \mathcal{C}$ such that for all $x, y \in \mathcal{L}$ with marginals $(x_1, \ldots, x_n)$ and $(y_1, \ldots, y_n)$, respectively:

$$\psi(x, y) = \sum_{i=1}^{n} \psi_{c_i}(x_i, y_i) + \sum_{i<j} \left[\psi_{c_i c_j}(x_i, y_j) - \psi_{c_i c_j}(x_j, y_i) \right].$$

Fishburn (1988) also provides the form of $\psi(x, y)$ if **F4** does not hold but **F5** does. It is however, difficult to establish a relationship between the individual utilities $u_i(x_i)$ and $\psi(x, y)$.

C   The analytic hierarchy process:
Hierarchic composition (Saaty, 1980)

To deal with multiple attributes in the AHP we introduce two concepts that are similar to the idea of utility independence. They are: *outer dependence* and *inner dependence*. The set of alternatives $\mathcal{A}$ is said to be outer dependent on a criterion C if there exists a $w_c \in W$ associated with them. If w_c does not exist then the alternatives do not depend on C and hence they are independent of each other with respect to C. The set of alternatives $\mathcal{A}$ is said to be inner dependent with respect to a criterion C if and only if the elements in $\mathcal{A}$ are outer dependent on themselves according to C. The third axiom of the AHP deals with these concepts. Given a hierarchy:

(**H3**):
- A level is outer dependent on the level above it.
- A level is inner independent with respect to all the elements in the level above it.
- A level is outer independent on the level below it.

(**H4**):   (Expectations)
When making a decision we always assume that the hierarchic structure is complete.

This fourth axiom states that if we assume that the hierarchy contains all the information in a particular situation, then we should be able to fulfill our expectations.

Let H_m be a hierarchy with m levels. Let $w(L_{i+1}|L_i)$ be the scales derived for the elements in the level $(i+1)$-st with respect to the elements in the i-th level. $w(L_{i+1}|L_i)$ is a matrix operator with the number of rows and columns equal to the number of elements in L_{i+1} and L_i, respectively.

Theorem 4: The axioms **H1–H4** hold if, and only if the scale associated with a level L_k is given by:

$$w(L_k|L_1) = w(L_k|L_{k-1}) \, w(L_{k-1}|L_{k-2}) \ldots w(L_2|L_1) \, w(L_1).$$

5 Synthesis from paired comparisons

In the case of AHP and Linear MAUT, this synthesis is already performed. However, in Fishburn's Non-linear MAUT, synthesis must be performed to obtain the utility function. In the transitive case we have:

$$\psi_{c_i}(x, y) = u_{c_i}(x) - u_{c_i}(y).$$

This decomposition is similar to the one in the AHP in the consistent case. If φ_{c_i} is consistent, then we have:

$$\varphi_{c_i}(A_h, A_k) = \frac{w_{c_i}(A_h)}{w_{c_i}(A_k)} \; .$$

Let $v_{c_i}(x) = e^{u_{c_i}(x)}$, we have:

$$e^{\psi_{c_i}(x,y)} = \frac{v_{c_i}(x)}{v_{c_i}(y)}$$

which would form a reciprocal consistent matrix as in the AHP, and in the inconsistent case the principal right eigenvector of the matrix:

$$\left[e^{\psi_{c_i}(x,y)} \right]$$

would yield the utility function synthesized from the paired comparisons. There is a problem with this approach. It is not intuitive how to provide paired comparisons for alternatives with respect to all the attributes at once. Consider two clusters C_1 and C_2, where C_1 is α times more important than C_2. Let A, B and D be three alternatives contained in C_1 and C_2 in the following amounts:

$$
\begin{array}{c c c c}
 & A & B & D \\
C_1 & a_1 & b_1 & d_1 \\
C_2 & a_2 & b_2 & d_2
\end{array}
$$

The judgment matrices are given by:

$$
\begin{array}{cc}
C_1 & C_2 \\
\begin{bmatrix}
1 & a_1/b_1 & a_1/d_1 \\
b_1/a_1 & 1 & b_1/d_1 \\
d_1/a_1 & d_1/b_1 & 1
\end{bmatrix}
&
\begin{bmatrix}
1 & a_2/b_2 & a_2/d_2 \\
b_2/a_2 & 1 & b_2/d_2 \\
d_2/a_2 & d_2/b_2 & 1
\end{bmatrix}
\end{array}
\tag{1}
$$

If we bypass the clusters and make judgments about A, B and D, the matrix of judgments would be:

$$
\begin{bmatrix}
1 & \dfrac{\alpha a_1 + a_2}{\alpha b_1 + b_2} & \dfrac{\alpha a_1 + a_2}{\alpha d_1 + d_2} \\[2mm]
\dfrac{\alpha b_1 + b_2}{\alpha a_1 + a_2} & 1 & \dfrac{\alpha b_1 + b_2}{\alpha d_1 + d_2} \\[2mm]
\dfrac{\alpha d_1 + d_2}{\alpha a_1 + a_2} & \dfrac{\alpha d_1 + d_2}{\alpha b_1 + b_2} & 1
\end{bmatrix}
\tag{2}
$$

which is obtained from the total amount of A, B and D in the clusters:

$$
A: \ \alpha a_1 + a_2; \qquad B: \ \alpha b_1 + b_2; \qquad \text{and} \qquad D: \ \alpha d_1 + d_2.
$$

How should one mix the judgments of A, B and D with respect to C_1 and C_2 given in (1) to obtain the judgments in the matrix given by (2)?

6   Conclusions

The technical difficulties pointed out above are just some of the problems one has attempting to extend UT to situations involving intransitivity of preferences. A more pressing difficulty is the question of how to deal with several levels of uncertainty. Despite the claims that some utility theorists make that MAUT can handle several levels of criteria, subcriteria and so on, the fact is that they cannot because to compare alternatives in an UT context one needs the range of values of the alternatives with respect to the attributes, and subcriteria may not have standardized scales. The Analytic Hierarchy Process is the only theory that has been developed to handle several levels of criteria and also interdependencies among not just the levels of a hierarchy but also the elements in the same level.

References

Colson, G. and De Bruyn, C. (1989). Models and Methods in Multiple Objectives Decision Making. *Math. Comput. Modelling*, 12, pp. 1201–1211.

Fishburn, P. (1988). Nonlinear Preference and Utility Theory. The Johns Hopkin University Press.

Keeney, R.L. and Raiffa, H. (1976). Decisions with Multiple Objectives. John Wiley.

Saaty, T.L. (1980). The Analytic Hierarchy Process. Mc-GrawHill International.

Nonexplicit-Utility-Function and Interactive Approach to Multiobjective Optimization

Yanzhang Wang and Zhongtuo Wang
Institute of Systems Engineering
Dalian University of Technology
116024 Dalian, P.R. China

Abstract

In the multiobjective optimization problems (MOP), the utility functions are not so easy to define, but some information about utility can be acquired easily from decision makers (such as weights of objectives, objective reference points, increments of objectives to be adjusted and so on). In fact, the information can be used to determine the optimal searching direction in objective space. On the basis of such information, the paper presents a searching model without explicit utility function. The model can exactly reflect the preferences of decision makers about objectives. Consequently Nonexplicit-Utility-Function and Interactive Approach (NUFIA) to multiobjective optimization is proposed. Finally, an example illustrating the approach is given.

1 Introduction

The main task in multiobjective optimization is to deal with the multiobjectives in a real problem. Evidently, if a utility function can be given, which correctly describes the preferences of decision makers to objectives, the multiobjective optimization problem can be changed into a single objective one and can be easily solved. But, unfortunately, it is difficult to construct a satisfactory utility function for a real multiobjective decision making problem, because the exact form of utility function in real world are difficult to define and their parameters are not so easy to be identified. In fact, the form and parameters of utility function mainly depends on the subjective value concepts of decision makers, and most of the concepts can not be measured. Although some methods of psychometrics have been given to learn about their subjective value concepts, most of decision makers are not willing to take part in psychometric experiments. Sometimes the decision makers have changing subjective value concepts over time. For these reasons, the methods relied on fixed utility functions cannot be implemented without difficulty. Therefore, interactive approaches of multiobjective optimization are widely noted (Sawaragi, 1985; Wierzbicki, 1988; Larichev, 1987) which can track the change of preferences of decision makers. A successful one of the approaches is reference-point method (Wang, 1988), by which many applications have been made.

In this paper a Nonexplicit-Utility-Function and Interactive Approach (NUFIA) to multiobjective optimization is proposed, where the information about preferences of decision makers are utilized as much as possible. At first, possible information from decision makers is analysed. From the information the mathematical ideas of NUFIA are discussed. Then the steps of NUFIA are given to nonlinear cases. Finally an example illustrating the NUFIA is studied.

For the convenience of statement, suppose multiobjective optimization problem is represented as

$$\text{MOP} \qquad \max Z_1 = f_1(X)$$
$$\max Z_2 = f_2(X)$$
$$\cdots \qquad \cdots$$
$$\max Z_p = f_p(X), \qquad X \in \mathcal{X}$$

or in vector form

$$\max Z = F(X) = [\, f_1(X) \; f_2(X) \; \ldots \; f_p(X)\,]$$

where $\mathcal{X}$ is a feasible solution set. Let $\mathcal{Z}$ denotes a set of objectives, namely $Z \in \mathcal{Z}$, and $K = \{1, 2, \ldots, p\}$.

2 Analysis of information about preferences of decision makers

It is well known that almost all of methods to multiobjective optimization need information support about preferences of decision makers, because practically treating or trading off multiobjectives is apparently a subjective action of decision makers. Therefore, it is the foundation of the research of multiobjective optimization to learn about information of preferences from decision makers. Perhaps, a successful method is one in which all of the informations are integrated to use.

1. Information from general utility theory

Some of common character of subjective value behavior of decision makers have been researched in general utility theory, and doubtlessly these are useful to the multiobjective optimization. For the cases of multiobjective optimization assume multiobjective utility function is

$$u = g(Z) = g(Z_1, Z_2, \ldots, Z_p), \qquad Z \in \mathcal{Z}.$$

Thus, the following conclusions from utility theory are always true for any practical multiobjective decision making problem.

(1) The nonsatiation axiom. Namely, for Z^1 and $Z^2 \in \mathcal{Z}$, if $Z^1 > Z^2$ then $u(Z^1) > u(Z^2)$. Also if $Z^1 \geq Z^2$ then $u(Z^1) \geq u(Z^2)$. In other words, this implies

$$\frac{\partial u(Z)}{\partial Z_i} > 0, \qquad \text{for } \forall i \in K.$$

(2) The law of diminishing marginal utility. That is

$$\frac{\partial^2 u(Z)}{\partial Z_i^2} < 0, \qquad \text{for } \forall i \in K.$$

This means that multiobjective utility function must be nonlinear. To the contrary, if the utility function is linear then marginal utility is constant, thus in this situation the optimization can be made according to the objective with the largest marginal utility and one objective dominating others will be happened. This is contradictory with the aspiration of decision makers in a real-world.

2. Information of preferences from decision makers

Except of above information from general utility theory, in practical multiobjective decision making problems some details of preference information of decision makers can be directly given by the decision makers through an interactive way or other suitable approaches. Up to now, the main information usually used in multiobjective decision making is as follows:

(1) Weighting coefficients, which are mainly used in the weighting coefficient method and given by decision makers on the basis of the judgment to the importance of objectives. In general, weighting coefficients are denoted by vector W, $W = [W_1, W_2, \ldots, W_p]$ and $\sum_{i \in K} W_i = 1$. It seems that weighting coefficient information is familiar to decision makers now because the weighting coefficient method is the most common one. However, most of decision makers usually do not know how to specify their preferences in terms of weighting coefficients. Before running a multiobjective model, some of them even have not an idea about their weighting coefficients. Sometimes the decision makers have changing over time preferences. So, acquisition of weighting coefficients from decision makers is often difficult.

(2) Reference points, which are state points of objectives decision makers expect, and these information are used in the reference point approach. For decision makers specifying their preferences in terms of reference points is easy because in every day decision makers think in terms of goals and aspiration levels, while the concepts and the probable quantities of objectives are familiar to decision makers.

(3) Increments of objectives to be adjusted. In a real-world multiobjective decision making process, when a noninferior solution is approached, namely a state point of objectives in objective space is given, judging the point decision makers can give an increment vector of objectives expected to be adjusted if the point is not satisfactory to the decision makers. The increment information is intuitive and can be easily given. In fact, for a state point of objective given if it is unsatisfied to decision makers they must be able to determine according to their experiences which of the objectives are expected to increase and which to decrease, namely the increments to be adjusted, at least the trend of increments elimination can be thought of by experiences.

In addition, there are also other information such as marginal rate of substitution of objectives and aspiration level of objectives. For the former it is very difficult to specify because the marginal rate of substitution is strictly a limit value so as to keep indifference relation, and evidently the limit operation seems beyond human ability. The latter is similar to reference point and it is easy to get it.

As a result, above information (2) and (3) are considered to be easily specified by decision makers, especially through an interactive procedure. In fact, the information can be changed into each other in condition given. For example, when a reference point, denoted as Z^r, is specified corresponding to a current state point of objectives represented as Z^0 given in an interactive process, a deviation vector ΔZ can be also got, namely

$$\Delta Z = Z^r - Z^0.$$

To the contrary, when Z^0 and ΔZ are given, we have

$$Z^r = Z^0 + \Delta Z.$$

3   Mathematical ideas of NUFIA

Most of the methods of multiobjective optimization adopt the ideas of changing multiobjective problem into single objective one so that the techniques of single objective optimization or decision making can be applied. Speaking strictly, this single objective is measure of aspiration to multiobjective such as utility or value function, distance function and so on. In fact, the measure function describes the tracks of aspiration change as objective states, and main contribution of the function to multiobjective optimization is that it can give the searching direction of optimization in objective space. Therefore, if the searching direction can be given through any way, the multiobjective optimization can be made. From this idea in this paper such information is used to determine the searching direction and a Nonexplicit-Utility-Function and Interactive Approach (NUFIA) is put forward.

Suppose that a state point of objectives Z^k and an increment vector of objectives expected to be adjusted ΔZ^k are given, and consider the optimization problem of utility function $g(Z)$ in objective space. In fact, the increment vector given ΔZ^k points out the searching direction of maximizing utility in objective space shown as Fig. 1. Thus, the adjustment of the state point Z^k can be made along the direction of ΔZ^k and a preferable state point of objectives Z^{k+1} can be approached, namely

$$Z^{k+1} = Z^k + w\Delta Z^k.$$

Here w is a searching step length. Furthermore, the problem of the optimization is how to determine an optimal step length. On the basis of general utility or value concepts of decision makers, the improvement of state point of objectives as possible along the direction is expected in intuition. In an ideal situation it is hoped that $w = 1$.

However, in general all the elements of Z, $Z_1, Z_2, \ldots, Z_p$ are dependent upon the alternate X, and $X \in \mathcal{X}$. Thus, in many cases, corresponding to feasible X, $w = 1$ cannot be reached, so we have $0 \leq w \leq 1$ or $w \in [0, 1]$. Apparently in the interval $[0, 1]$ the

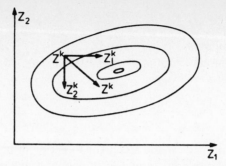

Figure 1: The searching direction in objective space

larger step length w is, the larger utility value u is. Therefore, in the interval optimizing utility u is equivalent to optimizing step length w. Therefore, the following model of single objective optimization can be constructed to solve step length w, alternate X and objective state Z.

$$\max \quad w$$
$$\text{s.t.} \quad F(X^{k+1}) - \Delta Z^k w \geq F(X^k)$$
$$X^{k+1} \in \mathcal{X}, \qquad w \in [0,1].$$

Up to now, we have described an interactive approach with the feature of rational division of works between man and machine. In the optimizing process, the search direction is determined by human according to their experience or intuition. The work to determine the step length is left to the machine. From the nonsatiation axiom it is known that when change of an objective does not effect other objectives, this objective can be solely improved and total utility value can be also increased. Therefore, the solution of above model usually is weak Pareto solution, and model is modified as follows

$$\max \quad \left[Mw + \sum_{i \in K} \rho_i \right]$$
$$\text{s.t.} \quad F(X^{k+1}) - \Delta Z^k w - \rho = F(X^k)$$
$$X^{k+1} \in \mathcal{X}, \qquad w \in [0,1], \qquad \rho \geq 0,$$

where $\rho \in R^p$, ρ_i is an element of ρ for $\forall i \in K$, and M is a number large enough to enable the Mw dominating the $\sum_{i \in K} \rho_i$. For convenience this model is called as Nonexplicit-Utility-Function Searching Model (NUFSM).

Theorem 1. If $[X^{*T} \ w^* \ \rho_1^* \ \rho_2^* \dots \rho_p^*]^T$ is the optimal solution of the NUFSM, then X^* is a noninferior solution of original MOP.

Proof: Since $[X^{*T} \ w^* \ \rho_1^* \ \rho_2^* \dots \rho_p^*]^T$ is the optimal solution of the NUFSM, we have $X^* \in \mathcal{X}$. Suppose X^* is not the optimal solution of the original MOP, then there exists a $X \in \mathcal{X}$ such that $F(X) \geq F(X^*)$ and existing at least one $i \in K$ such that

$f_i(X) > f_i(X^*)$. Therefore, we have $\rho'_i > \rho^*_i$ and $[X^{*T} \; w^* \; \rho^*_1 \; \rho^*_2 \ldots \rho^*_p]^T$ is a feasible solution of NUFSM, and

$$Mw^* + \sum_{j \in K \backslash \{i\}} \rho^*_j + \rho'_i > Mw^* + \sum_{j \in K \backslash \{i\}} \rho^*_j + \rho^*_i.$$

This is conflicting with the assumption that $[X^{*T} \; w^* \; \rho^*_1 \; \rho^*_2 \ldots \rho^*_p]^T$ is the optimal solution of NUFSM.

Owing to the optimization made along the direction of increment of objectives given by decision makers, the preferences or the subjective value concepts of decision makers can exactly reflected in the NUFSM. For a real application of the NUFSM, when the ideal point and the valley point of objectives of MOP are given, the other forms of the NUFSM can be used as follows:

(1) The NUFSM on the basis of the valley point of objectives. That is

$$\max \quad \left[Mw + \sum_{i \in K} \rho_i \right]$$
$$\text{s.t.} \quad F(X^{k+1}) - \Delta Z'w - \rho = F^-$$
$$X^{k+1} \in \mathcal{X}, \qquad \rho \geq 0.$$

Here F^- is the valley point of objectives, and

$$\Delta Z' = Z^r - F^-$$

or

$$\Delta Z' = \Delta Z + F(X^k) - F^-.$$

This form of NUFSM in linear cases have been used in NOSIA.

(2) The NUFSM on the basis of the ideal point objectives. Namely

$$\max \quad \left[-Mw + \sum_{i \in K} \rho_i \right]$$
$$\text{s.t.} \quad F(X^{k+1}) - \Delta Z'w - \rho = F^*$$
$$X^{k+1} \in \mathcal{X}, \qquad \rho \geq 0,$$

where F^* is the ideal point of objectives, and

$$\Delta Z' = F^* - Z^r$$

or

$$\Delta Z' = F^* - \Delta Z - F(X^k).$$

4 Procedure of NUFIA

The NUFSM can be solved by the methods of nonlinear programming with constraints. Here, suppose Lagrange Multiplier method is used, then we have the following Lagrange function

$$\max L = Mw + \sum_{i \in K} \rho_i - \lambda[F(X^k) - F(X^{k+1}) + \Delta Zw + \rho]$$

and

$$\frac{\partial L}{\partial w} = M - \lambda \Delta Z; \tag{1}$$

$$\frac{\partial L}{\partial \rho_i} = 1 - \lambda_i; \qquad \text{for } \forall i \in K \tag{2}$$

$$\frac{\partial L}{\partial X} = \nabla F^T(X)\lambda^T; \tag{3}$$

$$\frac{\partial L}{\partial \lambda^T} = F(X^{k+1}) - \Delta Zw - \rho - F(X^k). \tag{4}$$

Thus, for the MOP, a procedure of NUFIA can be summarized as follows:

Step 1. Solving decision support matrix D. D is defined as

$$D = [d_{ij}]$$

here

$$d_{ij} = f_i(X^{*j}) \qquad \text{for } \forall i,j \in K$$

and X^{*j} subject to $f_j(X^{*j}) = \max \{ f_j(X) \mid X \in \mathcal{X} \}$.

Meanwhile, the ideal point F^* and the valley point F^- can be given, namely

$$F^* = [f_1(X^{*1}) \; f_2(X^{*2}) \dots f_p(X^{*p})]^T$$

and

$$F^- = \left[\min_{j \in K} d_{1j} \; \min_{j \in K} d_{2j} \dots \min_{j \in K} d_{pj} \right]$$

Step 2. Starting the interaction of NUFIA. In this step the first noninferior solution is given, which is an effective solution suggested by NUFIA according to equal satisfactory degree. Set initial variables as

$$X^0 = \frac{1}{p} \sum_{i \in K} X^{*i}$$

$$\Delta Z^0 = F^* - F^-$$

$$\rho = 0, \qquad \lambda^0 = \Delta Z^{0T} / \sum_{i \in K} \left| \Delta Z_i^0 \right|$$

and set $l = 1$, $k = 1$ and $X^1 = F^-$.

Step 3. Iteration searching a noninferior solution. The iteration can be made by appropriate ways, here gradient method is used. In every time of iteration, with formulas (1–4) the variables can be improved by the following formulas

$$
\begin{aligned}
X^{k+1} &= X^k + \sigma \Delta F^T(X^k), & X^{k+1} &\in \mathcal{X} \\
\rho_i^{k+1} &= \rho_i^k + \sigma(1 - \lambda_i), & \text{for } &\forall i \in K \\
\lambda^{k+1} &= \lambda^k + \sigma[\, F(X^k) - \Delta Z w - \rho - F(X^1)\,]^T
\end{aligned}
$$

here is a step length of iteration, which can be determined by the method of nonlinear programming.

When every variable cannot be improved evidently, a noninferior solution is given, then stop iterating to next step. Otherwise, set $k = k+1$ and continue the iteration,

Step 4. Interacting with decision maker. If decision maker is satisfied by the noninferior solution, stop the procedure and a satisfied solution is current solution X^k. Otherwise decision maker can give increment of some objectives expected to be adjusted or a new reference point of objectives. Then set $l = l+1$, $X^l = X^k$ and substitute ΔZ by the new one. Return to step 3.

5   An example illustrating NUFIA

Suppose a MOP as

$$
\begin{aligned}
\max \quad & Z_1 = x_1^2 - 2x_2 \\
\max \quad & Z_2 = -x_1 + 1/2\, x_2^2 \\
\text{s.t.} \quad & 0 \le x_1 \le 10, \qquad 0 \le x_2 \le 20.
\end{aligned}
$$

The procedure solving the MOP by NUFIA is simply shown as follows:

Step 1. Computing the decision support matrix D, we have

$$
D = \begin{bmatrix} 100 & -40 \\ 10 & 200 \end{bmatrix}
$$

and

$$
F^* = \begin{bmatrix} 100 \\ 200 \end{bmatrix}, \qquad F^- = \begin{bmatrix} -40 \\ -20 \end{bmatrix}
$$

Step 2. Set

$$
Z = F^* - F^- = \begin{bmatrix} 140 \\ 210 \end{bmatrix}
$$

and generate he NUFSM below

$$
\begin{aligned}
\max \quad & [10000w + \rho_1 + \rho_2] \\
\text{s.t.} \quad & x_1^2 - 2x_2 - 140w - \rho_1 = -40 \\
& -x_1 + 1/2\, x_2^2 - 210w - \rho_2 = -10 \\
& 0 \le x_1 \le 10, \qquad 0 \le x_2 \le 20, \qquad \rho_1, \rho_2 \ge 0.
\end{aligned}
$$

Step 3. Solving the NUFSM, we have a noninferior solution as

$$X^+ = \begin{bmatrix} 10.00 \\ 17.647 \end{bmatrix}, \qquad F^+ = Z^+ = \begin{bmatrix} 64.706 \\ 145.710 \end{bmatrix}$$

and here $w = 0.74$.

Step 4. Judging the noninferior solution and the state of objectives, assume that the solution is unsatisfactory, and a new increment ΔZ is given as

$$\Delta Z = \begin{bmatrix} 100 \\ 160 \end{bmatrix}$$

Step 5. Modifying the NUFSM as

$$\max \quad [10000w + \rho_1 + \rho_2]$$
$$\text{s.t.} \quad x_1^2 - 2x_2 - 100w - \rho_1 \quad = \quad -40$$
$$-x_1 + 1/2\,x_2^2 - 160w - \rho_2 \quad = \quad -10$$
$$0 \le x_1 \le 10, \qquad 0 \le x_2 \le 20, \qquad \rho_1, \rho_2 \ge 0.$$

and solving it, we have

$$X^+ = \begin{bmatrix} 10 \\ 20 \end{bmatrix}, \qquad F^+ = \begin{bmatrix} 60 \\ 190 \end{bmatrix}$$

here $w = 1$ and $\rho_2 = 40$.

If this solution is also unsatisfied, we can continue the procedure.

References

Larichev, O. (1987). New Directions in Multicriteria Decision Making Research. WP–87–067, IIASA.

Lewandowski, A. and Grauer, M. (1982). The Reference Point Optimization Approach — Methods of Efficient Implementation. WP–82–26, IIASA.

Sawaragi, Y., Nakayama, H., Tanino, T. (1985). Theory of Multiobjective Optimization. Academic Press, Inc., Orlando.

Wang Yanzhang and Wang Zhongtuo (1988). Non-Objective-Submerged and Interactive Approach to Multiobjective Linear Programming. International Conference on Multiobjective Problems of Mathematical Programming (ICMPMP), Yalta.

Wierzbicki, A.P. (1979). A Methodological Guide to Multiobjective Optimization. WP–79–122, IIASA.

Wierzbicki, A.P. (1988). Dynamic Aspects of Multiobjective Optimization. ICMPMP, Yalta.

Introduction to Competence Set Analysis and Effective Suggestions*

Po Lung Yu, Dazhi Zhang

School of Business

University of Kansas

Lawrence, Kansas 66045-2003, U.S.A.

Abstract

For each decision problem there is a competence set consisting of ideas, knowledge, information and skills for its satisfactory solution. When a decision maker thinks he/she has already acquired and mastered the competence set as perceived, he/she will feel confident and comfortable making the decision and/or undertaking the challenge. The decision cycle is defined to be the time duration from the beginning of the decision problem to the end of its solution. The related habitual domains (including the perceived competence set) are evolving and expanding over the decision cycle. The proposed competence set analysis is new and based on a "set covering" concept instead of more traditional mathematical ordering and its maximization. The analysis may complement the existing methods for decision analysis.

1   Introduction

Why are some hunters not afraid of lions or tigers? Probably because they think they have acquired and mastered the needed skills to have the spontaneity to act quickly and effectively to protect themselves.

Why are newborn babies also not afraid of lions or tigers? Probably because in their memory there is nothing to be afraid of and there is no notion of danger and skill.

For each decision problem (from finding and selecting a job to corporate strategic planning and conflict resolution) there is a competence set, $Comp_t(E)$, consisting of ideas, knowledge, information and skills. When a decision maker thinks he/she has already acquired and mastered the competence set as perceived, he/she will feel confident and comfortable making the decision and/or undertaking the challenge. For the hunters, the competence set is acquired by hard work, practice and learning. For the babies, the competence set is empty, thus they have nothing to be afraid of. For most others as the competence set is only partially understood and not fully mastered, they would feel uncomfortable or fearful in hunting the dangerous animals.

*This research has been partially supported by NSF Grant No. IST-841 8863.

Through experience and learning, we have acquired a set of skills, information and knowledge, which on one hand makes our process of daily life more efficient, and on the other constrains our domains of thinking, responding and judgments. For each event or problem, denoted by E, we consciously or implicitly have a perception of a collection of what it takes to successfully solve the problem or handle the event. The collection will be denoted by $HD_t^*(E)$. We also have a perception of a collection of what skills, information or knowledge we have actually acquired for the problem E. This collection will be denoted by $Sk_t(E)$. Note that $HD_t^*(E)$ and $SK_t(E)$ are directly related to the competent set. At a point of time t, $HD_t^*(E)$ is our perception of the competence set for satisfactorily solving the problem E; while $Sk_t(E)$ is the perceived inventory of our skills, information and knowledge for solving the problem E. We use subscript t to emphasize that $HD_t^*(E)$ and $Sk_t(E)$ are evolving with time. They may be stable or steady most of the time but can be exploded at any moment when extraordinary events occur. Let us illustrate this concept by the following example.

EXAMPLE

A retiring Chief Executive Officer (CEO) invited to his ranch two finalists (A and B) from which he would select his replacement by a horse race. A and B, equally skillful in horseback riding, were given a black and white horse respectively. The CEO gave a course for the horse race and said "Starting at the same time, whoever's horse is **slower** in completing the course will be selected as the next CEO!" Finally, A jumped on B's horse and rode as fast as he could to the finish line. When B realized what was going on, it was too late! Naturally, A was the new CEO.

People would actually expect that the **faster** horse would be the winner in the horse race (a habitual domain). When a problem is not in our habitual domain, it is difficult to solve until our habitual domain is suitably expanded. Before the announcement of the rules of game, both A and B had their perception of $HD_t^*(E)$ and $Sk_t(E)$ to win the race (E). Upon the announcement, the players were shocked with unknown and uncertainty and began to expand their $HD_t^*(E)$ and $Sk_t(E)$ because the rules of the game were outside of their habitual domain and the players wanted to win. When A finally adequately expanded his $HD_t^*(E)$ and $Sk_t(E)$, all the unknown and uncertainty disappeared and he quickly executed his decision to win the race. Notice that without the expansion of $HD_t^*(E)$ and $Sk_t(E)$, the unknown and uncertainty cannot be clarified, and the problem cannot be solved. It always takes time to expand $HD_t^*(E)$ and $Sk_t(E)$. This raises the question of the concept of *decision cycle*: the time duration from the beginning of the decision problem to the end of its solution. In games and competitions, the players with shorter decision cycles usually have an upper hand over their slower opponents, with everything else being equal.

Effective ways to expand $HD_t^*(E)$ and $Sk_t(E)$ to clarify the unknown and uncertainty and to solve the problem E also lead to a new research area — suggestion theory. How can an expert guide his/her clients in expanding their $HD_t^*(E)$ and $Sk_t(E)$ effectively as to (1) clarify their unknown and uncertainty and (2) solve their problems within a minimum decision cycle?

Note, $HD_t^*(E)$ and $Sk_t(E)$ are habitual domains. They can be expanded and stabilized over time (Chan and Yu, 1985; Yu, 1985). In order to effectively expand $HD_t^*(E)$ and $Sk_t(E)$ we need to pay attention to habitual domains and learning processes as to be discussed in the next section. Effective ways of suggestion to help to expand the HDs will be discussed in Section 3. A conclusion is given by Section 4.

2 Habitual domains and learning processes

2.1 Cores of habitual domains

In abstract, our concepts and ideas may be represented by circuit patterns of the lit neurons in our brain (Yu, 1985, 1990). The concepts and ideas can be activated depending on our charge structures, attention allocation and the attended events. It has been recognized that (Chan and Yu, 1985; Yu, 1985, 1990) each human over time develops a set of fairly stable ideas or ways of thinking, judging and reacting to various events. This set is known as the habitual domain (HD). Through association and analogy, and our experience, given that an event has our attention, some ideas and concepts can be activated and some cannot. For instance, the event of talking about your boy/girl friend may trigger the activation of his/her name, image and some special memory about him or her. It may less likely activate the concepts of George Washington or your grandfather. Talking about an upcoming job interview may immediately activate the concepts of "be neat", "be knowledgeable", "be a good listener", etc. You would less likely activate the concept of icebergs or roosters fighting.

Given an event or a decision problem E which catches our attention at time t, the *propensity for an idea I to be activated* is denoted by $P_t(I, E)$. Like a conditional probability, we know that $0 \leq P_t(I, E) \leq 1$, that $P_t(I, E) = 0$ if I is unrelated to E or I is not an element of PD_t (potential domain) at time t, and that $P_t(I, E) = 1$ if I is automatically activated in the thinking process whenever E is presented.

Let us define the α-core of HD for E at time t, denoted by $C_t(\alpha, E)$, to be the collection of the ideas or concepts that can be activated with a propensity larger than or equal to α. That is,

$$C_t(\alpha, E) = \{I \mid P_t(I, E) \geq \alpha\}.$$

By the *core of HD for E* (with α absent), denoted by $C_t(E)$, we mean the collection of ideas or concepts that would almost surely be activated when E is presented. In other words, it is the α-core with $\alpha \to 1$. Sometimes, for convenience and to avoid confusion, the core of HD may simply mean the α-core with a high value of α. Thus if I is an element of the core of HD for E, then $P_t(I, E)$ is large (close to he limit of 1) for most of time t when E is present.

Now recall that $HD_t^*(E)$ is the perceived competence set for solving E, and the subscript t is used to emphasize its dynamics. Suppose that

$$HD_t^*(E) \subseteq C_t(\alpha, E)$$

with a large value of α (that is, α is close to its upper limit 1). In this case the decision maker would feel comfortable with the problem and could solve it with a high degree of efficiency, because he/she has acquired and almost mastered $HD^*(E)$.

If the above inclusion holds with $\alpha = 1$, then the decision maker has the needed spontaneity to solve this problem.

Note that when $HD_t^*(E)\backslash C_t(\alpha, E) = \emptyset$, the decision maker knows that further learning or training is needed to acquire and master the new ideas in order to achieve a certain degree of proficiency or confidence in solving the problem E. The relative size between $HD^*(E) \setminus C_t(\alpha, E)$ and $HD^*(E)$ can be a measurement of relatively how much more is needed to be learned or trained. It may also be a relative measure of the subjective proficiency or confidence in making the decision for E.

2.2 Learning processes — implanting, nurturing and habituating

In this subsection we discuss how the competence sets are acquired and mastered. This is a leaning process which includes implanting, nurturing and habituating.

2.2.1 Implanting

Given a decision problem E and an idea or skill I of $HD^*(E)$, suppose that $P_t(I, E) = 0$. That is, the decision maker does not associate I with E. Two possible cases could happen:

(i) the decision maker could have the circuit pattern of I in his/her potential domain, that is, $I \in PD_t$; and/or

(ii) the decision maker could have not learned I, that is, $I \notin PD_t$.

The purpose of implanting is to make a positive association between I and E. That is, $P_{t'}(I, E) > 0$ for some $t' > t$. This can be achieved through teaching, suggestion and/or training. If we play the expert's role, to be effective and to be sure that I is accepted, we must understand the decision maker's HD_t, and make a strong *connection* of I and HD_t and/or that of I and E.

Note that without a good connection, the idea I may be rejected right away. With a strong connection, however, the idea can be more easily accepted. Information which can increase and/or release our charges will usually catch our attention. For more details, see (Yu, 1990).

Once the idea I is accepted, we still need to make an effort to be sure that I is sufficiently rehearsed and/or practiced so as to have a strong circuit pattern representation. Otherwise, I may be stored in a remote area and be difficult to retrieve, which could prevent us from reaching $P_{t'}(I, E) > 0$ for some $t' > t$.

2.2.2 Nurturing

Once the idea I is implanted, $P_t(I, E)$ can be positive, yet still low. In order for I to have an impact on the decision maker, it needs to be high enough. To achieve this goal, we need to nurture the idea using training, practice and rehearsing. Like seedlings of a tree, without nurturing, the newly implanted ideas will wither and disappear.

Finally, we notice that "experiencing" and "self-suggesting", in addition to information inputs, are two important ways to strengthen our circuit patterns of new ideas. Our mind may not distinguish the sources. Both physical experience and mental exercise (or suggestion) are important in the nurturing process.

Thinking without doing may not push the ideas down to the very sensory and motor sections of the brain; thus the ideas may be less concrete. On the other hand, experiencing without thinking may not integrate the ideas extensively with the existing knowledge encoded in the existing HD_t; thus the ideas may not be as strong as they could be. They may even be rejected occasionally by part of the existing HD_t.

2.2.3 Habituating

Through repeated practice and nurturing, a new idea I could gradually become an element of the core of HD_t on the decision problem E. Thus, the propensity of activation of I is very high or, $P_t(I, E) \to 1$. That is, whenever our attention is paid to E, I would be almost surely activated. When we reach this stage for I, we say that I is a *habituating element* of HD_t on E.

Note that habituating elements have a strong influence on our decisions and behavior, consciously or subconsciously. Their influence may be insidious but so strong that we may not escape from their reach. One occasionally needs to detach himself from E and those habituating elements in order to jump out of HD_t and develop creative and innovative ideas.

Finally, we notice that the learning process of implanting, nurturing and habituating is not only applicable to self-learning, but also for suggestions to other people and/or training other people to acquire the competence set $HD^*(E)$.

3 Effective suggestions

A suggestion, S, is a set of ideas and/or operators. To help the decision maker reach decisions quickly (i.e., for the decision maker to have a shorter decision cycle), effective suggestions are extremely important.

From the dynamic behavior mechanism and habitual domain analysis (see Yu, 1985, 1990 for details), we have the following observations:

1. A suggestion can catch the attention only if it can create a relatively high level of charge on the decision maker. Although he/she has innate needs for external information, if the suggestion is unrelated to his/her charge structure (which is the collection of charges created by various events, see Yu, 1985, 1990 for details), it will be most likely ignored or neglected.

2. A suggestion cannot easily have a relatively high level of charge on the decision maker when the decision maker is preoccupied by other significant events (such as a grave illness or pressure to meet an important deadline unrelated to the suggestion).

3. A suggestion can be more easily accepted, if it already exists in the memory of the decision maker (thus only "retrieving" is needed for the acceptance, "encoding" is not needed), or it is *closely connected* to the significant memory of the decision maker (because of association and analogy in information processing).

4. A suggestion can receive a long duration of attention time if it can create a relatively high level of charge for a long duration, which occurs when the suggestion implants enthusiasm and confidence in the decision maker to achieve his/her burning desired goals. (Thus the suggestion not only creates a high level of charge, but also creates confidence for the release of charge).

5. Usually a suggestion perceived as highly related to important life goals of the decision maker, can easily obtain the attention of the decision maker because of 2–4.

6. If an accepted suggestion contains new ideas or knowledge, especially when S has a large intersection with the relevant domain $HD_t(E)$ (for simplicity, $HD_t(E)$ will be used to represent $Comp_t(E)$, $HD_t^*(E)$ or $Sk_t(E)$), the new ideas or knowledge will be integrated with the existing memory, and the memory will be expanded. Furthermore, $HD_t^*(E)$ and $Sk_t(E)$ will also be expanded. Yet they can be gradually stabilized, unless a new set of suggestions is encountered.

Now let us assume that $Comp_t(E)$ is fairly stable. Let $HD_t^*(E)$ and $Sk_t(E)$ simply be represented by $HD_t(E)$. Let $\{S_1, S_2, \ldots\}$ be a sequence of suggestions by the expert (S_i may be overlapping, i.e. $S_i \cap S_j \neq \emptyset$ and $S_i \neq S_j$). Let $HD_0 = HD_{t_0}(E)$ be the initial HD_t, and for $k = 1, 2, \ldots, HD_k$ be the $HD_t(E)$ after integrating S_k with HD_{k-1}. Then a *successful suggestion program* is a sequence of suggestion $S = \{S_1, S_2, \ldots\}$ so that as HD_k, $k = 1, 2, \ldots$, consecutively expanding, there is a finite number m so that $HD_m \supseteq Comp(E)$.

By assigning time and effort into S, one can study effective suggestion programs to create a successful program which minimizes time and effort by using models of multiple criteria decision making. When $Comp_t(E)$ varies with time and situations, the problem of effective suggestion can be modified, yet still remain similar to the situation above. However, the problem becomes far more complex because of the unknown and the uncertainty involved. This is a challenging research problem we are currently undertaking.

4 Conclusion

We have introduced the concepts of competence set analysis, effective decision, and suggestion theory. The primary concepts are grounded on set covering, not on traditional numerical ordering and maximization (for instance, see Fishburn, 1970; Keeney and Raiffa, 1976; Newell and Simon, 1972 and Von Neumann and Morgenstern, 1944). Many interesting and challenging problems are waiting for us to explore. For instance, how to effectively assess competence sets? the relevant HDs? and to effectively expand the relevant HDs? Some partial results are reported in (Yu, 1985, 1988, 1990; Yu and Zhang, 1989).

References

Chan, S. J. and Yu, P. L. (1985). Stable Habitual Domains: Existence and Implications. *Journal of Mathematical Analysis and Applications*, Vol. 110, No. 2, pp. 469–482.

Fishburn, P. C. (1970). Utility Theory for Decision Making. Wiley, New York.

Keeney, R. L. and Raiffa, H. (1976). Decision with Multiple Objectives: Preferences and Value Tradeoffs. Wiley, New York.

Newell, A. and Simon, H. A. (1972). Human Problem Solving. Prentice Hall Inc., Englewood Cliffs, NJ.

Von Neumann, J. and Morgenstern, O. (1944). Theory of Games and Economic Behavior. Princeton University Press, Princeton, NJ.

Yu, P. L. (1985). Multiple Criteria Decision Making: Concepts, Techniques and Extensions. Plenum, New York.

Yu, P. L. (1988). Effective Decision Making Using Habitual Domain Analysis. Tutorial Lecture delivered at ORSA/TIMS Joint National Meeting, Denver, Oct 23–26.

Yu, P. L. and Zhang, D. (1989). Competence Set Analysis for Effective Decision Making. In a special issue of

Yu, P. L. (1990). Forming Winning Strategies — an integrated theory of habitual domains. Springer-Verlag, Heidelberg, Berlin, New York. Control: Theory and Advanced Technology. Vol. 5, No. 4, pp. 523-547.

Part 2

Methods and Procedures for Multiple Criteria Decision Support

A Linear Programming Approach for Processing Approximate Articulation of Preference

Ami Arbel

Tel-Aviv University, Tel-Aviv, 69978, Israel

Abstract

This paper presents a new approach for priority derivation when preferences are expressed as interval judgments. Pairwise comparisons used in the Analytic Hierarchy Process (AHP) are point estimates and as such are inappropriate for certain choice problems. Such cases are common when a single decision maker, or a group of decision makers, cannot reach consensus on a scale value to represent preference. In these cases one is motivated to consider approaches where the decision maker is allowed to state his preference approximately through a range of scale values. This paper presents a linear programming approach for processing interval judgments for priority derivation. This approach generates a region (if one exists) that encloses all priority vectors derived from inequalities representing the original interval judgments. The approach is demonstrated through a numerical example.

1 Introduction

A new approach for priority derivation when preferences are expressed as interval judgments is presented. Interval judgment is a natural way for a decision maker (DM) to express his views when he is uncertain about his exact level of preference. This uncertainty may be the result of number of factors such as: unfamiliarity with the elicitation process and the scale used in its implementation, incomplete information or knowledge, and uncertainty about levels of intensity associated with his preference.

An approach for dealing with complex multicriteria decision problems is offered through Saaty's Analytic Hierarchy Process (AHP), (Saaty, 1980, 1982, 1988; Saaty and Vargas, 1982). As this methodology matures, it finds more and more application areas in which it is successfully applied to problem structuring, preference assessment and overall system analysis and selection (see, e.g., Harker, 1986; Saaty and Vargas, 1987a, 1987b). This constant exposure to testing by real decision making problems serves also to identify new directions for research. One such promising area is concerned with expanding the procedures currently available for deriving a priority structure associated with elements of a hierarchy.

The Analytic Hierarchy Process has three major components:

1. problem structuring,
2. preference assessment,
3. synthesis.

The second component, that of preference assessment, provides the focal point for the developments in this paper. As this is a major component of the AHP methodology this effort is quite worthwhile (Harker and Vargas, 1987; Saaty and Vargas, 1987a). Assessment of preference in the AHP is done by asking pairwise comparison questions about strength of preference between subjects of comparison. If preference can be articulated by a single value taken from the 1–9 preference scale, then one proceeds to fill a comparison matrix that summarizes these assessments and derives the priority vector given as the principal eigenvector of that matrix. While asking the decision maker to provide pairwise preference statements is easy to implement in most cases, this process may be met with some resistance in other cases. This resistance on the part of the decision maker does not necessarily stem from his reluctance to apply the AHP, or any other analytical approach, but rather reflects in most cases his own uncertainty as to the correct level of intensity to be assigned to a particular preference question. Therefore, it is useful to explore alternative methods of preference assessment — in the context of the AHP — to provide assistance aimed at overcoming such difficulties. In these cases one may consider approaches where the decision maker is allowed to state his preference as a range of scale values rather than a single one. The rationale for considering range of values in stating preferences and deriving priorities is to offer the decision maker an approach for dealing with his uncertainty in assigning "precise" preference numbers, while still seeking to determine his underlying preference structure.

The structure of this paper is as follows. Section 2 provides a short summary of AHP fundamentals that are relevant and necessary for the approach developed here. Section 3 describes the proposed approach, section 4 illustrates it with an example and section 5 provides a summary and suggestions for future research.

2   Preliminary discussions

A major component of the AHP methodology is concerned with deriving a priority structure associated with a hierarchy whose elements represent issues relevant to a specific decision problem. In deriving these priorities, a distinction is made between local and global priorities. A local priority reflects the importance (priority) of an element in a certain level with respect to an element in a level immediately above it. A global priority reflects the importance of an element with respect to the focus of the problem. Since this paper is concerned with the derivation of local priorities, the basic steps followed in his process are described briefly below.

The derivation of local priorities is carried out through the use of a comparison scale and a pairwise comparison matrix. A comparison matrix for deriving the priority vector $w^T = [w_1, w_2, \ldots, w_n]$, is associated with n elements in a specific level with respect to a single element in a level immediately above it. Such a matrix, denoted by A, is shown in (2.1).

$$A = \begin{bmatrix} w_1/w_1 & w_1/w_2 & \ldots & w_1/w_n \\ w_2/w_1 & w_2/w_2 & \ldots & w_2/w_n \\ \vdots & \vdots & \ddots & \vdots \\ w_n/w_1 & w_n/w_2 & \ldots & w_n/w_n \end{bmatrix} \tag{2.1}$$

In this matrix, every element a_{ij} is an answer to a pairwise comparison question inquiring as to the relative dominance (importance) of element i relative to element j. Obviously, if one compares the i-th element with the j-th element, a comparison is being made also of the j-th element with the i-th element. This causes the comparison matrix to be a *reciprocal* matrix satisfying $a_{ij} = 1/a_{ji}$. The answers to the pairwise comparison questions being asked during the elicitation process are provided by using the 1–9 comparison scale suggested by Saaty.

It is easily observed that for the matrix given in (2.1) the following relation holds: $Aw = nw$, where w is the priority vector and n is the number of elements being compared. This is the case of a perfectly consistent comparison matrix whose elements satisfy $a_{ij} = a_{ik}a_{kj}$ for all i, j, k. In this consistent case the priority vector, w, is the eigenvector associated with the largest eigenvalue which, in this case, equals the dimension of the matrix, n.

Since the consistent case is usually the exception rather than the rule, we have in general $Aw = \mu_{\max}w$, where $\mu_{\max}$ is the largest eigenvalue of the comparison matrix which can be shown to satisfy $\mu_{\max} \geq n$ with equality holding only in the perfectly consistent case. A consistency index (C.I) is now defined through C.I $= (\mu_{\max} - n)/(n - 1)$; this index will assume the value zero in the consistent case and will be positive otherwise. The introduction of a numerical measure of consistency is one of the distinctive features of the AHP in providing a tool that permits checking the answers provided by the decision maker and thus assessing the quality of the preference elicitation process. For a more detailed discussion of this and other related issues, the reader is referred to (Saaty, 1980, 1982, 1988; Saaty and Vargas, 1982).

The results shown above are applicable when the decision maker can articulate his preference by single scale values that serve as elements of a comparison matrix from which one derives later the priority vector. This paper is concerned with the case where one has to resort to approximate articulations of preference that still permits exposing the decision maker's underlying preference and priority structure.

3 Approximate articulation of preference

This section presents another approach for dealing with cases when judgments are provided as intervals rather than point estimates. That is ratio judgments are provided through:

$$l_{ij} \leq w_i/w_j \leq u_{ij}, \qquad 1 \leq i, j \leq n \tag{3.1}$$

where l_{ij} and u_{ij} are the lower and upper bounds, respectively, on the ij-th element of the comparison matrix.

To motivate the developments in this section, it is useful to start by considering a simple example of comparing only two objects. Let us assume that in expressing preference between these objects the following is obtained:

$$1 = l_{12} \leq w_1/w_2 \leq u_{12} = 2 \tag{3.2a}$$
$$w_1 + w_2 = 1 \tag{3.2b}$$

where l_{12} and u_{12} are the lower and upper bound, respectively, of the preference interval and condition (3.2b) is added to ensure that the resulting weights are normalized.

Clearly, the case summarized in (3.2) is quite general and contains more specific cases as well. For example, if the upper and lower bound approach each other, the interval becomes smaller until, in the limit, they intersect at one point (e.g., $w_1/w_2 = 2$) to yield the case where one has a point estimate of preference such as is done in the AHP:

$$\begin{aligned} w_1/w_2 &= 2 \\ w_1 + w_2 &= 1 \end{aligned} \tag{3.3}$$

Also, if one sets the lower bound, l, in (3.1) equal to zero a simple ranking statement: $w_1 \geq w_2$ is obtained.

The collection of preference statements described in (3.1) results in a set of inequalities that is converted to a standard form given by:

$$\begin{aligned} Aw &\leq 0 \\ w_1 + w_2 + \cdots + w_n &= 1 \\ w_1, w_2, \ldots, w_n &\geq 0 \end{aligned} \tag{3.4}$$

The system of inequalities is said to be *solvable* if there exist a solution vector, $w \in R^n$, that satisfies (3.4). Furthermore, every solution vector to (3.4) is a *generator* of a consistent matrix given by $w^T w$.

Since all solutions to the problem posed in (3.4) are restricted to lie on the simplex $w_1 + \cdots + w_n = 1$, the set of inequalities for a solvable system will form a convex region on this simplex.

The convex region on the simplex, if one exists, indicates that the system of inequalities is solvable and, therefore, that weak transitivity holds. The consistency index used in the AHP assumes the value zero when pairwise comparison judgments form a consistent set. Here, the consistent case is obtained when all constraints intersect at a single point on the simplex.

The problem of interest now is to find a characterization of solution vectors w that satisfy the problem stated in (3.4). An approach for this problem is provided by solving an auxiliary linear programming (LP) problem given by:

$$\begin{aligned} \text{Min } \ &w_0 \\ \text{subject to: } \ &Aw \leq 0 \\ &w_1 + w_2 + \cdots + w_n = 1 \\ &w_0, w_1, w_2, \ldots, w_n \geq 0 \end{aligned} \tag{3.5}$$

where w_0 is an artificial variable used to identify the existence of a feasible solution.

Theorem 3.1: The vertices of the feasible region for a solvable system of inequalities given by (3.4) are generators of completely consistent comparison matrices.

Proof: The vertices for the feasible region are found at unique intersection points of constraints that are active at that vertex. Since other inequalities do not intersect at this particular vertex they are inactive and, therefore, redundant for the solution obtained at this vertex. □

A related question is what happens to a solvable system when the ranges of preference shrink until inequalities of the type shown in (3.1) become equality constraints. Can we expect any relation on the eigenvector solution proposed by the AHP?

Theorem 3.2: When the upper and lower bounds of a solvable system of inequalities approach each other we have, in the limit, that the unique solution to (3.4) is the vector w that is the eigenvector to a consistent matrix.

Proof: When the bounds specified for a solvable system shrink until they become a point, the solvability property of the system of inequalities imply that all constraints intersect at a single point which is the solution for the priority vector of a consistent matrix. □

In many decision making situations, priorities are derived for establishing a rank ordering among the elements being compared. Can one expect a definitive rank order when preference is stated approximately as in (3.1)? This is answered next.

Theorem 3.3 (Rank order): If all q vertices of the solution subspace for a solvable system exhibit the same rank order, then any interior point will exhibit the same rank order too.

Proof: The solution subspace, Ω, for the problem posed in (3.4) is defined by $\Omega = \{ w \in R^n : Aw \leq 0, \ w_1 + \cdots + w_n = 1 \}$. Since this subspace forms a convex region, any convex combination of points in this region, belongs also to the region. Specifically, let the convex region describing the solution subspace of (3.4) have q vertices denoted by $w_1, w_2, \ldots, w_q$. Then for any collection of weights, α_i, where $0 \leq \alpha_i \leq 1$ and $\alpha_1 + \alpha_2 + \cdots + \alpha_q = 1$, the vector v, given by $v = \alpha_1 w_1 + \alpha_2 w_2 + \cdots + \alpha_p w_q$, belongs also to the solution subspace of (3.4). If the vertices to the solution subspace satisfy $w_i[k] \geq w_j[l]$, for all vertices $l \leq i, \ j \leq q$, and for some given components k and l, then it is easy to see that any internal point given by $v = \alpha_1 w_1 + \alpha_2 w_2 + \cdots + \alpha_p w_q$, will satisfy:

$$v[k] = \alpha_1 w_1[k] + \alpha_2 w_2[k] + \cdots + \alpha_p w_q[k]$$
$$v[l] = \alpha_1 w_1[l] + \alpha_2 w_2[l] + \cdots + \alpha_p w_q[l]$$

and clearly, $v[k] \geq v[l]$. □

4   A numerical example

We will demonstrate our approach with a simple example concerned with establishing priorities among three elements. An assessment process may result in the following approximate articulation of preference statements:

$$1 \leq w_1/w_2 \leq 2 \tag{4.1}$$
$$2 \leq w_2/w_3 \leq 3 \tag{4.2}$$
$$2 \leq w_1/w_3 \leq 6 \tag{4.3}$$

If one wanted to summarize these judgments in a matrix, the following will reflect these range assessment:

$$A = \begin{bmatrix} 1 & [1,2] & [2,6] \\ & 1 & [2,3] \\ & & 1 \end{bmatrix} \tag{4.4}$$

where the lower triangular part of this matrix is comprised, of course, of the reciprocals of these ranges. The approach we are proposing in this paper, however, is not concerned explicitly with this matrix but with the set of inequalities shown above.

If the system of inequalities shown in (4.1)–(4.3) is solvable, the inequalities are not contradictory and their intersection defines a region in the 3-dimensional priority space (contradictory inequalities result from violation of transitivity). Since the priorities satisfying (4.1)–(4.3) represent components of a normalized priority vector, we have the following additional equality constraint:

$$w_1 + w_2 + w_3 = 1 \tag{4.5}$$

Using (4.5), one can project the feasible region (if there exists one) defined by (4.1)–(4.3) on a subspace of smaller dimension than that of the vector $w^T = [w_1, w_2, w_3]$. It should be noted, however, that this reduction in dimensionality is not needed for the solution process but just to enable illustrating graphically the feasible region. Using (4.5) to replace w_3 with w_1 and w_2, (4.1)–(4.3) is now replaced by the set of inequalities shown in (4.6) involving w_1 and w_2 only.

$$
\begin{aligned}
(a): & \quad w_1 - 2w_2 && \leq && 0 \\
(b): & \quad w_1 - w_2 && \geq && 0 \\
(c): & \quad 3w_1 + 4w_2 && \leq && 3 \\
(d): & \quad 2w_1 + 3w_2 && \geq && 2 \\
(e): & \quad 7w_1 + 6w_2 && \leq && 6 \\
(f): & \quad 3w_1 + 2w_2 && \geq && 2
\end{aligned}
\tag{4.6}
$$

The vertices of the feasible region (i.e., the region in $w_1 - w_2$ satisfying the inequalities of (4.6)) are found by solving for the intersection points of the respective equalities that form the boundary for this region. Starting with the intersection of (b) and (c) and going clockwise around this region, the vertices are given below:

$$\text{Vertex } \#1: \quad w^T = [3/7 \ \ 3/7 \ \ 1/7]$$
$$\text{Vertex } \#2: \quad w^T = [6/10 \ \ 3/10 \ \ 1/10]$$
$$\text{Vertex } \#3: \quad w^T = [4/7 \ \ 2/7 \ \ 1/7]$$
$$\text{Vertex } \#4: \quad w^T = [2/5 \ \ 2/5 \ \ 1/5]$$

$$(4.7)$$

Note that the vertices of the feasible region exhibit a distinct rank order among themselves given by: $w_1 \geq w_2 \geq w_3$ and, therefore, by the theorem proven in section 3, every point internal to the feasible region maintains the same rank order.

5 Summary and conclusions

An approach for dealing with approximate articulation of preference has been presented. This approach may prove useful in allowing the decision maker to derive priorities to be used in an AHP analysis without forcing him to state his preference exactly as a single number taken from the 1–9 comparison scale. This approach may prove particularly useful at the initial phase of an elicitation process when difficulties in articulating preference are most common. Using this approach, the decision maker may get an appreciation for his preference structure and its underlying priorities. After this is done, one may use a comparison matrix to either obtain the required priority vector or, using the information contained in the vertices of the solution subspace, find (possibly through a comparison matrix) a weighting scheme that will identify an *interior* point through a convex combination of the vertices.

References

Harker, P.T., (ed.), (1986). The Analytic Hierarchy Process, (Special Issue). *Socio-Economic Planning Sciences*, Vol. 20, No. 6.

Harker, P.T. and Vargas, L.G. (1987). The Theory of Ratio Scale Estimates: Saaty's Analytic Hierarchy Process. *Management Science*, Vol. 33, No. 11, pp. 1383–1403.

Saaty, T.L. (1980). The Analytic Hierarchy Process. McGraw-Hill.

Saaty, T.L. (1982). Decision Making for Leaders. Lifetime Learning Publications, Belmont, CA.

Saaty, T.L. (1988). Multicriteria Decision Making: The Analytic Hierarchy Process. RSW Publications.

Saaty, T.L. and Vargas, L.G. (1982). The Logic of Priorities. Kluwer-Nijhoff Publishing.

Saaty, T.L. and Vargas, L.G. (1987a). Uncertainty and Rank Order in the Analytic Hierarchy Process. *European Journal of Operational Research*, Vol. 32, pp. 107–117.

Saaty, T.L. and Vargas, L.G., (eds.), (1987b). The Analytic Hierarchy Process: Theoretical Developments and Some Applications, (Special Issue). *Mathematical Modelling*, Vol. 9, No. 3–5.

MCDS under Poor Weighting Information: The Outweigh Approach

Carlos A. Bana E Costa

IST/CESUR–INIC, Technical University of Lisbon
Av. Rovisco Pais, 1000 Lisbon, Portugal

Abstract

Situations involving poor inter-criteria preference information are very common in the practice of decision aid. Nevertheless, there exists a significant lack of operational MCDA approaches explicitly devoted to support decision making under those circumstances. This paper shows how to overcome this draw-back, in the context of a cardinal additive multicriteria value function model.

Introduction: General focus and assumptions

It is not rare an analyst to be confronted with decision situations where it is difficult or even unrealistic to completely measure the relative importance of each criterion ($j = 1, \ldots, n$), due to a large variety of practical circumstances. Sometimes only ordinal information is available, such as partial preference relations between sub-sets or coalitions of criteria, or a rank-order of the weights (for instance, $w_1 > \ldots > w_j > \ldots > w_n$). In other situations, it is only appropriate to determine lower and upper interval bounds for each weight ($w_j^0 \leq w_j \leq w_j^*$), for reasons of imprecision, and/or uncertaintly, and/or inaccurate determination (see Roy, 1987), and/or because of the different preference systems of the actors involved.

In spite of that, traditional multicriteria methods are in the practice of decision aid only applied with stable and single weights: in the presence of poor weighting information the analyst usually forces the specification of a first vector of precise weights, and, afterwards, he makes a sensitivity analysis using other vectors, in order to conclude about the robustness and stability of the results obtained with the initial weights. But, one has to recognise that this procedure do not directly and specifically deals with imprecise weights.

The Outweigh Approach (OWA), presented in this paper, is an operational procedure conceived for direclty facing situations of prior partially available weighting information. The "outweigh concerns" were introduced in (Bana e Costa, 1988) and further developed in (Bana e Costa, 1989).

We assume an additively decomposable multiattributed value function has the basic aggregation model. Thus, being $A = \{a_1, \ldots, a_j, \ldots, a_m\}$ a set of alternatives, $X = \{X_1, \ldots, X_j, \ldots, X_n\}$ a set of attributes, $(x_1, \ldots, x_j, \ldots, x_n)$ the profile in X of

a general alternative $a \in A$ and $v_j(x_j)$ the partial (criterion) value of a for the attribute X_j $(j = 1, \ldots, n)$, the overall (or global) value $v(a)$ of a would be determined
by $v(a) = \sum_j w_j v_j(x_j)$, with $\sum_j w_j = 1$ and $w_j > 0$ for all j (along this paper and for
simplicity, the scaling constants w_j are designated by weights). OWA has been conceived
to be useful in practice after the phase of intra-attribute preference modelling, i.e., after
the construction of the criteria functions — the preference scales v_j $(j = 1, \ldots, n)$ —
which are assumed to be known.

First, we introduce the concept of *restricted dominance* for analysing which alternatives are guaranteed to be preferred to other alternatives under conditions of poor
inter-criteria information. This problem is well studied in the MAUT literature. Second,
to exploit in greater depth the information available and to investigate if it is possible to
enrich the conclusions of the restricted dominance analysis, usually too poor to support,
by itself, a final decision, we introduce the concept of *fuzzy outweigh relation*, derived from
the concept of fuzzy outranking relation, but significantly different from it, in terms of
methodological context, to justify a new designation, thus avoiding miss-understanding.
Basically, it searches for additional arguments to decrease the number of incomparability
cases.

In this way combining MAUT and outranking concepts, we make use of an example
(intentionally simple to permit a good illustration) to show how the Outweigh Approach
can be useful for decision aiding when the weights are not completely specified.

Restricted dominance analysis

OWA takes place in the R^{n-1} "space of the weights" where the set of conditions
$\sum_j w_j = 1$ and $w_j > 0$ $(j = 1, \ldots, n)$ defines a polyhedron that we call *general feasible
set* (Ω). Suppose for exemplification a decision situation with 5 alternatives and 3 attributes (see table I) characterised by the fact that only the following interval bounds for
the weights are available: $0.3 \leq w_1 \leq 0.5$, $0.2 \leq w_2 \leq 0.4$ and $0.3 \leq w_3 \leq 0.5$. These
conditions constrain the form of Ω to a smaller convex polyhedron — the *feasible set of
weights W*, $W \subset \Omega$ (see figure 1).

At each point P $(w_1^p, \ldots, w_j^p, \ldots, w_n^p)$ in W and for each pair of alternatives

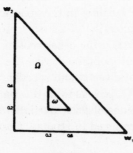

Figure 1

REFERENCE	E V A L U A T I O N S		
Alternatives	Criterion v_1	Criterion v_2	Criterion v_3
a_1	0.789	0	0.812
a_2	0.928	0.615	0.681
a_3	0.706	0.901	0.551
a_4	0.839	0.901	0.290
a_5	0.802	0.341	0.681
ideal	1	1	1
anti-ideal	0	0	0

Table I: Decision matrix

$a = (x_1, \ldots, x_j, \ldots, x_n)$ and $b = (y_1, \ldots, y_j, \ldots, y_n)$, one and only one of the following situations of global preference holds:

$$a \text{ strictly preferred to } b: \quad a >^p b \text{ iff } v^p(a) > v^p(b)$$
$$a \text{ indifferent to } b: \qquad\quad a \sim^p b \text{ iff } v^p(a) = v^p(b)$$
$$b \text{ strictly preferred to } a: \quad b >^p a \text{ iff } v^p(a) < v^p(b),$$

being $v^p(a) = \sum_j w_j^p v_j(x_j)$ and $v^p(b) = \sum_j w_j^p v_j(y_j)$ respectively the global values of a and b at the point P.

Let $\Gamma(a, b)$ be the subset of points of Ω to which corresponds a situation of indifference between a and b. If $\Gamma(a, b)$ does not intersect the set of feasible weights W ($W \cap \Gamma(a, b) = \emptyset$), one of the two alternatives will be always globally preferred to the other in W, and we will say that a situation of *restricted dominance* (Δ^r) occurs, even if neither a dominates b nor b dominates a (i.e., $\Omega \cap \Gamma(a, b) \neq \emptyset$) — see figure 2.$i$:

$$a \, \Delta^r b \text{ iff } \sum_j w_j^p \cdot [v_j(x_j) - v_j(y_j)] > 0 \text{ for all } P \in W.$$

Similarly, "restricted dominance" does not hold when $\Gamma(a, b)$ intersects somewhere the feasible set W ($\Gamma(a, b) \cap W \neq \emptyset$), thus defining on W two sub-sets $W(a, b)$ and $W(b, a)$ (see figure 2.ii):

$$W(a, b) = \left\{ P \in W : \sum_j w_j^p \cdot [v_j(x_j) - v_j(y_j)] > 0 \right\}$$

and

$$W(b, a) = \left\{ P \in W : \sum_j w_j^p \cdot [v_j(x_j) - v_j(y_j)] < 0 \right\}.$$

If $W(a, b) = W$, a restrictedly dominates b ($a \, \Delta^r b$). Similarly, if $W(b, a) = W$, b restrictedly dominates a ($b \, \Delta^r a$). Thus, under conditions of poor information available about the intercriteria preferences of the actors, represented by a feasible set of weights W, a is surely preferred to b if $W(a, b) = W$, that is, if $v^p(a) - v^p(b) > 0$, for all $P \in W$. This situation occurs if and only if $\min_W v^p(a) - v^p(b) > 0$.

Therefore, for the additive value function model, restricted dominance analysis between two alternatives a and b can be performed by a linear programming approach:

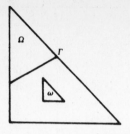 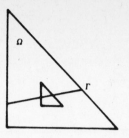

Figures 2.*i* and 2.*ii*

1. Solve the linear programme:

$$\min_{W} \sum_{j} w_j \cdot [v_j(x_j) - v_j(y_j)] = Z^* \, ,$$

subject to: $(w_1, \ldots, w_j, \ldots, w_n) \in W$

2. If $Z^* > 0$, then a is surely preferred to b. Otherwise a and b are incomparable.

The linear programme 1 is well studied in the literature (see Sarin, 1977; Malakooti, 1985; and Hazen, 1986). For example, in cases where interval bounds are available for the weights, the programme 1 is a linear knapsack problem solved by inspection by Sarin (1977). If a complete rank-order of the weights is defined, Hannan (1981) and Kirkwood and Sarin (1985) prove a very useful theorem for analysing additive restricted dominance between pairs of alternatives. Hazen (1986) proves an analogous theorem for the case of interval bounds for tradeoff values.

Normally, restricted dominance is a richer relation than (classical) dominance, because it tends to decrease the number of cases of incomparability, although usually not rich enough to completely rank-order the alternatives in A. In our example, only a_2 dominates a_5 but the output of the restricted dominance analysis is much more rich: the sub-set of alternatives $\{a_2, a_3\}$ is preferred to the subset of alternatives $\{a_1, a_4, a_5\}$. Within each of these two subsets the respective alternatives are incomparable, except that a_5 is preferred to a_1 .

The outweigh comparison procedure:
Degree of credibility and fuzzy outweigh relation

The concept of fuzzy outranking relation (Roy, 1977) embodies the contents of this section. Siskos et al. (1986) defines fuzzy outranking relation (S^d) in $A \times A$ as a membership function $d: A \times A \to [0,1]$ in which the different values $d(a,b)$ denote the strength of the relationship between any two actions a and b in A. Thus, as Roy (1977) indicates, $d(a,b)$ is the degree of credibility of the outranking of the action b by the action a.

We call *fuzzy outweigh relation* the particular fuzzy outranking relation constructed as follows, to deeper exploit the information contained in a feasible set of weights W:

If $W(a,b) = W$, that is, if a (restrictedly) dominates b, the degree of credibility $d(a,b)$ associated with the statement "a is at least as good as b" is maximum. On the other hand, if $W(a,b) = \emptyset$, $d(a,b)$ is minimum. But, if neither $a \Delta^r b$ nor $b \Delta^r a$, a natural measure of the degree of credibility $d(a,b)$ is given by the fraction of the volume of W where a is at least as good as b:

$$d(a,b) = \frac{V[W(a,b)]}{V[W]} = \frac{\int_{W(a,b)} \delta w_1, \ldots, \delta w_j, \ldots, \delta w_{n-1}}{\int_W \delta w_1, \ldots, \delta w_j, \ldots, \delta w_{n-1}}$$

where $V[W]$ and $V[W(a,b)]$ are respectively the volumes of the convex polyhedrons W and $W(a,b)$[1].

The following are the basic characteristics and properties of the "fuzzy outweigh relation" above constructed:

- $d: A \times A \to [0,1]$, that is, $0 \le d(a,b) \le 1$, for all pairs of alternatives (a,b);
- the fuzzy outweigh relation is reflexive: $d(a,a) = 1$, $\forall a \in A$;
- $d(a,b) + d(b,a) = 1$, for all pairs (a,b);
- $d(a,b) = 1$ iff a restrictedly dominates b $(a \neq b)$;
- $d(a,b) = 0$ iff b restrictedly dominates a $(a \neq b)$;
- d is a (max min) transitive relation, that is:
  $d(a,b) \ge \max_{c \in A} \min [d(a,c), d(c,b)]$, for all $a, b \in A$.
- $\Delta^r \subset S^d$.

Applying the concept of fuzzy outweigh relation to our example, the credibility degrees matrix of table II results. Of course, all the elements of this matrix corresponding to restricted dominance situations are equal to 1, but now the pairwise comparison information is much more rich.

Based on the fuzzy outweigh relation S^d, and to exploit in W the pairwise comparison information given by the membership function d, one can construct a sequence of crisp (non-fuzzy) transitive relations, $S^1 \subset S^2 \subset \ldots \subset S^s \subset \ldots$, of the following type:

$$a S^s b \text{ iff } d(a,b) \ge s, \text{ with } s \in]0.5, 1],$$

being the threshold (cut value) s as greater as it is weaker the strength of the arguments required to validate the assertion "a is at least as good as b".

[1] Within the context of the REGIME Analysis (Hinloopen et al., 1983) it is also proposed to associate the value of the credibility degree $d(a,b)$ with the relative size of $W(a,b)$.

	a_1	a_2	a_3	a_4	a_5
a_1	1	0	0	.133	0
a_2	1	1	.991	1	1
a_3	1	.009	1	1	1
a_4	.867	0	0	1	.678
a_5	1	0	0	.322	1

Table II: Credibility matrix

If "a outweighs b" ($a\,S^s\,b$) we will say that the actors are willing to accept that "a is at least as good as b", this act involving some "risk", a measure of which can be the value of $(1 - d(a, b))$. Under this reasoning, if $d(a, b)$ and $d(b, a)$ are both simultaneously lower than s, there are not sufficiently strong arguments to pairwise rank the alternatives a and b, and so, a and b are incomparable ($a\,?\,b$). Incomparability (?) reflects the fact that there are not enough strong arguments to make a choice between a and b.

Suppose that $s = 0.85$ is the minimum "degree of strength" accepted in our example. The crisp outweigh relation $S^{0.85}$ modelling the final preferences in A is represented by the pairwise comparison matrix of table III and by the partial global ordering of figure 3, thus enriching the restricted dominance analysis.

	a_1	a_2	a_3	a_4	a_5
a_1	–	0	0	0	0
a_2	1	–	1	1	1
a_3	1	0	–	1	1
a_4	1	0	0	–	0
a_5	1	0	0	0	–

Table III: Pairwise comparisons ($s = 0.85$)

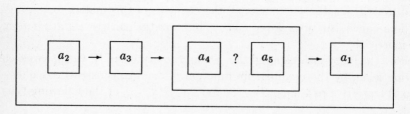

Figure 3

References

Bana e Costa, C.A. (1988). A methodology for sensitivity analysis in three-criteria problems: a case study in municipal management. *EJOR*, Vol. 33–2, pp. 159–173.

Bana e Costa, C.A. (1989). Une méthode pour l'aide à la décision en situations multicritères et multi-acteurs. *Document du Lamsade*, No. 59, Université de Paris-Dauphine, Paris.

Hannan, E.L. (1981). Obtaining nondominated priority vectors for multiple objective decisionmaking problems with different combinations of cardinal and ordinal information. *IEEE Trans. Syst., Man, Cybern.*, Vol. SMC-11, No. 8, pp. 538–543.

Hazen, G.B. (1986). Partial information, dominance, and potential optimality in multi-attribute utility theory. *Oper. Res.*, Vol. 34, No. 2, pp. 296–310.

Hinloopen, E., Nijkamp, P., Rietveld, P. (1983). Qualitative discrete multiple criteria choice models in regional planning. *Regional Science and Urban Economics*, Vol. 13, pp. 77–103.

Kirkwood, C.W., Sarin, R.K. (1985). Ranking with partial information: a method and an application. *Oper. Res.*, Vol. 33, No. 1, pp. 38–48.

Malakooti, B. (1985). A nonlinear multi-attribute utility theory. In Y.Y. Haimes, V. Chankong (eds.), Decision Making with Multiple Objectives, Springer-Verlag, Heilderberg.

Roy, B. (1977). Partial preference analysis and decision aid: the fuzzy outranking relation concept. In D.E. Bell, R.L. Keeney, H. Raiffa (eds.), Conflicting Objectives in Decisions, John Wiley & Sons, New York, pp. 40–75.

Roy, B. (1987). Main sources of inaccurate determination, uncertainty and imprecision in decision models. *Cahier du Lamsade*, No. 75, Université de Paris-Dauphine, Paris.

Sarin, R.K. (1977). Interactive evaluation and bound procedure for selecting multi-attributed alternatives. *TIMS Studies in Management Sciences*, Vol. 6, pp. 211–224.

Siskos, J., Lochard, J., Lombard, J. (1984). A multicriteria decision-making methodology under fuzziness: application to the evaluation of radiological protection in nuclear power plants. In H.-J. Zimmermann, L.A. Zadeh, B.R. Gaines (eds.), Fuzzy Sets and Decision Analysis, North-Holland, Amsterdam, pp. 261-283.

Visual Interactive Approaches for Bi-criteria Decision Making Problems

M. Murat Koksalan and Ozgur Oden
Department of Industrial Engineering
Middle East Technical University
Ankara 06531, Turkey

1 Introduction

A number of Multiple Criteria Decision Making (MCDM) methods that use computer graphics has been developed in recent years. Graphical representation is expected to aid the decision maker (DM) in better evaluating the solutions.

In this paper we consider the bi-criteria decision making problem. We conveniently represent the solutions graphically in the criterion space as we are dealing with only two criteria. Individuals are very familiar with this type of graphs and we expect that a DM can easily identify his/her preferences with the aid of such a visual representation.

In section 2 we develop a visual interactive approach for the discrete alternative case and in section 3 we discuss the continuous solution space case.

2 The discrete alternative case

The discrete bi-criteria decision making problem is simply the problem of choosing the DM's most preferred alternative among a set of alternatives where each alternative is defined by its scores in two criteria. For this problem any general MCDM method for discrete alternatives is applicable (see for example Green and Srinivasan, 1978, and Keeney and Raiffa, 1976). A visual interactive method has been developed by Korhonen (1988) for any number of criteria.

Here, we exploit the two criteria nature of the problem. Our approach is in the spirit of Korhonen et al. (1984), Koksalan et al. (1984) and Koksalan and Taner (1988). We assume that the DM has an underlying quasiconcave utility function of the two criteria. The DM is presented a pair of alternatives and is asked to choose the preferred one. The response of the DM is used to eliminate inferior alternatives that are identified using the properties of a quasiconcave utility function (see Korhonen et al. 1984). The procedure continues in the same manner until a single alternative is left. We next give the details of our visual interactive approach.

The Approach

In the interactive approach we develop, an analyst works with the DM. Provided that the DM has an underlying quasiconcave utility function and his/her responses are consistent with this function, the approach identifies the most preferred alternative as in (Korhonen et al. 1984) and (Koksalan et al. 1984).

Available alternatives are represented as points in the criterion space. The analyst can move the cursor among alternatives. The scores of the alternative that is pointed by the cursor are printed at the upper right part of the screen. The analyst chooses one of the alternatives, X, to be presented to the DM. Next, the analyst can move the cursor on the whole criterion space to choose another point, D. D can be an existing alternative or any other point (i.e., a dummy alternative) in the criterion space. Here, we extend the ideas of Koksalan et al. (1984) and Koksalan and Taner (1988). In the former study, dummy alternatives are constructed as convex combinations of existing alternatives whereas in the latter study dummy alternatives that are dominated by real alternatives are constructed. In our approach dummy alternatives can be constructed at any point in the criterion space. The choice of the dummy alternative is important since it affects the number of alternatives that can be eliminated from further consideration based on the response of the DM. Once X and D are chosen, the analyst is presented with a screen, an example of which is given in Fig. 1.

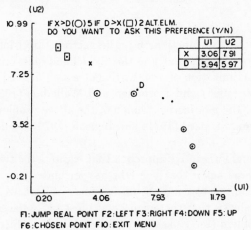

F1: JUMP REAL POINT F2: LEFT F3: RIGHT F4: DOWN F5: UP
F6: CHOSEN POINT F10: EXIT MENU

Figure 1: Eliminations conditional on the preference

The encircled alternatives are the ones that will be eliminated if the DM prefers X to D and the alternatives marked by a square will be eliminated if the preference is otherwise. Using the terminology of Korhonen et al. (1984), the encircled alternatives are in or dominated by the cone of inferior solutions if X is preferred to D and the alternatives marked by a square are in or dominated by the cone of inferior solutions if D is preferred to X. The analyst tries to choose X and D in such a way that many alternatives will be eliminated based on the preference of the DM between these alternatives. At this point the analyst may not be satisfied with the possible eliminations and may choose not to present these alternatives to the DM. In this case the analyst will go through the process of choosing new X and D. If the new X is the same as the previous one then the analyst sees on the screen the location of the previous dummy alternative which may guide him/her in choosing the new D. Once the new D is chosen, the analyst gets a screen similar to Fig. 1. In this case, information on additional number of eliminations compared to the previous D is also given on the screen. Once the analyst decides to present a pair of alternatives, X and D, to the DM, the DM indicates his/her preference by looking at both the locations of these alternatives in the criterion space and their scores shown on the screen. Based on the response of the DM either the encircled alternatives or the alternatives marked by a square are eliminated from further consideration. Then the analyst identifies new X and D among the remaining alternatives and this procedure is repeated until a single alternative is left. The procedure may be terminated at this point if the DM is satisfied with the chosen alternative or the whole process can be repeated if the DM is not satisfied.

3   Continuous solution space case

The problem we address here is:

$$\text{Maximize} \quad (f_1(x), f_2(x))$$
$$\text{subject to} \quad Ax = b$$
$$x \geq 0,$$

where $f_i(x)$ is the i-th objective function, x is the vector of decision variables, A is the matrix of technological coefficients and b is the right hand side vector. The quotation marks are used as the maximization of a vector is not a well defined operation.

Korhonen and Laakso (1986) and Korhonen and Wallenius (1988) developed visual interactive approaches for the p-objective version of the above problem. Geoffrion (1967), Walker (1978), Hocking and Shepard (1971) and Benson (1979) studied the two-objective problem.

Here we develop a visual interactive approach that exploits the two objective property of the problem. We assume again that the DM has an underlying quasiconcave utility function. The DM is required to compare an efficient solution with efficient solutions adjacent to it. It can be shown that there can be at most two adjacent efficient solutions for the two-objective problem (see Koksalan and Oden, 1989). Once the DM prefers an efficient solution to its adjacent efficient solutions, the DM is required to search for the best (possibly a non-extreme point) solution in a narrower region. This region is defined by the convex combinations of the preferred solution together with its adjacent efficient solutions. Tuncel (1988) proved that the best solution is in this region provided that there are two objective functions and the DM has an underlying quasiconcave utility function.

We illustrate our visual interactive approach on an example problem taken from Cohon (1978, p. 72). An initial efficient solution is found and presented to the DM graphically together with its adjacent efficient solutions as shown in Fig. 2. The DM can move the cursor among these solutions and the objective function values of the solution pointed by the cursor also appear on the screen.

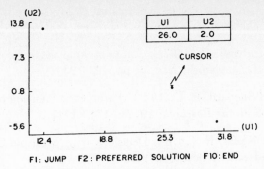

Figure 2: The initial display

After the DM chooses the preferred one of these solutions, a similar display appears on the screen showing the preferred solution together with its adjacent efficient solutions. If the DM's preferences are not consistent with a quasiconcave utility function, a warning appears on the screen but the DM may still continue with the approach. When the DM prefers a solution to its adjacent efficient solutions, the reduced solution space that contains the optimal solution appears on the screen as shown in Fig. 3. The DM may move the cursor on this region while the objective function values of the solution pointed by the cursor are printed on the screen.

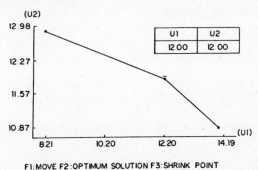

Figure 3: The display to search for the optimal solution

The movements of the cursor can be made as sensitive as desired by shrinking the region in which the search is made. The DM may terminate the search when he/she finds the optimal (or a satisfactory) solution. The DM may also choose to restart the whole process.

References

Benson, H. P. (1979). Vector Maximization with Two Objective Functions. *Journal of Optimization Theory and Applications*, **28**, pp. 253–257.

Cohon, J. L. (1978). Multiobjective Programming and Planning. Academic Press, New York.

Geoffrion, A. (1967). Solving Bicriterion Mathematical Programs. *Operations Research*, **15**, pp. 39–54.

Green, P. E. and Srinivasan, V. (1978). Conjoint Analysis in Consumer Research: Issues and Outlook. *J. Consumers Res.*, **5**, pp. 103–123.

Hocking, R. R. and Shepard, R. L. (1971). Parametric Solution of a Class of Nonconvex Programs. *Operations Research*, **19**, pp. 1742–1747.

Keeney, R. L. and Raiffa, H. (1976). Decisions with Multiple Objectives: Preferences and Value Tradeoffs. Wiley, New York.

Koksalan, M. M., Karwan, M. H. and Zionts, S. (1984). An Improved Method for Solving Multiple Criteria Problems Involving Discrete Alternatives. *IEEE Transactions on SMC*, **14**, pp. 24–34.

Koksalan, M. M. and Oden, O. (1989). Visual Interactive Methods for Bi-criteria Decision Making. Technical Report No. 89–11, Department of Ind. Eng., Middle East Technical University.

Koksalan, M. M. and Taner, O. V. (1988). An Approach for Finding the Most Preferred Alternative in the Presence of Multiple Criteria. Technical Report No. 88–01, Department of Ind. Eng., Middle East Technical University.

Korhonen, P. (1988). A Visual Reference Direction Approach to Solving Discrete Multiple Criteria Problems. *European J. Operations Research*, **34**, pp. 152–159.

Korhonen, P. and Laakso, J. (1986). A Visual Interactive Method for Solving the Multiple Criteria Problem. *European J. Operational Research*, **24**, pp. 277–287.

Korhonen, P. and Wallenius, J. (1988). A Pareto Race. *Naval Research Logistics*, **35**, pp. 615–623.

Korhonen, P., Wallenius, J. and Zionts, S. (1984). Solving the Discrete Multiple Criteria Problem Using Convex Cones. *Management Science*, **30**, pp. 1336–1345.

Tuncel, L. (1988). An Interactive Approach for Continuous Solution Space Multiple Criteria Problems. M.Sc. Thesis, Department of Ind. Eng., Middle East Technical University.

Walker, J. (1978). An Interactive Method as an Aid in Solving Bicriterion Mathematical Problems. *Journal of the Oper. Res. Soc.*, **29**, pp. 915–922.

PCCA and Compensation *

Benedetto Matarazzo
Università di Catania
Facoltà di Economia e Commercio, Istituto di Matematica,
Corso Italia 55, 95129 Catania, Italia

Abstract

The purpose of this article is to examine the characteristics of the original aggregation procedure by means of comparison by pairs of criteria with regard to compensation, making comparisons also with some other traditional multicriteria binary preference indices. It also underlines the particular compensatory logic on which the approach considered is based and the flexibility it affords in this field, also with reference to noncompensation, introducing the concept of PCCA-noncompensatory multiattribute preference structure and showing how compensatory and/or noncompensatory approaches may be used indifferently in the building phases of bicriteria and multicriteria preference indices.

1 Introduction

The notion of compensation, of major importance in all MCDM aggregation procedures, is sometimes used with different or controversial implications in specialized literature. Intuitively, the concept of compensation refers to the existence of "tradeoffs", that is, the possibility of offsetting the "disadvantages" on one or more attributes against sufficiently large "advantages" on one or more others. On the contrary, noncompensation is based on the idea that the global preference of an action a over an action b only depends on the disjoint subset of attributes on which there is partial preference of a over b and of b over a. In general, noncompensatory aggregation procedures only require "inter-attribute" information in terms of an importance relation and discordance set, and not necessarily tradeoffs between criteria, often very difficult to express. Moreover, noncompensatory aggregation procedures using the idea of veto effect tend to "rank" actions with "well-balanced" evaluations before actions which are evaluated highly on a number of attributes but very badly on others, while in some situations compensatory aggregation procedures may produce a reverse ranking (see Bouyssou, 1986 and Bouyssou and Vansnick, 1986).

In this work we shall illustrate some aspects of the particular aggregation procedure by means of comparison by pairs of criteria with reference to compensation. In particular

---

*Work partially supported by Italian Ministry of University, Scientific and Technological Research.

we shall underline the peculiar compensatory logic of this approach and the possibilities it offers on a methodological level.

After summarizing a general aggregation principle and the main binary preference indices which may be derived from it, we give a brief synthesis of the methodology and indices of our original aggregation procedures (Section 2), showing how it is possible to obtain a variety of aggregated binary indices with different characteristics from the point of view of compensation (Section 3), introducing also the concept of PCCA-noncompensatory preference structure (Section 4). The article concludes with some synthetic considerations of the more important results obtained, in order to show how, in our opinion, the approach presented may be considered a "mixed" method from the point of view of compensation (Section 5).

2 Multicriteria binary preference indices: classical aggregation procedures and the PCCA

With reference to an A. A. E. (Alternatives, Attributes, Evaluators) decisional model, let $A = \{a, b, \ldots\}$ the (finite) set of $|A|$ feasible actions or alternatives, and let $G = \{g_j | j \in J\}, |J| = m$, the set of criteria considered for the purpose of preference modelling, with $g_j : A \to R, \forall j \in J$, an interval scale of measurement.

A well–known aggregation model of monocriterion preferences, expressed by the pair of binary relations $\{P_j, I_j\}$, consists in building multicriteria binary preference indices $f(a, b), \forall (a, b) \in A^2$, not negative and independent of the irrelevant alternatives, which make it possible to obtain particular global binary relations, of the type I (indifference), P (preference), Q (weak preference) and R (incomparability). A general aggregation principle consists in choosing suitable monocriterion binary preference indices $\phi_j(a, b), j \in J$, characterized by certain properties, and in then associating with the set $\{\phi_1(a, b), \phi_2(a, b), \ldots, \phi_m(a, b)\}$ the two symmetric indices $f(a, b)$ and $f(b, a), \forall (a, b) \in A^2$ (see Jacquet-Lagrèze, 1982).

If $\lambda_j, j \in J$, indicates the normalized weight ($\sum_{j \in J} \lambda_j = 1$) associated with the criterion g_j, given:

$$
\begin{aligned}
J_{a>b} &= \{j \in J | g_j(a) > g_j(b)\}, \\
J_{a=b} &= \{j \in J | g_j(a) = g_j(b)\}, \\
J_{a\geq b} &= \{j \in J | g_j(a) \geq g_j(b)\}, \\
\Delta_j(a, b) &= g_j(a) - g_j(b),
\end{aligned}
$$

we may remember some well-known additive binary preference indices derived from classical aggregation procedures.

$$
-s(a, b) = \sum_{j \in J_{a \geq b}} \lambda_j \Delta_j(a, b) \qquad
\begin{aligned}
aPb &\Leftrightarrow s(a, b) > s(b, a); \\
bPa &\Leftrightarrow s(a, b) < s(b, a); \\
aIb &\Leftrightarrow s(a, b) = s(b, a);
\end{aligned}
$$

$$-w(a,b) = \sum_{j \in J_{a>b}} \lambda_j$$

$$aPb \;\Leftrightarrow\; w(a,b) > w(b,a);$$
$$bPa \;\Leftrightarrow\; w(a,b) < w(b,a);$$
$$aIb \;\Leftrightarrow\; w(a,b) = w(b,a);$$

$$-c(a,b) = \sum_{j \in J_{a \geq b}} \lambda_j$$

$$aSb \;\Leftrightarrow\; c(a,b) \geq c \; (0.5 \leq c \leq 1)$$
$$\text{and } w(a,b) \geq w(b,a)$$
$$\text{(outranking relation } S = P \cup I).$$

It is also possible to build multiple criteria binary preference indices with a methodologically different aggregation procedure, which consists first of all in comparing the feasible actions with respect to all the possible subsets of G containing $k, 2 \leq k < m$, of the m criteria considered, and then in suitably aggregating all the partial information thus obtained. In particular, it is possible to have $k = 2$, which seems to us the most significant case, so that in the first aggregation phase the comparisons are made by pairs of criteria (PCCA: Pairwise Criterion Comparison Approach, see Matarazzo, 1990). These comparisons may be made between one ranked pair of actions at a time (MAPPAC method, see Matarazzo, 1986) or between all the actions simultaneously (PRAGMA method, see Matarazzo, 1988a). In any case, we maintain that the greater number of calculations incurred is more than justified by the further partial information which may be obtained, and especially by the greater flexibility and the wider range of possibilities offered in the modelling phase (see Matarazzo, 1988b, 1990**). There is therefore not only none of the loss of information which is typical of MAUT decomposition but also an enrichment of the information obtained; moreover it is possible to underline also a sinergy between attributes, quite the opposite of a mechanicistic philosophy (see Starr and Zeleny, 1977). Finally, in our opinion, this approach may also be of great help in understanding the decision process itself.

Considering then a (ranked) pair of actions $(a, b) \in A^2$, we proceed with the normalization of the evaluations made by means of each criterion g_j introducing two suitable parameters a_j and b_j , $j \in J$, which represent respectively, in the decision maker's view, the "neutral" and "excellent" levels on each attribute. Then, we define

$$c_{xj} = \begin{cases} \frac{g_j(x) - a_j}{b_j - a_j} & \text{if } a_j < b_j \\ 0 & \text{if } a_j = b_j \end{cases} \quad \forall x \in A, j \in J.$$

With reference to the unranked pair of distinct criteria $g_i, g_j \in G$, in the first aggregation phase it is possible to calculate the following bicriteria binary indices, $\forall (a, b) \in A^2$:

$\pi_{ij}(a,b)$	$\pi_{ij}(b,a)$		
1	0		if $c_{ai} > c_{bi}$ and $c_{aj} > c_{bj}$
0	1		if $c_{ai} < c_{bi}$ and $c_{aj} < c_{bj}$
0.5	0.5		if $c_{ai} = c_{bi}$ and $c_{aj} = c_{bj}$
$\frac{\lambda_i(c_{ai}-c_{bi})}{\lambda_i(c_{ai}-c_{bi})+\lambda_j(c_{bj}-c_{aj})}$	$\frac{\lambda_j(c_{bj}-c_{aj})}{\lambda_j(c_{bj}-c_{aj})+\lambda_i(c_{ai}-c_{bi})}$	if	$\begin{array}{l} c_{ai} > c_{bi} \text{ and } c_{aj} \leq c_{bj} \\ c_{ai} = c_{bi} \text{ and } c_{aj} < c_{bj} \end{array}$
$\frac{\lambda_j(c_{aj}-c_{bj})}{\lambda_j(c_{aj}-c_{bj})+\lambda_i(c_{bi}-c_{ai})}$	$\frac{\lambda_i(c_{bi}-c_{ai})}{\lambda_i(c_{bi}-c_{ai})+\lambda_j(c_{aj}-c_{bj})}$	if	$\begin{array}{l} c_{ai} \leq c_{bi} \text{ and } c_{aj} > c_{bj} \\ c_{ai} < c_{bi} \text{ and } c_{aj} = c_{bj}. \end{array}$

$$(1)$$

If we assume

$$\hat{s}_{ij}(a,b) = \sum_{h \in \{i,j\} \cap J_{a \geq b}} \lambda_h (c_{ah} - c_{bh}),$$

(1) may be expressed (see Matarazzo, 1990**):

$$\pi_{ij}(a,b) = \begin{cases} \frac{\hat{s}_{ij}(a,b)}{\hat{s}_{ij}(a,b)+\hat{s}_{ij}(b,a)} & \text{if } \hat{s}_{ij}(a,b) + \hat{s}_{ij}(b,a) > 0 \\ 1/2 & \text{if } \hat{s}_{ij}(a,b) + \hat{s}_{ij}(b,a) = 0. \end{cases}$$

This index $\pi_{ij} : A \times A \to [0,1]$ is the image of a valued binary relation, complete, transitive, negatively transitive and ipsodual, and constitutes a complete valued preference structure on the set A (see Roubens and Vincke, 1985, Roubens, 1989). It is easy to represent geometrically and indicates the **credibility of partial dominance** of a over $b(aD_{ij}b)$, and may also be interpreted as a **basic preference index**, measuring the preference intensity of a over b. Indicating respectively with P_{ij} and I_{ij} the *partial* preference and indifference *binary relations*, that is with respect to the criteria g_i and g_j, we define:

$$aP_{ij}b \iff 0 \leq \pi_{ij}(b,a) < 0.5 < \pi_{ij}(a,b) \leq 1$$

$$aI_{ij}b \iff \pi_{ij}(a,b) = \pi_{ij}(b,a) = 0.5.$$

It may be demonstrated (see Matarazzo, 1984) that the preference relational system connected to the pair of relations $\{P_{ij}, I_{ij}\}$ is a complete preorder or a *weak order* on A. For further information regarding the possibility of considering suitable thresholds and areas of indifference, of introducing particular discordance indicators and carrying out specific conflict analyses, see Matarazzo, 1988b. In order to build the multicriteria binary preference index, then, we calculate all the possible partial indices $\pi_{ij}(a,b)$ (1) corresponding to the $\binom{m}{2}$ combinations of the criterion pairs, and then proceed with the aggregation of these.

The **aggregated preference index** introduced by us (see Matarazzo, 1986, 1990) is, with reference to each ranked pair $(a,b) \in A^2$:

$$\pi(a,b) = \frac{1}{m-1} \sum_{i,j;(i<j)} \pi_{ij}(a,b)(\lambda_i + \lambda_j) \qquad (2)$$

since

$$\sum_{i,j;(i<j)} (\lambda_i + \lambda_j) = (|J|-1)\sum_{h \in J} \lambda_h = m-1, \quad i,j \in J, \quad |J| \geq 2.$$

Such an index is therefore given by the weighted sum of all the bicriteria preference indices $\pi_{ij}(a,b)$, considering all the (unranked) pairs of distinct attributes. This may also be interpreted as the sum of the weights of each pair of attributes multiplied by the corresponding degree of credibility of the partial dominance of a over b. Since the index (2) then measures the intensity of the aggregated multicriteria preference of a over b, we define:

$$aPb \iff 0 \leq \pi(b,a) < 0.5 < \pi(a,b) \leq 1$$

$$aIb \iff \pi(a,b) = \pi(b,a) = 0.5.$$

From (2) (see Matarazzo, 1990**) it is easy to observe that $\pi(a,b) = 1 \iff aD_sb$; therefore $\pi(a,b)$ may also be interpreted as the **credibility index of the strict dominance** of a over b (D_s : strict dominance relation).

3 Other PCCA indices

It is now possible to make some comparisons between index (2) and other multicriteria binary preference indices, built according to the PCCA aggregation procedure. With reference to the (unranked) pair of criteria $g_i, g_j \in G$, we define the following bicriteria preference index (see Matarazzo, 1990**):

$$\pi'_{ij}(a,b) = \begin{cases} \frac{w_{ij}(a,b)}{w_{ij}(a,b)+w_{ij}(b,a)} & \text{if } w_{ij}(a,b) + w_{ij}(b,a) > 0 \\ 1/2 & \text{if } w_{ij}(a,b) + w_{ij}(b,a) = 0. \end{cases} \tag{3}$$

This partial index, too, shows the credibility of partial dominance of a over b, but assumes different values from those of the index $\pi_{ij}(a,b)$ (1) in the case of discordant evaluations, since it is based on a *logic of noncompensatory aggregation*.

From (3) we can therefore obtain the following aggregated binary index:

$$\pi'(a,b) = \frac{1}{m-1} \sum_{i,j;\,(i<j)} \pi'_{ij}(a,b)(\lambda_i + \lambda_j). \tag{4}$$

Given $p = |J_{a>b}|$, $n = |J_{b>a}|$ and $o = |J_{a=b}|$, we obtain (see Matarazzo, 1990*):

$$\pi(a,b) = \frac{1}{m-1}\Big[(p+o-1)\sum_{h\in J_{a\geq b}} \lambda_h - 0.5(o-1)\sum_{h\in J_{a=b}} \lambda_h +$$

$$+ \sum_{(r,s)\in J_{a>b}\times J_{b>a}} \pi_{rs}(a,b)(\lambda_r + \lambda_s)\Big], \tag{5}$$

$$\pi'(a,b) = \frac{1}{m-1}\Big[(p+o-1)\sum_{h\in J_{a\geq b}} \lambda_h - 0.5(o-1)\sum_{h\in J_{a=b}} \lambda_h +$$

$$+ \sum_{(r,s)\in J_{a>b}\times J_{b>a}} \pi'_{rs}(a,b)(\lambda_r + \lambda_s)\Big]; \tag{6}$$

(5) and (6) are different only by the last addenda, which have the respective value of

$$\sum_{(r,s)\in J_{a>b}\times J_{b>a}} \frac{\hat{s}_{rs}(a,b)}{\hat{s}_{rs}(a,b) + \hat{s}_{rs}(b,a)}(\lambda_r + \lambda_s)$$

and

$$\sum_{(r,s)\in J_{a>b}\times J_{b>a}} \frac{\sum_{h\in\{r,s\}\cap J_{a>b}} \lambda_h}{\sum_{h\in\{r,s\}\cap J_{a>b}} \lambda_h + \sum_{h\in\{r,s\}\cap J_{b>a}} \lambda_h}(\lambda_r + \lambda_s) = n\sum_{h\in J_{a>b}} \lambda_h,$$

so that (4) may be expressed:

$$\pi'(a,b) = \frac{1}{m-1}\Big[(m-1)\sum_{h\in J_{a>b}} \lambda_h + (p + \frac{o-1}{2})\sum_{h\in J_{a=b}} \lambda_h\Big]. \tag{7}$$

Given $i < j$, let $P_{ij}(a, b) = \{(i, j) \in J^2 | aP_{ij}b\}$ and $I_{ij}(a, b) = \{(i, j) \in J^2 | aI_{ij}b\}$, that is, these sets represent all the (unranked) pairs of distinct criteria by means of which respectively $\pi_{ij}(a, b) > 0.5$ and $\pi_{ij}(a, b) = 0.5$ are obtained. Further, we define

$$\pi^*(a, b) = \frac{1}{m - 1} \sum_{i, j; \ (i < j)} [\sum_{(i, j) \in P_{ij}(a, b)} (\lambda_i + \lambda_j) + 0.5 \sum_{(i, j) \in I_{ij}(a, b)} (\lambda_i + \lambda_j)]. \tag{8}$$

From (7) and (8) it is easy to observe that $\pi'(a, b) = \pi^*(a, b) \Leftrightarrow aD_s b$; therefore these indices too, like the index $\pi(a, b)$, measure the *credibility of the strict dominance* of a over b. Moreover, both these indices prove to have a value between 0 and 1 with a unitary sum, like $\pi(a, b)$. Observe however that the index $\pi'(a, b)$ (7) is explicitly defined – in analogy with index $c(a, b)$ – as a particular linear combination of the weights of the criteria belonging to sets $J_{a > b}$ and $J_{a = b}$, while the index $\pi^*(a, b)$ (8) is defined as a function of the weights of all the pairs of criteria such that $aP_{ij} \cup I_{ij}b$.

The addenda of both these indices, in fact, may be interpreted as indices of the relative importance of specific "coalitions of criteria" like the concordance index $c(a, b)$ of the ELECTRE I and II methods. Such coalitions, however, have as elements of $(g_i, g_j) \in G^2$, because of the peculiar characteristics of the PCCA. More precisely, considering the index $\pi'(a, b)$, the strength of these coalitions is represented by the sum of the weights of g_i and g_j, $g_i, g_j \in G$, if $aD_{ij}b$, by their half sum if $aI_{ij}b$ in the case of nondiscordant evaluation, by $\lambda_h \mid h \in \{i, j\} \cap J_{a > b}$, in the case of opposite preferences with respect to the two criteria g_i and g_j. In the case of the index $\pi^*(a, b)$ (8), on the other hand, this strength consists of the sum of the weights of the pairs of criteria $(g_i, g_j) \in G^2$ for which $aP_{ij}b$ (that is, $\pi_{ij}(a, b) > 0.5$) and of the half sum of the weights of the pairs of criteria $(g_i, g_j) \in G^2$ for which $aI_{ij}b$ (that is, $\pi_{ij}(a, b) = 0.5$), see Table 1.

Table 1: Example of a calculation of the binary indices $\pi(a, b)$, $\pi'(a, b)$ and $\pi^*(a, b)$.

Criteria	1	2	3	4	5	6
λ_h	0.15	0.20	0.10	0.20	0.15	0.20
$\Delta_h(a, b)$	0.4	0.3	0	0	-0.2	-0.3

Bicriteria basic indices:

$$\begin{aligned}
\pi_{12}(a, b) &= \pi_{13}(a, b) = \pi_{14}(a, b) = 1; \ \pi_{15}(a, b) = 2/3; \\
\pi_{16}(a, b) &= 0.5; \pi_{23}(a, b) = \pi_{24}(a, b) = 1; \ \pi_{25}(a, b) = 2/3; \\
\pi_{26}(a, b) &= \pi_{34}(a, b) = 0.5; \\
\pi_{35}(a, b) &= \pi_{36}(a, b) = \pi_{45}(a, b) = \pi_{46}(a, b) = \pi_{56}(a, b) = 0.
\end{aligned}$$

Subsets of J^2:

$$\begin{aligned}
P_{ij}(a, b) &= \{(1, 2), (1, 3), (1, 4), (1, 5), (2, 3), (2, 4), (2, 5)\}; \\
I_{ij}(a, b) &= \{(1, 6), (2, 6), (3, 4)\}; \\
P_{ij}(b, a) &= \{(3, 5), (3, 6), (4, 5), (4, 6), (5, 6)\}.
\end{aligned}$$

Binary indices:

$$\pi(a,b) = 0.522;$$
$$\pi'(a,b) = 1/5(5\lambda_1 + 5\lambda_2 + 2.5\lambda_3 + 2.5\lambda_4) = 0.5;$$
$$\pi^\star(a,b) = 1/5(4.5\lambda_1 + 4.5\lambda_2 + 2.5\lambda_3 + 2.5\lambda_4 + 2\lambda_5 + \lambda_6) = 0.565.$$

Comparing these binary indices of multicriteria preference with $c(a,b)$ we observe that the index $\pi^\star(a,b)$ uses an aggregation logic analogous to that of the ELECTRE I and II methods, but refers directly and instrumentally – as an intermediate step – to bicriteria complete valued preference relations, expressed by $\pi_{ij}(a,b)$. It is therefore based on a compensatory logic in the partial aggregation phase, even if only in order to identify which coalitions of criteria (pairs $(g_i, g_j) \in G^2$) must be considered and which discarded in the building of the aggregated index. Therefore, unlike index $c(a,b)$, this proves to be a function (weighted sum) also of $\lambda_h \mid h \in J_{b>a}$ and for which there exists at least one $j \in J_{a>b} \mid a P_{hj} \cup I_{hj} b$.

The index $\pi'(a,b)$ (4) on the other hand, while it uses an intermediate aggregation logic halfway between that of index $\pi(a,b)$ (2) and that of the ELECTRE I and II methods, proves to be a function only of the weights of the criteria belonging to set $J_{a>b}$, like index $c(a,b)$; more precisely – and more generally than $c(a,b)$ – it is a linear combination with non negative coefficients (see (7)) of the weights of the criteria belonging to sets $J_{a>b}$ and $J_{a=b}$. The indices $\pi'(a,b)$ and $\pi^\star(a,b)$, like the index $\pi(a,b)$, are also functions of p, n, o. The index $\pi(a,b)$ (2), as observed, is a function not only of the weights λ_h, $h \in J$, but also of the differences between the normalized evaluations of a and b by means of the criteria considered. It constitutes a complete valued preference relation on A and, from the perspective of the aggregation procedure, may be compared to the ELECTRE III method, making direct use of the valued partial preference relations $\pi_{ij}(a,b)$, which may be interpreted as a degree of credibility of the partial dominance of a over b, as weighting coefficients of each sum $\lambda_i + \lambda_j$ of the weights of all the pairs of distinct attributes.

4   Noncompensation and PCCA noncompensation

There is a fundamental distinction between the indices $\pi(a,b), \pi'(a,b)$ and $\pi^\star(a,b)$ considered here with reference to the concept of compensation. We remember that, given $P(x,y) = \{j \in J \mid x P_j y\}$, $\forall x, y \in A$, a multiattribute preference structure (MPS) is:

a) **totally noncompensatory** iff for all $a, b, c, d \in A$

A.1. $[(P(a,b), P(b,a)) = (P(c,d), P(d,c))] \Rightarrow [a P \cup I b \Rightarrow c P \cup I d]$,

A.2. $[P(a,b) \neq \emptyset$ and $P(b,a) = \emptyset] \Rightarrow a P b$.

b) **Noncompensatory** iff for all $a, b, c, d \in A$

B.1. $[(P(a,b), P(b,a)) = (P(c,d), P(d,c))] \Rightarrow [a P b \Rightarrow$ not $d P \cup I c]$ and $[a I b \Rightarrow$ not $d P c$ and not $c P d]$,

B.2. $[P(a,b) \neq \emptyset$ and $P(b,a) = \emptyset] \Rightarrow a P b$.

The conditions A.2. and B.2. could be omitted, but from a practical point of view only regular structures are of interest (see Bouyssou, 1986, Bouyssou and Vansnick, 1986, Fishburn, 1976, Keeney and Raiffa, 1976). In cases of noncompensation, therefore, the binary preference relations depend substantially on the subsets of J for which aP_jb or bP_ja result.

We say that an MPS is:

c) **PCCA-totally noncompensatory** iff for all $a, b, c, d \in A$

C.1. $[(P_{ij}(a,b), P_{ij}(b,a) = (P_{ij}(c,d), P_{ij}(d,c))] \Rightarrow [(aP \cup Ib \Rightarrow cP \cup Id)]$,

C.2. $[P_{ij}(a,b) \neq \emptyset$ and $P_{ij}(b,a) = \emptyset] \Rightarrow aPb$.

d) **PCCA-noncompensatory** iff for all $a, b, c, d \in A$

D.1. $[(P_{ij}(a,b), P_{ij}(b,a)) = (P_{ij}(c,d), P_{ij}(d,c))] \Rightarrow [aPb \Rightarrow$ not $dP \cup Ic]$ and $[aIb \Rightarrow$ not dPc and not $cPd]$,

D.2. $[P_{ij}(a,b) \neq \emptyset$ and $P_{ij}(b,a) = \emptyset] \Rightarrow aPb$.

In these definitions also, C.2. and D.2. may be omitted. Observe that if an MPS is (totally) noncompensatory then it is also PCCA-(totally) noncompensatory, but the converse is not necessarily true. In fact, noncompensation is valid for any subset of J (see Bouyssou and Vansnick, 1986) and therefore in particular for any pair $(i,j) \in J^2$ $(i \neq j)$. It may occur on the other hand that $aP_{ij}b$ and $cP_{ij}d$ while aP_ib, bP_ja and cP_jd and dP_ic, or vice versa, therefore $P_{ij}(a,b) = P_{ij}(c,d) \not\Rightarrow P(a,b) = P(c,d)$.

A PCCA-noncompensatory MPS is therefore more flexible than a corresponding noncompensatory structure.

It may then be observed that the index $\pi(a,b)$ (2), in analogy with the corresponding bicriteria index $\pi_{ij}(a,b)$, is *minimally compensatory* (see Bouyssou, 1986, Fishburn, 1976) and therefore, also on an aggregated level, it is necessary to treat the interattribute information according to a "trade–off reasoning" (see Vansnick, 1986). But the compensation due to the methodology of this index is very different from that obtained by the traditional weighted sum method, in which *all the differences* in evaluation of a and b by means of the true–criteria compensate one another *simultaneously*. It follows from the definition (1) of the index $\pi_{ij}(a,b)$, by means of which the differences in evaluation compensate one another *two at a time, if* and in so far as they are *opposed*. In (2) then, the weights of the criteria reappear explicitly, because in the aggregation phase by pairs of criteria the basic indices are normalized to underline the partial dominance, which is independent of the weights. Naturally $s(a,b)$ also may be formally written

$$s(a,b) = \frac{1}{m-1} \sum_{i,j;\ (i<j)} s_{ij}(a,b),$$

but this would not alter anything in its classical compensatory aggregation logic. The index $\pi'(a,b)$ on the other hand is a *totally noncompensatory* index, as may easily be deduced from (7). From this point of view, therefore, it is in analogy with the concordance indices of the ELECTRE I and II methods.

Finally, the index $\pi^*(a, b)$ is a *PCCA-totally noncompensatory index*, as may be observed from (8): it expresses the "coalition strength" of the pairs of criteria by means of which $aP_{ij}b$ or $aI_{ij}b$, and therefore the corresponding binary preference relations depend substantially on the weights of the subsets of G^2 such that $P_{ij}(a, b)$ or $I_{ij}(a, b)$.

This aggregation procedure is therefore, in our opinion, extremely flexible, since it permits the building both of MPS which allow for compensation only within preestablished preference differences with respect to each pair of criteria (see Luce, 1978), and of MPS in which the noncompensatory components derive from the specific methodology adopted (see Bouyssou, 1986), regardless of the entity of the differences in evaluation.

5 Final considerations

The binary indices built with the PCCA aggregation procedure characterize the credibility of strict dominance of a over b (see Matarazzo, 1990**) and make it possible to carry out suitable indifference and discordance analyses by means of pairs of criteria (see Matarazzo, 1988b). As a result of the particular aggregation methodology, moreover, the index $\pi(a, b)$ proves to be compensatory, but aggregates components (bicriteria indices) which are functions of the value, or only of the sign, of the differences between the weighted normalized evaluations of a and b (see Matarazzo, 1990*). In the initial phase of partial aggregation, then, the compensation does not take place globally, as with traditional compensatory indices, but according to a compensatory logic by means of pairs of criteria. In the second phase of aggregation, on the other hand, a traditional compensation logic is adopted, considering simultaneously all the partial indices previously obtained.

The peculiarity of the PCCA in subdividing the aggregation phase into two parts allows, in our opinion, for considerable flexibility also on the compensation modellization level. In fact it is possible to build preference indices which, in the first comparison phase by pairs of criteria, are compensatory, possibly admitting such a compensation within preestablished limits, or which are noncompensatory. In the aggregation phase of these bicriteria indices, then, it is possible to follow compensatory, noncompensatory or PCCA-noncompensatory procedures, and therefore to obtain MPS which correspond as closely as possible to the requirements expressed by the decision maker with reference to the specific problem considered. From the above considerations, we feel justified in stating that the PCCA may be considered a "mixed" or "intermediate" method with regard to compensation.

6 References

Bouyssou, D. (1986). Some remarks on the notion of compensation in MCDM, *European Journal of Operational Research* 26: 150-160.

Bouyssou, D., J.-Cl. Vansnick (1986). Noncompensatory and generalized noncompensatory preference structures, *Theory and Decision* 21:251-266.

Fishburn, P.C. (1976). Noncompensatory preferences, *Synthèse* 33:393-403.

Jacquet-Lagrèze, E. (1982). Binary preference indices; A new look on multicriteria aggregation procedures, *European Journal of Operational Research* 10: 26-32.

Keeney, R.L., H. Raiffa (1976). Decisions with Multiple Objectives: Preferences and Value Tradeoffs, J.Wiley and Sons, New York.

Luce, R.D. (1978). Lexicographic tradeoff structures, *Theory and Decision*, 9:187-193.

Matarazzo, B. (1984). Multicriteria analysis: the MAPPAC method, Università di Catania, Catania.

Matarazzo, B. (1986). Multicriterion Analysis of Preferences by means of Pairwise Actions and Criterion Comparisons (MAPPAC), *Applied Mathematics and Computation*, 18/2:119-141.

Matarazzo, B. (1988a). Preference Ranking Global Frequencies in Multicriterion Analysis (PRAGMA) *European Journal of Operational Research* 36/1:36-49.

Matarazzo, B. (1988b). A more effective implementation of the MAPPAC and PRAGMA methods, *Foundations of Control Engineering* 13:155-173.

Matarazzo, B. (1990). A Pairwise Criterion Comparison Approach: The MAPPAC and PRAGMA methods, in Bana e Costa, C. A. (ed.), Readings in Multiple Criteria Decision Aid, Springer–Verlag, Berlin–Heidelberg.

Matarazzo, B. (1990*). MAPPAC as a compromise between outranking methods and MAUT, forthcoming in *European Journal of Operational Research*.

Matarazzo, B. (1990**). PCCA and k-dominance in MCDM, in print in *Belgian Journal of Operations Research, Statistics and Computer Science*.

Roubens, M., Ph. Vincke (1985). Preference Modelling, Springer, Berlin-Heidelberg.

Roubens, M. (1989). Some properties of choice functions based on valued binary relations, *European Journal of Operational Research* 40: 309-321.

Starr, M.K., M. Zeleny (eds.) (1977). Multiple Criteria Decision Making, North-Holland, Amsterdam.

Vansnick, J.-Cl. (1986). On the problem of weights in multiple criteria decision making (the noncompensatory approach), *European Journal of Operational Research* 24: 288-294.

An Interactive Approach for MOLP Problems Analysis

Boyan Metev, Irena Yordanova

Institute of Industrial Cybernetics and Robotics

Bulgarian Academy of Sciences

Acad. G. Bonchev str., bl. 2, Sofia 1113, Bulgaria

Abstract

This paper includes basic theoretical aspects of an approach, that uses a reference point for multiple objective linear programming (MOLP) problems analysis. A short description of a possible interactive procedure, based on this approach, is proposed. An information about the respective computer realization and about the dialogue maintened with the user is also given in the paper.

1   Introduction

It is well known that the interactive procedures for solving the MOLP problems are very perspective because they are connected with active participation of the Decision Maker (DM) in the process of analysis and solving of the problem (when such problems are used for decision support). Among other interactive methods, the advantage of reference point methods consists in the fact that the Decision Maker can directly indicate points in the criterion space, reflecting in this way his preferences. Some possibilities for development and realization of an interactive procedure of this type are examined in the paper.

Further, theoretical foundations of the approach are given — a short description of the main properties of the single objective optimization problem used for analysing the MOLP problem. The possibility for realization of corresponding procedure is also described in brief. This procedure gives only nondominated points and ensures on each step improvement of the reached level of a chosen criterion, using a reference point appropriately chosen by the DM. In the procedure the dialogue with the user gives some recommendations about the choice of the reference point. The realized computer program is implemented on IBM-PC/XT.

The problem considered in this paper is:

(M1) $$\text{"max"} \quad [f_1(x), \ldots, f_m(x)]$$

$$\text{s.t.} \quad x \in X,$$

where X is the feasible set in the MOLP problem. We suppose that X is defined as follows:

$$X = \{\, x \in R^n \mid x \geq 0,\ g_i(x) \leq 0,\ i = 1,\ldots,r \,\}$$

and that X is a bounded set.

The m nontrivial linear functions $f_i(x)$, defined in X, are considered as formal criteria for optimization and should be maximized. Let $Z \subset R^m$ be the set of all feasible criterion vectors, i.e. the set of images of all $x \in X$:

$$Z = \{\, z \in R^m \mid z_i = f_i(x),\ x \in X,\ i = 1,\ldots,m \,\}.$$

The ideal point z^* and the opposite ideal point z^- are the points belonging to the criterion space Z, for which:

$$z_i^* = \max_{x \in X} f_i(x) \qquad i = 1,\ldots,m$$

and

$$z_i^- = \min_{x \in X} f_i(x) \qquad i = 1,\ldots,m.$$

2 Theoretical basis of the method

We will consider the following single criterion linear programming problem, which corresponds to the initial MOLP problem (M1):

(S1)
$$\min \left(d - \sum_{j=1}^{m} c_j e_j \right)$$

$$\text{s.t.} \quad x \in X$$

$$d \geq b_i[z_i^+ - f_i(x)] \qquad i = 1,\ldots,m$$

$$d \geq 0$$

$$f_i(x) - e_i = z_i^- \qquad i = 1,\ldots,m$$

$$e_i \geq 0 \qquad i = 1,\ldots,m$$

In this formulation: b_i $(i = 1,\ldots,m)$ are strictly positive real numbers (weights); c_j $(j = 1,\ldots,m)$ are sufficiently small positive numbers; $z^+ = (z_1^+,\ldots,z_m^+)$ is the reference point which may be an arbitrary point in the criterion space.

The problem defined in this way can be represented also in the following equivalent form:

(E1)
$$\min_x \left\{ \max \left\{ \max_i \left\{ b_i[z_i^+ - f_i(x)] \right\}, 0 \right\} - \sum_{j=1}^{m} c_j[f_j(x) - z_j^-] \right\},$$

where $x \in X$ and $i = 1,\ldots,m$.

This problem has the following sense.

If the reference point z^+ satisfies the conditions $z_i^+ \geq z_i^*$ for all $i = 1,\ldots,m$, then the linear programming problem (S1) /(E1)/, which corresponds to the initial MOLP problem (M1) is equivalent to the minimization of the modified weighted Tchebycheff distance:

$$\min_x \left\{ \max_i \left\{ b_i |z_i^+ - f_i(x)| \right\} - \sum_{j=1}^m c_j [f_j(x) - z_j^-] \right\},$$

where $x \in X$ and $i = 1, \ldots, m$.

The first part of this function is the usual weighted Tchebycheff distance to the reference point z^+ and the second one $(\sum_{j=1}^m c_j [f_j(x) - z_j^-])$ is a modification that assures the nondominance of the obtained solution.

If the reference point z^+ does not dominate the ideal point z^*, then it is possible that the following inequation is true:

$$b_i [z_i^+ - f_i(x)] < 0 \qquad \text{for some} \quad x \in X \quad \text{and for some} \quad i.$$

When for some $x \in X$ this inequation holds for all i $(i = 1, \ldots, m)$, the constraint $d \geq 0$ becomes important. If z^+ is dominated by all feasible points, then the constraint $d \geq 0$ is active for all points of X and the solution of (S1) /(E1)/ is such a point that maximizes the sum $\sum_{j=1}^m c_j [f_j(x) - z_j^-]$, i.e. the point that maximizes the weighted sum of deviations from the components of the opposite ideal point.

The solution of the problem (S1) is the vector of arguments x^m, the scalar d^m and the minimal value of the objective function $D^{\min} = d^m - \sum_{j=1}^m c_j [f_j(x^m) - z_j^-]$. The corresponding values of the criteria $f_i(x^m)$ $(i = 1, \ldots, m)$ may be determined, too. Then, the point z^m with components $z_i^m = f_i(x^m)$ $(i = 1, \ldots, m)$ is the solution of the problem (S1) in the criterion space.

The following theorem which concerns the problem (S1), defined and solved with an arbitrary reference point, can be proved:

Theorem 1: The solution z^m of the problem (S1) in the criterion space is guaranteed to be a Pareto point, independent of the position of the reference point z^+.

Proof: The following notation will be used for the value of the objective function in the problem (S1) /(E1)/ in each point $x \in X$:

(N1)
$$D(x) = \max \left\{ \max_i \left\{ b_i [z_i^+ - f_i(x)] \right\}, 0 \right\} - \sum_{j=1}^m c_j [f_j(x) - z_j^-],$$

where $i = 1, \ldots, m$.

Now, let suppose that the point z^m $(z_i^m = f_i(x^m), \ i = 1, \ldots, m)$ is dominated by the point $z^n \in Z$ with components $z_i^n = f_i(x^n)$ $(i = 1, \ldots, m, \ x^n \in X)$. Then:

$$f_i(x^n) > f_i(x^m) \qquad \text{for} \ i \in I_1,$$

$$f_i(x^n) = f_i(x^m) \qquad \text{for} \ i \in I_2,$$

$$I_1 \neq \emptyset,$$

$$I_1 \cup I_2 = \{1, \ldots, m\}.$$

This means that:

$$b_i[z_i^+ - f_i(x^n)] \le b_i[z_i^+ - f_i(x^m)] \qquad \text{for all } i \ (i = 1, \ldots, m)$$

and:

$$-\sum_{j=1}^m c_j[f_j(x^n) - z_j^-] < -\sum_{j=1}^m c_j[f_j(x^m) - z_j^-].$$

Therefore, using the notation (N1), we may write:

$$D(x^n) < D(x^m).$$

But x^m is the solution of the optimization problem (S1) /(E1)/ and therefore:

$$D(x^m) = D^{\min} = \min_{x \in X} D(x).$$

This means that the inequation $D(x^n) < D(x^m)$ can never be true. Therefore, it doesn't exist a point $z^n \in Z$, which dominates the solution z^m of the problem (S1) /(E1)/.

Q.E.D.

We will suppose now that the vector x^m (the solution of (S1) for a fixed reference point z^+) satisfies the inequation:

$$f_k(x^m) < \max_{x \in X} f_k(x).$$

Only in this case it makes sense to search a way for improvement of the obtained value of the objective $f_k(x)$. Further we will investigate the influence of the change in one of the coordinates of the reference point on the solution of the problem (S1). For this purpose we will define the following "pulled" problem:

(S2) $\qquad \min \ \left(d^\Delta - \sum_{j=1}^m c_j e_j\right)$

s.t. $\quad x \in X$

$\qquad d^\Delta \ge b_i[z_i^+ - f_i(x)] \qquad\qquad i = 1, \ldots, k-1, k+1, \ldots, m$

$\qquad d^\Delta \ge b_k[z_k^+ + \varepsilon - f_k(x)]$

$\qquad d^\Delta \ge 0$

$\qquad f_i(x) - e_i = z_i^- \qquad\qquad\qquad i = 1, \ldots, m$

$\qquad e_i \ge 0 \qquad\qquad\qquad\qquad\quad i = 1, \ldots, m$

The solution of this problem consists of three parts: the scalar $D^{\Delta \min}$, the vector $x^{\Delta m}$ and the corresponding point $z^{\Delta m}$ $(z_i^{\Delta m} = f_i(x^{\Delta m}), \ i = 1, \ldots, m)$ in the criterion space. Problem (S2) differs from the problem (S1) only by the k-th component of the reference point, which is equal to $z_k^+ + \varepsilon$ ($\varepsilon > 0$ and z_k^+ is the corresponding component in the reference point from the problem (S1)).

The equivalent form of the problem (S2) is the following:

$$(E2) \quad \min_x \left\{ \max \left\{ \max_i \left\{ b_i[z_i^+ - f_i(x)] \right\}, b_k[z_k^+ + \varepsilon - f_k(x)], 0 \right\} - \sum_{j=1}^m c_j[f_j(x) - z_j^-] \right\},$$

where $x \in X$ and $i = 1, \ldots, k-1, k+1, \ldots, m$.

Further, some transformations of (E1) and (E2) can be effected:

$$g_i(x) = b_i[z_i^+ - f_i(x)] \quad \text{for } i = 1, \ldots, m$$
$$g_{m+1}(x) = 0$$

It is clear that:

$$\max_i \{g_i(x)\} - \sum_{j=1}^m c_j[f_j(x) - z_j^-] = \max_i \left\{ g_i(x) - \sum_{j=1}^m c_j[f_j(x) - z_j^-] \right\}, \quad i = 1, \ldots, m+1.$$

We introduce the functions:

$$\Psi_i(x) = g_i(x) - \sum_{j=1}^m c_j[f_j(x) - z_j^-] \quad \text{for } i = 1, \ldots, m+1.$$

Therefore, (E1) can be represented in the following form:

$$(E1') \qquad \min_x \max_i \Psi_i(x), \quad x \in X, \quad i = 1, \ldots, m, m+1.$$

In a similar way it can be adopted that:

$$h_i(x) = \Psi_i(x) \quad \text{for } i = 1, \ldots, k-1, k+1, \ldots, m, m+1$$
$$h_k(x) = \Psi_k(x) + \varepsilon b_k$$

Then, for (E2) is obtained:

$$(E2') \qquad \min_x \max_i h_i(x), \quad x \in X, \quad i = 1, \ldots, m, m+1.$$

Using the equivalent representation of the problems (S1) and (S2) by (E1') and (E2') we can formulate the following assertions which are nearly obvious:

Assertion 1: $\quad D^{\Delta \min} \geq D^{\min}$

Assertion 2: $\quad D^{\Delta \min} \leq D^{\min} + \varepsilon b_k$

Let us suppose now, that we have solved the problem (S1) /(E1')/ and we have received the corresponding solution $D^{\min}$, x^m and that $f_k(x^m) < \max_{x \in X} f_k(x)$. We suppose, that in the point of the solution the restriction about the k-th criterion is active, i.e.:

$$D^{\min} = D(x^m) = \Psi_k(x^m).$$

Let us consider an open set $A(x^m)$ $(A(x^m) \subset X)$ and let x^m be an interior point of $A(x^m)$. We adopt that:

$$\inf_x \Psi_k(x) = D^{\min} - \eta_1, \qquad \eta_1 > 0, \qquad x \in A(x^m).$$

Therefore, a point $x^r \in A(x^m)$ exists, for which:

(I) $$\Psi_k(x^r) = D^{\min} - \eta, \qquad 0 < \eta < \eta_1 \text{ and } \eta \approx \eta_1 .$$

On the other hand, the value $\eta_2 \geq 0$ can be introduced in the following way:

(II) $$\sup_x \max_i \Psi_i(x) = D^{\min} + \eta_2,$$

where $x \in A(x^m)$ and $i = 1, \ldots, k-1, k+1, \ldots, m, m+1$.

We increase the k-th component of the reference point and solve (S2) /(E2')/. In this case the following assertion can be formulated for the values $D^{\min}$ and $D^{\Delta \min}$:

Assertion 3: For each positive number η, defined in (I), there is an ε, $\varepsilon b_k - \eta \geq 0$, that the following inequation is true:

$$D^{\Delta \min} \leq D^{\min} - \eta + \varepsilon b_k .$$

Proof: In the problem (S2) /(E2')/, where a "pull" of the k-th criterion is realized, it is obtained:

(III) $$h_k(x) = \Psi_k(x) + \varepsilon b_k .$$

Using (I) and (III), we can write:

(IV) $$h_k(x^r) = D^{\min} - \eta + \varepsilon b_k .$$

Let the chosen ε be such that the following is fulfilled:

(V) $$h_k(x^r) > \sup_x \max_i \Psi_i(x),$$

where $x \in A(x^m)$ and $i = 1, \ldots, k-1, k+1, \ldots, m, m+1$.

Then (V), (IV) and (II) assure, that the following inequation will be fulfilled:

$$D^{\min} - \eta + \varepsilon b_k > D^{\min} + \eta_2,$$

which is true if:

$$\varepsilon b_k > \eta_2 + \eta.$$

In this case, the following equation is true for the point x^r:

$$\max_i h_i(x^r) = D^{\min} - \eta + \varepsilon b_k , \qquad i = 1, \ldots, m, m+1.$$

Therefore: $$D^{\Delta \min} = \min_x \max_i h_i(x) \leq \max_i h_i(x^r) \leq D^{\min} - \eta + \varepsilon b_k ,$$
where $x \in X$ and $i = 1, \ldots, m, m+1$. $\hfill$ Q.E.D.

Now, the following theorem for the solutions of (S1) and (S2) can be formulated:

Theorem 2: In the problem (S2) ε may be chosen so that the following can be completed:

$$f_k(x^{\Delta m}) \geq f_k(x^m).$$

The proof of this theorem is based on the use of Assertion 3 in cases when the k-th constraint is active, or on the use of similar ideas, in cases when the k-th constraint is not active in the point x^m of the solution of the problem (S1). A similar theorem, but at stronger assumptions and restrictions for the position of the reference point has been proved in (Popchev et al., 1988).

It must be said, that Korhonen and Laakso (1986) have proposed a procedure for solving multiple objective optimization problems. This procedure uses single objective programming problem, that is in similar, but more general form than (S2).

3 Algorithm

The analyzed linear programming problem (S1) and its characteristics can be used in constructing a suitable interactive procedure for analysis and obtaining a solution of the initial multiobjective linear programming problem. Theorem 1 guarantees that nondominated solutions of the multiple criteria problem are obtained always through problem (S1). The purpose of the procedure is either to reach a satisfactory final nondominated solution through a few number of iterations, or to reject the possibility of finding any. In order to accomplish this, natural ways for improving the achieved level of the chosen by the Decision Maker criteria, are sought. Theorem 2 shows a way for improving the achieved level of a chosen criterion, but, of course, this is accompanied by worsening of the value of one or some other criteria. That's why when the procedure is constructed, a subsequent improvement of the values of the different criteria is supposed, i.e. at each iteration, the DM "pulls" (increases by $\varepsilon > 0$) only one component of the reference point which is corresponding to one of the criterial functions. The change of one component in the reference point means that only one of the restrictions of the initial problem (S1) is changed in the right part. Hence, the standard sensitivity analysis can be used for generating suitable recommendations to the DM.

If the DM wishes to improve the criterion value, having a corresponding nonactive restriction at the point of the current solution, then the sensitivity analysis shows the range in which the change according to the chosen criterion of a reference point component will not lead to a solution change, i.e. the level of this criterion will remain the same.

Besides, the sensitivity analysis of the problem shows these boundaries in which the problem's optimal basis remains unaffected. Usually, if the "pull" of the reference point coordinate is such, that it does not affect the problem's optimal basis, then the different formal criteria undergo unidirectional change during the transition from the initial problem's solution to the new problem's solution — the values of some criteria (including the number k criterion) are improved or kept unaffected, the others are worsened. But if the "pull" is beyond the limits in which the optimal basis of the initial problem remains unaffected, then at the point of changing the basis, the change of the directions for formal criteria alteration can take place — if the value of some criterion has been increasing up to this moment, at the new basis it may begin decreasing and vice versa. For this reason, the points at which the change of the basis takes place may be also subject of interest for the DM. By means of these points the DM can detect the changes in the values of the rest of the criteria (besides the number k criterion, which is guaranteed to be improved or to be unaffected), which take place during the transition from the solution of the initial problem to the solution of the new problem.

When a level of the number k criterion, satisfying the DM is reached, this is fixed in the problem's constraint system by adding an inequation of the kind $f_k(x) \geq \bar{f}_k(x) - \delta_k$. Here $\bar{f}_k(x)$ is the reached satisfactory value of the number k criterion and $\delta_k \geq 0$ is the appointed by the DM relaxation of this criterion. The value δ_k is greater than zero only in these cases in which the restriction $f_k(x) \geq \bar{f}_k(x)$ is rather severe and does not allow improvement of the values reached, according to the others criteria, Further the procedure continues with an attempt for improving the level of another criterion chosen by the user.

The weighting coefficients b_i $(i = 1, \ldots, m)$, used in problem (S1), can be calculated according to certain rules, using the ideal and the opposite ideal point components and the coefficients of the criterion functions. The user of the computer program has the possibility to choose an arbitrary vector of these coefficients, too. The small positive coefficients c_j $(j = 1, \ldots, m)$ are chosen, according to specified requirements, regarding the uniqueness of the solution of the single criterion problem, the restricting of the objective function's modification in a certain interval, etc.

This interactive procedure can converge to nonextreme final solutions and can be considered as a semistructered approach for generating a sequence of solutions. The procedure is designed to be used with conventional single criterion linear programming software.

4   Computer realization

The approach described in this work has been applied in the process of creating of the interactive computer system "POLINA". This system is designed for analysis and solving multiple criteria linear programming problems. The system offers to the user the following possibilities: to input and edit the MOLP problems; to find the ideal and the opposite ideal points of the problem; to check the compatibility of the inequations in the problem's system of constraints; to check the feasibility of an arbitrary point from the criterion space; to check the nondominance of an arbitrary feasible point from the criterion space; to find a solution of the MOLP problem using an interactive procedure, based on the above described ideas.

The work of the system consists of two basic phases — preparatory and operative. The first phase includes: input of the problem, constraints' compatibility check, ideal and opposite ideal point computing. The operative phase deals with finding a nondominated solution of the MOLP problem and realization of some additional functions as well, such as compatibility and nondominance check of a chosen point.

The system "POLINA" consists of three main components — data, models and dialogue, thus it possesses the features of the traditional Multiple Criteria Decision Support

Systems.

The system is implemented on IBM-PC/XT. The LINA-16 package is used, that solves linear single criterion programs. The minimum of 512 KB RAM is required.

5 Conclusion

Some theoretical and practical results in the field of MOLP problems analysis have been included in this paper. They can be used as base for constructing an improved procedure, which shall be the main purpose of our future efforts.

References

Korhonen, P. and Laakso, J. (1986). A Visual Interactive Method for Solving the Multiple Criteria Problem. *European Journal of Operational Research*, Vol. 24, No. 2.

Lewandowski, A. and Wierzbicki, A. (1987). Theory, Software and Testing Examples for DSS. IIASA, WP–87–26.

Popchev, I., Metev, B. and Yordanova, I. (1988). A Realization of Reference Point Method Using the Tchebycheff Distance. International Conference on: Multiobjective Problems of Mathematical Programming, Yalta, USSR, 26 Oct.–2 Nov., 1988.

Sawaragi, Y., Nakayama, H. and Tanino, T. (1985). Theory of Multiobjective Optimization. Academic Press, Orlando.

Steuer, R. (1986). Multiple Criteria Optimization: Theory, Computation and Application. John Wiley & Sons, N.Y.

Linear Interactive Maximizing (Minimizing) System LINA-16. User's Guide. Bulgarian Academy of Sciences, Institute of Industrial Cybernetics and Robotics, May 1986, (in Bulgarian).

Multiple Criteria Robust Interactive Decision Analysis (MCRID): A Tool for Multiple Criteria Decision Support

Herbert Moskowitz
Krannert Graduate School of Management

Paul V. Preckel
Department of Agriculture Economics

Aynang Yang
Department of Electrical Engineering

Purdue University
West Lafayette, IN 47907, U.S.A.

Abstract

A novel interactive procedure and Decision Support System (DSS) for performing decision analysis on the personal computer, called Robust Interactive Decision Analysis (RID), which avoids the difficult problems of precisely measuring utility and state probability information associated with traditional decision tree analysis has recently been developed. The RID method permits a decision maker (DM) to voluntarily and interactively express strong (viz; sure) binary preferences for actions, partial decision functions, and full decision functions, and only imprecise probability and utility function assessments. These inputs are used with various dominance operators to prune the state probability space, utility space, and decision space until an optimal choice strategy is obtained. Conceptually, the operation of the RID method can be regarded as a state-space pruning system and the computer implementation of the RID methodology can be viewed as a DSS. In this paper, we extend the RID concept and DSS to deal with multiple criteria decisions, circumventing the need to precisely assess attribute importance criteria/attribute weights. The approach is described and shown to be effective in eliminating inefficient alternatives. But, since the aggregate utility of each alternative is interval valued, it then becomes difficult to choose an optimal alternative from among the remaining efficient one, since the intervals are not defined by probability distributions. However, goal programming is used to vitiate this problem, thereby allowing the decision maker to choose an optimal alternative.

Introduction

Decision Analysis deals with making decisions in the face of uncertainty and multiple conflicting objectives, and can provide a potentially valuable conceptual and methodological tool for decision making in practice. However, to date, there has been a dearth of applications of these concepts. There are at least two reasons for this: (1) lack of user-friendly computer software support and (2) the often onerous measurement demands made on the decision maker (DM) to provide precise subjective input (probability, utility, and/or importance weight functions) to initiate and execute the analysis.

We have proposed an alternative approach to decision analysis that relaxes many of its stringent measurement requirements, thereby making it a potentially more accessible and viable tool for decision making in practice. The philosophical basis of the approach is one of exploiting robustness, thereby tolerating measurement vagueness or imprecision. Tolerating ambiguity and vagueness is somewhat contrary to traditional decision analysis principles, where precision in assessment is sought. Traditional decision analysis with decision trees, for example, requires obtaining explicit, precise, and complete information regarding a DM's beliefs (probability function) and tastes (utility function). Such information is often difficult and costly to obtain from a DM and is often unreliable and biased. This has limited the usefulness of applying decision analysis in practice (Hogarth, 1982; Moskowitz and Bunn, 1987). Moreover, since it has been shown that an optimal choice in many decision analysis problems is robust to the DM's probability and utility functions, limited and imprecise information may be all that is required to achieve optimality. Why then demand more precise information if it is costly to obtain and unnecessary to determine an optimal solution? This is the crux of Robust Interactive Decision-Analysis (RID), which obviates the measurement issue and exploits robustness by relaxing the stringent informational requirements of traditional decision analysis. The purpose of this paper is to extend this more relaxed approach to decision analysis applied to decision making under uncertainty to the multiple criteria decision making domain; hence the name multiple criteria RID (MCRID).

State of computer software development in multiple criteria decision analysis

Software systems for analyzing multiobjective decisions are plentiful and applied more in practice than decision tree analysis software for making decisions under uncertainty. EXPERT CHOICE, which is IBM PC compatible, is perhaps the most well known and most used of such packages. A similar and less powerful system, which takes advantage of the high resolution graphics capability and pull-down menus of the Macintosh PC is DECISION MAP. Both these and most other such software systems only consider the special case of an additive multiattribute value (utility) function. This offers simplicity, but may not fit the actual preference environment. Moreover, these systems require point estimates of importance weights as well as conditional performance values/utilities on the attributes associated with each alternative. Despite these and other criticisms, multiattribute utility analysis software is becoming increasingly popular. This popularity derives from the fact that most decisions are multiobjective in nature, the additive value model is simple to understand (particularly when uncertainty is not considered), and available software systems such as EXPERT CHOICE and DECISION MAP are very user friendly. A more recently developed PC-based package called ARIADNE, which permits relaxed (interval) estimates of importance weights and conditional performance values/utilities is more consistent with the spirit of MCRID than the above systems (Goicoechea, 1989). However, it is not an interactive procedure and does not deal formally with converging on an optimal choice, as does MCRID.

MCRID concept and methodology

The proposed MCRID approach, similar to RID, is based upon the premise that, in general, a DM can only consistently specify some imprecise knowledge about importance weights (e.g., ordinal or interval assessments regarding some (not necessarily all) of the attributes) and can only consistently articulate some strong preferences (e.g., action a is surely preferred to b) about some, but not necessarily all, pairs of possible actions. The information elicited from a DM is that about which he or she is certain about and elects to provide, to any degree of precision and completeness expressed. With the MCRID procedure, as in RID, importance weights (e.g., ordinal or interval) and strong (viz, sure) preferences are elicited interactively and progressively from the DM, which are used to prune the attribute weight space and ultimately the decision space, until an optimal action or subset of efficient (nondominated) actions is obtained (Moskowitz, 1989; Moskowitz, Preckel and Yang, 1990). As in RID, pruning is accomplished using vector dominance, preference dominance, and statistical dominance operators. The fundamental RID approach is suited for operationalization as an interactive computer decision support system (DSS), and is discussed and illustrated in (Moskowitz, Preckel and Yang, 1990), for the case of decision making under uncertainty.

We next use an example to illustrate how MCRID works. Be ware, however, that there are differences between the conventional RID and MCRID procedure. First, in the conventional RID procedure, after a strong preference is expressed, a cut is made in the decision and probability space (assuming utility function is known). In MCRID, however, an expressed strong preference only makes a pseudo cut in decision space for the purpose of generating a cut in attribute weight space. Secondly, instead of working with interval-valued conditional utility vectors generated by interval-valued attribute weights, to simplify the interactive choice preference, normalized point estimates of the attribute weights are computed in order to calculate specific expected utilities of actions as the procedure propagates up the attribute hierarchy. Preferences from the DM can then be more easily elicited, allowing us to progressively make cuts in attribute weight space at a higher level in the attribute hierarchy.

Example

An organization is seeking a qualified contractor to build an addition to one of its facilities. Nine prospective contractors are being considered and are to be evaluated based on four major criteria: (1) quality, (2) price, (3) performance history, and (4) construction capability. These criteria can be further partitioned into twelve individual subcriteria as shown in Figure 1. Assume, also that utility for each alternative on each of the twelve attributes has been determined via a spread sheet input. The MCRID procedure for analyzing this problem proceeds as follows.

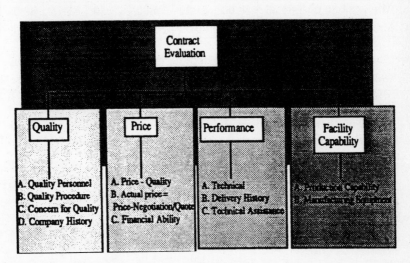

Figure 1: Hierarchy of criteria (attribute) for contractor evaluation

Step 1: Partition the problem into four subsets corresponding to the four major criteria (Quality, Price, Performance, and Facility Capacity). Apply MCRID to the portion of the spreadsheet associated with the subcriteria related to **Quality.**

Quality	Personnel	Procedure	Concern	Company History
C-1	85.0	80.0	80.0	90.0
C-2	82.0	88.0	83.0	88.0
C-3	90.0	85.0	70.0	75.0
C-4	78.0	90.0	75.0	85.0
C-5	95.0	75.0	85.0	70.0
C-6	75.0	82.0	85.0	80.0
C-7	90.0	82.0	75.0	80.0
C-8	70.0	90.0	90.0	85.0
C-9	75.0	78.0	90.0	82.0

Assume the DM states "Procedure" (P) is more important than "Personnel" (Pe), which is more important than "Concern of Quality" (C), which is more important than "Company History" (CH), namely, $w_P \geq w_{Pe} \geq w_C \geq w_{CH}$. Using these inputs the conditional weights is imputed via mathematical programming turn out to be $0.0 \leq w_{Pe} \leq 0.5$,

$0.25 \leq w_P \leq 1.0$, $0.0 \leq w_C \leq 0.333$, and $0.0 \leq w_{CH} \leq 0.25$. With this information and assuming an additive utility function, the aggregate conditional utility with respect to **Quality** for each contractor is as follows.

Contractor	1	2	3	4	5	6	7	8	9
Min	80.00	84.33	80.00	81.00	75.00	78.50	81.75	80.00	76.50
Max	83.75	88.00	87.50	90.00	85.00	82.00	86.00	90.00	81.25

Observe that alternatives $\{1, 6, 9\}$ are dominated, leaving only alternatives $\{2, 3, 4, 5, 7, 8\}$. Using the RID procedure, assume that the DM sequentially expresses the following set of binary preferences for the set of undominated alternatives: C 1 $\gg$ C 5, C 2 $\gg$ C 4, C 3 $\gg$ C 2 where C denotes contractor. Each of these preferences can be viewed as a constraint in a mathematical programming problem, which is used to redefine the feasible conditional weight space. For example, the constraint set for the DM's attribute weight input and binary preferences can be expressed as follows:

w_{Pe}	w_P	w_C	w_{CH}		
1.0	1.0	1.0	1.0	=	1.0
-1.0	1.0	0.0	0.0	>	0.0
1.0	0.0	-1.0	0.0	>	0.0
0.0	0.0	1.0	-1.0	>	0.0
-10.0	5.0	-5.0	20.0	>	0.0
8.0	-3.0	-13.0	-13.0	>	0.0
4.0	-2.0	8.0	3.0	>	0.0

This yields $0.294 \leq w_{Pe} \leq 0.35$, $0.57 \leq w_P \leq 68$, $0.0 \leq w_C \leq 0.04$, and $0.0 \leq w_{CH} \leq 0.04$. Now the utility ranges for each alternative are as follows:

Contractor	1	2	3	4	5	6	7	8	9
Min	81.47	85.71	85.71	85.02	81.04	79.61	84.19	82.86	77.00
Max	82.14	86.14	86.67	86.14	82.14	80.01	84.67	84.18	77.61

The following heuristic is then used to translate the interval-valued utilities into point estimates to simplify the interaction with the DM as the analysis propagates up the hierarchy. The mean value of each attribute weight interval is first determined and then normalized over their sum to assure that the computed weights sum to one, i.e., $w_i = \mu_i / \sum_{i=1}^{n} \mu_i$, where μ_i is the mean importance weight of attribute i (e.g., $w_{Pe} = 0.321/(0.321 + 0.624 + 0.020 + 0.020) = 0.324$). The point estimates of the conditional utilities associated with each alternative are thus:

Contractor	1	2	3	4	5	6	7	8	9
Utility	81.83	85.95	86.11	85.69	81.59	79.75	84.41	83.41	77.36

These values are then propagated to the next higher level for further evaluation and manipulation as shown in step 5.

Step 2: Apply the MCRID procedure to the subcriteria associated with **Price**.

Price	Price-Quality	Actual Price	Financial Ability
C-1	90.0	73.0	85.0
C-2	88.0	78.0	92.0
C-3	95.0	68.0	74.0
C-4	78.0	80.0	85.0
C-5	80.0	80.0	78.0
C-6	85.0	78.0	90.0
C-7	82.0	85.0	80.0
C-8	90.0	80.0	75.0
C-9	85.0	83.0	70.0

Assume that the DM sequentially states that $w_{PQ} > w_{AP} > w_{FA}$, and that $C\,5 \gg C\,4$, $C\,2 \gg C\,1$, $C\,2 \gg C\,3$, and $C\,6 \gg C\,9$. Similar to step 1, these statements yield the following attribute weights: $0.44 \leq w_{PQ} \leq 0.67$, $0.17 \leq w_{AP} \leq 0.44$, $0.08 \leq w_{FA} \leq 0.18$. The point estimates of the conditional utilities for each alternative propagated to the next level of the attribute hierarchy are as follows:

Contractor	1	2	3	4	5	6	7	8	9
Utility	84.08	85.43	83.90	79.53	79.74	83.48	82.67	84.95	82.43

Step 3: Apply the MCRID procedure to the subcriteria associated with **Performance**.

Perform	Technical	Delivery History	Technical Assistance
C-1	70.0	80.0	55.0
C-2	80.0	75.0	55.0
C-3	90.0	73.0	78.0
C-4	60.0	85.0	65.0
C-5	100.0	70.0	75.0
C-6	80.0	70.0	78.0
C-7	70.0	73.0	72.0
C-8	78.0	85.0	68.0
C-9	82.0	80.0	76.0

Assume that the DM states that $w_{TA} > w_T > w_{DH}$, and that $C\,4 \gg C\,2$, $C\,5 \gg C\,3$, $C\,6 \gg C\,9$, and $C\,8 \gg C\,7$. These statements yield $0.14 \leq w_T \leq 0.23$, $0.09 \leq w_{DH} \leq 0.23$, $0.54 \leq w_{TA} \leq 0.71$. The point estimates of the conditional utilities for each alternative propagated to the next level are as follows:

Contractor	1	2	3	4	5	6	7	8	9
Utility	61.99	63.09	79.48	67.33	78.97	77.07	71.78	72.72	77.81

Step 4. Apply the MCRID procedure to the appropriate portion of the spreadsheet associated with the subcriteria related to **Facility Capacity**.

Fac Capacity	Production Capacity	Manufacturing Equipment
C-1	85.0	70.0
C-2	80.0	83.0
C-3	78.0	90.0
C-4	65.0	95.0
C-5	55.0	100.0
C-6	80.0	77.0
C-7	75.0	85.0
C-8	83.0	79.0
C-9	78.0	70.0

Again assume that the DM progressively states that $w_{PC} > w_{ME}$, and that $C\,1 \gg C\,2$, $C\,7 \gg C\,9$, and $C\,3 \gg C\,2$. These statements yield $0.014 \leq w_{PC} \leq 0.23$, $0.09 \leq w_{ME} \leq 0.23$. The resulting conditional utility point estimates are shown below:

Contractor	1	2	3	4	5	6	7	8	9
Utility	81.25	80.75	81.00	72.50	66.25	79.25	77.50	82.00	76.00

Step 5. Apply MCRID to the next higher level of the attribute hierarchy, namely, the four major criteria in **Contractor** evaluation.

Contractor	Quality	Price	Performance	Facility Capacity
C-1	81.83	84.08	61.99	81.25
C-2	85.95	85.42	63.09	80.75
C-3	86.11	83.90	79.48	81.00
C-4	85.69	79.53	67.33	72.50
C-5	81.59	79.74	78.97	66.25
C-6	79.75	83.48	77.07	79.25
C-7	84.41	82.67	71.78	77.50
C-8	83.41	84.95	72.72	82.00
C-9	77.36	82.43	77.81	76.00

Assume that the DM states that $w_Q > w_{Pr} > w_{Pe} > w_{FC}$, and that $C\,4 \gg C\,5$, $C\,2 \gg C\,3$, $C\,6 \gg C\,5$, and $C\,7 \gg C\,6$. These statements infer that $0.15 \leq w_Q \leq 0.68$, $0.28 \leq w_{Pr} \leq 0.85$, $0.00 \leq w_{Pe} \leq 0.07$, and $0.00 \leq w_{FC} \leq 0.06$. This yields the aggregate utility intervals for each alternative and the weight intervals shown in Figure 2. Observe that 6 out of 9 contractors are eliminated. Of the three remaining candidate contractors, 2 and 3 appear more attractive than 8.

Contractor	1	2	3	4	5	6	7	8	9
Min	82.06	83.92	83.92	79.66	79.27	80.73	82.07	83.61	78.75
Max	83.75	85.78	85.38	83.66	80.98	82.93	83.84	84.72	81.67

Attr	Q/Pe	Q/P	Q/C	Q/CH	P/Q	P/AC
Min	0.044	0.085	0.000	0.000	0.122	0.047
Max	0.237	0.466	0.028	0.028	0.568	0.378

Attr	P/FA	P/T	P/DH	P/TA	FC/C	FC/CE
Min	0.021	0.000	0.000	0.000	0.000	0.000
Max	0.155	0.015	0.015	0.046	0.046	0.017

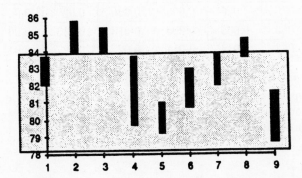

Figure 2: Final utility intervals for nine contractors

Our goal now is to select the best contractor from among the remaining three candidates. This can be accomplished using interactive goal programming.

Step 6.   Compute conditional utility point estimates of the remaining candidate alternatives.

This yields utilities of 84.69, 84.04 and 83.78 for contractors 2, 3 and 8, respectively. We next use goal programming (GP) to determine how far weights can be relaxed such that the alternative with the optimal utility point estimate still remains optimal. Namely, we

$$\text{Max}\ \ Z = d$$

$$\text{subject to}\ \ w_i + \delta_i^+ + \delta_i^- + \delta = w_{i,0} \qquad i = 1,\ldots,12 \qquad (1)$$

$$w_i \geq w_{i,0}^- \qquad i = 1,\ldots,12 \qquad (2)$$

$$w_i \leq w_{i,0}^+ \qquad i = 1,\ldots,12 \qquad (3)$$

$$84.69 - \max\{E[A_i]\} \geq 0, \qquad i = 3,8.$$

$$\sum_{i=1}^{12} w_i = 1\,,$$

where $w_{i,0}^+$ and $w_{i,0}^-$ are the upper and lower bounds of the attribute weights, and $w_{i,0}$ is the point weight function for attribute i determined heuristically, as indicated previously. (These could also be estimated by the DM). In this example, there are $3*12+2+1 = 39$

total constraints in the system. The resulting solution is $d = 0.072$, with the weight point estimates and intervals shown in Figure 3.

Wei	Q/Pe	Q/P	Q/C	Q/CH	P/Q	P/AC
pt	0.121	0.238	0.012	0.012	0.298	0.183
Min	0.114	0.231	0.005	0.005	0.290	0.176
Max	0.128	0.245	0.019	0.019	0.305	0.191

Wei	P/FA	P/T	P/DH	P/TA	FC/C	FC/CE
pt	0.076	0.006	0.006	0.020	0.020	0.007
Min	0.069	0.000	0.000	0.013	0.013	0.000
Max	0.083	0.014	0.014	0.027	0.027	0.014

The DM can change the point estimates of the weights by modifying constraints (1)–(3). For example, he/she might say that the point estimates should be a changed (in (1)), the upper bound is too high/low (in (2)), or the lower bound is too high/low (in (3)), and resolve interactively until satisfied with the result.

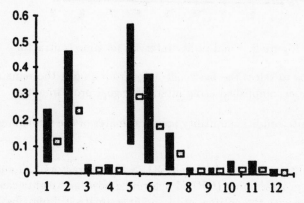

Figure 3: Final weight intervals such that optimal alternative remains optimal

Summary

In this paper, we have extended RID to deal with multiple criteria decisions. MCRID circumvents the need to precisely assess attribute importance weights, using the RID dominance operators to define an efficient set of alternatives, from which an optimal decision is selected using an interactive GP formulation. We plan to further extend the MCRID procedure in incorporate interval-valued performance values/utilities. The resulting integrated RID/MCRID software system should be an appealing tool for DMs, in the sense that it can solve decision problems under uncertainty and with multiple criteria.

References

Goicoechea, A. (1989). On the Use of Multiple Attributes and Imperfect Information with ARIADNE to rank Alternative Systems. *Applied Mathematics and Computation Journal*.

Hogarth, R.M. (1982). From Romanticism to Precision to..., *Decision Sciences*, 13, 4, pp. 543–546.

Moskowitz, H. (1989). Decision Analysis in Contemporary Organizations: Problems and Prospects. In Ira Horowitz (ed.): Organization and Decision Theory, Kluwer-Nijhoff.

Moskowitz, H., Preckel, P.V. and Yang, A. (1990). Robust Interactive Decision Analysis (RID): A Tool for Information Systems Evaluation. In J.R. Marsden and D. Pingrey (eds.): Advanced in Intelligent Information Technology.

Multicriteria Optimization (Linear and Nonlinear) Using Proxy Value Functions

Asim Roy, Patrick Mackin

Dept. of Decision and Information Systems
College of Business
Arizona State University
Tempe, Arizona 85287, U.S.A.

1   Introduction

This paper presents a new method for multicriteria optimization for both linear and nonlinear objective and constraint functions. The method is based on obtaining answers to a sequence of pairwise comparison questions. During each question-answer phase, the Decision Maker is asked $(p+1)$ pairwise comparison questions, where p is the number of criteria functions. After each question-answer phase, the method uses all of the previous responses to approximate the value function of the Decision Maker. In this approximation procedure, each pairwise comparison is set up as a constraint and a feasible set of parameters for a proxy value function is solved for using a mathematical programming system. If the proxy value function used is linear, this problem is an LP; if it is nonlinear, the problem is nonlinear. This problem is solved $(p+1)$ times to get $(p+1)$ extreme feasible sets of parameters for the proxy value function, given the responses. These $(p+1)$ proxy value functions are then used to generate $(p+1)$ solutions to the multicriteria problem and these solutions are then presented to the DM for pairwise comparison. This sequence continues until either the $(p+1)$ solutions converge or the DM is satisfied with the current solution.

The method combines the good features of many of the existing algorithms. It uses Steuer's (1986) idea of presenting well-dispersed points on the efficient frontier for pairwise comparison. This way, the DM gets an idea of the range of solutions available at each stage. It also uses Oppenheimer's (1978) and Zionts and Wallenius' (1976) idea of constructing a proxy value function (linear or nonlinear) from the preference answers and using it to generate a new solution consistent with the old answers.

Many interactive methods have been devised to solve various types of multicriteria optimization problems. Surveys of such methods are given by Stadler (1979), Zionts (1979), Roy (1971), Rosenthal (1985) and Steuer (1986), among others. The method of Zionts and Wallenius (1976) is limited to multiple objective linear programming problems. It has subsequently been generalized to nonlinear problems by Roy and Wallenius (1989).

The Geoffrion, Dyer and Fienberg (1972) (GDF) method can solve a general nonlinear multicriteria problem, but is awkward and time consuming since it requires the DM to provide "local" marginal rates of substitution between criteria. Recent extensions of the GDF method have been done by Loganathan and Sherali (1987). Other related work includes that of Boyd (1970), Oppenheimer (1978), Benayoun et al. (1971), Contini and Zionts (1968) and Zionts and Wallenius (1983).

2   The multicriteria decision problem

The problem under consideration involves a set of n decision variables represented by the vector X constrained by m (possibly) nonlinear constraints. We represent the constraints algebraically as follows:

$$
\begin{aligned}
g_k(X) &= 0, & k &= 1, \ldots, m, \\
l_j &\leq X_j \leq u_j, & j &= 1, \ldots, n,
\end{aligned}
\tag{1}
$$

where l_j and u_j are given lower and upper bounds. The vector X contains both the structural and the slack variables. The constraint functions $g_k(X)$ are assumed to be continuously differentiable and the feasible set defined by (1) is assumed to be a nonempty, compact, and convex subset of R^n. If $m = 0$, the problem becomes unconstrained. The decision situation involves a single decision-maker who has p continuously differentiable and concave objectives. We write these objectives as $u = f(X)$, where $f(X)$ is a vector of real-valued objective functions, whose components are $f_i(X)$, $f_i : R^n \to R$, $i = 1, \ldots, p$. Without loss of generality, we assume that the objectives are all to be maximized. A DM is assumed to have only an implicit function of these multiple objectives and no explicit knowledge of the value function that he/she wishes to maximize. Let $U(f_1(X), \ldots, f_p(X))$ be the unknown, implicit value function, assumed to be concave and continuously differentiable. The DM is interested in maximizing his/her value function $U(f_1(X), \ldots, f_p(X))$ subject to the constraints in (1).

3   An outline of the algorithm

The proposed algorithm is described below.

(1) *Construct Payoff Matrix*

A Payoff Matrix is found by maximizing each of the objectives individually. From this matrix the DM can see the most he/she can obtain for each objective, thereby educating the DM on the range of possible outcomes (Benayoun et al., 1971). Solve p problems of the form:

$$
\begin{aligned}
\text{Max} \quad & f_i \\
\text{s.t.} \quad & g_k(X) = 0, & k &= 1, \ldots, m, \\
& l_j \leq X_j \leq u_j, & j &= 1, \ldots, n.
\end{aligned}
\tag{2}
$$

Let the rth solution define the vector $S_r = (f_1^r, f_2^r, \ldots, f_p^r)$ where $r = 1, 2, \ldots, p$.

(2) Determine the coefficients a_i of the hyperplane (in the criterion space) that passes through all p of the vectors S_r.

(3) Solve a problem of the form:

$$\text{Max} \quad \sum a_i f_i$$
$$\text{s.t.} \quad g_k(X) = 0, \qquad k = 1, \ldots, m, \tag{3}$$
$$l_j \leq X_j \leq u_j, \qquad j = 1, \ldots, n.$$

Let the solution be $S_{p+1} = (f_1^{p+1}, f_2^{p+1}, \ldots, f_p^{p+1})$.

(4) Ask the decision maker to answer pairwise comparison questions for all solution pairs of the form (S_r, S_{p+1}) where $r = 1, \ldots, p$. That is, present solution vectors S_r and S_{p+1} to the DM and ask him/her to indicate one of following preferences:

(a) S_r is strongly preferred to S_{p+1} or vice versa;

(b) S_r is weakly preferred to S_{p+1} or vice versa;

(c) The DM is indifferent between S_r and S_{p+1}.

At this point, if the DM is satisfied with one of the solutions presented, then the process is terminated. If not, proceed to step 5.

(5) Determine p sets of λ-values by solving p problems of the following form:

$$\text{Max} \quad \lambda_i \quad (i = 1, \ldots, p)$$
$$\text{s.t.} \quad \sum_{i=1}^{p} \lambda_i(f_i)_{S_r} - \sum_{i=1}^{p} \lambda_i(f_i)_{S_t} \geq \varepsilon \tag{4}$$

for all pairwise comparisons in which a solution S_r was preferred to S_t. Let the qth solution set be the vector $\lambda^q = (\lambda_1^q, \lambda_2^q, \ldots, \lambda_p^q)$ where $q = 1, 2, \ldots, p$.
Note: At present the indifference and weak preference responses are ignored.

(6) Solve p problems of the form:

$$\text{Max} \quad \sum \lambda_i^q f_i \qquad \text{for} \quad q = 1, 2, \ldots, p$$
$$\text{s.t.} \quad g_k(X) = 0, \qquad k = 1, \ldots, m, \tag{5}$$
$$l_j \leq X_j \leq u_j, \qquad j = 1, \ldots, n.$$

Let the solution vectors S_r, $r = 1, \ldots, p$, be as defined in step 1. Go to step 2.

4 Comments on the proposed algorithm

(1) The basic idea of the proposed method is to present a sequence of pairwise comparison questions (step 4) based on well-dispersed solutions on the efficient frontier.

From the answers given, approximations (or proxies) to the DM's preference function is constructed that are consistent with these answers (step 5). These proxy preference functions are then used to generate new sets of solutions (step 6) for pairwise comparison and the process is repeated until the DM is satisfied with a solution that maximizes his or her overall utility.

(2) Presenting well-dispersed solutions on the efficient frontier for pairwise comparison is from (Steuer, 1986). Construction of proxy preference functions consistent with DM's answers is from the methods of Roy and Wallenius (1989), Zionts and Wallenius (1976) and Oppenheimer (1978). A global proxy function is constructed like Roy and Wallenius (1989) and Zionts and Wallenius (1976); Oppenheimer (1978) constructs only a local proxy function. The proxy functions can be linear or nonlinear (e.g. exponential), even though the algorithm shown uses a linear proxy. The proxy function is used to guide the algorithm to the preferred solution by generating new solutions that are closer to it.

(3) Steps 1, 3 and 6 involve a problem of mathematical programming, which existing algorithms, such as Lasdon et al. (1974), can be used to solve. Since the feasible region defined by (1) is assumed to be convex and the objective functions to be maximized in these steps are concave, the optimization problems in these steps are convex programming problems and a local maximum is also a global maximum. For more general nonlinear programming problems, only local maximums are generated in these steps.

(4) When an optimal solution lies on a hyperplane, a linear proxy cannot be used to find it. Typically, the method would cycle from one extreme point solution to another. In such a case, we should switch to a nonlinear proxy (Oppenheimer, 1978). Then the problem in step 5 would be set up differently.

(5) If a DM is inconsistent in the responses, then the lambda problem in step 5 becomes infeasible. Hence inconsistency is immediately detected and reported by the method and the DM can correct such inconsistent responses. Since inconsistency arises especially when it is difficult to make a clear-cut choice on preference (yes or no), the DM should use the indifference response (which is ignored) in such cases and avoid the risk of being inconsistent. Thus, he/she should respond yes or no to a tradeoff question only when absolutely sure.

5 An example (source: Lasdon et al., 1974)

Consider the following set of constraints:

$$x_1 - x_2 \geq 0$$
$$-x_1^2 + x_2 \geq 0$$
$$x_1 + x_2 \geq 1$$
$$x_1 \geq 0, \qquad 0 \leq x_2 \leq 0.8$$

and the following objective functions, both to be maximized:

$$f_1 = -2x_1^2 - 2x_2^2$$
$$f_2 = 4x_1 + 3.2x_2 - 3.28$$

For the example, assume that the (implicit) value function is $0.999f_1$, $+0.001f_2$, but only use the knowledge of this function in answering the preference questions. Initially, at iteration 1 (Table 1), the payoff matrix is found by assigning the highest weight (0.999) to each objective function in turn and maximizing that value function (step 1 of the algorithm). Then a middle point (in the criterion space) is found by constructing a hyperplane through these solution points (step 2) then maximize the hyperplane (step 3). This middle solution is the last one shown in iteration 1 (Table 1). The 3 solutions in iteration 1 are presented to the DM and asked to indicate the most preferred one. Using the value function stated above (the computed values are shown in the last column of the table), the first solution is preferred (indicated by an asterisk). To find p ($p = 2$ here) sets of λ-values consistent with these answers (step 5), p problems of the following form are solved, where ε is a small constant:

$$\begin{aligned}
\max \quad & \lambda_i \quad (i = 1, 2) \\
\text{s.t.} \quad & 1.88015\lambda_1 - 2.5378\lambda_2 \geq \varepsilon \\
& 0.80012\lambda_1 - 1.25972\lambda_2 \geq \varepsilon \\
& \lambda_1 + \lambda_2 = 1, \qquad \lambda_1, \lambda_2 \geq 0.001
\end{aligned} \tag{6}$$

The optimal solutions are ($\lambda_1 = 0.99999$, $\lambda_2 = 0.00001$) and ($\lambda_1 = 0.61157$, $\lambda_2 = 0.38844$), as shown by iteration 2 lambda values in Table 1. New solutions are found with these weight vectors, and then a middle solution is found, as shown in iteration 2 (Table 1). The last solution in each iteration is the middle solution. The 3 solutions in iteration 2 are then presented to the DM. Using the value function stated above, the first solution is again preferred. The two new constraints,

$$\begin{aligned}
0.32316\lambda_1 - 0.56651\lambda_2 &\geq \varepsilon \\
0.06729\lambda_1 - 0.14204\lambda_2 &\geq \varepsilon
\end{aligned} \tag{7}$$

are added to (6). Two new λ-vectors are then found and the process continued.

At iteration 4, the criteria values are very close and the DM would probably stop there, having obtained a close-to-optimal solution. We used a tighter tolerance to go to iteration 5 and then stop. The solutions at iterations 4 and 5 are very close.

DM's Value (or Utility)
$U = .99 * Obj\ 1 + .01 * Obj\ 2$

Iteration	Lambda Weights		Optimal Objective Values		Utility Value**
	Obj 1	Obj 2	Obj 1	Obj 2	
(1)	0.99900	0.00100	-1.00000	0.32008	-0.98680*
	0.00100	0.99900	-2.88015	2.85788	-2.82277
	0.57443	0.42557	-1.80012	1.57980	-1.76632
(2)	0.99999	0.00001	-1.00000	0.32000	-0.98680*
	0.61157	0.38844	-1.32316	0.88651	-1.30106
	0.63677	0.36323	-1.06729	0.46204	-1.05200
(3)	0.99999	0.00001	-1.00000	0.32000	-0.98680*
	0.67859	0.32141	-1.00897	0.35789	-0.99531
	0.80852	0.19148	-1.00224	0.33895	-0.98883
(4)	0.99999	0.00001	-1.00000	0.32000	-0.98680*
	0.89461	0.10539	-1.00056	0.32942	-0.98726
	0.94438	0.05563	-1.00014	0.32471	-0.98689
(5)	0.99999	0.00001	-1.00000	0.32000	-0.98680*
	0.97341	0.02659	-1.00003	0.32219	-0.98681
	0.98653	0.01348	-1.00001	0.32109	-0.98680
	True Weights		Optimal Objective Values		Optimal Utility
	0.99000	0.01000	-1.00000	0.32081	-0.98680

** Computed using the value function used to answer the preference questions.
* Preferred solution of the 3 solutions presented at each iteration.

Table 1: Sequence of solutions presented to the Decision Maker

134

References

Benayoun, R., De Montgolfier, J., Tergny, J. and Laritchev, O. (1971). Linear Programming with Multiple Objective Functions: STEP Method (STEM). *Mathematical Programming*, Vol. 1, No. 3, pp. 366–375.

Boyd, D. (1970). A Methodology for Analyzing Decision Problems Involving Complex Preference Assessments. Ph.D. Dissertation, Stanford University.

Contini, B. and Zionts, S. (1968). Restricted Bargaining for Organizations with Multiple Objectives. *Econometrica*, Vol. 16, No. 1, pp. 397–414.

Geoffrion, A.M., Dyer, J.S. and Feinberg, A. (1972). An Interactive Approach for Multicriterion Optimization with an Application to the Operation of an Academic Department. *Management Science*, Vol. 19, No. 4, pp. 357–368.

Lasdon, L., Fox, R.L. and Ratner, M. (1974). Nonlinear Optimization Using the Generalized Reduced Gradient Method. *R.A.I.R.O.*, 3, pp. 73–104.

Loganathan, G.V. and Sherali, H.D. (1987). A Convergent Cutting-Plane Algorithm for Multiobjective Optimization. *Operations Research*, 35, pp. 365–377.

Oppenheimer, K.R. (1978). A Proxy Approach to Multiattribute Decision-Making. *Management Science*, Vol. 24, No. 6.

Rosenthal, R.E. (1985). Principles of Multiobjective Optimization. *Decision Sciences*, 16, pp. 133–152.

Roy, A. and Wallenius, J. (1989). Nonlinear Multiple Objective Optimization: An Algorithm and Some Theory. *Mathematical Programming*, (forthcoming).

Roy, B. (1971). Problems and Methods with Multiple Objective Functions. *Mathematical Programming*, Vol. 1, No. 2, pp. 239–266.

Stadler, W. (1979). A Survey of Multi-Criteria Optimization or the Vector Maximization problem, Part I: 1776–1966. *JOTA*, Vol. 29, pp. 1–53.

Steuer, R. (1986). Multiple Criteria Optimization: Theory, Computation, and Application. Wiley, New York.

Zionts, S. (1979). Methods for Solving Management Problems Involving Multiple Objectives. Working Paper No. 400, School of Management, State University of New York at Buffalo.

Zionts, S. and Wallenius, J. (1976). An Interactive Programming Method for Solving the Multiple Criteria Problem. *Management Science*, Vol. 22, No. 6, pp. 652–663.

Zionts, S. and Wallenius, J. (1983). An Interactive Multiple Objective Linear Programming Method for a Class of Underlying Nonlinear Utility Functions. *Management Science*, Vol. 29, No. 5, pp. 519–529.

Part 3

Multiple Criteria Decision Support Systems

A Knowledge-Based Approach to DSS Development

Bojil Dobrev
Institute for Information Technologies
1000 Sofia, Volov 2, Bulgaria

1 Introduction

The development of DSS could be considered as an evolution of Information Systems development and nowadays is influenced by the knowledge-based systems in different ways. A good overview of the ways for KB systems incorporation into decision support environment is presented by Raghavan and Chaud (1987). KB systems could be used in problem representation and problem-solving methods of Expert systems for developing decision structuring facilities, using knowledge representation techniques for symbolic models of reasoning, for capturing domain specific knowledge and making it available for suggesting alternatives to the decision makers, for improving the user interface. KB system capabilities can be used also in the DSS development and one approach is proposed in this paper. The goal of the proposal is to provide the user with information and knowledge in two aspects. First, in the case that the user is searching for an existing DSS which could help him to solve the problem. Second, in the case, that the user has to design a specific DSS, providing him with the rules for the DSS design according to the DSS design methodology.

As a tool which covers the both aspects, a KB advice-giving system is presented.

2 DSS development methodology

The DSS development methodology is based on the main stages presented in (Er, 1988) and is shown on Fig. 1.

It consists of the following stages:

- Preliminary study;
- Global DSS design;
- DSS concept evaluation and software selection;
- Detailed DSS design;
- Prototype development and evaluation;
- Implementation.

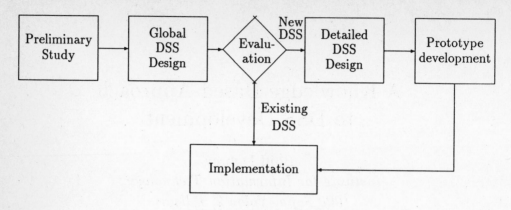

Figure 1

The methodology of the DSS development is presented as a linear set of modules, presenting the DSS design phases. Each phase is decomposed into steps and each step includes several activities. The phase description consists of the folowing topics:

- Phase goal — the tasks which have to be solved and the expected results are described;

- Phase scope and structure — the included steps are listed and the links between them are pointed;

- Performance reguirements — the necessary conditions in organization, information and legal aspects are stressed;

- Check-points — those steps, which require evaluation of intermediary results and possible decision making during the design process are pointed.

The step description includes:

- Step goal — the tasks which have to be solved and the expected results;

- Performance requirements — the required previous steps and their result are described;

- Operations — the set of activities is listed;

- Results — the expected results and the form of their presentation and documentation are described.

According to this model, the Preliminary Study stage could be presented in the following way:

Step 1: Problem analysis.

Performance requirements:

−Type of decision making;

−Application of decision making;

Result: Problem specifications.

Step 2: Decision making analysis.

Performance requirements:

−Type of decision making;
−Stages of decision making;
−Level of decision making;
−Decision makers;
−Required data.

Result: Decision making model, including:

−key decisions,
−decision activities flowchart,
−data requirements,
−model requirements.

Step 3: Data analysis.

Performance requirements:

−Data requirements;
−Data sources;
−Data flow.

Result: Information model.

Step 4: Resources analysis.

Performance requirements:

−Technical resources;
−Finanial resources;
−Staff.

Result: Resources estimation.

Step 5: Manager reguirements.

Performance requirements: Time, costs and quality.

−Time;
−Costs;
−Quality.

Result: Goals.

For the global DSS design stage the Performance requirements are the results from the previous stage as:

− Problem specification;
− Decision making model;
− Information model;

- Resources estimation;
- Goal.

The result consists of a DSS Concept, including:

- DSS functions;
- DSS users;
- Data requirements;
- Method requirements;
- User interface requirements;
- Organization requirements;
- Time and costs requirements.

The DSS Concept evaluation is presented on Fig. 2.

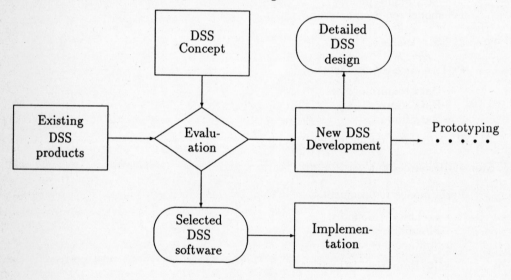

Figure 2

The Detailed DSS design includes the following main steps:

- Data Base Design;
- Model Base Design;
- User Interface Design.

The Protype Development and Evaluation includes:

- Scoping of prototype;
- Define evaluation criteria;
- Software realisation;
- Testing;

- Demonstration;
- Evaluation.

The Implementation stage includes:

- DSS features study;
- Training;
- Providing technical and organization requirements;
- Data preparation;
- DSS elements implementation;
- DSS testing and evaluation;
- DSS maitenance.

3   KB advice-giving system

The structure of the system is shown on Fig. 3.

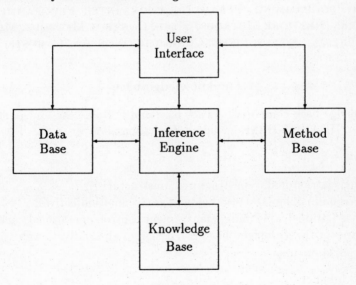

Figure 3

The proposed KB advice-giving system consists of:

- – Data base;
- – Method base;
- – Knowledge base.

Data base

The data base contains metadata about the available information resources for the decision making. The groups of information are as follows:

- Internal: corporation level, division level, department level

- External: national, regional and firm level

In each group the information is devided in subgroups according to the activities of the organization /production, planning, distribution etc. and the semantic of the data (indicators, key words). There are also data about the information sources, data organisation and access capabilities.

Method base

The method base consists of a list of methods and information about their application area, input and output data and software organisation.

In (Ivanek, 1986) the following methods are suggested: LINEAR PROGRAMMING, NON-LINEAR PROGRAMMING, PARAMETRIZATION, INTER PROGRAMMING, GRAPHS AND NETWORKS, NETWORK METHODS, STOCK CONTROL METHODS, MULTIPLE CRITERIA EVALUATION, ANTAGONISTIC CONFLICTS, NON-ANTAGONISTIC CONFLICTS, RISK AND UNCERTAINTY.

The knowledge base

The knowledge base consists of a Fact base and a Rule base and is organized as a semantic net. THE FACT BASE includes information about:

– Problems –

- Types (structured, semistructured, unstructured);
- Decision making (DM) (individual, group, multiobjective);
- Level (strategic, planning, managemant control, operational control);
- Stages of DM (problem diagnosis, design of alternatives, evaluation, choice);
- Application area.

– and DSS products –

- Functional capabilities;
- Modeling tasks and methods;
- Data bases;
- User interface tools;
- Data management tools;
- Graphics;
- Hardware/software reguirements;
- Maintenance, training and support;
- Price.

The rule base contains the description of the set of the modules for DSS design according to the described methodology and the general rules for usage of the available DSS products, presenteted as production rules:

THE INFERENCE engine of the system should serve as a tool for selection and interpretation of the rules to be applied. It should provide forward and backward chaining depending on the results of the different steps in the DSS design and DSS products usage. Additional information is provided from the DATA BASE and THE METHOD BASE if it is required.

THE USER INTERFACE allows the users of the system to carry out the following functions of interaction:

- Accepting a user guestion;

- Access to the Data base and Method base

- Access to the Knowledge base via the Inference engine

- Answers presentation

The KB advice-giving system performs the following functions:

- Problem identification and analysis

- Specifying the methods and data for the problem solving

- Selection of the available DSS software products providing the required methods and data

- Providing information about the existing information resources and methods

- Supporting the DSS development by providing the user information and knowledge how to perform the DSS development steps

4 Conclusions

- A module set presentation of DSS development methodology is proposed.

- A KB advice-giving system is presented which can be used for improving the performance of DSS development and for training in DSS development methodology.

- The described KB advice-giving system is under software development for PC using the Expert System Development Environment INFOTEX (IIT, Bulgaria).

- An implementation of the system in the IIASA Project "Methodology and Software for Interactive Decision Support" is suggested.

- Future directions of research work will be a detailed specification of the relations between the requirements of each DSS element and the design methodology steps applied to each DSS element.

References

Doukidis, D. I. (1988). DSS Concepts in Expert Systems: An Empirical Study. *Decision Support Systems*, **4**, pp. 345–354.

Er, M. C. (1988). DSS: A summary, Problems and Future Trends. *Decision Support Systems*, **4**.

Ivanek, J. (1986). An expert system recommending suitable mathematical decision method. *Computers and Artificial Intelligence*, **5**, p. 3.

Raghavan, S. A. and Chaud, D. R. (1987). Expert systems and Decision Support Systems. FGCS Symposium, Madras.

Ramesh, R. and Sekar, G. (1988). An integrated Framework for Decision Support in Corporate Planning. *Decision Support Systems*, **4**, pp. 365–375.

Distributed Decision Support System and Information Technologies of Controlling the Development

Valery A. Irikov, Oleg I. Dranko
Moscow Institute of Physics and Technology
141700 Moskovskaya oblastj
gorod Dolgoprudnyi
Institutskyi pereulok 9
Moscow, U.S.S.R.

Vasily N. Trenev, Andrey V. Galuzo
Institute for Energy Researches
Moscow, U.S.S.R.

Abstract

The paper is devoted to the problem of the distributed distributed multiple criteria decision support system (MCDSS) of development control of distributed organizing system. The typical subtasks of the general problem of industry or corporation development are given. The specialist groups are described and the main needed programming means are declared. The way of management system saticfactory construction for user is proposed. The short description of such a system is given. Prototyping is used instead of the technical specifications. This approach reduces manifold the labour intensiveness of the system developing. The scientific foundation of proposed methods and algorithms is discussed.

Keywords: Multiple criteria decision support systems; management systems; disributed control; man-machine information technology; prototyping.

1 Introduction

The practical procedures of planning and management are multicriterial (MC) and disributed processes (Pospelov et al., 1985; Irikov, 1985) in such a sense that subtasks of a common complex task (e.g. the planning of the industry or corporation development), competence, authority, information and its processing procedures are distributed, dispersed among many workers (specialized working places). Each subtask is solved by the worker comparatively independently using his own criteria and a heuristic approach, which helps him to substantiate the results. At each working place only part of objects and criteria is considered. The coordination of the task as a whole is carried out in the process of the iterative interaction of the workers.

An example of such a complex task is the task of developing long-term and average plans and programs of the industry or corporation development. The examples of strategic control subtasks are the choice of a structural policy (the nomenclature and the volume of production, proportions in output development), scientific and technical policy (the definition of the priority scientific and technical programs), investment policy (the share of accumulation and consumption, the distribution of resources among production, reproduction, science, the main programs) etc. These subtasks are further divided into the typical multicriterial subtasks of balance forming, scheduling etc., each having a well-defined procedure of solution and a technology of information processing using DSS.

2 Definitions

The general and detailed working definitions of information technology (IT) are used below.

1. Information technology (IT) is a way of organizing the process and the means of obtaining the data, which decrease the uncertainty degree of the knowledge, necessary for solving the given task.

2. IT is a regulated information process, defining the way of presenting the data and the order of carrying out elementary operations (search, storage, grouping etc.) of information processing by people and technical means, which leads to the solution of the task.

IT giving the solution of the general original task is referred to as the complex information technology (CIT). CIT consists of elementary information technologies (EIT), i.e. a set of elementary operations, which does not require further detailization for the given user.

Formally the CIT may be described in the following way. Let X be a space of the simulated system indices, P — a multitude of index designations, $q = \langle 1, 2, 3, 4, 5, 6, 7, 8 \rangle$ — a multitude of typical tasks, described below. Then the EIT is described as $T = \langle P_1, P_2, Z_1, Z_q, Z_1 \rangle$ and presents a union of three ordered problems Z_1, Z_q, Z_1 (two problems of analysis, comparison and information correction and a task of data processing) and two multitudes P_1, P_2 of the input and output indices. CIT in this case represents an ordered set of the EIT: $CIT = \langle T_1, \ldots, T_i, \ldots \rangle$.

3 The examples of typical information technologies

Besides, the presence of typical management subtasks and typical IT is characteristic of solving concrete tasks. For example, for respective planning these tasks are as follows:

1. data grouping, analysis, correction, comparison. This is mainly connected with the creation of working forms and interactive means of data correction, convenient for the user.

2. "calculation type" — the perfomance of standard actions (the criteria calculation) using a standard method.

3. summary index calculation, which is connected with the aggregation procedures according to different signs in the hierarchical information structures and by multi-criterial estimation of final results and efficiency.

4. "balance type", formaly connected with the necessity of the search for the allowed solution of the system of equations; and actually connected with the coordination of particular product balances, powers and resources formed by different subunits (Trenev, 1988).

5. taking into account the prospect of R and D and other means of development. Formally this is connected with the necessity of the purposeful change of the balance model parameters; these are the problems of MC system optimization, actually connected with the procedures of eliminating the bottlenecks (Irikov and Trenev, 1985).

6. the analysis of the life cycle of the objects under investigation. This is connected with taking account of the dynamics in net models and scheduling models.

7. disaggregation. These are the problems of taking decision as to the distribution of the resources, the apportionment of the product tasks etc., connected with the information detalization and decision procedures.

8. choice of rational informational structure, connected with the construction of adequate information model of minimal complexity.

4   The specialist groups

A number of peculiarities of the development control tasks and requirements to the distributed man-machine (M–M) decision support system (DSS) are given by Irikov and Pospelov (1985). The implementation and usind by 40–50 terminal users of the first turn of such a system ("STRATEC") is given by Pospelov (1985). The main system-forming function is performed by multilevel information structure, describing a set of objects and information processes in them. The knots of the information structures are elementary information models of the information processes, corresponding to particular subtasks (a list of indices, connections and algorithms of their processing). The algorithms (of aggregation, disaggregation, etc.) are defined on the ribs of the information structure, corresponding to the connections between elementary models. The experience of developing the second turn of the system ("ROSSIA"), oriented on IBM PC, shows that the rational application of such a system is connected with the division of functions between four groups of specialists:

- managers (terminal users) — knowing the contents of the problems and responsible for their solution. From their point of view the DSS is percieved as a comparatively small set of typical IT, permitting to solve the greater part of the current content subtasks, referring to the given working place. The terminal users are not specialists in mathematics, programming etc. and prefer simple and convenient means of interaction with the computer (the indication of the content subtask in the menu).

- designers of IT, who work out and together with the terminal users in a short time correct the IT solutions of the typical subtasks and give recommendations as to the complex technologies of complex problem solution. For them the DSS is a flexible information technology design system (ITDS).

- system analysts, knowing the content statement of the problems, models and methods of their solution. They carry out complex multicriterial analysis and single out the key problems (the bottlenecks of the development), single out a set of the most important indices and connections, which should be considered at the working place of the the construction of the CIT and its elements. For the analist analyst the DSS is a flexible means of forming and investigating the model complexes (the automized modelling system — AMS).

- programmers of basic means for AMS and ITDS, new types of models and methods of the main problem solution. The results of their work must provide a single basis for the creation and continuous development of the basic programming means (BPM) for automation of the elementary data processing operations.

5   The main parts of DSS

Thus, one can single out four constituent parts in the distributed DSS:

- the final result ("the upper part of the iceberg"): the information technologies of the complex problem solution

- the information technology desigh system (ITDS)

- the automized modelling system (AMS)

- the basic programming means (BPM)

The BPM includes

1. the command analyser, which carries out the syntax analysis and the operations of the command language of the system;

2. the local database;

3. the distribution support module, which provides the information exchange between PC using any local net;

4. menu support module, which consists of different menu generators and connection modules between the menu and the command analyser;

5. working form editor, which includes the tabular editor, designed to process standard and generate new types of documents (forms), the means of graphic interpretation of the results obtained, the means of the electronic tables function emulation;

6. the generator of the imitator algorithms, allowing the user to correct or create the imitation models of the information processes.

The AMS includes part of the basic means, the library of standard algorithms (multi-criterial analysis, aggregation and disaggregation, linear programming, statistic processing etc.), the library of application programs, designed for a definite subject sphere. The AMS allows the user to efficiently correct each separate elementary information model as described by Pospelov (1985), corresponding to the subtask. The input and exclusion of the indices, their connection, the recalculation algorithms, the creation of the new model require not more than an hour. The construction of the composite multilevel model (the input of connections, typical aggregation and disaggregation algorithms) also takes about an hour. Thus, each imitation model, constructed with the help of the AMS includes both the object model and the information process model.

The ITDS includes the means of interaction with the AMS, which helps to construct the EIT, and the intelligent preprocessor, which allows to obtain the CIT from the EIT.

The ITDS can be realized, for example, as a semantic net, each peak being the frame, displayed on the user' screen. Each slot of such a frame contains the information about the character of the typical elementary problem and a sign of the typical technology or algorithm of this solution. If the problem described is not elementary, the slot contains a reference to the frame, which contains a further detailization of the problem.

Working with such a constructor, the IT designer and the user must resolve the general task into elementary content subtasks, point out the desired sequence of the problem solution as a way on the frame structure of the constructor (as a sequence of the menu points) and fix this way in the form of its parts, leaving the points of the dialogue. As a result the CIT of the initial problem solution will be constructed, which will be a sequence of the EIT. Each EIT may be ascribed a set of signs, characterizing both the technology itself and the conditions of its application. The sets of signs, represented by a frame structure, may be modified in the process of work by the user or the system analyst and constitute the situational description. Using it, the system may select one or several EIT sets, providing an optimal solution, that is the CIT.

6 The problem of the scientific foundations

The problem of the CIT construction automation may be divided into two parts.

A. Creation of a minimal sufficient set of the EIT (for a certain subject sphere or a certain group of users).

B. Selection of the EIT sequence, leading to the solution of the problem, set by the user.

Problem "A" is solved using the AMS, for which multitudes of indices, objects, connections, which are taken into account and investigated, are singled out; a multitude of information objects — working forms (an object, a set of indices and connections) are constructed and for each of the constructed information objects a set of formal typical tasks Z_q is determined expertly.

The solution of problem "B" for simple problems of the Z_1, Z_2, Z_3 type ordering may take place on the basis of the descriptive approach and then specified in the process of calculation experiment using ITDS.

In complex subproblems, connected with decisions making by a manager, in coordinating the problem solution as a whole a normative approach, providing the fulfilment of the CIT quality requirement (the correspodence of the aim, convergence etc., see Pospelov, 1985) is necessary. For example, for the reglamentation of the typical task solution Z_5, for the ordering of the typical IT in the multilevel organization structure the coordination procedure based on the exposure and elimination of the bottlenecks is used. The theorems and algorithms, connected with the MC system optimization model, are its scientific foundation and they are described by Irikov and Trenev (1985), Pospelov (1985).

The typical subproblems Z_4 are based on the theorems and algorithms (Trenev, 1988) of forming a summary balance on the basis of separate balances or according to the multicriterial optimization concession scheme. The possibility for the chief to solve the problem autonomously at his working place and to coordinate it with the specialists' solution is based on the theorem of the necessary and sufficient conditions of the aggegated model solution permissibility with the data detalization. The selection of the heuristic algorithm library and the resource distribution EITs is based on the theorem of the possibility to synthetize correct algorithms out of incorrect ones for certain classes of problems.

Correct foundations, however, are obtained only for certain concrete types of tasks and in general the problem of creating regular methods and techniques of the EIT ordering in the framework of the complex IT is yet to be solved.

7   Prototyping

A complex IT for typical task of development planning is formed on the basis of the ITDS without programmers in 1 or 2 days, with using DSS "STRATEC" (Pospelov, 1985) or "ROSSIA" It takes 7–10 days if we use AMS. Some years ago it took 2 months (with the use of basic means). Before the appearance of the basic means the creation of the IT model for the realization of the cycle "technical specifications — programming — polishing — implementation" took 1 or 2 years with the participation of 4–5 skillful programmers.

Thus, new conditions, that have appeared recently (the elavation of the effective means of the man-machine IT designing, massive appearance of PCs at working places of the terminal users, increasing social orders for the industrial methods of M–M IT elaboration) make it reasonable and possible to use the CIT prototyping. The main purpose of prototyping is to provide a sufficient correspondence of the management M–M IT to the content requirements of the real process of management. The main criterion of prototype sufficiency is the user's ability to work with M–M system without system developers. The quality of the programs must not be high, it is important that there must be a gain in comparison with hand work. The prototype is really the technical specifications for the industrial system. The prototype is used to teach and adapt to the AMS the terminal users and to solve real problems at the working places in the process of the experimental implementation. This may lead to the substitution of the cycle "IT prototyping — experimental industrial implementation, coinciding in time with programming — implementation".

According to preliminary estimates and experience this may yeild a 3 or 4- fold reduction of time before the use of M–M IT by the terminal user, a 10- fold reduction of programming labour intensiveness on the 1st stage of prototyping, a 2, 3- fold reduction of the period and volume of work of the professional programmers (and in the future with the development of the ITDS — a 10- fold reduction).

This provides the grounds for the transition to the industrial methods of the solution of the problem of the mass computerization maximum response.

References

Irikov, V. A. (1985). Distributed systems of taking decisions in planning and management. The proceedings of the conference "Problems and methods of decision taking in organizing management systems", Moscow, All-union Scientific and Research Institute for Systems Researches, pp. 23–35.

Irikov, V. A. and Trenev, V. N. (1985). Algorithms for goal oriented formations of the parameters of a model for the development of an industry. *Soviet Journal of Computer and System Sciences* (formerly *Engineering Cybernetics*), **29**, pp. 106–114.

Pospelov, G. S., Irikov, V. A. and Kurilov, A. E. (1985). Procedures and algorithms of complex program construction. Moscow, Science.

Trenev, N. N. (1988). Certain algorithms for coordinated solutions formation in distributed system. *Kibernetika*, **6**, pp. 62–65, (in Russian).

Multicriteria Decision Making Using Personal Computers

Vahid Lotfi and Jeffrey E. Teich
School of Management
State University of New York at Buffalo
Buffalo, New York 14260

1   Introduction

Multiple criteria decision making (MCDM) refers to decision making in presence of two or more, usually conflicting and non-commensurate, criteria or objectives. The problem involves selection of an alternative, from among a set of alternatives, with acceptable values (judged by a decision maker) on all of the relevant criteria. MCDM has a wide range of applications and in fact the literature is abundant with the type of problems which pertain to MCDM. Further, within the last decade, many methods have been developed to solve various types of MCDM problems. Only recently, some of these methods have been implemented on the personal computer (PC) and are available for use by decision makers who may not have extensive quantitative and/or computer skills. The availability of the personal computer to most managers, at various levels within a firm, renders the possible use of these methods a viable quantitative decision making tool.

We present an overview of some of the recent PC-based MCDM implementations. Our main goal is to familiarize the reader with the available methodology and associated software, the type of problems addressed, capability of the software, and its cost and availability. We do not perform a formal computational study, comparing algorithmic performance of these methods. Indeed, that would be an extensive study in itself. In addition, most of the packages included in this study are designed to solve different types of MCDM problems with different characteristics and assumptions.

We have selected eight of the most recently developed MCDM methods to be included in this study (see Table 1). In two instances, we had access to the production versions of commercially available software and we used the production versions for evaluation. These included Expert Choice (EC) and Visual Interactive Support System for MCDM (VIG). In what follows, we utilize the terminology presented in (Zionts, 1987).

2   Comparisons of the selected approaches

The eight MCDM approaches included in this study are designed to solve different type of problems. Table 1 presents a summary of the type of problems each software is intended for. It also shows the hardware requirements and maximum problem size for each package. Although some of the packages can be used on a computer with just a monochrome display, the programs utilize graphics and/or color to enhance their effectiveness. We have identified these packages by specifying more than one display type. The remainder of this section consists of an overview of the selected approaches and the associated software.

AIM — Aspiration-Level Interactive Method

Aspiration-Level Interactive Method (AIM) is designed to solve the discrete alternative MCDM problem. Alternatives are described in terms of their performance on multiple objectives (or criteria). AIM can solve problems with maximizing, minimizing, and/or target type objectives. With each of the three objective types, there may be associated satisficing thresholds. The decision maker is effectively indifferent to values above or below the threshold (in the case of the first two objective types) or within the range of threshold values in the third case.

AIM utilizes levels of aspiration to explore the set of non-dominated solutions. The aspiration levels are initially set at the median values for each objective. The DM can then use the arrow keys to change the aspiration levels and is provided instantaneous feedback with respect to the reasonableness of these levels. The program provides items such as the nadir point, ideal point, next better and next worse (compared with the current aspiration levels), and fraction of alternatives satisfying these levels. A "nearest solution" to the current aspiration levels is determined by using a scalarizing function (Wierzbicki, 1980); with a weight on objective i defined as the normalized distance between the aspiration level and the ideal value for objective i. The weight reflects the increasing importance attached to objective i as the aspiration level is moved closer to the ideal value. AIM provides several additional options for further exploring the solution space. These include: display of dominated/nondominated alternatives; descriptive statistics for the entire data base; the set of outranking alternatives (a simplified version of ELECTRE (due to Roy, 1968); and a bar chart of the criterion weights.

ARIADNE

ARIADNE is a discrete alternative Multi-Criteria Decision Making (MCDM) model developed by Goicoechea (1988). ARIADNE is an extension of an earlier work by Sage and White (1984). The criteria themselves can either be deterministic or stochastic. In addition, there may be uncertainties surrounding the values of the criteria and the associated weights. These uncertainties allow the users to input a range on the values, and on the weights in either a single level or multiple level hierarchy.

The marginal value functions are determined either by using a straight line approximation, or by specifying the range of possible utility values for the alternatives. The maximum and minimum possible utility values for every alternative are obtained by solving a series of linear and/or nonlinear programs. The utility information is then conveniently reported to the user in the form of a bar graph. One bar for each alternative, that shows these minimum and maximum values. The bar graph can be used to identify and discard the dominated alternatives.

EC — Expert Choice

Expert Choice (EC) is based on the Analytic Hierarchy Process (AHP) (Saaty, 1980). EC is designed to solve hierarchical decision problems. The method utilizes a decision tree where the root node represents the goal (to be achieved) and the subsequent nodes, at the lower levels, represent criteria, sub-criteria, or alternatives. At each level of the tree (other than the root), up to seven nodes may be defined for a maximum of seven levels.

EC uses a matrix of pairwise comparisons to determine the relative importance of each criterion (sub-criterion) relative to the goal (the criterion). The rows and columns of this matrix are the criteria (sub-criteria) comprising the goal (criteria). The matrix entries are the pairwise ratings (based on a 9 point scale) of the row and column criterion (sub-criterion). Once all of the pairwise comparisons have been completed, EC will compute the weights associated with each sub-criterion. The weights are the elements of the normalized eigen-vector associated with the largest eigen-value of the ratings matrix. The weights are then presented using a bar chart showing their relative sizes.

Alternatives are added to the model either by direct entry (as lower level nodes of the tree) or through the "rating module". Alternatives are also compared (pairwise) in relation to a given criterion (or sub-criterion). After completing the preference ratings of all the alternatives with respect to all the criteria, EC can be used to determine a total weighted score for every alternative. The alternative having the highest weighted score is the most preferred one according to the preference structure.

MATS — Multi-Attribute Tradeoff System

Multi-Attribute Tradeoff System (MATS) is a discrete alternative MCDM software package designed to help the DM develop multi-attribute value functions based on certainty (deterministic) information. The value functions are then used to evaluate the alternative "plans" and rank them (see Brown et al., 1986 for more details).

The program allows the attributes or "factors" to be either continuous or dichotomous. The marginal value functions can be input either through interrogation or by specification. If a user chooses interrogation, he must answer a series of questions to determine the 50th percentile point in value. Then, a piecewise linear function connects the nadir point to the 50th percentile and to the ideal point for that attribute. A piecewise linear value function with several break points may be formed through direct input.

The criterion weights are determined for the issues through interrogation, or through specification. The interrogation option consists of pairwise comparison, trading off on two attributes at a time. The program allows the DM to input data relating to the factors or alternatives. MATS can then be used to determine a weighted score for every alternative. Clearly, better alternatives have higher scores.

PCPDA — Personal Computer Programs for Decision Analysis

Personal Computer Programs for Decision Analysis is a software package designed to solve the single and multi-attribute utility assessment problems. The package has been developed by Kirkwood and van der Feltz (1986) and consists of two programs. The first program, referred to as Exponential Utility Function (EUF) calculator, is designed to solve the single attribute utility assessment problem which in turn may be utilized in decision analysis. The second program called Multiplicative Utility Analysis (MUA), solves the multi-attribute utility analysis problem with additive or multiplicative utility functions. Both programs assume that for any alternative the attributes as well as their utilities are mutually independent (probabilistically). Consequently, the joint probability distribution function of the attributes/utilities is equal to the product of the marginal distributions. The attributes are assumed continuous.

EUF solves the single-attribute utility assessment problem involving constant risk aversion. It is designed to determine the various parameters of a utility function such as risk attitude and scaling constants. EUF utilizes the Pearson-Tukey approximation to calculate the expected utility. The utility functions can be increasing or decreasing. The risk attitude constant can be either specified or calculated using a certainty equivalent for a two fork lottery.

MUA is a multi-attribute version of the EUF and enables the user to determine the expected utility for deterministic and stochastic alternatives. Once the utility functions are determined, the user can proceed by entering the information regarding the marginal cumulative probability distributions for the alternatives. A three-point estimate is used to realize each distribution. After completing the problem definition, the user can request a list of alternatives, rank-ordered according to their expected utility values. The alternative with the highest expected utility is considered the most preferred one.

P/G% — Policy/Goal Percentaging

P/G%, also known as Best-Choice, is another discrete alternative MCDM package that can be used either with deterministic or stochastic information (Nagel, 1988). We used the Plato version of the package which comes on three disks. The program is also available in a lotus version that is basically a large macro file. The program initially allows a user to set up a data file with alternatives, then the multiple criteria with their associated weights, and finally the data matrix. Users can either input raw data into the matrix, or input ordinal or cardinal performance scores for any or all criteria.

The primary analysis shows the overall score for each of the alternatives. The alternative with the highest score would be the most preferred one. The intermediate analysis shows how the scores in the primary analysis were calculated. The package transforms the original data into "part-whole percentages" by dividing the alternative score on a criteria by the summation of all alternative scores for that criteria. The part-whole percentages are calculated in order to compare the differing units of measures across criteria (raw data, cardinal or ordinal scales). The total score for an alternative is calculated by multiplying the percentages by the assigned weight for that criteria and summing these products across criteria.

VIMDA — Visual Interactive Method for Discrete Alternatives

VIMDA is a multiple criteria decision support system designed for use with discrete alternatives. VIMDA allows the DM to interactively search the database by iteratively setting and resetting the aspiration levels on various criteria to find a desired solution.

Once the alternatives are defined, the user specifies the direction of preference on the criteria, either maximization or minimization. In addition, he specifies aspiration levels for each of the criteria. VIMDA calculates a current solution by optimizing one of the criteria, and uses the aspiration levels to calculate a reference direction. An achievement function based on the reference direction is formulated which then enables the program to calculate a subset of efficient solutions. This method is similar to the reference point solution as suggested by Wierzbicki (1980).

The subset of alternatives selected are then presented to the DM. The values of the criteria are presented both numerically and graphically for the subset of alternatives. A line graph presenting the criterion levels for the subset is also displayed. The y axis represents criterion levels and the x axis represents the subset of alternatives. The DM can use the cursor to select an alternative among the subset, and see a vertical line cross the criterion lines at the selected alternative. The criterion values for that alternative is also presented numerically at the top of the screen along with a key that identifies the type of line and the color that represent each criterion in the graph. The current most preferred alternative (or starting) is presented on the right side of the graph. At each iteration, the DM selects the most preferred alternative from the subset, then resets the aspiration levels. A new subset of alternatives is presented and the process repeats.

VIG — A Visual Interactive Support System for MCDM

VIG is marketed by NumPlan and is based on the earlier work referred to as "Parato Race", (see Korhonen and Wallenius, 1988 and Korhonen, 1988a). The software is designed to solve the multiple objective linear programming (MOLP) problem. Through the use of computer graphics, the decision maker can examine various parts of the efficient frontier and eventually determine the most preferred solution.

VIG conceptualizes the MOLP as a set of goals which are either "flexible", or "rigid". The rigid goals are those which *must* be achieved and the flexible goals are those which are *desirable* to be achieved. Rigid goals are analogous to the constraints in an MOLP and flexible goals are the objectives with prespecified aspiration levels. Once the model has been entered, the user may identify one or more of the rows (up to 10) as flexible goals or objectives with the directions of inequalities indicating the type of optimization (i.e., ">" for maximization and "<" for minimization). A row with an equal to relation cannot be used as an objective.

The model may be solved in one of two ways. First, the user may specify a set of aspiration levels and then request a solution. In this case, VIG uses a scalarizing function to determine the nearest non-dominated solution to his aspiration levels. The user can then return to the edit mode and change the aspiration levels and request another solution. This process is repeated until an acceptable solution is found. Alternatively, one can use the initial solution as a starting point and examine various non-dominated solutions on the efficient frontier. VIG uses computer graphics and provides a mechanism for traversing the efficient frontier.

Software	Source	System required	Problem size	Price
AIM	Lotfi, Stewart, and Zionts, Jacobs Management Center SUNY at Buffalo, Buffalo, NY 14260	R = 512 D = M/C/G	10 obj. 150 alt.	$15
Ariadne	Ambrose Goicoechea, IS&Sys. Engineering Department, George Mason University, Fairfax, Virginia	R = 256 D = C/G	15 att. 10 alt.	$40
Expert Choice	Decision Support Software, Inc., 1300 Vincent Place, Mc-Lean, Virginia 22101	R = 320 D = M/C/G	49 obj. 125 alt.	$495*
MATS	Bureau of Reclamation, US Department of Interior, Denver, Colorado 80225	R = 256 D = M/C/G	40 obj. 40 alt.	Free
PCPDA	Kirkwood and van der Feltz, Dept. of Decision and Info. Sys., College of Business, Arizona State University, Tempe, Arizona 85287	R = 76 D = M	20 obj. 20 alt.	$20
P/G%	Decision Aids, Inc., 361 Lincoln Hall, University of Illinois, Urbana, Ill 61801	R = 256 D = M	15 obj. 15 alt.	$20
VIMDA	NumPlan, P.O. Box 128, SF-03101 Nummela, Finland	R = 256 D = C/G	10 obj. 500 alt.	$?
VIG	NumPlan	R = 256 D = C/G	10 obj. 100 rows. 96 vars.	$400@

Table 1: Developers and Prices

? unknown at the time of this report
* list price, educational institutions may qualify for a discount
@ academic price, price for industry is $1,900.

3 Conclusions

Several MCDM approaches and associated software, designed for use on the IBM Personal Computer or compatible, were discussed. The types of MCDM problems addressed ranged from the discrete alternative to multi-attribute expected utility assessment problem. The choice of software depends directly on the type of MCDM problem at hand. The potential user, who does not have an extensive knowledge of the MCDM methodology, can benefit from acquiring several of the packages which are available at a nominal charge to gain familiarity with the problem and associated methodology.

References

Brown, C. A., Stinson, D. P. and Grant R. W. (1986). Multi-Attribute Tradeoff System: Personal Computer Version User's Manual. Bureau of Reclamation, U.S. Department of Interior, Denver, Colorado.

Goicoechea, A. (1988). On the Use of Multiple Attribute and Imperfect Information with ARIADNE to Rank Alternative Systems. *Applied Mathematics and Computation Journal*, forthcoming.

Goicoechea, A., Hansen, D. R. and Duckstein L. (1982). Multiobjective Decision Analysis with Engineering and Business Applications. John Wiley & Sons, New York.

Kirkwood, C. W. and van der Feltz, L. C. (1986). Personal Computer Programs for Decision Analysis, Volume 1: User Manual. Technical Report DIS–86/87–4, Department of Decision and Information Systems, College of Business, Arizona State University.

Korhonen, P. J. (1988a). VIG — A Visual Interactive Support System for Multiple Criteria Decision Making. Helsinki School of Economics, Helsinki, Finland.

Korhonen, P. J. (1988b). A Visual Reference Direction Approach to Solving Discrete Multiple Criteria Problems. *European Journal of Operational Research*, **34**, pp. 152–159.

Korhonen, P. J., and Wallenius, J. (1988). A Pareto Race. *Naval Research Logistics*, **35**, pp. 615–623.

Lotfi, V., Stewart, T. and Zionts, S. (1988). An Aspiration-Level Interactive Method for Multiple Criteria Decision Making. Working paper, School of Management, State University of New York, Buffalo, New York.

Nagel, S. S. (1988). P/G% Or Best-Choice Tutorials: Introductory, Intermediate, and Advanced Levels. University of Illinois.

Roy, B. (1968). Classement et Choix en Presence de Points de Vue Multiples (La Methode ELECTRE). *Revue d'Informatique et de Recherche Operationelle*, **8**, pp. 57–75.

Saaty, L. T. (1980). The Analytical Hierarchy Process. McGraw-Hill, New York.

Sage, A. P. and White, C. C. (1984). ARIADNE: A Knowledge-Based Interactive System for Planning and Decision Support. *IEEE Transactions*, **SMC-14, 1**.

Wierzbicki, A. P. (1980). The Use of Reference Objectives in Multiobjective Optimization. In: G. Fandel and T. Gal (Eds.), Multiple Criteria Decision Making Theory and Application, Springer-Verlag, New York.

Zionts, S. (1987). Multiple Criteria Mathematical Programming: An Updated Overview and Several Approaches. School of Management, State University of New York at Buffalo, Buffalo, New York.

HYBRID–FMS: an element of DSS for designing Flexible Manufacturing Systems

Marek Makowski

International Institute for Applied Systems Analysis,

A-2361 Laxenburg, Austria.[*]

Janusz S. Sosnowski

Systems Research Institute, Polish Academy of Sciences,

Newelska 6, 01-447 Warsaw, Poland.

Abstract

Hybrid-FMS is a dedicated optimization package which allows for formulation and solution of a multicriteria problem related to a selection of a Flexible Manufacturing System taking into account different criteria such as productivity, cost and flexibility.

1 Introduction

Flexible Manufacturing Systems (FMS) have been playing an increasingly important role in the effort to improve productivity (Buzacott and Yao, 1986), (Ranta and Alabian, 1988). Among the basic features of such systems there is the ability to produce variations of products of different degrees of complexity, easy change of production volumes and batch sizes. The design of FMS is a multilevel and multicriteria task. Hybrid-FMS is aimed at multicriteria optimization of the model developed at the Computer Integrated Manufacturing Project at IIASA (Ranta and Alabian, 1988). So far this is still a prototype of an element which will be included into a DSS which is planned to assist the designing process of a FMS.

Hybrid-FMS runs on a PC compatible with IBM PC. It is assumed that a user need not to be skilled in computer usage. However, good knowledge of the FMS model and an understanding of multicriteria optimization basics are essential for rational use of the software. The package accepts the standard MPSX format of LP problem formulation

---

[*]on leave from the Systems Research Institute of the Polish Academy of Sciences, Warsaw.

but it also offers an option to read original data from an ASCII file (in a free format that may easily be generated by any DBMS). In the latter case it is possible to interactively modify all coefficients of the FMS model defined by (Ranta and Alabian, 1988) and the corresponding optimization model is generated by the package. Such an approach allows for avoiding the cumbersome procedure of generating and updating an LP or bilinear model.

Hybrid-FMS allows for generation of the simplified LP model in which a group of variables is fixed. This option corresponds to the initial formulation the FMS model which has been solved by LP packages (cf Kuula and Stam, 1989). The main purpose of Hybrid-FMS however is to generate and solve a multicriteria non-linear (bilinear) problem.

The formulation and solution of the multicriteria problem is based on the reference point approach (cf Makowski and Sosnowski, 1989) which allows for conversion of the multicriteria problem to a single criterion one. Therefore the multicriteria problem is solved as a sequence of parametric single objective optimization problems – modified by a user in interactive way upon analysis of previous results.

Solution of a single objective bilinear optimization problem is based on a technique which combines a Newton type method for finding solutions which satisfies Kuhn–Tucker (K–T) conditions with the augmented Lagrangian method.

2   Formulation of the FMS Model

2.1   Basic assumptions

The model formulation follows the model described in (Ranta and Alabian, 1988) therefore only short summary is provided here. It is assumed that a FMS consists of m machines which are to produce n different parts. Parts of the same type are grouped into batches. The planning period is equal to one year.

Let j – denote index of part and i – index of machine. We assume the following notation:

x_j – number of batches of j-th part per year.

y_j – batch size of j-th part.

v_j – production volume of j-th part per year.

Since the obvious dependencies between variables $v_j = x_j y_j$ hold, there are only two groups of decision variables, namely: numbers of batches (for each type of part) and the corresponding batch size. For the simplified LP model the batch sizes are fixed and given.

The resulting mathematical formulation of the FMS model is described below, whereas original formulation of the FMS model is given by (Ranta and Alabian, 1988). Modification of the later model and computations using different packages have been made by (Stam and Kuula, 1989) and (Kuula and Stam, 1989).

2.2 Criteria

The following three criteria have been selected for the Hybrid-FMS. This list may be easily extended (cf Kuula and Stam, 1989).

1. Maximization of production

$$q_1 = \sum_{j=1}^{n} \omega_j v_j \tag{1}$$

2. Minimization of cost

$$q_2 = \sum_{j=1}^{n} (\alpha_j x_j + \beta_j y_j) \tag{2}$$

3. Maximization of flexibility (or complexity potential)

$$q_3 = \sum_{j=1}^{n} \gamma_j v_j \tag{3}$$

2.3 Constraints

1. Machine time limitation

$$\sum_{j=1}^{n} a_{ij} v_j \leq b_i \qquad i = 1, \ldots, m \tag{4}$$

2. Line time limitation

$$\sum_{i=1}^{m} \sum_{j=1}^{n} a_{ij} v_j + \sum_{j=1}^{n} d_j x_j \leq T \tag{5}$$

3. Definition of additional variables

$$v_j = x_j y_j \qquad j = 1, \ldots, n \tag{6}$$

4. Simple constraints for variables

$$0 < l_j \leq v_j \leq u_j \qquad j = 1, \ldots, n \tag{7}$$

$$0 < \underline{x}_j \leq x_j \leq \overline{x}_j \qquad j = 1, \ldots, n \tag{8}$$

$$0 < \underline{y}_j \leq y_j \leq \overline{y}_j \qquad j = 1, \ldots, n \tag{9}$$

3 Multicriteria optimization

We formulate the multicriteria problem as finding a local Pareto-optimal solution for criteria (1), (2) and (3) subject to constraints (1)–(9). A Pareto solution can be found by the minimization of the scalarizing function in the form:

$$\max_{i=1,2,3} (w_i(q_i - \bar{q}_i)) + \varepsilon_m \sum_{i=1}^{3} w_i q_i \tag{10}$$

on the set of variables (q, x) which fulfill the constraints (1)–(9).

In the function (10) the following notation is used:

$\bar{q}_i$ is the aspiration level for i-th criterion (i.e. values desired by a user for each criterion),

w_i is a weight associated with i-th criterion (a weight is internally made negative for criteria which are to be maximized),

ε_m is a given small non-negative parameter which is introduced to avoid weakly Pareto optimal solution in certain situations (cf Kallio et al., 1980).

The approach adopted in the Hybrid–FMS may generally describe as follows:

1. A user may specify an aspiration level $\bar{q} = (\bar{q}_1, \bar{q}_2, \bar{q}_3)$ and weights w_i for each criterion. A recommended alternative is to compute first so called *utopia point* which is calculated as a result of single criterion optimization for each criterion separately. Utopia point components provides very useful information, i.e. an upper bound evaluation of each criterion value (which is usually not attainable) that can be expected from multicriteria optimization.

2. The scalarizing function (10) is minimized subject to constraints (1)-(9).

3. The user explores various Pareto-optimal points by changing either the aspiration level $\bar{q}$ or/and weights attached to criteria or/and parameters related to the definition of the criteria.

5. The procedure described in points 2 and 3 is repeated until a satisfactory solution is found.

4 Solution technique

The scalarizing function (10) is nondifferentiable but it can be transformed to a differentiable one by the introduction of an additional variable δ and auxiliary constraints:

$$-\delta + w_i q_i \leq w_i \bar{q}_i \qquad i = 1, 2, 3 \tag{11}$$

The objective function for the auxiliary problem takes the form:

$$\min \delta + \varepsilon_m \sum_{i=1}^{3} w_i q_i \tag{12}$$

The following notation will be used for a more compact description of the solution technique and of the applied algorithm:

$\|x\|$ – denotes the Euclidian norm of vector x

$\|x\|_1$ – denotes the L_1–norm of vector x

$\|x\|_\infty$ – denotes the L_∞–norm of vector x

$(u)_+$ – denotes the vector composed of the non-negative elements of vector u (where negative elements are replaced by zeros)

$diag(x_iy_i)$ – denotes a diagonal matrix which i–th diagonal element is x_iy_i.

I – denotes the unit matrix

e – denotes the vector with all elements equal 1.

$z = (x, y, v, \delta)$ – denotes a vector composed with $x \in R^n, y \in R^n, v \in R^n, \delta \in R$ respectively.

The auxiliary problem of minimization function (12) subject to the constraints (1)–(9), (11) may be reformulated as follows:

$$\min c^T z$$

$$Az \le b$$

$$diag(x_iy_i)e - v = 0$$

$$l \le z \le u$$

The ordinary Lagrange function takes form:

$$l(z, \lambda, \sigma) = c^T z + \lambda^T (Az - b) + \sigma^T (diag(x_iy_i)e - v)$$

We note that the simple constraints are not included into Lagrange's function. The augmented Lagrangian function to the auxiliary problem may be formulated in the following way:

$$L(z, \lambda, \sigma, \rho) = c^T z + \left(\|(\lambda + \rho(Az - b))_+\|^2 + \|\sigma + \rho(diag(x_iy_i)e - v)\|^2 - \|\lambda\|^2 - \|\sigma\|^2 \right) / (2\rho)$$

A nonconvex problem often has a duality gap and the value of the dual problem is less than the value of primal problem. But under regular conditions (Rockafellar, 1974), there exists such $\bar{\rho}$, that for $\rho \ge \bar{\rho}$ the augmented Lagrangian has a saddle point and there is possible application of primal–dual method for solving nonconvex problem.

We introduce L_1 penalty function (Fletcher, 1981),

$$P_r(z) = c^T z + r \left(\|(Az - b)_+\|_1 + \|diag(x_iy_i)e - v\|_1 \right)$$

where $r > 0$ is a penalty parameter which will be defined in the description of the algorithm.

For given $\lambda^k \ \sigma^k$ and $\rho^k > 0 \ z^k$ and matrix B^k we define the following function:

$$F^k(z) = c^T z + (z - z^k)^T B^k (z - z^k) + \left(\|(\lambda^k + \rho^k(Az - b))_+\|^2 + \right.$$

$$\left. \|\sigma^k + \rho^k(diag(y_i^k)x + diag(x_i^k)y - v - diag(x_i^ky_i^k)e)\|^2 \right) / (2\rho^k)$$

Where the matrix B^k is Levenberg's modification of Hessian computed for the Lagrangian function in the point $(z^k, \lambda^k, \sigma^k)$.

$$B^k = \partial l(z^k, \lambda^k, \sigma^k)/\partial z + (1/\gamma^k)I$$

4.1 Algorithm

The algorithm consists of the following steps:

0. Assume $\beta_1, \beta_2, \eta_1, \eta_2 > 1$, $0 < \mu, \theta < 1$.

1. Choose $\lambda^0, \sigma^0, \rho^0, \gamma^0 > 0$, and a initial point z^0 such that $l \leq z^0 \leq u$. Compute B^0; set $k = 0$.

2. Compute

$$\bar{z}^k = \arg\min F^k(z), \quad l \leq z \leq u$$

$$\bar{\lambda}^k = (\lambda^k + \rho^k(A\bar{z}_k - b))_+$$

$$\bar{\sigma}^k = \sigma^k + \rho^k(diag(y_i^k)\bar{x}^k + diag(x_i^k)\bar{y}^k - v - diag(x_i^k y_i^k)e)$$

$$r = \max\left(\|\bar{\lambda}^k\|_\infty, \|\bar{\sigma}^k\|_\infty\right)$$

3. If

$$P_r(\bar{z}^k) \leq P_r(z^k) - \mu\|\bar{z}^k - z^k\|$$

then we set:

$$z^{k+1} = \bar{z}^k, \quad \lambda^{k+1} = \bar{\lambda}^k, \quad \sigma^{k+1} = \bar{\sigma}^k,$$

$$\rho^{k+1} = \beta_1 \rho^k, \quad \gamma^{k+1} = \eta_1 \gamma^k,$$

$k := k + 1$ and go to step 2

4. Armijo linesearch in direction $d^k = \bar{z}^k - z^k$ for function $L(z, \lambda^k, \sigma^k, \rho_k)$.

$$L(z^k + \alpha_k d^k, \lambda^k, \sigma^k, \rho_k) \leq L(z^k \lambda^k, \sigma^k, \rho_k) + \theta\alpha_k(\partial L(z^k, \lambda^k, \sigma^k, \rho_k)/\partial z)^T d^k$$

If α_k is chosen step then set:

$$z^{k+1} = z^k + \alpha_k d^k$$

5. If z^{k+1} is a minimizer of $L(\cdot, \lambda^k, \sigma^k, \rho_k)$ then set:

$$\lambda^{k+1} = (\lambda^k + \rho^k(A\bar{z}_k - b))_+$$

$$\sigma^{k+1} = \sigma^k + \rho_k(diag(x_i^{k+1}y_i^{k+1})e - v^{k+1})$$

and set:

$$\rho^{k+1} = \beta_2 \rho^k, \quad \gamma^{k+1} = \eta_2 \gamma^k,$$

$k := k + 1$ and go to step 2

6. Set

$$\lambda^{k+1} = \lambda^k, \quad \sigma^{k+1} = \sigma^k,$$

$k := k + 1$ and go to step 2

The above algorithm combines Newton's type method for constrained minimization problems with the multiplier method. In the Step 2, the preconditioned conjugate gradient and active set strategy method are used in the way as described in (Makowski and Sosnowski, 1989).

5 Implementation

The Hybrid-FMS is designed for users who know the FMS model as defined by (Ranta and Alabian, 1988) but who are not necessarily specialists in multicriteria optimization. It is assumed that a user will be given a short introduction to multicriteria optimization technique. The package provides a context sensitive help which enables its usage by a user who has little computer experience.

The package is written in C and can be run on a standard configuration of a PC IBM compatible. It requires less then 1 MB space on a hard disk (more space may be needed if storage of many scenarios is requested). A math coprocessor is strongly recommended since the solver runs about 5 times slower without a 80x87 chip.

The package is composed of the following mutually linked modules:

- Driver: this module controls the usage of all other modules, loads them and executes, analyses the status of a problem being solved and provides tools for storing, retriving and modification of different models and of different tasks (a task is an instance of a model for which objectives and all parameters are selected); driver is also loaded and executed by each of other modules after the execution of the latter is completed,

- Preprocessor, which serves for formulation of the model (more exactly it generates constraints that define admissible set of solutions) and allows for interactive modifications of model formulation. A user has to choose one of the two provided preprocessors:

  - The one that processes input that conforms to the MPSX standard for LP problems formulation.

  - The one that is specialized for the FMS model. It reads a free format ASCII file with all coefficients of the model (such a file can be easily generated by any data base management system). Therefore it is possible to modify original model coefficients which have well understood for a user meaning (contrary to the "standard" approach of generating LP models which enables modifications of matrix coefficients which usually have no easy interpretation). According to user choice either a bilinear or simplified linear model is generated.

- Task generator allows for definition of criteria. A user may interactively select criteria and parameters of a multicriteria optimization (such as reference point, weights etc). After a user defines a multicriteria problem the corresponding optimization problem is generated.

- Solver that is capable to solve the generated optimization problem (which is either bilinear or linear depending on the user choice of the model).

The chosen method of allocating storage in the memory takes maximal advantage of the available computer memory and of the features of typical real-word problems. Memory is dynamically allocated, space for data is adjusted to actual size of data and memory is released when it is no longer required. Functional division among the modules is a result of a trade-off between the speed of the program execution and memory usage. Each module loads a next one in a memory space occupied by itself which allows (together with a technique for storing sparse matrices) for formulation and solution of relatively large problems.

6 Conclusions

Hybrid-FMS is still a pilot-type of software. In its current state it can be applied only to the FMS as formulated by (Ranta and Alabian, 1988) using three predefined criteria. The authors agree with suggestions made in (Kuula and Stam, 1989) for making the package more flexible. Further development of Hybrid-FMS depends however on the actual demand for its usage and on experience by specialists on FMS modeling.

References

Buzacott, J.A. and D.D. Yao (1986). Flexible Manufacturing Systems: A Review of Analitical Models. *Management Science* , 32(1986) 890–905.

Fletcher, R. (1981). Practical methods of optimization, vol II, Constrained optimization, Wiley, New York.

Kuula, M. and Stam A. (1989). A nonlinear multicriteria model for strategic FMS selection decisions, WP-89-62, IIASA, Laxenburg, August 1989.

Makowski, M. and J. Sosnowski (1988). User Guide to a Mathematical Programming Package for Multicriteria Dynamic Linear Problems HYBRID Version 3.1, WP-88-111, IIASA, Laxenburg, December 1988.

Makowski, M. and J. Sosnowski (1989). Mathematical Programming Package HYBRID. In Aspiration Based Decision. Eds. A. Lewandowski, A.P. Wierzbicki Lecture Notes in Economics and Mathematical Systems Vol.331.Springer-Verlag.Berlin 1989

Ranta, J. and A. Alabian (1988). Interactive Analysis of FMS Productivity and Flexibility, WP-88-098, IIASA, Laxenburg, October 1988.

Rockefellar R.T (1974). Augmented Lagrange Multiplier Functions and Duality in Nonconvex Programming. *SIAM Journal on Control and Optimization* , 12(1974) 268–285.

Stam A. and Kuula, M.(1989). Selecting a flexible manufacturing system using multiple criteria analysis WP-89-48, IIASA, Laxenburg, July 1989.

N-tomic: A Support System for Multicriteria Segmentation Problems

Roberto Massaglia and Anna Ostanello

Politecnico di Torino - Dip. Automatica e Informatica

Corso duca degli Abruzzi 24 - 10129 Torino, Italy

1   Introduction

Evaluation of a number of candidates (individuals or objects) applying (or proposed) for some qualifications, has been generally dealt with as a selection or a ranking problem in the MC literature. Practice and the analysis of actual evaluation cases show, however, that such processes possess certain special features which substantially differentiate them from both choice and ranking problem formulation. These features may be summarized as follows:

a) **Decision problem formulation** is **Segmentation** (Roy, 1981). Each candidate is expecting a justified answer, in terms of acceptance/rejection or of class assignment; such an answer is normally deduced through a process where some specifications or reference levels have been defined, enabling post-decisional justification by the decision makers (DM).

b) The **set of candidates** is not generally "given" in the classic sense, but **evolves**. Candidates generally do not appear all at once, but either one by one or in echelons, and thus do not compete against each other directly, at least explicitly.

c) Different points of view must be taken for the evaluation; the integration of sometimes dishomogeneous evaluations on multiple attributes or criteria is performed, in effect, with **logics** that seldom correspond to any algebraic rule (cf, for instance, the "Elimination by Aspects" framework (Tversky, 1971)).

Moreover the evaluation criteria, the reference levels and the aggregation logic may evolve during the process, for instance, depending on the number of candidates, the tenure of the decision makers, and for different reasons such as the different personalities of new candidates or modifications in the DM's **attitude** toward acceptance or rejection.

The question of judgment **coherence**, at least in a given interval of time, and of transparency of the evaluation process is crucial and may be critical in many actual processes where any candidate may appeal against the results (for instance, competitions within public institutions).

Few "pioneer" works, to our knowledge, exist on MCDA methods for evaluation with reference profiles (for instance: Le Boulanger and Roy, 1968; Benayoun and Boulier, 1972; Hyenne and Moscarola, 1972; Moscarola and Roy, 1977; Norese and Merighi, 1979; Merighi, 1980; Roy, 1981). A common feature of most of these methods, one generally placing some limits in their utilization by potential applicators of real organizations, consists in focusing on the segmentation stage of the decision process without integrating its other more unstructured stages, such as structuring of an available information base and specification of levels providing a clear definition of the conditions of acceptance and rejection.

Systems to support the different stages of multicriteria segmentation processes are not common. This paper introduces an interactive system, **nTOMIC**, which is designed to support all stages of a segmentation process. The system is based on an empirically derived model enabling a routine articulation of the process. A procedure to support the structuring of a reference frame is the core of the system. Global evaluations of the candidates can be deduced from this frame by selecting possible aggregation logics.

2 Structure of the Support System

With reference to a framework introduced in Norese and Ostanello (1988), process representation is based on three principal routines: **search and structuring, specification, evaluation.** nTOMIC is divided into three main modules. Each module, Mi (i=1,2,3), corresponds to a routine and can be applied to different data bases, on which some modelling and decision activities may be performed as summarized below.

M1) Search and Structuring: This module supports the construction of a set of criteria with the corresponding evaluation scales (MC model), working on the available information base. This task may be performed by DBIII Plus. If a given data base relates to a set of sub-criteria, constituting the disaggregation of a nominal criterion, then a qualitative scale for this criterion can be structured with the procedure in M2.

M2) Specification: This module consists of a procedure for structuring both a reference frame and the segmentation classes. The activity domain is an MC evaluative model. The procedure can support to assess the classes and their qualifications, according to the DM's agreement on the class characterization by selected flexible profiles of potential candidates. To facilitate a flexible frame definition and meaningful candidate discriminations, some kinds of uncertainty may be dealt with: for instance, uncertainty about the specification levels or the qualifications of certain classes; possible different DM's attitudes towards acceptance and rejection may be also made explicit.

M3) Evaluation: By this module, a global evaluation can be automatically assigned to each candidate of either a given or an evolving set. The candidate's MC evaluation is confronted with the reference model; a judgement on each candidate would correspond to the qualification of one of the classes established by M2. Feedbacks and shifting from one module to another are always possible without complex input procedures.

3 Procedure for structuring a reference frame

The core of nTOMIC is a procedure that can be applied both, globally, to assess a reference frame for the evaluation and, locally, to structure the qualitative scale of a criterion.

Starting input to the procedure is a set of structured criteria, $g = [g_j : j \in J]$, with numerical scales, E_j. The assumption of numerical scales is not very restrictive in practice.

Three routines (or sub-routines) can be used, each allowing specification, aggregation and structuring to be conducted by steps, as specified below.

3.1 Specification routine

Step 1 - Level specification: Assuming preference monotonically not decreasing on the scale $Ej, \forall j \in J$, two correlated levels of the scale may be defined: b_j, to specify the concept of "good" or "acceptable" score, and c_j to specify the concept of "bad" or "refusable" score, so that $c_j < b_j$. These levels should represent two thresholds on the scale beyond or below which, respectively, a potential candidate could be considered locally either "certainly acceptable or good" or "certainly rejectable or bad". Even only one of these levels may be defined, depending on the attribute and on its relevance to characterize a frame profile. Each of the levels may activate some conditions of veto, both to rejection (b_j) and to acceptance (c_j) at a successive step of the procedure.

Step 2 - Definition of uncertainty thresholds: A single point definition of the specification levels may not allow judgement flexibility or convergence, within uncertainty or conflict situations. Thus the reference levels may be "fuzzified" by the introduction of two thresholds, $0 \leq q \leq s$, called of: **indifference, q**, and **discrimination, s** (cf Roy, 1978). With preference monotonically not decreasing on the scale E_j, the thresholds may be specified as follows:

i) b_j thresholds "on the left", $s_j^- \geq q_j^- \geq 0$, so that any level $e \in E_j$ could be qualified, respectively, as:

"certainly good"   if $e \geq b_j$ or $(b_j - e) \leq q_j^-$

"fairly good"   if $q_j^- < (b_j - e) < s_j^-$

"not good"   if $(b_j - e) \geq s_j^-$;

ii) c_j thresholds "on the right", $s_j^+ \geq q_j^+ \geq 0$, so that any level $e \in E_j$ could be qualified, respectively, as:

"certainly bad"   if $e \leq c_j$ or $(e - c_j) \leq q_j^+$

"fairly bad"   if $q_j^+ < (e - c_j) < s_j^+$

"not bad"   if $(e - c_j) \geq s_j^+$.

For coherence reasons, the thresholds must satisfy the relation: $c_j + s_j^+ \leq b_j - s_j^-$. The possible elements e, $e \in [c_j + s_j^+, b_j - s_j^-]$, are qualified as "neither good nor bad".

If the preference is monotonically not increasing with the scale E_j, then the thresholds are defined: "on the right" for b_j and "on the left" for c_j and the qualification relations are coherently modified.

Step 3 - Marginal indices: For the purpose of formulating aggregated judgements, two marginal functions, $d_j(., b_j)$ and $D_j(c_j, .)$, are defined on each scale E_j for any pair (c_j, b_j) of correlated specification levels. They are called, respectively, **goodness and badness credibility** index. These functions are introduced to give automatically an estimate of the credibility of the statements "e is at least as good as b_j" and "e is at least as bad as c_j" for every level e of the scale. Their definition is suggested by the fuzzy outranking model of ELECTRE III (Roy, 1978).

More formally, they are real valued functions, endowed with the following properties:

a) range: $\quad\quad\quad\quad\quad 0 \leq d_j(.,b_j) \leq 1,\, 0 \leq D_j(c_j,.) \leq 1;$

b) complementarity: $\quad\quad d_j(.,b_j) * D_j(c_j,.) = 0;$

c) monotonicity: $\quad\quad$ - d_j not decreasing with E_j, so that:

$\quad\quad\quad\quad\quad\quad\quad\quad\quad\quad d_j(e,b_j) = 1 \Leftrightarrow e$ is "certainly good"

$\quad\quad\quad\quad\quad\quad\quad\quad\quad\quad d_j(e,b_j) = 0 \Leftrightarrow e$ is "not good"

$\quad\quad\quad\quad\quad\quad\quad\quad\quad\quad 0 < d_j(e,b_j) < 1 \Leftrightarrow e$ is "fairly good";

$\quad\quad\quad\quad\quad\quad\quad\quad$ - D_j not increasing with E_j, so that:

$\quad\quad\quad\quad\quad\quad\quad\quad\quad\quad D_j(c_j,e) = 1 \Leftrightarrow e$ is "certainly bad"

$\quad\quad\quad\quad\quad\quad\quad\quad\quad\quad D_j(c_j,e) = 0 \Leftrightarrow e$ is "not bad"

$\quad\quad\quad\quad\quad\quad\quad\quad\quad\quad 0 < D_j(c_j,e) < 1 \Leftrightarrow e$ is "fairly bad";

d) continuity, with $s_j > q_j > 0$.

A graphical representation of the two indices is given in Fig.1, assuming continuity and linear interpolation.

3.2 Aggregation routine

Step 1 - Relative importance of the attributes: The criteria may be of varying importance in the formulation of a global judgement. Thus the procedure requires a numerical estimate of the "weights", $p_j > 0, \forall j$. In default they are all made equal to 1.

Step 2 - Aggregated indices: Aggregations of the marginal credibility indices can be performed by two approaches: with or without compensation.

a) Aggregation without compensation:

The following models have been assumed to represent both goodness credibility, $d(.,b)$, and badness credibility, $D(c,.)$:

$$d(.,b) = \sum_{j \in J} p_j d_j(.,b_j), \text{ with } b = \{b_j : j \in J\} \quad (1)$$

$$D(c,.) = \sum_{j \in J} p_j D_j(c_j,.), \text{ with } c = \{c_j : j \in J\} \quad (2)$$

The following properties are evident, with normalized "weights":

$$0 \leq d(.,b) \leq 1, \quad 0 \leq D(c,.) \leq 1 \text{ and } d(.,b) + D(c,.) \leq 1 \quad (3)$$

b) Aggregation with compensation: The aggregated indices may be differently defined in cases where a candidate has a singular score (either especially "good" or "bad") on some attribute, so as to induce the decision makers to take more careful consideration.

- Credibility of goodness, $d^*(.,b)$: The following index model is assumed to take into account particular negative scores on at least one criterion of an identified subset $J^* \subseteq J$:

$$d^*(.,b) = d(.,b) \prod_{j \in J^*} \frac{1 - D_j(c_j,.)}{1 - d(.,b)} \quad (4)$$

with $j \in J^*$ so that $D_j(c_j,.) > d(.,b)$ (cf Roy, 1978).

It is $0 \leq d^* < d$ and it may be $d^* = 0$, in cases where on even one criterion of J^* the candidate is "certainly bad" $(D_j = 1)$ (Veto activation to the statement "e is potentially good").

- **Credibility of badness,** $D^*(c,.)$: Similarly if, for at least one attribute of an identified set $J^{**} \subseteq J$, it is $d_j(.,b_j) > D(c,.)$, then the aggregated credibility of badness may be modeled by:

$$D^*(c,.) = D(c,.) \prod_{j \in J^{**}} \frac{1 - d_j(.,b_j)}{1 - D(c,.)} \quad (5)$$

It is $0 \le D^* < D$ and it may be $D^* = 0$, in cases where on even one attribute of J^{**} the candidate is "certainly good" ($d_j = 1$) (Veto activation to the statement "e is potentially bad").

Step 3 - Attitude assumption: The decision makers' attitude to acceptance or rejection may be made explicit at this level of the procedure. Three possible attitudes: **neutral, prone to accept, prone to reject**, have been distinguished (cf Moscarola and Roy, 1977). They may imply the adoption of different aggregated indices as in Table 1.

Table 1 - Possible index selection by attitude

	NEUTRAL	PRO-ACCEPTANCE	PRO-REJECTION
Index of "goodness"	$d(.,b)$	$d(.,b)$	$d^*(.,b)$
Index of "badness"	$D(c,.)$	$D^*(c,.)$	$D(c,.)$

3.3 Class structuring routine

Both number and qualifications of the classes are specified by this routine. If the procedure is applied to structure a criterion, then the scale grades may be set here. The routine works by two steps which are not independent, but linked by a structure of decision logics.

Step 1 - Definition of class number and qualifications: The number, n, of classes ranges between 3 and 8 (or 12) in the present version of nTOMIC; $n=3$ would correspond to a trichotomic segmentation of the set $A(t)$ into: "acceptable or good", "not acceptable or bad", "uncertain" candidates. The max number of classes, $n=8$, is not an upper limit of the system; it has, however, been regarded as sufficient for practical cases. The "uncertain" class is always present to embrace profiles not clearly qualifiable as "good" or "bad" (for instance, so that: $d = D = 0$). The number of classes may increase with a second-order segmentation of the "uncertain" class.

The qualifications should define a preference ranking on the classes. The segments that can be defined by nTOMIC correspond to a qualification scale as follows: 3 "lower level" classes (qualified by default as: "very bad", "bad", "insufficient"); 4 "upper level" classes (qualified by default as: "sufficient", "fairly good", "good", "very good"); 1 "intermediate" class, which could be segmented into 5 sub-classes, each associated with different statements of uncertainty on the qualification of a candidate. These last sub-classes may be particularly interesting: they can point out some particular behaviour of the candidates relating to the defined reference frame, and may thus allow possible considerations on the frame itself or on the attitude to be assumed for a final decision on each candidate.

Step 2 - Definition of separation thresholds: Let's define **Aggregated Evaluation Space (AES)** the subset of the cartesian plane (d, D), defined by the relations (3). d and D denote the aggregated credibility indices as defined either by (1) and (2) or by (4) and (5) if explicitly specified. Then a segmentation model would correspond to a possible partition of AES. That could be operatively performed by the joint definition of adequate thresholds on d and D.

Considering that candidates located in the "proximity" of the axis d or D would belong to different evaluation classes pertaining, respectively, to a "potentially good" and a "potentially bad" category, while those with a different location could belong to the "uncertain" category, then a separation within each of these categories may be defined by the introduction of a couple of separation thresholds, (α, β). Such thresholds would represent specific levels of the credibilities, respectively d and D, which may enable a characterization of different policies both towards potentially acceptable candidates and potentially rejectable ones.

The separation thresholds are subjectively defined by the decision makers in such a way that:

a) For potentially acceptable candidates, $\alpha > \beta \geq 0$, with α "rather large" and β "sufficiently small". Varying the threshold levels may allow different policies of acceptance to be made explicit, with different levels of risk; thus, for instance, $\alpha = 1$ and $\beta = 0$ would correspond to a policy of accepting only "ideal" candidates, certainly and unanimously "good"; lowering the value of α would imply a certain acceptance of candidates "somehow less good" but which do not have "certainly bad" scores on any attribute if $\beta = 0$. "Fairly bad" behaviour is tolerated at the increasing of $\beta > 0$, up to a level that the decision makers estimate a limit for a still positive global judgement.

b) For potentially rejectable candidates, $\beta^1 > \alpha^1 \geq 0$, with β^1 "rather large" and α^1 "sufficiently small". Different policies of rejection may be made explicit, similarly to the acceptance case.

The AES segmentation resulting from a threshold definition could be differently interpreted by the decision makers with regard to the segment qualifications. An example of possible qualifications is shown in Fig. 2: potential candidate positions, so that $d > D$, are segmented, assuming a non-compensatory logic. Different qualifications could result with the same thresholds, by taking attitudes other than "neutral" (cf Table 1). In order to raise the max number of segmentation classes, second-order (or weak) thresholds could be defined.

Evaluative logics - The different qualifications may be deduced by following certain logics of association of the evaluative elements within an assumed policy. These elements are summarized as: marginal indices, $d_j(., b_j)$ and $D_j(c_j, .)$, for every $j \in J$; aggregated indices, $d(., b)$ and $D(c, .)$, $d^*(., b)$ and $D^*(c, .)$; separation thresholds; class number. The logics actually introduced in nTOMIC are connected in a tree structure which is not presented for lack of space.

Qualifications other than those by default may be assigned by the user. Such an assignment must fit the paths in the tree structure.

4 Implementation characteristics and Application

The system is implemented on a personal computer. The program requires the following hardware and software features: PC IBM compatible, 640 Kbytes of RAM memory, hard disk, V.G.A. graphic card and colour monitor, DOS- version 2 or following, Editor (EDIT, PE2, E, WS etc).

The program permits working on data bases that DB III Plus can deal with. Special attention has been given to the user interface; data insertion and modification are very flexible. All the potentialities offered by the program are always directly usable through the main menu so that the user is not constrained to follow complex input sequences. The potentialities of the VGA graphic card are widely exploited.

An application of the system has been performed to assign qualitative evaluations to more than one hundred written tests (Operations Research course). Some properties of the system could be tested such as: adequacy in promoting the assignment of coherent evaluations to "relatively" similar candidates; capacity to separate candidate typologies; flexibility confronted with some changes, for instance those concerning potential candidate types or the evaluation policy; ability to help in identifying suitable classes, in terms of both number and qualifications, so as to allow decisions to be congruent with the decision makers' assumptions about preference and the available candidate base. The main advantage of using nTOMIC consisted in the ability to maintain coherence in the sequential evaluation of so many tests, without a further time-consuming and stressful process of test comparison to identify distinct similarity classes. Some developments of the system are in progress.

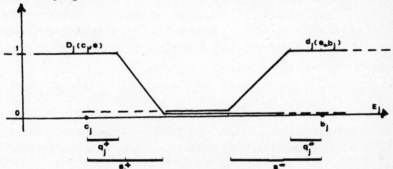

Figure 1. Marginal credibility indices.

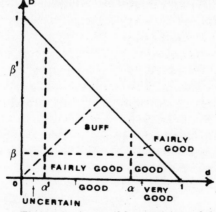

Figure 2. A possible partition of AES, $d > D$

References

Benayoun, R. and Boulier, C. (1972). *Approches rationnelles dans la gestion du personnel*, Dunod, Paris.

Hyenne, J. and Moscarola, J. (1972). Méthode trichotomique de choix multicritère, Memoire 3ème Cycle, Sciences des Organisations, Université de Paris IX Dauphine.

Le Boulanger, H. and Roy, B. (1968). L'entreprise face à la sélection et à l'orientation des projets de recherche: une méthodologie en usage dans le groupe SEMA. *Revue METRA*, vol.VII, n.4, 641-669.

Merighi, D. and Norese, M.F. (1979). Lay-out comparative evaluation (in Italian). *Atti AIRO '79*, vol.II: 67-82.

Merighi, D. (1980). An evaluation model with given reference sets (in Italian). *Ricerca Operativa*: 31-52.

Moscarola, J. and Roy, B. (1977). Procédure automatique d'examen de dossiers fondée sur une segmentation trichotomique en présence de critères multiples. *RAIRO - Recherche Opérationnelle* 2: 145-173.

Norese, M.F. and Ostanello, A. (1988). Decision Aid Process typologies and operational tools. In Centro di Ricerca IBM Pisa (ed): *Atti AIRO '88*: 661-680.

Roy, B. (1978). ELECTRE III. Un algorithme de classement fondé sur une représentation floue des préférences en présence de critères multiples. *Cahier du Centre d'Etudes de Recherche Opérationnelle*, vol.20.

Roy, B. (1981). A multicriteria analysis for trichotomic segmentation problems. In P.Nijkamp and J.Spronk (eds): *Multiple Criteria Analysis*, Gower Publ. Comp.: 245-257.

Tversky, A. (1971). Elimination by aspects : a Theory of choice. *Psychological Review* 79: 281-299.

MDS a Decision Support Software for Evaluation of Discrete Alternatives

Peter Parizek, Imrich Bertok, Tomas Vasko
Institute for Applied Cybernetics
Hanulova 5a
844 16 Bratislava, Czechoslovakia

Abstract

The aim of this contribution is to describe the latest stage of development of the software package MDS, which is a decision support system (DSS) devoted to support evaluation of finite set of alternatives which are generated by the group of experts. The qualitative properties and relations of alternatives are described in criteria-attributes and rules. System supports individual and group decision making and provides table and graphic output. The paper describes the typical decision problems to be solved with help of the package, the philosophy and main ideas of system development and computer implementation as well as some experience gained from system usage.

1 Problem description

There are two basic types of "evaluation of alternatives" problem.

The first one assumes description of the problem by using some kind of an analytical model of the situation (e.g. multiobjective linear or nonlinear programming model) which implicitly generates possible alternatives, in many cases an infinite number of them. Problems of this type require often some special mathematical knowledge from the decision maker to become familiar with the system. On the other hand, the system designer-model analyst must know all the details of the modeled system to set up all the constrains and objective functions of the model.

The second type of decision problem, on the other hand assumes, that the decision maker (or a group of them) defines a final number of alternatives and agree upon criteria and rules for their evaluation. Problems of this type occur more often, do not require special mathematical knowledge from decision makers and the decision procedure is more understandable for all participants.

The MDS represents a general software environment for solving of problems of the second type. For group decision making problems a person called manager or moderator of the procedure is responsible for running the system with some special duties devoted to him. In individual decision problems the decision maker runs the system in the role of manager. The procedure of treating a decision with the help of MDS consists of following stages:

1. Problem definition

   - setting up the group of experts and their voting power (duty of the manager)
   - setting up the alternatives
   - setting up the attributes and their ranges
   - selection of appropriate methodology for evaluation of attribute weights, ranking of alternatives, aggregation, disagreement analysis and processing the rules

2. Definition of the model

   - evaluation of attributes (depends on methodology)
   - setting up the rules
   - aggregation of individual settings (manager)
   - disagreement analysis (duty of the manager)

3. Evaluation of alternatives

   - setting up the values of alternatives which are not due to expert evaluation (duty of the manager)
   - setting up the values for alternatives according to other criteria
   - aggregation of individual settings (manager)

4. Results

   - final ranking of alternatives I (with respect to criteria)
   - final ranking of alternatives II (with respect to rules)
   - final ranking of alternatives III (with respect to both criteria and rules)
   - analysis of individual and group results
   - display and printouts of results

The steps which are due to the manager in stages 1., 2., and 3. are usually performed only in case of group decision making. The manager, who is responsible for running the procedure, has access to all data; other participants of the expert evaluation have limited rights to access the data (i.e. they cannot look at the evaluation data of other members of the decision committee). Therefore the computer implementation has to provide different facilities for the manager and other members.

2   The main ideas of system development

The all-purpose nature of MDS is characterized by the following properties:

- it enables a simultaneous solution of several independent decision-making problems which are freely organized into groups

- the system is open towards the used methods, which means that an unlimited number of them may be included in the system

- the individual algorithms — methods may be implemented in any programming language and they are not a direct part of the shell of the system.

The system is hierarchically divided into two levels:

a. — level of programs $P(1), \ldots, P(p)$
b. — level of goals $G(1), \ldots, G(g)$

Under the term "program" we understand complex areas of evaluation, i.e. areas managed by the same person covering a list of decision problems. Every program $P(i)$ may incorporate any number of goals.

Under the term "goal" we understand a concrete evaluation problem to be solved to reach the goal, i.e. to find the appropriate alternative from the proposed set. The goal is characterized by attributes (criteria) $C(1), \ldots, C(c)$, eventually rules $R(1), \ldots, R(r)$, whereas alternatives $A(1), \ldots, A(a)$ are the objects of evaluation. Further characteristics of the goal may if necessary be created in the system with the help of special methods. Attributes together with rules describe the characteristic of the goal. The selection of appropriate attributes is made by experts $E(1), \ldots, E(e)$ or by the manager of the decision process. From the point of view of the decision-making process we divide the attributes into two groups depending on their values which may be either objectively measurable (which means they may be numerically expressed and input beforehand, e.g. technical parameters, numbers, weight etc.) or they may be the object of evaluation by experts.

By the means of rules experts express general characteristics of the goal, which can not be expressed by the values of attributes or if this makes considerable difficulties. Rules serve to define borders, limitations, eventually relations between attributes. Rules are of the IF-THEN type, where the conditional and active part consist of attributes or some numerical values combined into relational expressions. Every rule has an allocated weight, which influences the final evaluation of alternatives. The rules are discussed and set up by experts together or by the manager of the procedure. Every goal may be reached by any number of alternatives.

The aim of the MDS is to specify the optimal ranking of alternatives with the help of the knowledge expressed in attributes and rules, in their weights and in the methods of multi-criteria evaluation which process the common meaning of the group of experts.

Experts from the given field participate in the definition of the decision-making task and its solution. Their responsibility is to choose the attributes and general rules for the given goal, to evaluate the weights of the attributes and to evaluate the scores of alternatives according to attributes which are due to expert evaluation.

The standard version of the system contains some basic methods for all parts of evaluation with necessary supporting facilities such as printouts, graphic outputs for all kinds of results, etc. The shell implementation enables to include into the system several types of methods for evaluation of weights of attributes (i.e. metfessels allocation, pairwise comparison methods, aspiration level methods), different types and approaches for final ranking of alternatives (utility function methods, achievement function methods, pairwise comparison type methods, risk assessment methods) as well as several ways of evaluation of rules and different ways of aggregation of individual assessments (e.g. average value with or without extremes). The standard version contains the Metfessel's allocation method and the Scale allocation method for evaluation of attribute weights, later the Basic alternative method and Linear utility function method for final ranking of alternatives and forward chaining approach for evaluation of rules and both types of aggregation mentioned above.

The linear utility function method has been partially modified within MDS. Aspiration and reservation values have been introduced for all attributes. The evaluation algorithm takes as upper and lover limit for computing of partial linear utility functions the aspiration and reservation values, except the maximal and minimal value reached by alternatives.

The new idea of MDS is the introduction of rules as a tool for representation of expert knowledge of the problem. Formulation and definition of rules is fully menu driven using the set of attributes, several types of relational operators and predefined numerical values. There are two possible ways of using the rules for final evaluation. They depend on two different approaches for the final ranking. We may either aggregate individual evaluation and then compute the final ranking or compute individual ranking for each expert and then aggregate them for the final result.

1. The alternatives are ranked according to the experts' opinion and a method used for final multicriterial ranking. The particular result of this procedure are aggregated evaluations $V(i,j)$ of each alternative i according to each attribute j. The evaluation by rules feature uses these values to check the rules. The rules in general set up a relation required between some values $V(i,j)$. The weight of the rule k, $r(k)$ is a number $0 < r(k) \leq 100$. It is set up within the definition of rules procedure and is a duty of the manager. The quantitative evaluation of the relation expressed by rule k is a function $f(k)$. The value of $f(k)$ is higher if the level of fulfilling of the rule is better. The function f may be a constant, or exponential function or a composition of both. The final evaluation of alternatives is computed as the mean value of evaluation by attributes and evaluation by rules.

2. The rules are defined by the manager, but the weights of rules are set up together with weights of attributes. Evaluation of weights is then a common step for both attributes and rules. After evaluation of alternatives according all attributes, the rules are evaluated with respect to individual evaluations of $V(i,j)$ for each expert. The result of evaluation of a rule is a value $f(k)$, where f is the same function as in the case 1. This value is then included into evaluation of a particular alternative in the same way as evaluations according to attributes within the procedure for individual ranking of alternatives. Individual assessments are finally aggregated for

common group ranking. This approach is suitable in cases if an analysis of individual assessments is required.

The first approach of aggregation and ranking is implemented in the standard version of MDS.

3 PC implementation ideas

The MDS system is a heterogeneous system, as far as the programming tools are concerned, which means that various parts may be programmed in different programming languages. The unifying environment is formed by the system databases of dBASE III format and by two communication modules programmed under the database system CLIP-PER. All further modules, programmed in different programming languages, are called from the communication modules with the use of the command RUN which is a part of the CLIPPER language. The cooperation of the various modules takes place through the databases. The methods of reading and writing these databases are known, as their structure is described in dBASE III+ manual.

There were several reasons to form such a heterogeneous system, built from databases and independent routines:

- an effort to process data with the help of a professional database system, e.g. CLIP-PER, so that it would not be necessary to undergo the time-consuming programming of subroutines in some of the common programming languages to obtain functions such as editing of data, seeking for data or data retrieval. This approach ensures some degree of comfort in the system with the possibility of archivation, copying, import from text files, eventually employing data from other professional software packages which recognize the dBASE III+ data structure

- an aim to create a communication environment with a modular concept to enable the use of various subroutines written in any programming language. These subroutines may include the algorithms or supporting subroutines, e.g. for graphic output.

- a further required property of the system was a possibility of increasing the number of employed methods. By complying these requirements an all-purpose system was created which actually forms an environment for the tasks of multi-criteria selection of discrete alternatives.

The standard shell data structures of the system (dBase III+ databases) contain the resulting data of the used methods, individual methods may require using additional data files

The system is implemented on the IBM PC–XT/AT with 640KB RAM. The communication modules are able to operate independently on the used video controller, the modules for graphic output depend on the used software package, which must respect the configuration of the video controller. In regard of the size of the whole system and in order to increase operation speed the use of a hard disk is recommended. The maximum number of attributes and experts is 1020. The number of programs, goals, rules and alternatives is limited by the maximum database size in the CLIPPER database system, i.e. approximately one milliard records. From the above mentioned it is clear, that the size and number of solved tasks is practically limited only by the disk memory size of the computer.

A special graphic representation package has been developed to represent all types of results providing 2D and 3D bar charts, line and pie graphs.

4 Experience and case studies

The preliminary phases of MDS development were initialized by the need of a DSS system for management of research and development. Thus the real life implementation started in the problems of R&D planning. One of the case studies required ranking of project proposals for implementation of CAD/CAM hardware in various organizations and companies throughout the country. As the government supported financially buying of large number of working stations, it was necessary to evaluate these projects according to government's requirements (attributes) given ahead. Here was nothing to be evaluated by experts (attributes were clearly described and evaluated using quantitative values and scales), so this was a single user problem with up to 15 attributes and over one hundred alternatives. There were no major differences between the weights of attributes and no rules or further limits for evaluation were given. The result was used by the Slovak Commission for Planning, Research and Development as a background for distribution of working stations for CAD/CAM applications. The case study proved the system's ability to solve simple problems with large number of alternatives.

Another problem area for which MDS have been used was selection of appropriate computer technology for an information and database center. This was a typical group decision problem with 12 experts, 10 attributes and 4 alternatives. there were a few quantitative attributes related to price and performance, all other attributes were due to expert evaluation. Some IF-THEN rules relating the price and performance and simple rules making limits for price were also included. As there were two naturally divided groups of experts who preferred their special technology, the procedure of evaluation of attribute weights led to a high level of disagreement for some important attributes. Running the ranking procedure without the feedback information of disagreement analysis caused huge complains of one group of experts about manipulation of results. Everything was understood when we used the disagreement analysis facility of the system. This example showed the high importance of disagreement analysis for attributes and the necessary feedback of this information. It also showed the power of evaluation according to rules. MDS is also introduced in some planning and decision activities in large industrial companies. It was offered as a computer aided tool for industrial planning within the UNIDO/UNIDPLAN program with a special focus on environmental impacts of industrial planning. It is expected that the basic version will be in case of special needs enlarged with additional methodology together with expertise resulting also in setting up of attributes and rules.

5 Summary

Such a broad-concept, open system with a modular structure offers a wide variety of practical use. For specific applications it is possible to create versions which are exactly "tailored to suit the needs" for one or several problems in a short span of time but nevertheless with all comfort required for software products of this kind, which also has a big importance from the commercial point of view. A combination of this system with an real expert system is expected in near future which will further improve the quality of this system and will enable a wider application in the field of selection of discrete alternatives. At present a library of standard methods is being created and a knowledge base for the selection of appropriate methods for MDS applications is being built. A first user version of MDS with standard methods described above is now available. It is a well documented English version with a user manual.

References

Fotr, J. and Pisek, M. (1986). Exact Methods for Economical Decisions. Academia, Prague.

LIGHTYEAR, (1984). The Decision Support Software. Lightyear, Inc.

Lewandowski, A., Johnson, S. and Wierzbicki, A. P. (1986). A Prototype Selection Committee Decision Analysis and Support System, SCDASS: theoretical background and computer implementation. Working Paper WP–86–27, IIASA, Laxenburg, Austria.

Lewandowski, A. and Wierzbicki, A. P. (1987). Interactive Decision Support Systems — the Case of Discrete Alternatives for Committee Decision Making. Working Paper WP–87–38, IIASA, Laxenburg, Austria.

Lewandowski, A. and Wierzbicki, A. P. (1988). Aspiration Based Decision Analysis and Support, Part I.: Theoretical and Methodological Backgrounds. Working Paper WP–88–03, IIASA, Laxenburg, Austria.

Parizek, P. (1988). Planning and Management of Research and Development as a Multicriteria Decision Problem. A contribution submitted for the VIIIth International MCDM Conference, Manchester, UK.

Parizek, P. and Vasko, T. (1987). MDS — an Interactive System for Multicriteria Evaluation of Alternatives — a Prototype Version, (short announcement). In: Methodology and Software for Interactive Decision Support, A. Lewandowski, I. Stanchev (eds.), Proceedings from the International Workshop held in Albena, Bulgaria, Springer-Verlag.

Parizek, P. and Vasko, T. (1988). Computer Aided Decision Support for Planning and Management of Research and Development. Proceedings of the International Workshop on Interactive Decision Support Systems, Yalta, USSR.

Sprague, R. H. and Carlson, C. (eds.) (1982). Building Effective Decision Support Systems. Prentice Hall, Inc.

Decision Support in Artificial Intelligence Environment

Ahti Salo and Raimo P. Hämäläinen

Systems Analysis Laboratory
Helsinki University of Technology
Otakaari 1 M, 02150 Espoo

Abstract

This paper discusses the potential of artificial intelligence technology in supporting decision making. Special attention is given to the early phases of decision making, particularly problem structuring. In this context the role of decision analytic methods is emphasized, since these methods have been developed to help the decision maker address problems with no evident structure. Finally a prototype system containing three decision analytic tools is described.

1   Introduction

Due to the rapid evolution of new computer technology and with the increasing number of reports of successful applications, artificial intelligence (AI) is now acknowledged as an appropriate approach to solving problems in business and management (Leinweber, 1988). Typical AI applications employ knowledge representation schemes such as rules and semantic networks to capture expert knowledge (Winston, 1984). This knowledge is then applied to tackle problems in the domain of the encoded expertise. The solution is in many applications obtained by reasoning along similar lines as the expert. In order to attain high performance it is crucial that expert knowledge is carefully elicited and implemented.

This paper points out that the technology that has evolved with AI provides new opportunities also for implementing tools which do not a priori contain expert knowledge (see also Lehner, Probus and Donnell, 1985). Such tools are common for instance in the field of decision analysis (DA), where the purpose of the tools is to provide the decision maker (DM) with a framework for structuring and analyzing decision problems (Winterfeldt and Edwards, 1986). In the course of the modelling process the DM must carefully consider relevant aspects of the problem from different perspectives, whereby he learns to undestand the problem more clearly. Ultimately the process aims at improving the quality of the DM's decisions.

In decision analytic tools it is particularly important that the user-interface be clearly structured, because the DM himself is in charge of problem structuring and analysis. Conceptual clarity and ease of use also help to minimize the time needed for learning the operation of the tools and encourage the DM to use them. In tools for DA domain knowledge cannot be encoded in advance. Consequently complex knowledge representation schemes are not as useful as they are in large-scale AI applications.

AI workstations provide advanced programming facilitites, which are helpful in building tools for DA. With these facilities it is possible to implement tools where the user can interactively construct and modify models in a given framework. Since no single framework is suitable for all problems it is desirable to have several tools available, each providing the DM with a different framework. He can then choose among the different alternative ways of approaching the problem, or perhaps analyze the same problem with more than one tool.

In the sequel those aspects of the AI technology that make the technology particularly amenable for implementing tools for DA are emphasized. The rest of the paper describes a prototype system developed to test some of the ideas in a real life application.

2 Artificial intelligence environment

In this paper the term AI environment is used to refer to the types of advanced programming tools that have previously been available on AI workstations only. For example, on an AI environment tailored reasoning mechanisms and knowledge representation schemes can be utilized to describe the problem domain. User-interaction is often superior to that of other computers, featuring multiple windows and mouse-driven menus on a large screen. Several programs can be run concurrently, and the user can easily switch between the different applications.

From the programmer's point of view AI workstations have several advantages over other computing environments. Programs can be developed more quickly; each new piece of code can be tested without delay because no compilation is required. For AI workstations there are several object-oriented languages available, which provide modularity and reusability of code (Shefik and Bobrow, 1986). These characteristics are particularly helpful in the design of user-interfaces. The object-oriented approach is also suitable for creating a robust framework for large programs so that these can be modified and extended with less effort (Ramamoorthy and Sheu, 1988). As a result AI workstations are especially appropriate for development by prototyping, where revised versions of the system must be quickly available.

However, the AI workstations have some notable drawbacks, too. The operating systems and the programming tools differ markedly from the environments that programmers are usually accustomed to. Without an educational background in knowledge engineering a fair amount of time and effort is needed before the workstation can be used effectively.

In many cases applications running on an AI workstation cannot be easily converted into other computer environments. Moreover, AI workstations are expensive in comparison to other computer environments such as PCs, especially if the costs incurred by the need to convert the code are accounted for. In view of these observations, AI workstations should be reserved only for applications where the potential cost savings are significant and where the powerful features of the AI environment are truly needed to solve the problem.

3   Decision analytic tools

Decision analysis provides a tested methodology for problem structuring and analysis, which is still relatively unknown to DSS practitioners (Stabell, 1986). Specifically it addresses problems where several noncommensurate factors must be considered. The focus in DA is on the process where the DM structures and analyzes the problem in a suitable framework. During this process he must consider what the key factors in the decision making situation are and how these relate to each other. The DM must state his values and assumptions explicitly, whereby he can gain additional insights into the problem (Hämäläinen and Karjalainen, 1989).

The decision analytic approach to problem structuring results in a model which captures the DM's knowledge about the problem. Building such a model is in fact a way of encoding expert knowledge (Lehner, Probus and Donnel, 1985).

The choice between different methods, not only those of DA, depends on the problem characteristics. A subjective preference model is a good choice in problems where values are important or when objective information is either impossible or hard to come by. What-if-simulations are helpful in semi-structured problems where parts of the problem can be quantitatively modelled. The optimization techiniques of operations research are applicable to problems with a well understood structure (Smart, Vertinsky and Vertinsky, 1984; Fry and Spiguel, 1986).

4   A prototype of a decision maker's workstation

The system contains three decision analytic tools and a large domain specific tool for supporting the financial planning of a telecommunications service. In this paper the focus is on the decision analytic tools. An account of the domain specific tool can be found in Salo and Hämäläinen, 1989. All tools were implemented on a Xerox 1186 AI workstation with the Loops-object-oriented programming environment using InterLisp-D.

4.1   Graphic modelling tool

Many of the functional features of the graphic modelling tool are similar to those found in advanced spreadsheet packages. With this tool, the user can interactively build quantitative models for simulation purposes. These models can be used to study how the values of different variables would evolve given the user's assumptions about the underlying structure of the model and the initial values of the variables.

In the graphic modelling tool, the model is visualized as a directed graph, where the arrows show the dependencies between the variables. For example, an arrow from variable X to variable Y indicates that the value of Y at any period depends on the value of X. Thus the graphical display gives the user an overview of the structure of the model, so that he can more easily understand the interdependencies between the variables (Pracht, 1986).

The quantitative dependencies between the variables are specified as a set of equations where variables are referred to by their proper names. The equations

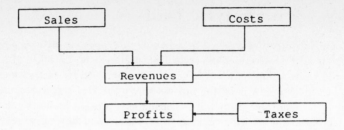

Figure 1: Visualizing a model as a directed graph

are presented to the user in an easy-to-read format showing how the value of each variable is calculated from the values of the preceding period.

There is a connection between the graphic modelling tool and the domain specific tool. In this sense the different tools are not separate from each other, as data can be transferred from one tool to another in order to derive further decision support.

4.2 Hierarchical preference analysis

The analytical hierarchy process (AHP) is a method for decomposing a problem into its constituents and deriving weights reflecting the DMs preferences (Saaty, 1980; Golden, Wasil and Levy, 1989). In AHP the relevant factors for the decision are organized as a hierarchy, where the topmost element stands for the overall goals of the decision, and the elements below it represent the different subgoals. The subgoals may be further decomposed until the hierarchy is a sufficiently detailed description of the decision problem.

The tool for hierarchical preference analysis has the following novel features. First, the large screen of the workstation permits the user to view the entire hierarchy (say, upto 5 levels) at a time. In the display the lines connecting elements on adjacent level are of varying thickness. The thicker the line connecting the two elements, the greater the local weight of the lower level element at the upper level element. This feature helps to visualize the flow of weight in the hierarchy, since the user can easily get an overview of which factors are the most important ones (see Fig. 2).

Second, the tool for hierarchical preference analysis allows the user to enter local weights directly via distributions. Each distribution consists of a set of columns showing the local weights of the lower level elements (see Fig. 3). The user can modify the heights of the columns with the mouse, whereafter the tool automatically computes updated results. In this sense the tools supports sensitivity analysis as well.

4.3 Preference analysis via value functions

The third decision analytic tool is aimed at a user who is interested in investigating the likely choices of independent DMs given assumptions about their preferences. For example, a vendor might want to know how the different customer groups view the product he is selling in contrast to the competing products.

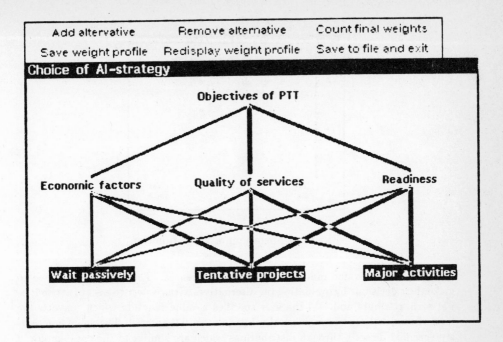

Figure 2: An example of a hierarchy

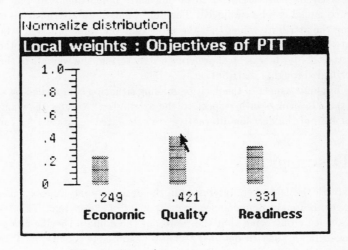

Figure 3: A distribution for specifying local weights

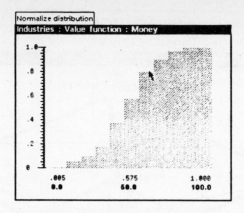

Figure 4: Specifying a value function

The tool uses value functions to model preferences. The DMs are assumed to make their decisions by evaluating the alternatives with respect to a set of attributes. For each attribute and DM the user specifies a value function which converts the level of an attribute to a numerical value between 0.0 and 1.0. The value functions are specified directly through distributions which are similar to the ones employed in the tool for hierarchical preference analysis. For more on value functions, see e.g. Winterfeldt and Edwards, 1986.

The attributes are assumed to be mutually independent so that an additive preference model can be employed. The final value of an alternative is obtained by summing the attribute values (i.e. the value that the value function attaches to the attribute level of an alternative) multiplied by the relative weight of the attribute. Like in the tool for hierarchical preference structuring, the weights of the attributes are specified through a distribution.

The dynamic aspect of the decision making situation is modelled by allowing the alternatives to evolve with respect to the attributes. Results showing the overall value of each of the decision alternative are calculated separately for each period.

5 Discussion

Even though the DMs were interested in the decision analytic tools, they were still more eager to use the domain specific component of the system. This tendency can be explained by observing that the results of the domain specific component were based on a large body of detailed technical knowledge. Thus the DMs probably considered the results given by the domain specific component more credible than those of the other tools. The DMs were also already familiar with the concepts and terms of the domain specific components. The decision analytic tools, on the other hand, required the DM to learn new terminology and concepts before providing any results.

From the point of view of implementing DA tools, the AI workstation proved to be an asset in several ways. Previous versions of the tools could be modified

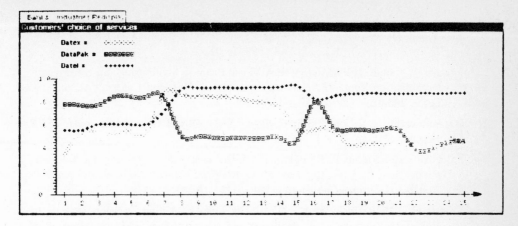

Figure 5: Result showing the value of the alternatives over time

quickly, which helped to keep the expert interested in the development of the tools. Even though the tools were designed to accomplish different tasks, large portions of code, especially code pertaining to the user- interface, could be shared among the different tools. The object-oriented approach made it easy to logically organize the structure the programs. In summary, the experiences acquired in the project gave support for the purported advantages of the AI technology.

With the cost of hardware and software declining, it seems that programming tools for the the development of tools such as the ones we have described will soon be available on other computing environments as well. This trend will in part resolve the question whether or not dedicated AI technology should be relied on to develop DSSs, since powerful PCs will in time provide most of the capabilities now found on AI workstations only. At the moment, the falling sales of AI workstations can be seen as a sign of this trend.

References

Fry, James and Claudio P. Spiguel (1986). A Model-Based Information System: A Framework and Architecture. *Proc of the 19th Annual Hawaii International Conference on Systems Sciences*, 416-424.

Golden, Bruce L, Edward A. Wasil and Doug E. Levy (1989). Applications of the Analytic Hierarchy Process: A Categorized Annotated Bibliography. In Golden, Wasil and Harker (eds): *The Analytic Hierarchy Process: Applications and Studies*, Springer-Verlag, Heidelberg, 37-58.

Hämäläinen, Raimo P. and Risto Karjalainen (1989). Structuring the Risks of Energy Production.*Proc Multiobjective Problems of Mathematical Programming Conference*, Yalta, USSR, Oct 26 - Nov 2, 1988 Springer-Verlag (to appear).

Lehner, Paul E. , Matthew A. Probus and Michael E. Donnell (1985). Building Decision Aids: Exploiting the Synergy Between Decision Analysis and Artificial Intelligence. *IEEE Trans on Systems, Man and Cybernetics*, vol. 15, no.

2, 469-474.

Leinweber, David (1988). Knowledge-Based Systems for Financial Applications. *IEEE Expert*, vol. 3, no. 3, Fall 1988, 18-31.

Pracht, William E. (1986). GISMO: A Visual Problem Structuring and Knowledge-Organization Tool. *IEEE Trans on Systems, Man and Cybernetics*, vol. 16, no. 2, 265-270.

Ramamoorthy, C. V. and Phillip C. Sheu (1988). Object-Oriented Systems. *IEEE Expert*, vol.3, no. 3, Fall 1988, 9-15.

Salo, Ahti and Raimo P. Hämäläinen. A Decision Aid for Supporting Telecommunications Investments. *Proc of the 1989 IEEE International Conference on Systems, Man and Cybernetics*, Vol I, 115-118.

Smart, C. , I. Vertinsky and P. Vertinsky (1984). Aiding Decision Making in Uncertain Environments: Problems and Prescriptions. *INFOR - Journal of the Canadian operational research society*, vol. 22, no. 2, 141-154.

Stefik, Mark and Daniel E. Bobrow (1986). Object-Oriented Programming; Themes and Variations, *AI Magazine*, Vol. 6 No. 4, 40-64.

Winston, Patrick H. (1984). *Artificial Intelligence*, 2nd ed. Addison-Wesley Publishing Company Inc., Reading, MA.

Winterfeldt, Detlof von and Ward Edwards (1986). *Decision Analysis and Behavioral Research.* Cambridge University Press, Cambridge, 604 p.

A Hierarchical Multiobjective Approach to Project Management

M.Grazia Speranza
Dipartimento di Matematica e Informatica
Università di Udine
Via Zanon, 6 - I-33100 Udine

Carlo Vercellis *
Dipartimento di Economia e Produzione
Politecnico di Milano
Piazza L. da Vinci, 32 - I-20133 Milano

Abstract

We propose a multiobjective model-based methodology for nonpreemptive multi-project management problems, based on a hierarchical two-stage decomposition of the planning and scheduling process. The performance criteria consist of multiple objectives: the net present value, which includes investment costs and operating costs, revenues and penalties for late completion; the service levels, expressing the agreement between the completion times of the different projects and the customer needs. The resulting models and algorithms are incorporated into a decision support system which is thought to assist the planners in understanding the interrelations among the allocation of resources, the timing of the different activities, the cash flows, the slack in usage of the available resources.

1   Introduction

Careful planning is generally regarded as one of the most critical factors in determining the success of companies operating in the project business. Planning activities range from the tactical level — in which milestones and due dates have to be determined, along with the allocation of limited resources, for a number of projects within the same organization, to the operational level — in which the scheduling of specific activities must be established in light of an appropriate trade-off between time, cost and resource usage.

This paper deals with the planning process in a multi-project environment, and gives particular emphasis to the methodologies for achieving a high degree of integration between tactical and operational stages of the decision process.

---

*Partially supported by Project "Construction Building" of the National Research Council.

In the project management practice, planners are generally concerned with a number of different decision criteria, often contrasting among each other. The intrinsic multi-objective nature of the decision processes involved in project management emerges with particular evidence in conjunction with the tactical planning phases, over medium to long term time horizons. Hence, this conflict of objectives appears particularly relevant in the early stages of analysis of the project plan, when establishing milestones for bidding proposals and allocating scarce resources among different projects or subprojects. Indeed, even if the productivity performance is of major concern to most project managers, other factors, such as the service time to the customer and the reliability in meeting the promised delivery dates, should be explicitly taken into account.

Furthermore, when dealing with tactical planning analysis, project managers are mostly interested in understanding how the controllable key decisions, such as timing, costs and resources usage for the different activities, do interact in determining the resulting performances in terms of productivity, service and reliability. This means that, in general, every activity can be performed in one among several alternative *modes*, each one corresponding to a different combination of time duration, cost and absorbtion of resources. Thus, planners are requested to determine, for each activity, the most appropriate mode of accomplishment, in order to obtain an acceptable level of performance in terms of the multiple conflicting objectives.

It turns out that the resulting planning activity, considered in its whole complexity, is overwhelmingly difficult to manage, involving the interactions among several key decisions, such as the allocation of limited resources among different projects or subprojects competing for their usage, the determination of milestones, the attribution of the modes of realization to the various activities, as well as the timing of these latter.

At least in principle, one might draw a mathematical model representing variables, objectives and constraints of the planning process as an almost straightforward exercise. Yet, the multiobjective nature of the resulting model makes it ill-defined, and not amenable to standard optimization paradigms. Furthermore, even if a single criterion model can be derived by giving higher priority to a specific objective, the large dimensions determined by realistic sized multi-project problems would put the model far beyond the boundaries of computational tractability, at least by means of currently available mathematical programming techniques.

In front to the complexity of the outlined decision processes, the large majority of models proposed in the OR literature, as well as the available commercial software for project planning and scheduling, tend to disregard the multiobjective character of the planning phases of project management. One exception is represented by (Slowinski, 1981), in which, however, the attention is confined to the case of preemptive scheduling problems. On the other side, several papers have been devoted to nonpreemptive project scheduling problems with limited resources, addressing issues of model formulation (Balas, 1970), of computational complexity (Blazewicz et al., 1983), of exact (Christofides et al., 1987), (Davis and Heidorn, 1971), (Doersch and Patterson, 1977), (Gorenstein, 1972), (Patterson and Huber, 1974), (Patterson, 1984), (Pritsker et al., 1969), (Talbot and Patterson, 1978) and approximate (Davis and Patterson, 1975), (Norbis and Mac Gregor Smith, 1988), (Patterson, 1976), (Russel, 1986) solution algorithms. However, very limited attention has been paid to the analysis of the case in which activities can be performed in alternative modes, a notable exception being represented by (Talbot, 1982). With respect to the planning time horizon, a few authors, such as those maximizing the net present value (Doersch and Patterson 1977), (Elmaghraby and Herroelen, 1988), (Russell, 1970), (Russell, 1986), seem to adhere, more or less explicitly, to the tactical level of analysis. Most of the others, generally aimed at the minimization of the completion time, seem to place their methodologies at the operational level. There not exist, to our knowledge, any effort to develope a structured quantitative approach addressing the issue of integration between the two stages of the planning process.

To partially overcome these limitations, in this paper we propose a multiobjective model-based methodology for nonpreemptive multi-project management problems, which results in a hierarchical two-stage decomposition of the planning and scheduling process. The performance criteria consist of multiple objectives: the net present value, which includes investment costs and operating costs, revenues and penalties for late completion; the service levels, i.e. the agreement of the completion times of the different projects with the customer needs. The resulting models and algorithms are incorporated into a decision support system which is thought to assist the planners in understanding the interrelations among the allocation of resources, the timing of the different activities, the cash flows, the slack in usage of the available resources.

The methodology we propose hierarchically decomposes the project planning decision process in two stages, to a large extent corresponding to the tactical and operational levels of analysis. Decisions at both levels do interact by means of an explicit coordination scheme: at the higher level, decisions are influenced by an approximate evaluation of the future effects determined at the lower level by current choices; on the other hand, when higher level decisions have been taken, they influence future decisions through the constraints incorporated into lower level models. Our approach seems to achieve a number of advantages. For example, by attributing different objectives to the two stages, it has the effect that the resulting models at each stage are in a well-posed single objective optimization form, and that their sizes are significantly reduced with respect to the size of the planning model considered in its entirety. Furthermore, this decomposition scheme is likely to reflect the temporal and organizational division of the decision process within a company operating in the project business. More specifically, the first stage corresponds to determining due dates for the projects or subprojects and allocating the limited resources among them, with the productivity objective dominating the other criteria. The second stage deals with determining the actual modes and timing of the activities within each project or subproject, with the service level as the main objective.

In our model resources are grouped into three categories, which reflect the possibility that a resource is constrained on a period by period basis, or on the whole lifetime of the project, or both. Activities can be performed according to alternative modes, corresponding to different combinations of resource consumption, cost and time duration. Starting from an *activity on nodes* network representation of the multi-project, it will be assumed that a set of node-disjoint subnetworks can be identified by the planner, corresponding to individual projects or specific subprojects. In general, each of these projects or subprojects refers to its own organizational unit, which is responsible for the resources allocated to it. Moreover, it acts as an accounting unit, with associated start-up costs for investments, revenues corresponding to due dates milestones, penalties for delayed finish. Referring to the hierarchical decomposition of the decision process, the tactical stage of analysis considers an aggregated network whose nodes correspond to entire projects or subprojects, and are therefore regarded as *macro-activities*. These macro-activities, in turn, will be disaggregated in elementary activities during the subsequent stage, corresponding to the operational analysis.

2   The multiobjective resource constrained project planning problem

In the Introduction we have been referring indifferently to projects and subprojects as the macro-activities of the planning process at the tactical level. In order to simplify the description, in the sequel of the paper only the term project will be used.

We will consider a discrete-time model, in which the integer T denotes the total length of the time horizon, measured in a suitable time unit — which in most cases ranges between the week and the month.

In this paper, a project s will consist of a given set V_s of activities, on which a partial order relation, denoted by $\prec$, is defined. We say that $i \prec k$ whenever activity i must be finished before starting activity k. The set V_s includes two dummy activities, b_s and e_s, representing the start and the end of the project, respectively. An activity-on-node representation of a given project relies on the definition of an oriented acyclic graph $G_s = (V_s, P_s)$ in which the set of vertices V_s is identified with the set of activities of project s. An arc $(i, k) \in P_s$ exists whenever $i \prec k$ for the corresponding activities.

In order to be performed, each activity requires the usage of a given amount of specific resources, whose availability over time is generally limited for the entire program. In particular, it will be assumed that a set of renewable resources $\mathcal{R}$ is given, such that an amount W_r of resource $r \in \mathcal{R}$ is available in each time period. In addition, a set of non-renewable resources $\mathcal{N}$ is given as well, such that the amount Q_r of resource $r \in \mathcal{N}$ is available over the whole life-time of the program. The unit cost of resource $r \in \{\mathcal{R} \cup \mathcal{N}\}$ will be denoted by c_r^U. In order to model situations in which the availability of a resource involves a fixed cost, to each unused unit of a resource $r \in \mathcal{R}$ will be inputted a cost c_r^N.

We will assume that each activity i can be carried out in n_i modes, each mode corresponding to different resource requirements and to a different processing time. Thus, due to the previous assumptions relative to the cost of the resources, it follows that different modes of accomplishment correspond also to different costs for each activity. Specifically, if activity i is carried out in mode j, an amount w_{ijrt} of resource $r \in \mathcal{R}$ is consumed at time t, where the time index is computed relative to the starting time of activity i. The corresponding amount q_{ijr} of a nonrenewable resource $r \in \mathcal{N}$ is consumed by the execution of activity i according to mode j, irrespective to the time dimension. The corresponding duration of activity i carried out according to mode j will be denoted by d_{ij}. It is further assumed that the absorbtion of resource $r \in \mathcal{N}$ over time is constant, which means that if activity i is performed in mode j the consumption of resource $r \in \mathcal{N}$ at each discrete time interval is given by q_{ijr}/d_{ij}. Relative to the dummy activities, there is associated a single mode, denoted as 1, which does not require any resource, and whose durations are given by $d_{b_s 1} = 0$ and $d_{e_s 1} = 0$.

Each project is part of a program constituted by a set S of projects, whose cardinality will be denoted by S. The projects are interrelated and influence each other in two ways: at a general level, they are in competition for the use of the limited resources $\{\mathcal{R} \cup \mathcal{N}\}$; moreover, at least in specific cases, they can be related by a partial order relation. We say that project s precedes project z whenever $e_s \prec b_z$. The program can be represented by an oriented acyclic graph $G = (V, P)$. The set of vertices $V = \cup_{s \in S} V_s \cup b \cup e$ includes two dummy vertices b and e which represent the start and end of the entire program. Again, these dummy activities have a single mode, denoted as 1, and time durations $d_{b1} = 0$ and $d_{e1} = 0$. The set of arcs $P = \cup_{s \in S} P_s \cup P_S$ is composed by the precedence arcs P_s for each project $s \in S$, and by additional arcs P_S which are introduced for three different reasons. First, there are arcs expressing precedence relationships between projects. Such an arc $(e_s, b_z) \in P_S$ exists whenever project s precedes project z. Then, there are arcs connecting the beginning and the end of some projects to the dummy nodes b and e, respectively: an arc $(b, b_s) \in P_S$ exists whenever project s is not preceded by any other project and analogously an arc $(e_s, e) \in P_S$ exists whenever project s does not precede any other project.

Two different types of deadline can be associated to each project s. If a project s will not be completed by h_s (penalty deadline), a penalty p_s will be paid, while if project s will be completed by a_s (revenue deadline), a revenue f_s will be gained. The amount of the investment for project s will be denoted by c_s^I and is independent from the modes of the activities of the project. It is assumed that such amount has to be paid at the beginning of the project.

The solution of the project planning and scheduling problem corresponds to determining, for each activity, the mode of execution and the starting time. In order to formulate the constraints in linear form, it is convenient to introduce the following binary decision variables:

$$x_{ijt} = \begin{cases} 1 & \text{if activity } i \text{ starts at time } t \text{ in mode } j \\ 0 & \text{otherwise.} \end{cases}$$

As already mentioned in the Introduction, in this planning problem multiple criteria appear of interest. The multiobjective problem G can be formulated as follows, where two different types of criteria — the net present value of the whole program and the duration of each project — will be explicitly considered.

(O1) *Criterion type 1*: The net present value represents the most relevant criterion of optimality for the planning problem over a medium to long term time horizon. In particular, an appropriate timing of the cash flows appears to be a critical factor of success in connection to a wide typology of projects, such as those relative to the construction building industry. In the sequel, we will denote by α the discount rate.

The variable coefficients of the net present value criterion have the following expressions

$$C_s^R = \sum_{t=1}^{a_s} f_s x_{e_s 1 t}$$

$$C_s^P = \sum_{t=h_s+1}^{T} p_s x_{e_s 1 t}$$

$$C_{irt}^{UN} = \begin{cases} \sum_{j=1}^{n_i} \sum_{\tau=t-d_{ij}+1}^{t} w_{ijr(t-\tau+1)} x_{ij\tau}(c_r^U - c_r^N) & \text{if } r \in \mathcal{R} \\ \\ \sum_{j=1}^{n_i} \sum_{\tau=t-d_{ij}+1}^{t} q_{ijr} x_{ij\tau}(c_r^U - c_r^N)/d_{ij}) & \text{if } r \in \mathcal{N} \end{cases}$$

where C_s^R is the positive cash flow due to the revenues, C_s^P is the negative cash flow due to the penalties and C_{irt}^{UN} is the cost of the resource $r \in \{\mathcal{R} \cup \mathcal{N}\}$ at time t due to the accomplishment of activity i.

Criterion 1 (net present value):

$$\max \sum_{s \in \mathcal{S}}(C_s^R e^{-\alpha(a_s+1)} - c_s^I e^{-\alpha T_{bs}} - C_s^P e^{-\alpha(h_s+1)}) - \sum_{i \in V} \sum_{r \in \{\mathcal{R} \cup \mathcal{N}\}} \sum_{t=1}^{T} C_{irt}^{UN} e^{-\alpha t}. \quad (1)$$

It is worth to observe, for the development of solution procedures for the project planning problem, that the nonlinear form of the net present value criterion in (1) is only apparent, since simple algebraic manipulations can reduce it to a linear form, due to the discrete nature of the variables. We will assume hereafter that this reduction takes place whenever required by the solution algorithms, such as the branch-and-bound procedure used for solving the multi-project model in Section 3.

(O2) *Criterion type 2*: The duration of each project should be kept as short as possible, in order to provide the customer a good level of service. Although the economic advantage of completing a project within its deadlines is already taken into account by means of the net present value criterion (1) over a medium to long term planning horizon, time control by itself becomes one the most critical issues for project managers at the operational level, leading to the objective of minimizing the time durations of the various projects. This gives rise to S criteria, each corresponding to the minimization of the time duration of a project:

$$\text{Criterion } s+1 \text{ (duration of project } s): \min T_{e_s} \qquad s = 1, \ldots, S, \quad (2)$$

where T_i represents the starting time of activity i and can be expressed as

$$T_i = \sum_{j=1}^{n_i} \sum_{t=1}^{T} t\, x_{ijt} \qquad \forall i.$$

A number of constraints must be satisfied by a solution to the project planning problem. In order to simplify their formulation, we will introduce an additional variable D_i denoting the duration of activity i, as defined by (3).

$$D_i = \sum_{j=1}^{n_i} d_{ij} \sum_{t=1}^{T} x_{ijt} \qquad \forall i \quad (3)$$

$$T_k - T_i \geq D_i \qquad \forall (i,k) \in P \tag{4}$$

$$\sum_{i \in V} \sum_{j=1}^{n_i} q_{ijr} \sum_{t=1}^{T} x_{ijt} \leq Q_r \qquad \forall r \in \mathcal{N} \tag{5}$$

$$\sum_{i \in V} \sum_{j=1}^{n_i} \sum_{\tau=t-d_{ij}+1}^{t} w_{ijr(t-\tau+1)} x_{ij\tau} \leq W_r \qquad \forall r \in \mathcal{R}, \forall t \tag{6}$$

$$\sum_{j=1}^{n_i} \sum_{t=1}^{T} x_{ijt} = 1 \qquad \forall i \tag{7}$$

$$x_{ijt} \in \{0,1\} \qquad \forall i, \forall j, \forall t \tag{8}$$

Inequalities (4) express the precedence relationships between pairs of activities, as defined by the relation $\prec$. Constraints (5) and (6) take into account the limitations on the availability of the renewable and nonrenewable resources, respectively. Of course, doubly constrained resources can be modeled by inclusion of a corresponding pair of constraints of type (5) and (6). Finally, equalities (7) stipulate that each activity must be started exactly once, in a given time period and for a given mode of accomplishment.

As already mentioned in the Introduction, at least two main difficulties arise as one attempts to devise a solution methodology for solving this project planning and scheduling problem. On one side, the different criteria described, relative to either a monetary unit or a time unit, do not appear easily amenable to a single optimization objective. On the other hand, even if admittedly one might succeed in identifying a single criterion optimization model, instances of the multi-project planning problem of realistic size will turn out very easily as computationally intractable, at least for the current state of development of exact methods. These difficulties in solving the multi-criteria planning problem motivates the decomposition approach proposed in the next section as our solution methodology.

3   The decomposition approach

As a preliminary remark, observe that each of the time duration criteria, i.e. criteria $s+1$ ($s = 1, 2, \ldots S$), is relative to a single project, whereas the net present value criterion depends on the whole set of projects. Moreover, the net present value criterion is expected to have higher priority at the multi-project planning stage, over medium to long term time horizons, while the time duration criteria seem more appropriate for shorter horizons, at the project scheduling level.

These two remarks naturally lead to the following decomposition scheme for the multi-project planning problem. At the higher level, corresponding to the tactical planning stage, a single objective optimization model is considered by restricting the attention to an aggregate multi-project network in which each node represents a whole project. This model, referred in what follows as the *multi-project model*, will have the net present value as its objective function and will be aimed at determining the timing of the projects and the allocation of the resources to each project.

Since the multi-project model regards an entire project as a single macro-activity, without decomposing it in its elementary activities, one is required to develope a model designed to describe the time-cost-resources trade-off characterizing the aggregate behaviour of each macro-activity. Specifically, each macro-activity (project) will be described by a set of *macro-modes* of accomplishment, corresponding to different time durations and different levels of usage of the resources, therefore resulting in different costs. As the number of these macro-modes is probably too high in realistic sized multi-projects, the corresponding *shrinking model* described below plays the key role of selecting only that subset of macro-modes which identify the curve of most efficient time-cost trade-off.

Finally, as the multi-project model assigns to each project a starting time and a resource requirement profile, a third model is required at the operational level for determining the detailed assignment of modes and starting times to the elementary activities which compose each project. This *detailed project model* is therefore applied to each project, independently from the others, and results in a single objective optimization model in which the project time duration has to be minimized, subject to the limitations on resources availability which derive from the higher level allocation among the different projects.

The multi-project model

In the multi-project model an oriented acyclic graph $G^S = (V^S, P^S)$ is considered which represents the precedence relations among the projects. The set of vertices V^S consists of the set of projects to which two dummy projects b and e have been added, representing the start and the end of the program, respectively. The set of arcs P^S is in a one-to-one correspondence with the set of arcs P_S defined in Section 2. This means that an arc $(s, z) \in P^S$ is associated to the arc $(e_s, b_z) \in P_S$, while an arc $(b, s) \in P^S$ or an arc $(z, e) \in P^S$ corresponds to the arc $(b, b_s) \in P_S$ or the arc $(e_s, e) \in P_S$, respectively. We will refer to a project represented by a single vertex in graph G^S as a macro-activity.

The number N_s of modes to perform a macro-activity s, that is an entire project composed by its elementary activities, is obviously given by the cardinality of the Cartesian product of the modes corresponding to the elementary activities, i.e.

$$N_s = \prod_{i \in V_s} n_i.$$

Unfortunately, this number grows very large for realistic sized multi-project planning problems. In order to keep the aggregate network model of moderate size, one would like to take into account, for each macro-activity, only those macro-modes of accomplishment which are likely to correspond to the optimal selection of modes, at the operational level, for the elementary activities composing project s. The shrinking model presented in the next subsection has precisely the objective of determining, from the total number of N_s macro-modes, only a small subset of modes of "maximum efficiency", in a sense that will be precised below. Therefore, we will assume hereafter that each macro-activity s can be carried out in $\tilde{n}_s < N_s$ macro-modes, each one corresponding to a given processing time and resource requirement profile. Using a notation similar to the one adopted in Section 2, we will denote by $\tilde{d}_{sj}$ the duration of macro-activity s carried out in macro-mode j, by $\tilde{q}_{sjr}$ the requirement of resource $r \in \mathcal{N}$ and by $\tilde{w}_{sjrt}$ the requirement of resource $r \in \mathcal{R}$ at time t, respectively. Let us define the following binary decision variables:

$$\tilde{x}_{ijt} = \begin{cases} 1 & \text{if project } i \text{ starts at time } t \text{ in macro-mode } j \\ 0 & \text{otherwise.} \end{cases}$$

We can therefore formulate the following optimization model, denoted as problem M in the sequel, in which the net present value is taken as the objective function.

$$\max \sum_{s \in \mathcal{S}} (C_s^R e^{-\alpha a_s} - c_s^I e^{-\alpha T_{bs}} - C_s^P e^{-\alpha h_s} - \sum_{r \in \{\mathcal{RUN}\}} \sum_{t=1}^{T} C_{srt}^{UN} e^{-\alpha t})$$

$$\tilde{D}_s = \sum_{j=1}^{\tilde{n}_s} \tilde{d}_{sj} \sum_{t=1}^{T} \tilde{x}_{sjt} \qquad \forall s$$

$$\tilde{T}_s = \sum_{j=1}^{\tilde{n}_s} \sum_{t=1}^{T} t \, \tilde{x}_{sjt} \qquad \forall s$$

$$\tilde{T}_z - \tilde{T}_s \geq \tilde{D}_s \qquad \forall (s,z) \in P^S$$

$$\sum_{s \in \mathcal{S}} \sum_{j=1}^{\tilde{n}_s} \tilde{q}_{sjr} \sum_{t=1}^{T} \tilde{x}_{sjt} \leq Q_r \qquad \forall r \in \mathcal{N}$$

$$\sum_{s \in \mathcal{S}} \sum_{j=1}^{\tilde{n}_s} \sum_{\tau = t - \tilde{d}_{sj} + 1}^{t} \tilde{w}_{sjr(t-\tau+1)} \tilde{x}_{sj\tau} \leq W_r \qquad \forall r \in \mathcal{R}, \ \forall t$$

$$\sum_{j=1}^{\tilde{n}_s} \sum_{t=1}^{T} \tilde{x}_{sjt} = 1 \qquad \forall s$$

$$\tilde{x}_{sjt} \in \{0,1\} \qquad \forall s, \ \forall j, \ \forall t$$

A solution of problem M corresponds to selecting for each macro-activity s a macro-mode and a starting time. In other words, problem M schedules the projects over the time horizon taking the resource constraints into account and at the same time allocates the resources globally available among the different projects in such a way that the net present value is maximized. Denoting by $\tilde{x}^*$ an optimal solution to problem M, the amount $\tilde{Q}_r$ of resource $r \in \mathcal{N}$ required by project s is given by

$$\tilde{Q}_r = \sum_{j=1}^{\tilde{n}_s} \tilde{q}_{sjr} \sum_{t=1}^{T} \tilde{x}_{sjt}^*$$

while the corresponding amount $\tilde{W}_{rt}$ of resource $r \in \mathcal{R}$ required by project s at time t is

$$\tilde{W}_{rt} = \sum_{j=1}^{\tilde{n}_s} \sum_{\tau = t - \tilde{d}_{sj} + 1}^{t} \tilde{w}_{sjr(t-\tau+1)} \tilde{x}_{sj\tau}^*.$$

Since the accuracy in solving problem M is particularly relevant for the success of the whole decomposition approach, a branch-and-bound algorithm for its solution has been developed. The adoption of an exact method is also justified by the fact that the size of problem M can be made tractable by restricting the number $\tilde{n}_s$ of macro-modes considered for each project.

The shrinking model

The shrinking model is applied to each of the projects constituting the multi-project environment. As noticed, the aim of this model is that of transforming a project into a single macro-activity, to be incorporated into the higher level multi-project model. Therefore, in designing the shrinking model, one should try to balance two conflicting requirements: on one side, in order to make the decisions of the multi-project model consistent with the detailed project characteristics, the model should transform each project into a single macro-activity which maintains as many detailed informations about the project as possible; on the other hand, to keep the size of the multi-project model moderate, the shrinking model should select as few macro-modes as possible.

Since the actual timing of the projects will be decided at the higher level by the multi-project model, it turns out that the cost relative to resources consumption is the only economic quantity which remains of interest within the shrinking model.

Obviously, the mode selection for the activities of a project depends on the other projects through the limitations on resource availabilities. Hence, a model which minimizes time duration of a single project disregarding these interrelations might result in a violation of the resource constraints when the solutions derived in this way are considered at the multi-project level.

Therefore, the shrinking model presented here is aimed at identifying the maximum efficiency frontier between time duration and cost of each single project. This is done by solving a sequence of optimization models, which correspond to determining the minimum project duration for different selected values of budget monetary availability.

More specifically, a set K^s of cost values are selected, which represent a reasonable discretization of the possible budget limitations for project s. Then, for each project s, the following problem has to be solved for each element $k_v^s \in K^s$, $v = 1, 2, \ldots \tilde{n}_s$, where $\tilde{n}_s = |K^s|$. The problem will be referred to as problem $A(s, v)$, to express the dependence from the project index s and from the index of the budget limitation k_v^s.

$$\min T_{e_s}$$

$$\sum_{i \in V_s} \sum_{r \in \{\mathcal{R} \cup \mathcal{N}\}} \sum_{t=1}^{T} C_{irt}^{UN} \leq k_v^s \tag{9}$$

$$D_i = \sum_{j=1}^{n_i} d_{ij} \sum_{t=1}^{T} x_{ijt} \qquad \forall i \in V_s$$

$$T_i = \sum_{j=1}^{n_i} \sum_{t=1}^{T} t \, x_{ijt} \qquad \forall i \in V_s \tag{10}$$

$$T_k - T_i \geq D_i \qquad \forall (i, k) \in P^s$$

$$\sum_{i \in V_s} \sum_{j=1}^{n_i} q_{ijr} \sum_{t=1}^{T} x_{ijt} \leq Q_r \qquad \forall r \in \mathcal{N}$$

$$\sum_{i \in V_s} \sum_{j=1}^{n_i} \sum_{\tau=t-d_{ij}+1}^{t} w_{ijr(t-\tau+1)} x_{ij\tau} \leq W_r \qquad \forall r \in \mathcal{R}, \forall t$$

$$\sum_{j=1}^{n_i} \sum_{t=1}^{T} x_{ijt} = 1 \qquad \forall i \in V_s$$

$$x_{ijt} \in \{0,1\} \qquad \forall i \in V_s, \ \forall j, \ \forall t$$

Constraint (9) expresses the limitation on the available budget for project s. The solution of problem $A(s,v)$, for a given level k_v^s of cost limitation, consists in a project duration and in a corresponding resource requirements profile, that is in the specification of a macro-mode v of accomplishment for the macro-activity s. The profile of resource requirements of the macro-activity s in mode v is found from an optimal solution $\bar{x}$ to problem $A(s,v)$ as follows. The resource requirement of the nonrenewable resource $r \in \mathcal{N}$ is given by

$$\tilde{q}_{svr} = \sum_{i \in V_s} \sum_{j=1}^{n_i} q_{ijr} \sum_{t=1}^{T} \bar{x}_{ijt},$$

while the resource requirement of the renewable resource $r \in \mathcal{R}$ at time t is expressed by

$$\tilde{w}_{svrt} = \sum_{i \in V_s} \sum_{j=1}^{n_i} \sum_{\tau=t-d_{ij}+1}^{t} w_{ijr(t-\tau+1)} \bar{x}_{ij\tau}.$$

Obviously, the duration of the macro-activity s in mode v is given by $\tilde{d}_{sv} = T_v$. Notice that the starting times $\bar{T}_i$ determined by substituting $\bar{x}$ in the relations (10) are not definitive. The actual starting times for the activities of s depend from the solution of the multi-project model as well as from the solution of the detailed project model, described in a subsection below.

Notice that the constraints on the resources availability, taking into account for project s the global limitations Q_r and W_{rt}, are only apparently loose. In fact, the resources are indirectly limited through the limitation k_v^s on the resources cost. A tight limitation in this budget constraint will determine a macro-mode of accomplishment for project s, which is likely to be quite fast but also resources consuming; on the contrary, a lower budget value, if feasible, will correspond to a macro-mode which is slower but less resource consuming. Consistently with our hierarchical decomposition, the appropriate global combination of these macro-modes is determined at the tactical planning level, within the previous multi-project model, by means of the net present value maximization.

A heuristic approach has been adopted for the solution of problem $A(s,v)$. Two reasons motivated the choice of a fast heuristic approach over a slower exact method. First, the number of problems $A(s,v)$ which have to be solved equals the sum of the number of selected budget limitations $\tilde{n}_s$ for the different S projects constituting the multi-project environment, and can therefore be quite large. Furthermore, the solution of such problems represents only a preliminary insight into the program structure, to be used at the higher level by the multi-project model, while the final decisions are taken by means of the multi-project and the detailed project models. In particular, a simulated annealing approach has been chosen for solving problem $A(s,v)$, since it allows the user to specify an appropriate balance between accuracy of the solution and computing time, in dependence of the problem characteristics.

The detailed project model

While the multi-project model identifies the resource requirement profile and the starting time for each project s, a detailed project model is required to determine modes of accomplishment and starting times for the single activities of each project. As the financial objectives of the multi-project have been taken into account over the medium term horizon by the tactical planning stage, within the multi-project model, the detailed project model takes the duration of the project as its objective function. The allocation of resources $\tilde{Q}_r^s$ and $\tilde{W}_{rt}^s$ to project s have been determined through the multi-project model. Obviously, $\tilde{W}_{rt}^s \neq 0$ only for t belonging to the particular time interval in which project s has been scheduled. For each project s the following problem D(s) has to be solved.

$$\min T_{e_s}$$

$$D_i = \sum_{j=1}^{n_i} d_{ij} \sum_{t=1}^{T} x_{ijt} \qquad \forall i \in V_s$$

$$T_i = \sum_{j=1}^{n_i} \sum_{t=1}^{T} t \, x_{ijt} \qquad \forall i \in V_s$$

$$T_k - T_i \geq D_i \qquad \forall (i,k) \in P^s$$

$$\sum_{i \in V_s} \sum_{j=1}^{n_i} q_{ijr} \sum_{t=1}^{T} x_{ijt} \leq \tilde{Q}_{rt}^s \qquad \forall r \in \mathcal{N}$$

$$\sum_{i \in V_s} \sum_{j=1}^{n_i} \sum_{\tau=t-d_{ij}+1}^{t} w_{ijr(t-\tau+1)} x_{ij\tau} \leq \tilde{W}_{rt}^s \qquad \forall r \in \mathcal{R}, \forall t \qquad (11)$$

$$\sum_{j=1}^{n_i} \sum_{t=1}^{T} x_{ijt} = 1 \qquad \forall i \in V_s$$

$$x_{ijt} \in \{0,1\} \qquad \forall i \in V_s, \forall j, \forall t$$

Observe that problem D(s) differs from problem A(s,v), since the former does not include the constraint (9) on the budget limitation. Notice also that this constraint can be dropped because it is replaced by the set of constraints (11), which limit the usage of renewable resources on a period by period basis, as for renewable resources, due to the optimal allocation of resources through the various projects derived from the multi-project model. Yet, the heuristic algorithmic procedure developed for problem A(s,v) can be easily adapted to the solution of problem D(s).

4   Conclusions

As remarked in the Introduction, the models described in Section 2, as well as the corresponding solution algorithms, have been incorporated into a decision support system which is thought to assist the project managers in the planning process at the tactical and operational levels. The decision support system should be seen as a tool aimed at facilitating the multi-project analysis by the planners, and should stay on top of a project management information system used in executing, monitoring and controlling the projects during their lifetime.

We have already indicated the main features of the analysis allowed by the support system, such as allocating scarce resources among projects or subprojects and evaluating different cash flows, in light of the net present value maximization; identifying the most appropriate modes of accomplishment of the various activities; scheduling the elementary activities and the entire projects over the planning horizon.

In conclusion, the decomposition methodology proposed in this paper seems to be particularly suited to fit into the decision processes involved in multi-project planning. Further developments of the proposed approach will lead to incorporate a third type of criteria, related to the project plan dependability, i.e. the reliability in actually meeting the scheduled dates.

References

Balas, E. (1970). Project scheduling with resource constraints, In *Applications of Mathematical Programming Techniques*, Carnegie-Mellon Univ., Pittsburgh, 187-200.

Blazewicz, J., Lenstra, J.K. and Rinnooy Kan, A.H.G. (1983). Scheduling subject to resource constraints: classification and complexity, *Discrete Applied Mathematics*, 5:11–24.

Christofides, N., Alvarez-Valdez, R. and Tamarit, J.M. (1987). Project scheduling with resource constraints: a branch and bound approach, *European J. of Operational Research*, 29:262–273.

Davis, E.W. and Heidorn, G.E. (1971). An algorithm for optimal project scheduling under multiple resource constraints, *Management Science*, 17(B):803–816.

Davis, E.W. and Patterson, J.H. (1975). A comparison of heuristic and optimal solutions in resource-constrained project scheduling, *Management Science*, 21:944–955.

Doersch, R.H. and Patterson, J.H. (1977). Scheduling a project to maximize its present value: a zero-one programming approach, *Management Science*, 23:882–889.

Elmaghraby, S.E. and Herroelen, W.S. (1988). *The Scheduling of Activities to Maximize the Net Present Value of Projects*, Technical Report OR 222, North Carolina State Univ.

Gorestein, S. (1972). An algorithm for project (job) sequencing with resource constraints, *Operations Research*, 20:835–850.

Norbis, M.I. and Mac Gregor Smith, J. (1988). A multiobjective, multi-level heuristic for dynamic resource constrained scheduling problems, *European J. of Operational Research*, 33:30–41.

Patterson, J.H. (1984). A comparison of exact approaches for solving the multiple constrained resource, project scheduling problem, *Management Science*, 30:854–866.

Patterson, J.H. (1976). Project scheduling: the effects of problem structure on heuristic performance, *Naval Research Logistics Quarterly*, 23:95–123.

Patterson, J.H. and Huber, W.D. (1974). A horizon-varying, zero-one approach to project scheduling, *Management Science*, 20:990–998.

Pritsker, L.J., Watters, A.A.B. and Wolfe, P.M. (1969). Multiproject scheduling with limited resources: a zero-one programming approach, *Management Science*, 16:93–108.

Russell, A.H. (1970). Cash flows in networks, *Management Science*, 16:357–373.

Russell, R.A. (1986). A comparison of heuristics for scheduling projects with cash flows and resource restrictions, *Management Science*, 32:1291–1300.

Slowinski, R. (1981). Multiobjective network scheduling with efficient use of renewable and nonrenewable resources, *European J. of Operational Research*, 7:265–273.

Talbot, F.B. (1982). Resource-constrained project scheduling with time-resource trade-offs: the nonpreemtive case, *Management Science*, 28:1197–1210.

Talbot, F.B. and Patterson, J.H. (1978). An efficient integer programming algorithm with network cuts for solving resource-constrained scheduling problems, *Management Science*, 24:1163–1174.

Part 4

Design of Multiple Criteria Decision Support

Flexible Method Bases and Man-Machine Interfaces as Key Features in Interactive MOLP Approaches

Joao Climaco and C. Henggeler Antunes
Department of Electrical Engineering
University of Coimbra
3000 Coimbra, Portugal

Abstract

The experience acquired with the study of power expansion planning problems using several interactive multiple objective linear programming (MOLP) methods led us to conclude that it is not possible to state that any of them is better than the others in all the circumstances. So we started to develop an interactive MOLP method base which presently includes STEM, Zionts-Wallenius, Interval Criterion Weights, Pareto Race and TRIMAP methods. On the other hand, the quality of man-machine interfaces has also revealed to be crucial, not only to facilitate the dialogue with the decision maker (DM) within the framework of interactive MOLP methods, but also to make flexible the formulation of the power planning problem by performing an automatic formulation of the linear objective functions and constraints.

> "... a good decision aid should help the DM explore not just the problem, but also himself. It should bring to his attention possible conflicts and inconsistencies in his preferences so that he can think about their resolution."

(S. French, 1984)

1 Introduction

The experience acquired with the computer implementation and the application of interactive MOLP methods as well as the consequent evaluation of their conceptual characteristics led us to the development of a more flexible tool. Different interactive MOLP methods have been integrated in the same computer package which enables the exchange of information among them and the sharing of a common interface and input data. For further details on the computer implementation see (Antunes et al., 1989).

The study of power systems expansion planning problems (where cost, reliability and environmental impact objective functions were considered) by means of different interactive MOLP methods helped us understanding the reasons why there is not, in absolute, a method better than all the others. For details see (Climaco and Antunes, 1990).

Whenever possible (namely in Zionts-Wallenius, Interval Criterion Weights and TRI-MAP methods) the analysis of the weighting space revealed to be a fundamental step in the interactive decision aiding process. Based on this analysis we concluded that in power planning problems there are large regions of the weighting space for which the variation of the objective function values of the corresponding solutions is very small, and steep variations among those regions also occur. Therefore, even in the same problem there are methods more suited than others to different phases of the decision process. For example, the DM may not be willing to make pairwise comparisons before having some more knowledge about the problem by previously performing a more global strategic search.

In these circumstances we decided to develop a method base as flexible as possible making it possible advantage to be taken of the interaction among different type of interactive MOLP methods. This undoubtedly contributes not only to knowledge acquisition but also to the emergence of new intuitions about the problem. The underlying principle is to support interactively the DM in the progressive narrowing of the scope of the search. As more knowledge about the problem is gathered in each interaction, the system of preferences of the DM is progressively evolving, thus making the DM to reflect upon his previous search directions, or even to revise his system of preferences.

2　An interactive MOLP method base

The MOLP method base plays the key role in a decision aiding structure which includes a procedures toolbox, a dialogue base and a data management module. The MOLP method base integrates at present STEM, Zionts-Wallenius (ZW), Interval Criterion Weights (ICW), Pareto Race and TRIMAP interactive MOLP methods. The methods can be used either in a standard manner or in any sequence. Special emphasis has been placed on the creation of an intuitive and user-friendly environment for interacting with the DM. The so-called procedures toolbox includes a set of useful functions for finding all the non-dominated extreme points or all nondominated extreme points adjacent to a given extreme solution and for filtering a sample of solutions to be presented to the DM. These procedures are intended to be used at specific stages of the interactive decision aiding process, namely after the scope of the search has been sufficiently reduced. The data management module deals with data input, data editing and output of the results, enabling to correct the input data and reformulate the problem.

It is always possible to make a transition from one method to another in any interaction with the DM. However, according to the type of situation, different "degrees of learning" with the previous experience can be distinguished :

- the decision of changing from one method to another at a given moment of the interactive process means, from the point of view of the new method, to reiniciate the process (eg. Zionts-Wallenius-STEM);

- based on previous experience it may be decided that constraints should be placed on the search region, namely as a result of lower bounds for the objective function values (eg. TRIMAP), or to contract the gradient cone of the objective functions (eg. ICW);

- starting from the solution obtained in the previous iteration whether there is or not a reduction in the search region (eg. TRIMAP-Pareto Race, TRIMAP-ZW, Pareto Race-TRIMAP).

It is possible in all the situations to abandon immediately whatever has been changed by the application of the current method, and return to the abandoned state of the previous method. It is also possible to revise previous decisions during the application of each method.

In certain cases, a method is used as a procedure with different objectives from those defined in the originally developed method. Some examples are:

- STEM executing one (or several) iterations having in mind only to establish bounds for the objective function values.

- Zionts-Wallenius used locally, starting from a given efficient extreme point and executing pairwise comparisons and/or tradeoff judgments, enabling to establish constraints on the weighting space; this implies that bounds on the search region of the polyhedron be established, implicitly.

Although not compulsory it is usual practice (in an initial search phase) to start by using methods where the "learning" of preferences by the DM consists in limiting the future search to a more restricted region of the feasible polyhedron (eg. STEM, ICW, TRIMAP). Only in the final stage of the process we should opt for a type of search where the information required from the DM is directional (eg. Zionts-Wallenius, Pareto Race).

We would like to emphasize that by using the method base we seek a progressive learning of the system of preferences of the DM, having in mind to find satisfactory solutions (Simon, 1969). The system of preferences of the DM (considered himself as a component of the decision process) is progressively evolving in each interaction, as he learns more about the problem. In this context the designation of "psychological convergence" (quoting Vincke's words) seems to us quite appropriate!

There are several ways of characterizing the interactive methods. We will now briefly refer the five methods which are included in this first version of the MOLP method base (implemented on Macintosh II), the interface being dedicated, at the present stage, mainly to three-objective problems:

STEM (Benayoun et al., 1971)

- Feasible region reduction method.
- Preference information: aspiration levels.
- Scalarization function: a weighted Tchebycheff metric.

Zionts-Wallenius (Zionts and Wallenius, 1976)

- Weighting space reduction method.
- Preference information: pairwise comparison of alternatives and tradeoff judgements.
- Scalarization function: weighted sum of the objective functions.

Interval Criterion Weights (Steuer, 1977)

- Criterion cone reduction method.

- Preference information: comparison among various alternatives, leading to the choice of one of them.

- Scalarization function: weighted sum of the objective functions (used $2p + 1$ times per iteration).

Pareto Race (Korhonen and Wallenius, 1988)

- Directional scanning method.

- Preference information: aspiration levels perturbation.

- Scalarization function: achievement scalarizing function and right-hand side parametric programming.

TRIMAP (Climaco and Antunes, 1989)

- It combines feasible region reduction with weighting space reduction, translating feasible region reductions into weighting space reductions.

- Preference information: establishing minimum levels for the objective functions values and imposing constraints directly on the weighting space (this just in special cases).

- Scalarization function: weighted sum of the objective functions.

3　An illustrative example

In the first iteration we use ICW, with sample size 3. In each iteration $2p + 1$ (p being the number of objective functions) linear problems are solved. The points inside the weighting space represent the dispersed convex combinations of the objective functions (weighting vectors).

Let us suppose that solution 4 in fig. 1 was selected for performing the criterion cone contraction.

There are two ways of entering TRIMAP from the ICW method:

- To consider the contracted cone and using TRIMAP as usual (fig. 2a).

- To translate the weighting space corresponding to the problem with the contracted cone, onto the weighting space of the original problem (fig. 2b).

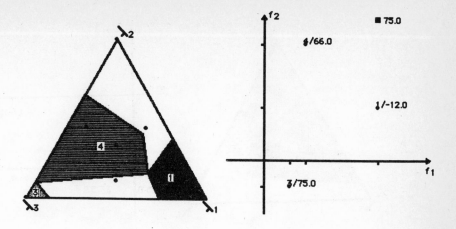

Fig. 1: Interval criterion weights method

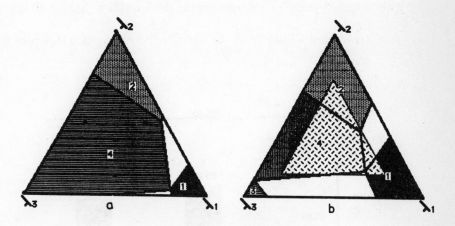

Fig. 2: Fom ICW to TRIMAP

(Due to space limitations only the weighting space is shown.)

Let us suppose that TRIMAP has been used according to the second option.

TRIMAP is specially useful for establishing inferior bounds on the objective function values. This information is "translated" onto the weighting space, displaying the regions corresponding to Pareto optimal solutions satisfying those additional constraints imposed by the DM (see fig. 3, where the constraint $f_2(\underline{x}) \geq 40$ was introduced).

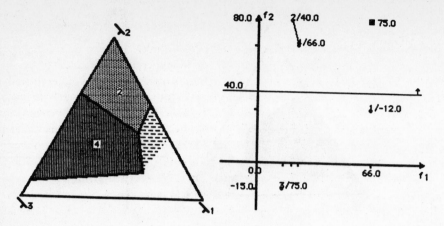

Fig. 3: Using TRIMAP to visualize on the weighting space the additional constraints on the objective function values

We make a transition to STEM, considering the limitation $f_2(\underline{x}) \geq 40$ imposed within TRIMAP.

The first iteration of STEM (with the additional constraint) is shown in fig. 4.

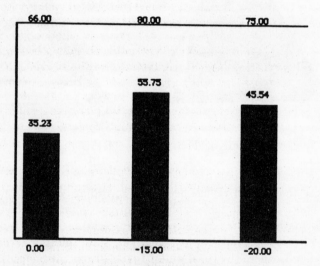

Fig. 4: Using STEM

Suppose it was decided to relax $f_1(\underline{x})$ by 15 and continue the search in a more reduced region using TRIMAP, by introducing the constraints $f_1 \geq 20.23$, $f_2 \geq 55.75$, $f_3 \geq 45.54$.

In fig. 5a the sub-regions of the weighting space corresponding to each constraint are filled with different patterns which overlap, thus enabling to visualize the zones where the additional constraints have their intersection.

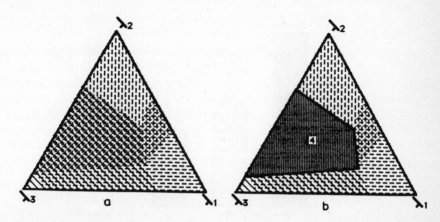

Fig. 5: The regions in the weighting space satisfying the additional constraints

Solution 4 in fig. 5b is the only Pareto optimal extreme point satisfying all the limitations on the objective function values simultaneously.

Starting from this solution we now make a transition to Zionts-Wallenius method (fig. 6).

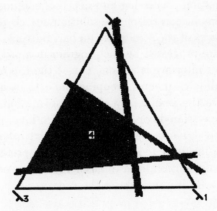

Fig. 6: The weighting space showing the constraints resulting from the responses to pairwise comparisons in Zionts-Wallenius method

Suppose the DM does not accept the pairwise comparisons between the solution 4 and the adjacent solutions. If he does not accept any of the proposed tradeoffs too, then this solution is the final one. We can enter Pareto Race method from this solution by selecting a direction of improvement of one objective function and then proceeding in the usual manner according to this method by using the controls at the user's disposal (fig. 7).

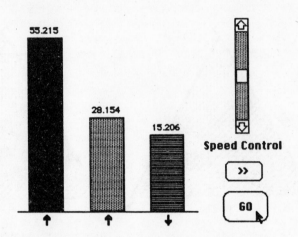

Fig. 7: Using Pareto Race method

4   Man-machine interface

The interface offers the DM a flexible and user-friendly human-computer interaction which is easy to learn and intuitive to use in order to capture better his preferences and enhance his capabilities of information processing and decision making.

The user always keeps in control of the solution search process just by clicking the mouse in appropriate places of the screen (menu bar, buttons, etc.). These actions generate input events which are processed by the program in a orderly way. The fundamental structure of the computer interface is a menu bar at the top of the screen which lists the titles of the available pulldown menus, grouping the actions available to the user. Overlapping windows improve the availability of the information, being used for displaying graphical (weighting space triangle or any of its projections, projections of the objective function space, static and dynamic bar graphs) and text information. Pictorial controls provide the user with an intuitive tool for specifying his preferences. Dialogue boxes are used to request further information from the user before a given command can be carried out or to convey some useful information to the user.

5   Some conclusions

(Larichev and Nikiforov, 1987) evaluated the interactive methods taking into consideration the possibilities of eliciting reliable information from people and the consistency of the method requirements. By estimating the "correctness" of the interactive methods, they concluded that, in general, good methods use in the dialogue with the DM information relative to the objective function values, in order to create a system of preferences.

Note that this may lead to two different ways of acting. According to the terminology by (Nakayama, 1985):

- to fix aspiration levels close to the ideal value (optimistic point of view);

- to fix minimum allowable levels (pessimistic point of view): eg. TRIMAP.

Operations like pairwise comparisons (as used in Zionts-Wallenius) and the choice of one among several alternatives (used in ICW) are considered very complex for the DM.

This type of considerations must be taken into account when a method or a sequence of methods is chosen to be applied to a given problem. The method base must still serve for the evaluation and/or confirmation of the conditions (different stages of the decision process or type of decision problems) for which each method is more effective.

The graph representing the weighting space is important specially because, besides being easy to understand, it enables that informations, resulting from the use of the various methods during the interactive decison aiding process, be accumulated.

Despite the fact that the philosophy of this package contradicts the idea that the interactive process aims at converging to the optimum of the DM's implicit utility function, whenever it is justified to carry out a local search (using for example Zionts-Wallenius) it may be interesting to implement a procedure of the type proposed by (Steuer and Liou, 1988) in order to reduce the searching region of the weighting space around the departure point.

6 Developments in progress

Besides continuing the experiments with the interactive MOLP method base namely as far as engineering problems are concerned work is currently in progress under the following directions:

- Development of a rule-based system that will be able to support the DM in the task of deciding how and when to change from method to method. Here we do not seek to replace the DM in the "learning" of his system of preferences, but just to develop a tool for aiding him in the choice of methods or sequence of methods to be applied to a given kind of problem, namely by making him some suggestions.

- Extension of the method base to new methods, for more than three objective functions by developing a suitable interface and to new computational environments.

References

Antunes, C. H., Alves, M. J., Silva, A. L. and Climaco, J. N. (1989). A computer implementation of an interactive MOLP model base with applications to energy and telecommunications planning. Proc. of the Int. Conf. on MCDM, Bangkok, Thailand.

Benayoun, R., de Montgolfier, J., Tergny, J. and Larichev, O. (1971). Linear programming with multiple objective functions: step method (STEM). *Mathematical Programming*, **1**, pp. 366–375.

Climaco, J. and Antunes, C. H. (1989). Implementation of a user friendly software package — a guided tour of TRIMAP. *Mathematical and Computer Modelling*, **12**, pp. 1299–1309.

Climaco, J. and Antunes, C. H. (1990). A comparison of microcomputer implemented interactive MOLP methods based on a case study. Selected proc. of the Third International Summer School on MCDA. Springer-Verlag, (in press).

French, S. (1984). Interactive multi-objective programming: its aims, applications and demands. *Journal of the Operational Research Society*, **35**, pp. 827–834.

Korhonen, P. and Wallenius, J. (1988). A Pareto race. *Naval Research Logistics*, **35**, pp. 615–623.

Larichev, O. and Nikiforov, A. (1987). Analytical survey of procedures for solving multicriteria mathematical programming problems. In: "Towards interactive and intelligent decision support systems", vol. **1**, Springer-Verlag, pp. 95–104.

Nakayama, H. (1985). On the components in interactive multiobjective programming methods. In: "Plural rationality and interactive decision processes". Springer-Verlag.

Simon, H. (1969). The sciences of the artificial. MIT Press.

Steuer, R. (1977). An interactive multiple objective linear programming procedure. *TIMS Studies in the Management Sciences*, **6**, pp. 225–239.

Steuer, R. (1986). Multiple criteria optimization: theory, computation and application. Wiley.

Steuer, R. and Liou, F. (1988). Grid point weighting vectors for convergence control in multiple objective programming. Presented at the Int. Conf. on Multiobjective Problems in Mathematical Programming, Yalta, USSR.

Zionts, S. and Wallenius, J. (1983). An interactive multiple objective linear programming method for a class of underlying nonlinear utility functions. *Management Science*, **29**, pp. 519–529.

The Foundations of Multi-Criteria Interactive Modelling: Some Reflections

Mordechai I. Henig

Faculty of Management

Tel Aviv University, Tel Aviv, 69978, Israel

Abstract

The accumulation in recent years of a considerable body of theoretical and practical knowledge on interactive processes in decision making, makes it possible to try now and answer some of the methodological issues raised in the past. Instead of posing these methodological issues directly, I shall revisit three decision problems: in the private, public and personal sectors, in an effort to determine how interactive modelling can help the decision maker in multi-criteria decision making.

1 Introduction

The title of my talk is similar to that of White's (1983) article in which he raised several questions, some of them still open. I have simply replaced "programming" by "modelling" and "questions" by "reflections".

By interactive programming we usually mean a decision-maker-analyst dialogue where the decision maker (DM) expresses his (subjective) preferences in a given set of alternatives or attributes. In interactive modelling the dialogue encompasses three phases of the traditional decision-making process — constructing the model, assessing the preference system and selecting the best alternative — and it may require the participation of other sources of information. The reasons for extending the role of the interactive process, the meaning of assessment, and the types of information will become clear in the sequel.

"It has been recognized", White observed, "that decision makers may change their minds, or formulate their preferences as a result of the interactive process, but that is all, and the methods all take the descriptive view point and base the analysis on actual responses without question to a large extent ... Is it likely that a random method ... would be the 'best' general method?"

We all agree that interactive modelling can aid the DM in learning and understanding his preferences. Furthermore, this is a natural way to make decisions in complicated situations, when an ambiguity surrounds the problem. Thus, the motive and justification for using interactive modelling is its acceptability by the DM, a motivation which is somehow different from other approaches, such as that of utility theory.

Indeed, many interactive methods (IM) have been developed in response to a need to solve specific problems, rather than as a response to methodological issues. It seems that too often, when an analyst is asked to help solve a multiple-criteria decision making (MCDM) problem he develops a method, if he does not have one already. Usually, the method works. Does this mean that every analyst-MCDM problem-DM trio is unique and requires its own unique method of solution or at least modification of an existing method?

Imagine the response of a DM or a practitioner to the following statement in "A User-Oriented Listing of Multiple-Criteria Decision Methods" by Despontin et al. (1983): "Although initially present, the authors rapidly left the intention of comparing, or even classifying the methods ... Decision situations can vary so much in quantity, quality and preciseness of information that most methods do not even fit in a large classification scheme." One still hears, too, that "in order to be sure of the solution, several methods should be applied".

Researchers in DSS and artificial intelligence have recognized the imperative for integration of these technologies with IM as an aid in decision-making. This is demonstrated by the number of papers on the subject that have appeared in the literature. In a recent study, Javalgi and Jain (1988) write "The ultimate goal of the MCDM methods is to find the most-preferred nondominated solution". Is this true?

In my opinion, since White first raised the questions, much theory and practice has accumulated and we can now answer most of them and formulate a methodology of interactive modelling, which, among other things, will classify IMs.

Instead of raising methodological issues directly, I shall reexamine three well-known decision problems in an effort to determine how interactive modelling can help the DM in MCDM. My representation will be in the spirit of French (1984), who believes that "a good decision aid should help the decision maker explore not just the problem, but also himself. It should bring to his attention possible conflicts and inconsistencies in his preferences so that he can think about their resolution. ... While acceptability and ease of use is a necessary prerequisite for a good decision aid, it is not a sufficient condition. The aid must also be based upon sound logical and methodological foundations which are compatible with our empirical knowledge".

2 Three examples

The private sector: Wallenius (1975) and Buchanan and Daellenbach (1987) presented an LP production-scheduling problem with three criteria: operating costs; average number of stockouts; and average percentage of the labor force temporarily laid off.

Formally, since the criteria are given, any of the many known IMs can be applied. The question is which one. The authors suggest evaluating the methods according to:

1. DM's confidence in the final solution.
2. Ease of use of the method.
3. Ease of understanding the logic of the method.
4. CPU time.
5. Elapsed time to find the most preferred solution.
6. Relative preference for using each method.

The last item seems to be an aggregate of the other five.

In the research of these authors, four IMs were compared in a "laboratory" setting: two "sophisticated" methods, those of Zionts and Wallenius (1976) and Haimes and Hall (1974), make use of a value function; the others, those of Steuer and Choo (1983) and a naive method, do not. The last two were judged favorable. Wallenius claims that the DM does not accommodate well to sophisticated methods. Buchanan and Daellenbach (1988) conclude that IMs should be unstructured, to allow free and even random search.

All methods, including naive ones and even a random search, teach the DM something about his system of preferences, but only some of them present it explicitly. Surprisingly, those which do not assess the preference system at all gave DM the impression that he was learning his preferences better than did the sophisticated method. At the same time, the DM showed higher confidence in methods that accommodate previously revealed preferences in the selection of further alternatives from a given set, in the process of searching for an acceptable alternative.

It seems that the methods which select alternatives according to, and simultaneously with, assessing a value function, failed to convince the DM that he was learning his preferences, because they are too structured, technical and formal. He wants to discover the preferences at his own pace and according to his own level of conviction. However, the DM wants more than a naive method or a random search. In the words of Buchanan and Daellenbach (1988): "First, users preferred methods that allowed them sufficient time to explore the solution space before homing in on the preferred solution. Second, users wanted to be in control of the solution search, rather than relinquish control to the 'computer' ... The meaning of 'interactive' in MCDM should thus not be taken as synonymous with 'interactive' in a computer science context of real-time response."

Will the decision process benefit from making the preference system explicit? The answer to this question have been several, the most common being:

1. No, the DM is not interested and it may confuse him.
2. There is no such system.
3. No. The best alternative can be found without knowing the preference system.
4. Yes, but it is expensive and time consuming.

In my opinion, forming a system of preferences will benefit the decision-making process. Furthermore, that is exactly what the DM expects of an IM: to let him KNOW his preferences, knowledge being information expressed explicitly. The question is how this system of preferences can be expressed. As Roy (1987) so succinctly put it, the DM has a story in his mind and the analyst helps him write it.

Since the production-scheduling problem is repetitive in nature, identifying a preference system in terms of a value function is very helpful. But two methods which assess a value function have failed?! This is because the methods are formal and structured to work on a given set of alternatives and attributes, without really giving the DM the flexibility and freedom to explore himself.

The production-scheduling problem is an example taken from a large class of one-criterion problems in the private sector where the criterion for judging alternatives is profit. It is solved as a multi-attribute problem mainly because this criterion is a priori not well defined. However, preferences are a function of profit only, and the goal of the IM is to assess the criterion by forming a profit function over the attributes. The criteria of operating costs, stockouts and lay-offs in the scheduling problem may be seen as attributes of profit, and in a real problem there may be other attributes as well. The second and the third attributes do, however, contain the hint that there may be other criteria, disjoint from profit; these may be related to reputation, ethics or traditions concerning shortage and unemployment. But this can be exposed only by appropriate interaction with the DM.

Finding the criteria and the attributes is part of the interactive method. Whenever a DM reveals his preference there follows a routine check on whether the set of criteria or attributes have to be modified.

In the production-scheduling problem an IM method should start with understanding the meaning of "profit" and why operating cost is not its equivalent. This may be so because operating costs do not reflect long-term costs and benefits of the schedule. Then attributes like stockout and lay-off, which are related to future costs, are introduced. Thus the reason for the ambiguity is lack of knowledge about the attributes and how they affect the criteria.

Objective information and subjective opinion regarding how the attributes affect the "profit" are collected interactively. Objective information can be obtained through simulation, mathematical models, inference from past data, from experts and the experience of the DM. It may be revealed that the ambiguity in the problem is due to uncertain future or unclear temporal preferences. In the first case, the problem is no longer deterministic, and states of nature and probabilities have to be explored. In the second case, preferences over time must be explored. Subjective information reflects intuition, emotions and beliefs of the DM concerning the attributes and their effect on "profit". This information is important because it sums up the experience of the DM in making good decisions, and it is impossible or expensive to obtain otherwise.

Such a value function summarizes the current objective and subjective knowledge regarding how the attributes affect the criterion. It is used to derive alternatives which are consistent with the objectives of the organization as the DM conceives of them. Consistency over time is also retained by modifying the function as more information is collected. **The public sector:** The example given is one of decision problems in a fire department, such as location of stations, types of engines and ladders, and operating policy etc. The criteria are in the main the same for every problem: loss of life and injuries, property damage and various other costs. The respective attributes are: annual number of deaths and injuries, annual dollar value of property damaged or destroyed, and annual budget of the fire department. Keeney and Raiffa (1976) approximated a utility function over the proxy attributes of response times of engines and ladders, mainly because fire fighters express their preferences in terms of response time.

In the public sector an explicit preference system is important to let the public and its representatives know, understand, judge and modify the preferences. A value function over the attributes defines the overall objective of the department and enables a consistent decision-making process. Simulation and mathematical models, as well as intuition and experience of the fire fighters are required to evaluate the alternatives in terms of the attributes. However, the value function over the attributes is subjective and reflects society's beliefs and ideology concerning the value of life, responsibility of the authorities for security, and availability of public funds.

Who determines this function? Practically, it is determined by the chief of the department and his colleagues through an IM which articulates their preferences. It reflects the status quo and their beliefs, experience, and intuition on what the public considers to be adequate security.

The personal sector: The example is buying a car. Common criteria are costs, traveling time, reliability, comfort, safety and appearance. The set of alternatives is frequently not well defined and IMs may have to generate alternatives that are unknown a priori. The system of preferences is not easily evaluated in terms of a value function but must nevertheless be explicit in order to generate good alternatives. It is possible to evaluate a value function over the attributes, but an individual will refrain from doing so because it is tedious and because of qualitative objectives.

In any case, the key question whenever the DM reveals his preference is "Why?". Why is a car needed? Why do you like this car? Why do you prefer car A to car B? and new alternatives should be generated according to the answers. Even when the DM likes the appearance of a car, it is possible sometimes to understand what property attracts him in the appearance and to look for other alternatives with similar properties. When I put this question to friends, who were seeking my advise on this matter, their answers revealed two new criteria: freedom of movement and the pleasure of driving, causing the search for their "ideal" car to be productive.

3   Conclusions

It is clear that in the above examples, as in the many others which appear in the literature, the DM benefits from an interactive method. What he might have in his mind, when he first approaches the problem, is a confusion of thoughts and ideas which reflect his experience, intuition, emotions and beliefs. He desperately seeks some objective mechanism to apply those thoughts rationally in the decision process.

We are concerned not only with a process of learning the problem, but also with learning the preferences and understanding the DM himself. It is an open and unstructured learning process. A good IM should gather information while minimizing the stress due to the many criteria, and the many alternatives, as well as the stress of the learning process itself. "The spirit is one of Socratic discovery — of unfolding what you really believe, of convincing yourself, and of deciding" (Keeney and Raiffa, 1976).

The goal of IM is to make the system of preference as explicit as possible. Each problem and each DM (and each analyst) have their own features, and inquiry into the reasons for and the source of preferences is what IM is all about.

The advantages of having a value function over the attributes have been made clear here, especially in the first two examples. However, there is a clear difference between the one that aggregates, as objectively as possible, the attributes into "profit" and the one that reflects subjective opinions and beliefs of the public. A successful assessment of a value function is the best way to achieve the goal of IM.

Will the DM cooperate? In my opinion, this is exactly what the DM is seeking when he calls in an analyst to help. We know that the DM does not necessarily want to optimize, and that optimality is expensive to obtain. However, only when one knows the preferences can one select an optimal, approximately optimal, heuristically optimal or satisficing decision.

References

Buchanan, J. T. and Daellenbach, H. G. (1987). A Comparative Evaluation of Interactive Solution Methods for Multiple Objective Decision Models. *European Journal of Operational Research*, **29**, pp. 353–359.

Buchanan, J. T. and Daellenbach, H. G. (1988). Desirable Properties of Interactive Multi-Objective Programming Methods. Presented at the MCDM international conference in Manchester, England.

Despontin, M., Moscarola, J. and Spronk, J. (1983). A User-Oriented Listing of Multiple Criteria Decision Methods. *Revue Belge de Statistique, d'Informatique et de Recherche Operationnelle*, **23**.

French, S. (1984). Interactive Multi-Objective Programming: Its Aims, Applications and Demands. *J. Opl. Res. Soc.*, **35**, pp. 827–834.

Haimes, Y. Y. and Hall, W. A. (1974). Multiobjectives in Water Resources Systems Analysis: The Surrogate Worth Trade-Off Method. *Water Resour. Res.*, **10**, pp. 615–623.

Javalgi R. and Jain, H. (1988). Integrating Multiple Criteria Decision Making Models into the Decision Supporting Systems Framework for Marketing Decisions. *Naval Research Logistics*, **35**, pp. 575–596.

Keeney R. L. and Raiffa, H. (1976). Decisions with Multiple Objectives: Preferences and Value Tradeoffs. John Wiley & Sons.

Roy, B. (1987). Meaning and Validity of Interactive Procedures as Tools for Decision Making. *European Journal of Operational Research*, **31**, pp. 297–303.

Steuer, R. E. and Choo, E. U. (1983). An Interactive Weighted Tchebycheff Procedure for Multiple Objective Programming. *Mathematical Programming*, **26**, pp. 326–344.

Wallenius, J. (1975). Comparative Evaluation of Some Interactive Approaches to Multicriteria Optimization. *Management Science*, **21**, pp. 1387–1396.

White, D. J. (1983). The Foundations of Multi-Objective Interactive Programming — Some Questions. In: P. Hansen (Ed.): Essays and Surveys on Multiple Criteria Decision Making, Springer Verlag, pp. 406–415.

Zionts, S. and Wallenius, J. (1976). An Interactive Programming Method for Solving the Multiple Criteria Problem. *Management Science*, **22**, pp. 652–663.

Modelling with MCDSS: What about Ethics ?

Tawfik Jelassi and Bernard Sinclair-Desgagné*
Technology Management Area
INSEAD
Boulevard de Constance
77305 Fontainebleau, France

Abstract

Modelling the preferences of a decision maker requires that: 1) all the criteria and attributes relevant for making a choice be thoroughly considered, 2) the available alternatives be listed and ranked with respect to each criterion, and 3) the various rankings be combined to yield a global evaluation of the alternatives. The decision maker, even when he/she uses sophisticated decision aids, is often found to have difficulty with these requirements.

In this paper we argue that the decision maker's hesitation might be due to a lack of understanding of the role each criterion should play in the global judgment. A careful look at ethics — as the discipline that considers the justifications people offer for the principles and values they hold — , in conjunction with the development and usage of multiple criteria decision support systems (MCDSS), would then help enlightening the decision maker.

1 Introduction

> "Le décideur attend généralement de l'aide à la décision qu'elle l'éclaire sur la manière la plus "juste" de faire intervenir les critères dans le choix d'une stratégie."
>
> [Roy, 1985, p. 402]

Over the last decade, there has been an increasing interest in building and using multiple criteria decision support systems (MCDSS) to solve a variety of practical problems. One reason for this development is the greater availability of sophisticated, yet affordable,

*We would like to thank the participants of the International Workshop on Multiple Criteria Decision Support (held in Helsinki, Finland, August 7–9, 1989), especially Professors Vladimir Ozernoy and Rudolf Vetschera, for their helpful comments. This research was supported by the INSEAD R & D Division, Grant #2146R.

hardware and "user-friendly" software. A wide spectrum of managerial decisions can now be supported through systematic generation and evaluation of alternatives and criteria.

Despite their performance, multiple criteria decision support systems are often met with skepticism. The diffusion of this technology on a wide basis remains relatively slow, and one cannot blame it only on a natural resistance to novelty. The fact is that existing MCDSS may be well suited for listing decision criteria and storing information about alternatives, but they still provide insufficient means for helping decision makers to **structure** their goals and values. In this respect most MCDSS rather constitute a rigid tool that sometimes leaves decision makers rather confused.

In this paper we reflect on how to make multiple criteria decision support systems more helpful for structuring values. The next section describes the current state of MCDSS. The third section highlights some features of actual MCDSS that should be improved. Section 4 contains a brief presentation of how MCDSS may benefit by explicitly considering ethics — as the discipline that deals with the justifications people offer for the principles and values they hold. Section 5 summarizes the paper and indicates avenues for future research.

2 State of the art in MCDSS

First MCDSS were designed and implemented as "stand-alone" systems, each consisting of a mathematical algorithm (corresponding to a given decision model), a rudimentary user interface supporting the human-computer dialogue, and a data file of the application at hand. They fell short, however, of fulfilling several generally recognized requirements, such as ease of use, response to changes in the user, task, or environment, and support of learning by the decision maker or information sharing among data files and decision models. (Bonczek et al., 1981; Sprague and Carlson, 1982)

Subsequent implementations of MCDSS tried to alleviate some of these shortcomings. The main improvements dealt with the management of data. They were due to technological advances in the database field and the commercial availability of corresponding software packages. (For more details, see Jelassi, 1987).

As there was a growing awareness of the crucial importance of the user interface in information systems in general and in DSS applications in particular (Bennett, 1983), the management of user/computer dialogue is another area where significant progress was made. A greater understanding of the behaviorial aspects of human/computer interactions helped formulating more effective approaches to computer-supported decision making (Schneiderman, 1980; Byrer and Jelassi, 1990). Also, innovations in hardware and software (e.g. "mouse", touch screens, light pens, color graphics, hypermedia/hypertext technologies) made the development of "friendlier" user interfaces possible.

Finally, numerous DSS studies have focused on model management. Model management aims at building, within the DSS framework, a handy supply of decision models (MCDM, simulation, time series, etc.). Dictionaries would provide information about the stored models (e.g. model name, required data inputs, possible outputs, techniques used, allowed linkages, etc.). Special software would handle a "model base" — the analogue of a database. To be satisfactory, however, model management still awaits further breakthroughs (see, for example, Blanning, 1986; Dolk, 1986; Liang, 1985).

3 Explaining the users' hesitation

Decision makers usually have difficulty finding a suitable rule for **their** multi-criteria decision problem. So, given the present status of model management, several MCDSS focus on a particular class of MCDM rules. In this class, numerical weights are assigned to criteria and rankings along each criterion (i.e. local rankings) are expressed on a numerical scale, each alternative receives a number of points equal to the weighted sum of its local ranks, and the alternative(s) receiving the highest number of points is (are) selected. Such rules have several advantages:

1. They are simple and familiar for decision makers,

2. Since they let decision makers select the weights, they are interactive and they take advantage of the information available in particular contexts.

Such aggregation rules, however, are very sensitive to the weights. But for a given decision maker, these "are always subject to considerable fluctuations from one day to the next, even from one hour to the next!" (Arrow and Raynaud, 1986, p. 14) By measuring the consistency of the assessed weights, one may hope to stabilize them. But the existing consistency checks, in addition to being sometimes controversial, overlook the fact that the decision maker's attitude may evolve over time while the assessed weights at each period remain perfectly consistent.[1]

The translation of local rankings into a numerical scale is also arguable. Someone who uses an MCDSS is usually expected to provide local rankings in an ordinal fashion. However, when a decision maker says that, with respect to criterion α, she prefers item A to item B, some MCDSS "conclude" that, thanks to criterion α, item A brings the decision maker x units of satisfaction more than item B. First, this automatic interpretation of the decision maker's input might not be logically correct (see Debreu, 1983). Second, it entails comparisons and trade-offs between local rankings, and this feeds back the decision maker with a (classical) utilitarian picture of her preferences (Harsanyi, 1979) which might be inaccurate and misleading.

Even if the local rankings are taken as they are stated by the decision maker, i.e. as ordinal rankings, there might still be problems. Imagine that a criterion represents a type of voter, that a numerical weight on a criterion corresponds to the number of voters of this type, and that a local ranking is the preference profile of a voter. Then,

---

[1]Consistency is a legitimate norm for decision making, but decision analysts and MCDM researchers should not focus exclusively on it. As (Sen, 1987, p. 69) argues: "Recent empirical studies of behaviour under uncertainty have brought out what has appeared to be systematic inconsistencies in the evaluation of risk and in the comparative assessment of alternative decisions. Many of these results have been interpreted, perhaps with some justice, as simply 'mistakes' in perception of reasoning. Even if that view is fully accepted, the prevalence of such behaviour indicates the case for making room for departures from the usual requirement of 'rationality' in understanding actual behaviour. But **it is also arguable that some of these so-called 'mistakes', in fact, only reflect a different view of the decision problem**, in contrast with that formalized in the standard literature".(emphasis added)

the above aggregation rules are formally identical to majority voting. Hence, they share the advantages, but also the well-known drawbacks of majority voting: i.e., a frequent failure in finding an outstanding alternative, and a consequent sensitivity of the decision to the order in which pairwise comparisons are made at the elicitation phase. (Arrow and Raynaud, 1986)

These remarks may explain some of the difficulties that MCDSS users often encounter. Decision makers would perhaps better accept MCDSS if they were given the possibility to construct **their own** rules for global ranking. The challenge for MCDSS developers is then to provide decision makers with more perspective or support in choosing a way to combine their various criteria.

4   From doubt to resolution

In order for MCDSS to better meet users' expectations, focus must be put on the so-called "agency aspect" of decision makers, "recognizing and respecting ...[their] ability to form goals, commitments, values, etc." (Sen, 1987) This leads to considering ethics and moral reasoning.

The term **ethics** has two meanings (Sherwin, 1983). In a popular sense, ethics refers to a set of moral standards or values to guide behavior. In a more fundamental sense, ethics is the discipline that considers the justifications people provide for the principles and values they hold. This latter meaning of ethics matches the philosophy of decision support systems.

Ethics could contribute to MCDSS in the following ways:

1. It could provide **a frame for the dialogue** between the user and the system concerning global and local rankings. Ethics has been studied for centuries. There is now an accessible language of ethics, a well-known body of ethical concepts, a wealth of cases, examples, and metaphors, that could stimulate the decision maker's thinking about multi-criteria decisions.

2. Favoring the development of a coherent, integrated dialogue management in MCDSS, ethics could help the decision maker **formulate precise requirements for a global ranking**.

3. Given the decision maker's requirements, ethics could finally help **suggest appropriate aggregation rules** for multi-criteria decision making.

Imagine, for example, a decision maker using an MCDSS that offers the features listed above. After interacting with the system, he/she could conclude that his/her local rankings can be compared to some extent, but that they must be taken as ordinal rankings. The MCDSS could then recommend using aggregation rules that fulfill the maximin principle[2] (see Sen, 1970).

We claim that features 1 and 2 listed above could be provided by the current MCDSS technology. Offering the third feature, however, would require further developments of

---

[2]The maximin principle stipulates that one should try to maximize along the least satisfied criterion. It is often considered as the cornerstone of "justice as fairness" (see Rawls, 1971).

model management and expert systems in the multi-criteria decision making context. Knowledge about aggregation rules should be acquired from MCDM experts and built in the system (Jelassi and Ozernoy, 1989). An "intelligent" system should then advise the decision maker on the most appropriate aggregation technique or rule to use, thereby supporting him/her in the modelling phase of multi-criteria decision making.

5 Concluding remarks

> "Some sense of the individuals that may lie behind an abstraction must always be recognized."

> [Arrow, 1973, p. 28]

This paper first overviewed the state of the art and potential of Multiple Criteria Decision Support Systems. A special focus was given to modelling decision makers' preferences and the associated difficulties encountered by the system users. Some MCDSS provide inadequate support for combining the criteria used to evaluate the available alternatives. They arbitrarily impose on the decision maker a type of aggregation rule — a weighted average — that, although simple, may be inaccurate and misleading. These MCDSS must instead recognize the ability of the user to make global judgments. Through appropriate support, the decision maker should be to find a suitable rule for aggregating local rankings. Ethics — as the field that considers the justification people bring for the judgments they hold — could underlie such decision support. Database and expert systems techniques may be used here as the underpinning technologies that store and provide, when needed, appropriate ethical knowledge for guiding the decision maker in his/her interaction with the MCDSS.

References

Arrow, K. J. (1973). The Limits of Organization. W. W. Norton & Company, New York.

Arrow, K. J. and Raynaud, H. (1986). Social Choice and Multi-criterion Decision-Making. MIT Press.

Bennett, J. L. (1983). Analysis and design of the user interface for decision support systems. In: J. L. Bennett (ed.): Building Decision Support Systems, Addison-Wesley.

Blanning, R. W. (1986). An entity-relationship approach to model management. *Decision Support Systems: The International Journal*, **2**, pp. 65–72.

Bonczek, R. H., Holsapple, C. W. and Whinston, A. B. (1981). Foundations of Decision Support Systems. Academic Press.

Byrer, J. K. and Jelassi, M. T. (1990). The impact of language theories on DSS dialogue. *European Journal of Operational Research*, forthcoming.

Debreu, G. (1983). Mathematical Economics: Twenty Papers by Gérard Debreu. Cambridge University Press.

Dolk, D. R. (1986). Data as models: an approach to implementing model management. *Decision Support Systems: The International Journal*, **2**, pp. 73–80.

Harsanyi, J. C. (1979). Bayesian decision theory, rule utilitarianism, and Arrow's impossibility theorem. *Theory and Decision*, **11**, pp. 289–317.

Jelassi, M. T. (1987). MCDM: From 'Stand-Alone' methods to integrated and intelligent DSS. In: Y. Sawaragi, K. Inoue and H. Nakayama (eds.): Toward Interactive and Intelligent Decision Support Systems, Springer.

Jelassi, M. T. and Ozernoy, V. (1989). A framework for building an expert system for MCDM models selection. In: A. G. Lockett (ed.): Improving Decision Making in Organizations, Springer.

Keeney, R. L. (1988). Building models of values. *European Journal of Operational Research*, **37**, pp. 149–157.

Liang, T. P. (1985). Integrating model management with data management in decision support systems. *Decision Support Systems: The International Journal*, **1**, pp. 221–232.

Rawls, J. (1971). A Theory of Justice. Harvard University Press.

Roy, B. (1985). Méthodologie Multicritère d'Aide à la Décision. Economica, Paris.

Schneiderman, B. (1980). Software Psychology: Human Factors in Computer and Information Systems. Little, Brown and Co, Boston.

Sen, A. K. (1970). Collective Choice and Social Welfare. Holden-Day, Cambridge, MA.

Sen, A. K. (1987). On Ethics and Economics. Basil Blackwell, Oxford, UK.

Sherwin, D. S. (1983). The ethical roots of the business system. *Harvard Business Review*, pp. 183–192.

Sprague, R. H. Jr. and Carlson, E. D. (1982). Building Effective Decision Support Systems. Prentice Hall.

Dynamic BIPLOT as the Interaction Interface for Aspiration Based Decision Support Systems

Andrzej Lewandowski
Temple University, Philadelphia, USA
Janusz Granat
Warsaw University of Technology
Warsaw, Poland

Abstract

The important problem in designing DSS software regards graphic presentation of results and graphic interaction. The interface should make possible insight into data generated by the system and should provide tools for their analysis. Since the user is interested in analysis of data which are points in high dimensional space, methods for dimensionality reduction must be used. This paper presents a technique for using BIPLOT for performing such reduction of dimensionality as well as a methodology for building graphical interactive user interface utilizing BIPLOT.

1   Graphics in Decision Support Systems

Although Decision Support Systems are understood as interactive systems, not too much attention has been paid towards analysis of the role of graphics in building man–machine interfaces, designing architecture of these interfaces and principles of their operation. These issues are especially important due to availability of efficient computer hardware, modern computational algorithms and user friendly interface which allow (and stimulate) to use Decision Support System as a generator of large amount of information. The amount of information is usually too big to allow full insight into all quantitative aspects of the decision problem being solved. Therefore, the basic idea of Decision Support Systems as a device supporting feedback between decision maker and formalized model is frequently not sufficiently explored.

There are two different aspects of graphical information presentation in Decision Support Systems:

- Presentation of large amount of data in graphic form to improve understanding of data, their internal structure as well as relationships between components of the decision problem being solved (objectives, decision variables etc.),

- Providing support for dynamic interaction between user and Decision Support Systems. This function contributes to the learning process by allowing analysis of the history of interaction process which has resulted in achieving the current state of the decision making process. The other function of the graphic interface is simplifying planning consecutive steps in elaborating a decision with help of Decision Support System.

Most of research in the field of graphic perception and graphic interaction design has been directed towards first of the mentioned above aspects of information presentation. Several guidelines for good graphic presentation of data have been proposed (for definition of *graphic excellence* see Tufte, 1983). Experimental study of graph perception has been performed by several researchers. Cleveland and McGill (1984) investigated the *graphical perception* as the *ability of visual decoding of information encoded on graphs*. On the basis of several experiments they have determined efficiency of various forms of graphic presentation as well as possible ways of improvement of graphic presentation style.

Lucas (1981) analyzed the impact of computer–based graphics on efficiency of decision making. The experimental task consisted of selecting quarterly reorder quantities for an importer under condition of uncertain demand, using both graphic and tabular data presentation. Results of this research do not give precise answer regarding comparison of tabular and graphical data presentation. According to the author, in *analytic situation,* tabular presentation gives more precise insight into data, in *heuristic situation,* graphic presentation simplifies reasoning when exact analytic model of the decision situation is not sufficiently well known.

The most complete investigation of the role of graphic presentation in decision making has been performed by DeSanctis (DeSanctis, 1984, Dickson at all., 1986). According to the results of carefully designed experiments they state, that the generalized claims of superiority of graphic presentation are not well justified, at least for decision related activities. Results of experiments performed by DeSanctis suggest that the effectiveness of the data display format is largely a function of the characteristics of the task being solved.

The further study, including these performed by Jarvenpaa and Dickson (1986) and Simkin and Hastie (1987) also does not provide clear answer regarding comparison of various types of data presentation in decision–making context. Nevertheless, several conclusions regarding proper form of graphs as well as selection of tasks where graphic presentation is more adequate than tabular one, can be derived from these experiments.

The mentioned above research has been limited to tasks not being especially adequate to type of questions which appear when using interactive Multiple Criteria Decision Support Systems. Dickson and DeSanctis have investigated such tasks like *summarizing data, showing trends, comparing points and patterns, showing deviations* and *point–value reading.* The mentioned above tasks can constitute important parts of data analysis performed during interactive decision analysis and contribute to the mentioned above *static aspect of problem solving*, but several other aspects of data analysis are of bigger importance. These aspects include the following questions which can be formulated by a decision maker:

- What are *similarities* and *dissimilarities* between solutions obtained on different stages of decision making process,

- What are *relationships* between important components of decisions like values of objectives and decision variables obtained on different stages of decision making process,

- What conclusions regarding consecutive steps of the interactive decision making process can be derived from the cumulated data.

The similarity of task of data analysis in DSS context with standard task of data analysis in statistics must be emphasized. In recently formulated principles of the *Exploratory Data Analysis* (see Hartwig and Dearing, 1989) it is stated that *the underlying assumption of the exploratory approach is that the more one knows about data, the more effectively data can be used to develop, test and refine theory*. Thus, this approach to data analysis seeks to maximize what can be learned from data, supporting questions like *what these data can tell me about important relationships* rather than *do the data confirm my hypothesis about important relationships*. The first mode – an *exploratory* one is typical for interactive work with DSS in contrast to the second one – *the confirmatory* mode typical for statistical data analysis.

2 Interactive graphics for MCDM

According to the principle of exploratory data analysis, the graphical user interface should allow to perform a quick analysis of properties of data obtained in the process of solving decision problem with support of DSS. The situation is, however, different than in statistics – in DSS context the user can deal with historical data, but can also perform an *active experiment* running the DSS software to obtain new data to validate or invalidate his hypothesis. Therefore, the graphical data analysis interface should also provide access to all features of DSS.

However most of existing DSSs are equipped in modules for graphical data presentation, not too many of them are oriented towards exploratory data analysis.

The VISA approach proposed by Belton (1988) utilizes the concept of visual interactive modeling. According to Bell (see Belton, 1988 for further references) the Visual Interactive Modeling is the *process of building and using a visual interactive model to investigate issues important for decision maker*. The Visual Interactive Model has three essential components: a mathematical model, a visual display of the status of the model and an interaction device that permits the status of the model to be changed. The basic idea of VISA is the animation which allows displaying of changes of solution simultaneously with changes of certain parameters of the decision problem performed by the user (weighting factors).

The TRIMAP approach developed by Climacao (Climacao at all., 1988) has been designed for solving problems with 3 criteria. In each iteration two graphs are presented to the decision maker: the first one shows regions in weight space corresponding to each of the already known Pareto optimal vertices, the second one presents projections of Pareto solutions on a plane.

Korhonen and Laakso proposed extension of the *reference point* optimization to *reference direction* optimization (Korhonen and Laakso, 1986a, 1986b). Similar approach utilizing linear parametric programming has been proposed by Lewandowski and Grauer (Lewandowski and Grauer, 1982). The basic idea of this method is as follows:

- Decision maker specifies the reference direction, starting from the most recently obtained solution,

- The reference direction vector is projected on the Pareto surface and a curve traversing across the efficient frontier is obtained,

- Values of objectives along the projected reference vector are plotted on the screen using a distinct color or line pattern for each objective. The graphic cursor can be moved to any point on the curve and the corresponding numerical values of objectives are displayed.

In this way the decision maker can obtain an overview of the behavior of the objectives across the efficient frontier.

Further improvements of this concept have been implemented in the Pareto Race procedure (Korhonen, 1987, Kananen at all., 1990). Pareto Race is a dynamic version of the mentioned above method and allows interactive exploration of the Pareto surface.

However all the mentioned above methods provide various forms of dynamic interaction with Decision Support System, they do not support exploratory data analysis. These methods allow to use the interactive graphic interface to formulate questions about the problem being solved and to enter these questions to a computer to obtain answer, but they do not allow to investigate the *process of interaction*, since historical data are not stored and tools for their analysis are not available. Therefore, important questions regarding conflicts in objectives, their dependency and redundancy cannot be supported.

3 Reduction of dimensionality

The basic difficulty in visualization of results of MCDM analysis is created by the fact that dimensionality of the objective space is usually higher than 2. Therefore, several attempts have been made to perform 2 dimensional presentation of data located in higher dimensional space. This is not the goal of this paper to discuss all possible methods of such presentation. It is necessary, however, to mention two possible approaches:

- The *iconic approach*, when every point in n dimensional space is represented as an *icon* parametrized by values of coordinates of this data point. This technique has been adapted by Korhonen (1988) in his Harmonious Houses approach and implemented in VICO (Visual Multiple Criteria Comparison) system,

- The *projection approach*, when every point in n dimensional space is projected on a plane. The projection operator is selected in such a way that all important properties of data in n dimensional space (distance, correlation) are preserved for points projected on a plane with as high accuracy as possible. This technique is known as *Multidimensional Scaling* (see Kruskal and Wish, 1989) and has been adopted for MCDM by Marechal and Brans (1988) as a non–interactive data analysis procedure.

The iconic approach possesses several disadvantages. The iconic representation is not unique, since the same data can be transformed to an icon in many possible ways.

Moreover, the analyst can "like" or "dislike" some shapes, even if these shapes are purely abstract and have no well defined meaning. In the case of houses or faces the bias can be even higher. Moreover, the only analytic technique for deriving conclusions about data being analyzed is a highly subjective visual inspection which cannot bring information about important quantitative characteristics of data, like correlation.

However the projection technique is not free of problems, it can provide much more deep insight into structure of data. Among many existing projection techniques the *biplot* seems to be the best tool which ensures preservation of many characteristics of data important for decision making.

3.1 Principal component biplot

The *biplot* has been proposed by Gabriel (1971) as a convenient technique for graphical presentation of matrices of rank 2. Such a matrix Y of dimensions $m \times n$ can be factorized as a product of two matrices G and H

$$Y = GH' \tag{1}$$

where G is $n \times 2$ matrix and H is $m \times 2$ matrix. From the above formula follows that

$$y_{ij} = g_i' h_j \tag{2}$$

Therefore, this factorization assigns vectors $g_1, ..., g_n$ to rows of Y and vectors $g_1, ..., g_n$ to columns of Y. Since the vectors g and h are vectors of order two, they can be plotted on a plane giving a representation of the $m \times n$ elements of the matrix Y by means of the inner products of the corresponding vectors. Such a plot is called a *biplot* since it allows the rows and columns to be plotted jointly.

Let us consider the $n \times m$ matrix Y of data. In our case this matrix represents set of nondominated solutions of the MCDM problem with columns corresponding to objectives and rows corresponding to solutions.

It is well known, that such a matrix can be represented using the singular value decomposition

$$Y = \sum_{\alpha=1}^{r} \lambda_\alpha p_\alpha q_\alpha' \tag{3}$$

where λ_α denotes the singular values of the matrix Y, p_α denotes the singular column and q_α denotes the singular row satisfying the following relations:

$$p_\alpha' Y = \lambda_\alpha q_\alpha' \tag{4}$$

$$Y q_\alpha' = \lambda_\alpha p_\alpha' \tag{5}$$

$$YY' p_\alpha = \lambda_\alpha^2 p_\alpha \tag{6}$$

$$Y'Y q_\alpha = \lambda_\alpha^2 q_\alpha \tag{7}$$

It ia also known, that the matrix M of rank s

$$M_{(s)} = \sum_{\alpha=1}^{s} \lambda_\alpha p_\alpha q_\alpha' \tag{8}$$

can be considered as the least-squares optimal rank s approximation of matrix M, i.e. $M_{(s)}$ minimizes the functional

$$\| Y - M \|^2 = \sum_{i=1}^{n} \sum_{j=1}^{m} (y_{ij} - m_{ij})^2 \tag{9}$$

The absolute measure of the goodness of fit of the above approximation can be expressed as

$$\rho_s^2 = \frac{\sum_{\alpha=1}^{s} \lambda_\alpha^2}{\sum_{\alpha=1}^{r} \lambda_\alpha^2} \tag{10}$$

Let us assume that the matrix Y is normalized, i.e. mean value of each objective has been subtracted from the corresponding column of the matrix Y, then

$$S = \frac{1}{n} Y'Y \tag{11}$$

can be interpreted as the variance-covariance matrix. Let us consider the rank 2 approximation of matrix Y

$$M_{(2)} \sim Y \tag{12}$$

and let $\{\lambda_1, \lambda_2\}$ denote two largest singular values. Than the matrix $M_{(2)}$ can be factorized as

$$M_{(2)} = GH' \tag{13}$$

where

$$G = (p_1, p_2)\sqrt{n} \tag{14}$$

$$H = \frac{1}{\sqrt{n}}(\lambda_1 q_1, \lambda_2 q_2) \tag{15}$$

Therefore, if we consider definition of the matrix $M_{(2)}$, the following conclusions can be derived from the general properties of the singular values decomposition and factorization

$$Y \sim GH' \tag{16}$$

$$YS^{-1}Y' \sim GG' \tag{17}$$

$$S \sim HH' \tag{18}$$

where $\sim$ stands for *is approximated by means of a least squares fit of rank two*. Therefore, we can establish the following approximation for values of matrix Y

$$y_{ij} \sim g_i'h_j \tag{19}$$

as well as for covariances, variances and correlation

$$s_{j,g} \sim h_j'h_g \tag{20}$$

$$s_j^2 \sim \| h_j \|^2 \tag{21}$$

$$r_{j,g} \sim \cos(h_j, h_g) \tag{22}$$

Moreover, the Euclidean distance between vectors $\{g_i\}$ approximates the standardized (Machlanobis) distance between observations

$$d_{i,j} \sim \| g_i - g_j \| \tag{23}$$

where

$$d_{i,j} = (y_i - y_j)' S^{-1} (y_i - y_j) \tag{24}$$

The expression

$$\frac{1}{n} \sum_{i=1}^n (y_{ij} - y_{ig})^2 \sim \| h_j - h_g \|^2 \tag{25}$$

gives an approximation to the average squared difference between variables.

It is necessary to point out similarity between the biplot and principal component analysis (Jolliffe, 1986). Namely, the expression (7) defines vectors $\{q_i\}$ as eigenvectors of covariance matrix S what coincides with definition of *principal components*. Therefore, the biplot can be interpreted as projection technique where all data points are projected on a linear manifold spanned by first s principal components of a covariance matrix.

Especially important for interpreting biplot are relationships (19) – (22). According to these formulas:

- elements of data matrix can be approximated as orthogonal projections of vectors h on principal component directions,

- correlation coefficients between variables are approximated by angle between vectors h,

- variance of variable is approximated by length of corresponding vector h.

It is necessary to point out that the factorization of $M_{(2)}$ can be performed in many other ways, but only the factorization (13) – (15) ensures preserving the mentioned above properties of data.

4 Dynamic BIPLOT interaction in aspiration based DSS

Recently, the methodology for Aspiration–Led DSS have been advanced (Lewandowski and Wierzbicki, 1989) and several software products implementing this methodology have became available. According to the Aspiration–Led DSS methodology the interaction loop consist of the following steps:

- specification of aspirations,

- computation of corresponding Pareto solution,

- evaluation of results by decision maker and return to first step.

The last step requires a lot of effort from the decision maker. If the most recent solution cannot be accepted as satisfactory, the decision maker must change his aspirations. To support this task, it is necessary to analyze the most recent solution as well as other solutions obtained during interaction with the system, including answering the following questions:

- What are similarities between the most recently obtained solution and other solutions? What are similarities, dissimilarities or clusters in the set of solutions?

- If there are solutions similar or dissimilar to the most recent one, how these solutions have been evaluated?

- What are reasonable directions for modifying aspirations? What objectives can be improved simultaneously and which cannot? What will be the consequences of modified aspirations?

If solutions collected during interaction with the DSS are considered as data points and objectives as variables, the biplot technique can be used to provide the following information:

- *Clusters.* Since distance between solutions (data points) on biplot plane approximate these in original space (24), clusters are easily visible and can be detected by visual inspection of the biplot. Therefore, it is possible to analyze similarities and dissimilarities between solutions with Machlanobis distance as similarity measure.

- *Variance.* Length of vector h approximates variance of the objective. This value can be interpreted as *flexibility* or *sensitivity* of the objective.

- *Correlation.* The angle between vectors h represents correlation between objectives. Analysis of correlation can support deriving the following conclusions:

  - *Redundancy of objectives.* If some objectives are highly positively or negatively correlated, they can be replaced by one or by lower number of objectives,

  - *Conflicts between objectives.* Let us consider objectives h_i. If we denote by Λ the following cone

$$\Lambda = \sum_i \alpha_i h_i, \qquad \alpha_i \geq 0 \tag{26}$$

  than these objectives are in conflict if

$$\Lambda^* = \{0\} \tag{27}$$

where Λ^* denotes the dual cone of the cone Λ. In such a case it is not possible to improve all these objectives simultaneously.

5 Implementation

The BIPLOT interface implements the formulas presented above and provides tools for graphical visual interaction. The objectives are scaled according to the principles of DIDAS methodology, i.e. using the *utopia* and *nadir* points (Lewandowski and Wierzbicki, 1989). Both h and g vectors are presented on the screen. The user can move a cursor (using mouse or keyboard); simultaneously a point representing cursor is projected on directions generated by h vectors, giving values of objectives corresponding to this point. The center of coordinates can be located in a point corresponding to mean values of objectives or moved to a point corresponding to selected solution. In the later case it is possible to analyze improvements of objectives with respect to a selected solution (Figure 2). Several other options are available:

- Comparison of two solutions,

- Selection and removing a group of points,

- Displaying of h of g vectors separately.

To illustrate application of BIPLOT interface, the *Frankfurter Blending Problem* analyzed by Steuer (1986) will be considered. The complete formulation of the problem will be not discussed here, since for presentation of BIPLOT it is enough to know only the list of objectives:

1. Cost/lb	2. Color (on a scale of 0 to 10)
3. % Meat use	4. % Fat
5. % Protein	6. % Moisture
7. Beef-to-meat use (%)	8. Pork-to-meat use (%)

Of the above criteria, cost and % fat are to be minimized. To be maximized are % meat use, % protein, and color. Beef to meat use and pork to meat use are goal criteria with target values of 55% and 45%, respectively. Moisture is a free-floating variable which does not need to be minimized nor maximized. Steuer publishes data obtained during analysis of this problem using the ADBASE program. These data have been used for producing the biplot.

On Figure 1 only h vectors corresponding to objectives (variables) are presented. The following conclusions can be deducted from this plot:

- The Cost and % Protein objectives are highly correlated. This means that it would be not reasonable to request improvement only one of them with the second one constant or decreasing. Moreover, it is possible to conclude that the problem is not correctly formulated, since due to high correlation one of these objectives could be eliminated. Such reformulation of the problem would reduce dimensionality of the objective space and, therefore, would result in simplification of the problem.

- The Beef-to-meat and Pork-to-meat objectives are highly negatively correlated. It is not possible to increase both of them simultaneously. Due to high correlation it would be possible to eliminate one of these objectives.

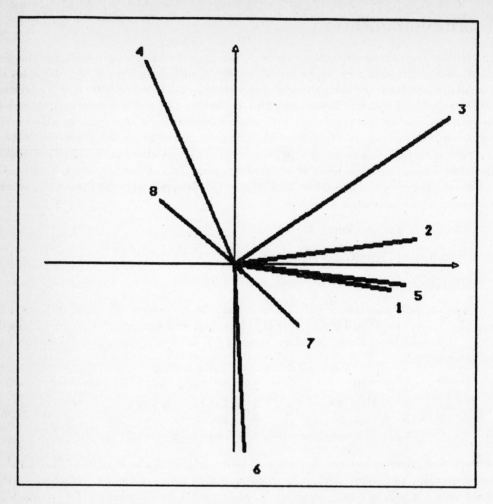

Figure 1: Analysis of correlation between objectives using BIPLOT

- The Moisture is almost not correlated with Color and Cost and Protein.

- % Meat use and % Fat are almost not correlated.

- There exist several conflicts among objectives. For example, the conflict appears between elements of the following triplet: Cost, % Meat use and % Fat. Simultaneous improvement of Cost and % Fat will cause decrease of % Meat use (which should be maximized). Similarly, improvement of two of these objectives will result in worsening the third one. Several other conflicting triplets can be selected. This information provides valuable feedback for the decision maker regarding admissible changes of his aspirations: these requirements should not be in conflict with correlation pattern between objectives.

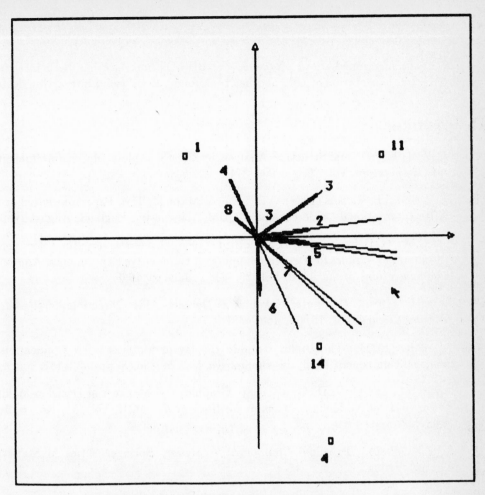

Figure 2: Interactive analysis of objectives

6   Conclusions

The Dynamic BIPLOT constitutes essential improvement of graphical interaction for DSS compared with standard approaches like bar charts, line plots etc. Unfortunately, this approach is not free of problems:

- Accuracy of approximation is not high if number of data points is low. Moreover, various characteristics of data set are represented with different accuracy. With the factorization presented in this paper, the most accurate is representation of correlations. The less accurate is approximation of Machlanobis distance between objectives. Moreover, Machlanobis distance is difficult to interpret and standard Euclidean distance would be more appropriate. Therefore, all conclusions regarding clusters must be treated with care.

- Interaction is performed on 2 dimensional plane, therefore certain paradoxes can occur. In particular, it is not possible to consider constraints on objectives.

Despite all the mentioned above problems, the BIPLOT interface has been integrated with several implementation of DSS and has been found as an useful interaction device.

References

Baaske, W. (1988). Visual Structure Analysis by Cluster Biplots. *Applied Mathematics and Computation*, Vol. 26, pp. 303–314.

Belton, V. and S.P. Vickers (1988). V.I.S.A. – VIM for MCDM. Paper presented at the VIIIth International Conference on MCDM, Manchester, England, August 1988.

Dickson, G.W., G. DeSanctis and D.J. McBride (1986). Understanding the Effectiveness of Computer Graphics for Decision Support: A Cumulative Experimental Approach. *Communications of the ACM*, Vol. 29, No. 1, January 1986.

DeSanctis, G. (1984). Computer Graphics as Decision Aids: Directions for Research. *Decision Science*, Vol. 15, pp. 463 – 487.

Gabriel, K.R. (1971). The Biplot Graphic Display of Matrices with Application to Principal Component Analysis. *Biometrika*, Vol. 58, No. 3; pp. 453–467.

Jarvenpaa, S.L. and G.W. Dickson (1988). Graphics and Managerial Decision Making: Research Based Guidelines. *Communications of the ACM*, Vol. 31, No. 6, June 1988.

Jolliffe, I.T. (1986). Principal Component Analysis. Springer Series in Statistics, Springer Verlag.

Hartwih, F. and B.E. Dearing (1989). Exploratory Data Analysis. Sage University Paper No. 16, SAGE Publications.

Kananen, I., P. Korhonen, J. Wallenius and H. Wallenius (1990). Multiple Objective Analysis of Input–Output Models for Emergency Management. *Operations Research*, Vol. 38, No. 2, March–April 1990.

Korhonen, P.J. and J. Laakso (1986a). A visual interactive method for solving the multiple criteria problem. *European Journal of Operational Research*, Vol. 24, pp. 277–287.

Korhonen, P.J. and J. Laakso (1986b). Solving generalized goal programming problems using a visual interactive approach. *European Journal of Operational Research*, Vol. 26, pp. 355–363.

Korhonen, P.J. (1987). On Using Computer Graphics for Solving MCDM Problems. In: *Towards Interactive and Intelligent Decision Support* Systems, Y. Sawaragi, K. Inoue and H. Nakayama, Eds. Proceedings of the Seventh International Conference on Multiple Criteria Decision Making, Kyoto, Japan, August 1986. Lecture Notes in Economics and Mathematical Systems, Vol. 286, Springer Verlag.

Korhonen, P. (1988). Using Harmonious Houses for Visual Pairwise Comparison of Multiple Criteria Alternatives. Working Paper F–203, Helsinki School of Economics, Helsinki, Finland, December 1988.

Korhonen, P. (1988). A visual reference direction approach to solving discrete multiple criteria problems. *European Journal of Operational Research*, Vol. 34, pp. 152–159.

Kruskal, J.B. and M. Wish (1989). Multidimensional Scaling. Sage University Paper No. 11, SAGE Publications.

Lewandowski, A. and M. Grauer (1982). The reference point optimization – methods of efficient implementation. In: *Multiobjective and Stochastic Optimization*, M. Grauer, A. Lewandowski and A.P. Wierzbicki, Eds., CP–82-S12, International Institute for Applied Systems Analysis, Laxenburg, Austria.

Lewandowski, A. and A.P. Wierzbicki (Eds.) (1989). Aspiration Based Decision Support Systems: Theory, Software and Applications. Lecture Notes in Economics and Mathematical Systems, Vol. 331, Springer Verlag.

Lucas, H.C. (1981). An Experimental Investigation of the Use of Computer–Based Graphics in Decision Making. *Management Science*, Vol. 27, No. 7, July 1981.

Marechal, B. and J.-P. Brans (1988). Geometrical Representation for MCDA. *European Journal of Operational Research*, Vol. 34, pp. 66–77.

Simkin, D. and R. Hastie (1987). An Information–Processing Analysis of Graph Perception. *Journal of the American Statistical Association*, Vol. 82, No. 398, June 1987.

Steuer, R.E. (1986). Multiple–Criteria Optimization: Theory, Computation and Application. Willey Series in Probablilty and Mathematical Statistics.

Tufte, E.R. (1983). The Visual Display of Quantitative Information. Graphic Press, Chestire, Connecticut.

Developing an Interactive Decision Support for Discrete Alternative MCDM Method Selection

Vladimir M. Ozernoy

School of Business and Economics
California State University, Hayward
Hayward, California 94542 U.S.A.

Abstract

In this paper, a prototype MCDM knowledge-based system is described and discussed. The system uses the information about available discrete alternative MCDM methods to guide the user through an analysis of the decision situation.

1 Introduction

In (Ozernoy, 1989), a conceptual framework was developed for a rule-based expert system that would assist the decision maker or analyst to justify the selection of the most appropriate discrete alternative MCDM method in a given decision situation. The purpose, structure, and possible applications of the expert system were also discussed.

There are three major steps in the development of an MCDM expert system:

(1) MCDM knowledge identification,

(2) MCDM knowledge acquisition, and

(3) MCDM knowledge representation.

This paper describes one of these major steps: MCDM knowledge representation. An expert system prototype developed is characterized and some screens of a sample consultation are demonstrated. A small prototype called "MCDM Advisor" was developed in order to

(1) investigate the possibility of using the expert system technology to formalize knowledge about discrete alternative MCDM methods, and

(2) test the basic structure and concept of an MCDM expert system before committing substantial resources for its development.

2 "MCDM Advisor": an overview

"MCDM Advisor" was developed using a microcomputer based expert system shell called VP-Expert (Hicks and Lee, 1988). The knowledge base contains eight MCDM methods, including both compensatory and noncompensatory methods. These are: disjunctive method (Coombs, 1964), conjunctive method (Coombs, 1964), dominance (Keeney and Raiffa, 1976), lexicographic method (Fishburn, 1964), weighted-additive evaluation function with partial information (Kirkwood and Sarin, 1984), simple multiattribute rating technique (Edwards, 1977), aspiration level interactive model (Lotfi et al., 1988) and ELECTRE-1 (Roy, 1971).

In the MCDM knowledge base, backward chaining is used to find the appropriate MCDM method. With this approach, the system starts with the hypothesis that a particular method is appropriate for a given decision situation, then reasons backward, looking for facts and rules to support it. If the first hypothesis fails, the system switches to another.

The MCDM knowledge base is composed of three parts or blocks (see Hicks and Lee, 1988 for more detail). The first block, the Actions Block, controls the user consultation session. The Rules Block contains the IF/THEN rules that represent the basic logic of the system. The last block, the Statements Block, contains messages that direct the interaction with the user to elicit the information about the decision problem as well as the decision maker's preference information.

The Actions Block is quite simple (Fig. 1). The only actions are to display an opening message, find the value of the goal variable Advice and then display that value. The Find clause instructs the inference engine to seek the value of Advice, which becomes the goal variable for the consultation.

When all the instructions in this section of the knowledge base have been performed, the consultation will be complete.

The Rules Block contains rules written in an IF/THEN format (Fig. 2). The inference engine first looks for a rule having the final goal, Advice, in its conclusion. Next, it tests the conditions for the rule as specified in the IF part of the rule. These constitute sub-goals for the search. Some of these sub-goals are satisfied directly by asking the user questions. Other sub-goals are determined through other rules. This process continues until all the conditions of the original goal, Advice, have been satisfied. If at any point in this search process a sub-goal cannot be satisfied, the inference engine "backs up" and looks for another rule to satisfy the goal. If no other rules can be found, it makes attempts to obtain the value from the user. If this approach does not work, the search fails and no value is found.

The final block in the MCDM knowledge base is the Statements Block (Fig. 3). This block contains the ASK statements and any special conditions associated with them. The presence of a CHOICES statement indicates that the user will be presented with a menu of available values, from which he or she selects an answer by positioning the cursor. If an ASK statement does not have an accompanying CHOICES statement, the user will be expected to enter a value.

3 A sample consultation session

When the user starts the dialogue, the inference engine begins by displaying the welcome message in the DISPLAY cause (Fig. 4) and then processing the FIND clause. The inference engine uses backward chaining to find the value of the goal.

Fig. 4 shows the structure of the consultation screen. The upper window is the Consultation Window. The program will display messages to the user in this location, such as requests for information and displays of results.

The left window is the Rules Window. It displays the value that is now sought and the rule that is being evaluated.

The right window is the Results Window. It tells the user which variables have obtained values, what those values are, and what confidence factor is given to each value.

The first question to the user in the consultation is about the type of the user's decision (Fig. 5). The question displayed in the Consultation Window can be answered by moving the lightbar to the correct answer. In the sample consultation session, the choice is 1, "To find the preferred alternative".

The Rules Window provides the user with a trace of the rules presently being used in the consultation. In this window, the user can see which rule is being evaluated. The Results Window shows the current status of the reasoning.

The second question in the sample consultation is "Are you willing to make tradeoffs between attributes?" (Fig. 6). The answer is NO.

At this point, all of the windows are active, and we can observe the progress of the consultation.

The third question is "Can you rank-order all the attributes in decreasing order of importance?" The answer is YES.

The fourth question in the sample consultation is "Is an alternative acceptable if the attribute levels of the chosen alternative exceed the cutoff values ('levels of aspiration') of each of the attributes?" The answer is YES.

The preceding questions remain on the screen until they are scrolled off by subsequent questions. The last question (Fig. 7) is "Would you like to explore the nondominated frontier by allowing the user to establish and adjust levels of aspiration?" The answer is YES.

If the answer is YES, there will be no request for additional information. Instead, the message states that the goal has been reached. The best advice that this MCDM knowledge base has for the user is AIM — the Aspiration Level Interactive Model.

If the answer to the last question were NO, the goal would not have been reached and the Advice would have been "The recommended method is not found in the MCDM knowledge base" (Fig. 8).

Once the rules have been entered, a convenient way of monitoring their execution is a decision trace. The system records the steps taken in a consultation and can display a trace after the consultation has been completed. Two forms of traces are used to show the consultation process: the Graphics display or the Text display. Fig. 9 shows the Text display corresponding to the selection of the AIM method/model. The display clearly shows the path of the inference engine and the values that it obtains as it tests various rules.

Several options are available during a consultation. For example, the WHY? option shows why a question is asked or why a specific recommendation has been made.

In an additional sample consultation session, the first question to the user is about the type of the user's decision problem. The choice is 3 — "To find all acceptable alternatives".

The second question is: "Are you willing to make tradeoffs between attributes?" The answer is NO (Fig. 10).

The third question is: "Is an alternative acceptable if at least one attribute level of the chosen alternative exceeds a desirable level?" The answer is NO (Fig. 10).

And the fourth question is: "Is an alternative acceptable if the attribute levels of the chosen alternative exceed the cutoff values of each of the attributes?"

If the user asks WHY at this point, the display will be as shown in Fig. 11. Thus, the WHY? option shows why a question was asked.

4   Summary

A small prototype advisory MCDM expert system called "MCDM Advisor" was developed using a microcomputer based expert system shell called VP-Expert. Experiments with "MCDM Advisor" indicate that the basic structure of the system and the interrelationship of its components will permit the development of a comprehensive MCDM expert system. Experimentation has already shown that an increase in the number of MCDM methods in the knowledge base did not result in a significant increase of the consultation time.

As VP-Expert interfaces with external programs (such as dBaseII and Lotus 1-2-3) that may offer greater possibilities to the knowledge base designer, these capabilities can be used both in consultation and in computer-aided instruction. Subsequently, a fifth-generation MCDM decision support system can be developed based on a stand-alone advisory system. It would allow not only recommending but also executing the recommended MCDM method.

References

Coombs, C. H. (1964). A theory of data. Wiley, New York.

Edwards, W. (1977). Use of multiattribute utility measurement for social decision making. In D. E. Bell, R. L. Keeney and H. Raiffa (eds.), Conflicting objectives in decisions. Wiley, New York, pp. 247–276.

Fishburn, P. C. (1974). Lexicographic order, utilities and decision rules: a survey. *Management Science*, 20, pp. 1442–1471.

Hicks, R. and Lee, R. (1988). VP-Expert for business applications. Holden-Day, Inc., Oakland.

Keeney, R. L. and Raiffa, H. (1976). Decisions with multiple objectives. Wiley, New York.

Kirkwood, C. W. and Sarin, R. K. (1985). Ranking with partial information: a method and an application. *Operations Research*, 33, pp. 38–48.

Lotfi, V., Stewart, T. J. and Zionts, S. (1988). An aspiration-level interactive model for multiple criteria decision making. Working Paper No. 701, Department of Management Science and Systems, School of Management, State University of New York at Buffalo, Buffalo, New York 14260.

Ozernoy, V. M. (1989). Some issues in designing an expert system for multiple criteria decision making. In: B. Rohrman, L. R. Beach, C. Vlek and S. R. Watson (eds.), Advances in Decision Research. North Holland, Amsterdam, pp. 237–254.

Roy, B. (1971). Problems and methods with multiple objective functions. *Mathematical Programming*, 1, pp. 239–266.

```
! MCDM.KBS
! Actions Block
ACTIONS
        DISPLAY  "Welcome to the MCDM Advisor!
                 This is a prototype advisory MCDM knowledge-based
                 expert system.

                 The following consultation will help you to determine
                 the most appropriate discrete alternative MCDM method
                 for your decision problem.

                 Press 1 to begin the consultation."
        GETCH Consultation
        Consultation = 1
        FIND Advice
        DISPLAY "The best advice we have for you is as follows:
           the recommended MCDM method is {#Advice}.";
```

Figure 1: Actions Block — introductory screen, concluding screen, and goal statement of MCDM Advisor knowledge-base file.

```
!Rules Block
RULE 1
IF      Problem = 3
        AND Tradeoffs = No
        AND One_cutoff_value = Yes
THEN    Advice = Disjunctive_Method
BECAUSE "Will_be_explained_later.";

RULE 2
IF      Problem = 3
        AND Tradeoffs = No
        AND All_cutoff_values = Yes
THEN    Advice = Conjunctive_Method
BECAUSE "Will_be_explained_later.";

RULE 3
IF      Problem = 4
        AND Tradeoffs = No
        AND Dominance = Yes
THEN    Advice = Dominance_Method
BECAUSE "Will_be_explained_later.";

RULE 4
IF      Problem = 1
        OR Problem = 2
        AND Tradeoffs = No
        AND Rank_attributes = Yes
        AND Sequential_screening = Yes
THEN    Advice = Lexicographic_Method
BECAUSE "Will_be_explained_later.";
```

Figure 2: Rules Block — IF-THEN rules of MCDM Advisor knowledge-base file.

```
'Statements Block
ASk Problem: "Please identify the type of your decision problem
               1 - To find the preferred alternative
               2 - To rank-order feasible alternatives
               3 - To find all acceptable alternatives
               4 - To identify all nondominated alternatives
               5 - To partially order nondominated alternatives";
CHOICES Problem:  1, 2, 3, 4, 5;

ASK Tradeoffs:
"Are you willing to make tradeoffs between attributes?";
CHOICES Tradeoffs: Yes, No;

ASK One_cutoff_value:
"Is an alternative acceptable if at least one attribute level
of the chosen alternative exceeds a desirable level?";
CHOICES One_cutoff_value: Yes, No;

ASK All_cutoff_values:
"Is an alternative acceptable if  the attribute levels of the chosen
alternative exceed the cutoff values for each of the attribute?";
CHOICES All_cutoff_values: Yes, No;

ASK Dominance:
"Is an alternative nondominated if there exist no other alternative
that will yield an improvement in one attribute without causing a
degeneration in at least one other attribute?";
CHOICES Dominance: Yes, No;

ASK Rank_attributes:
"Can you rank-order all the attributes in decreasing order of importance?";
```

Figure 3: Statements Block — user questions of MCDM Advisor knowledge-base file.

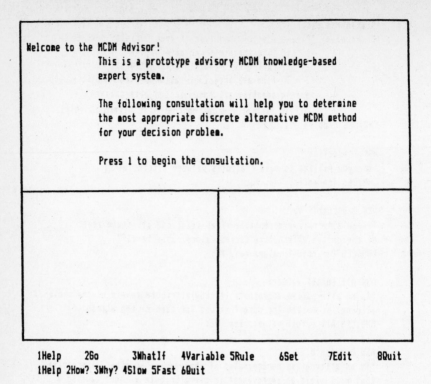

Figure 4: Initial consultation screen for MCDM knowledge base.

```
               Press 1 to begin the consultation.
Please identify the type of your decision problem
               1 - To find the preferred alternative
               2 - To rank-order feasible alternatives
               3 - To find all acceptable alternatives
               4 - To identify all nondominated alternatives
               5 - To partially order nondominated alternatives
 1 ◁                          2                          3
 4                            5
```

```
Testing 1                        Consultation = 1 CNF 100
RULE 1 IF                        Consultation = 1 CNF 100
Problem = 3 AND
Tradeoffs = No AND
One_cutoff_value = Yes
THEN
Advice = Disjunctive_Method CNF 100
Finding Problem
```

```
   Enter to select   END to complete   /Q to Quit   ? for Unknown
```

Figure 5: First question in the sample consultation.

```
Are you willing to make tradeoffs between attributes?
  Yes                     No ◁

Can you rank-order all the attributes in
decreasing order of importance?
  Yes ◁                   No

Is an alternative acceptable if  the attribute levels of the chosen
alternative exceed the cutoff values for each of the attribute?
  Yes ◁                   No
```

Problem = 1 AND Tradeoffs = No AND All_cutoff_values = Yes AND Change_cutoff_values = Yes THEN Advice = AIM-Aspiration_Level_Interacti ve_Model CNF 100 Finding All_cutoff_values	Pause = 1 CNF 100 Pause = 1 CNF 100 Problem = 1 CNF 100 Tradeoffs = No CNF 100 Rank_attributes = No CNF 100

```
    Enter to select   END to complete   /Q to Quit   ? for Unknown
```

Figure 6: Second, third, and fourth questions in the sample consultation.

```
Yes   ◁              No

Would you like to explore the nondominated frontier by allowing the
user to establish and adjust levels of aspirations?
Yes   ◁              No

The best advice we have for you is as follows:
         the recommended MCDM method is AIM-Aspiration Level Interactive Model
CNF 100.
```

```
Tradeoffs = No AND              Pause = 1 CNF 100
All_cutoff_values = Yes AND     Problem = 1 CNF 100
Change_cutoff_values = Yes      Tradeoffs = No CNF 100
THEN                            Rank_attributes = No CNF 100
Advice = AIM-Aspiration_Level_Interacti   All_cutoff_values = Yes CNF 100
ve_Model CNF 100               Change_cutoff_values = Yes CNF 100
Finding All_cutoff_values       Advice = AIM-Aspiration_Level CNF 100
Finding Change_cutoff_values
```

```
1Help    2Go     3WhatIf  4Variable 5Rule    6Set     7Edit    8Quit
1Help 2How? 3Why? 4Slow 5Fast 6Quit
```

Figure 7: Last question and advice in the sample consultation.

```
Yes    ◁           No

Would you like to explore the nondominated frontier by allowing the
user to establish and adjust levels of aspirations?
 Yes                    No   ◁

The best advice we have for you is as follows:
         the recommended MCDM method is not found in the MCDM knowledge base C
F 100.
```

Advice <> KIrkwood_&_Sarin_Method AND	Consultation = 1 CNF 100
Advice <> SMART AND	Problem = 1 CNF 100
Advice <> AIM-Aspiration_Level_Interact	Tradeoffs = No CNF 100
ive_Model AND	Rank_attributes = No CNF 100
Advice <> Electre_I	All_cutoff_values = Yes CNF 100
THEN	Change_cutoff_values = No CNF 100
Advice = not_found_in_the_MCDM_knowledg	Advice = not_found_in_the_MCD CNF 100
e_base CNF 100	

```
 1Help    2Go     3WhatIf   4Variable 5Rule    6Set    7Edit    8Quit
 1Help 2How? 3Why? 4Slow 5Fast 6Quit
```

Figure 8: Advice when the goal has not been reached.

```
Testing b:\MCDM.kbs
(= yes CNF 0 )
(= 1 CNF 100 )
!   Advice
!   !   Testing 1
!   !   !   Problem
!   !   !   !   (= 1 CNF 100 )
!   !   Testing 2
!   !   Testing 3
!   !   Testing 4
!   !   !   Tradeoffs
!   !   !   !   (= No CNF 100 )
!   !   !   Rank_attributes
!   !   !   !   (= No CNF 100 )
!   !   Testing 5
!   !   Testing 6
!   !   Testing 7
!   !   !   All_cutoff_values
!   !   !   !   (= Yes CNF 100 )
!   !   !   Change_cutoff_values
!   !   !   !   (= Yes CNF 100 )
!   !   (= AIM-Aspiration_Level_Interactive_Model CNF 100 )
```

Figure 9: Example of a decision trace.

```
Are you willing to make tradeoffs between attributes?
  Yes                    No   ◁

Is an alternative acceptable if at least one attribute level
of the chosen alternative exceeds a desirable level?
  Yes                    No   ◁

Is an alternative acceptable if  the attribute levels of the chosen
alternative exceed the cutoff values for each of the attribute?
  Yes                    No
```

```
Testing 2                          Consultation = 1 CNF 100
RULE 2 IF                          Consultation = 1 CNF 100
Problem = 3 AND                    Problem = 3 CNF 100
Tradeoffs = No AND                 Tradeoffs = No CNF 100
All_cutoff_values = Yes            One_cutoff_value = No CNF 100
THEN
Advice = Conjunctive_Method CNF 100
Finding All_cutoff_values
```

```
Enter to select   END to complete    /Q to Quit   ? for Unknown
```

Figure 10: Second, third, and fourth questions in a sample consultation.

```
┌─────────────────────────────────────────────────────────────────────┐
│ Are you willing to make tradeoffs between attributes?                 │
│   Yes                    No                                           │
│                                                                       │
│ Is an alternative acceptable if at least one attribute level          │
│ of the chosen alternative exceeds a desirable level?                  │
│   Yes                    No                                           │
│                                                                       │
│ Is an alternative acceptable if  the attribute levels of the chosen   │
│ ──────────────────────────[ WHY ]──────────────────────────          │
│   │ The question is being asked because:                          │  │
│   │ If you want to classify the decision alternatives into acceptable/│
│   │ not acceptable categories AND an alternative is acceptable for you│
│   │ if attribute levels of the chosen alternative exceed the cutoff values│
│   │ for each of the attributes AND tradeoffs between attributes are not│
│   │ permitted, then the appropriate MCDM method is CONJUNCTIVE METHOD.│
│   │ (Press Any Key To Continue)                                   │  │
│   │                                                               │  │
│   │                                                               │  │
│                                                                       │
├───────────────────────────────────┬───────────────────────────────────┤
│ Finding All_cutoff_values         │                                   │
│                                   │                                   │
└───────────────────────────────────┴───────────────────────────────────┘

  1Help    2How?    3Why?    4Slow    5Fast    6Quit
  Ask why a question was asked
```

Figure 11: WHY? option.

Interactive System for Multicriterial Analysis — Some Aspects and One Application

Ivan Popchev, Loreta Markova
Institute of Industrial Cybernetics & Robotics
Acad. G. Bonchev str., Bl. 2
1113 Sofia, Bulgaria

Abstract

The described system solves discrete multicriterial problems with a finite set of alternatives. The system has realizations of several methods for multicriterial choice. It is implemented on IBM PC/XT compatible computer. The computational properties of the system are described on the base of analysis of numerical experiments. An approach for analysing the sensitivity of the results with respect to some parameters is proposed. Some information about real applications is given, too.

1 Some general information and realised methods

The system can be used in such practical cases, when it is necessary to select some elements from a finite set — for example to select technologies, research themes or investment projects. These elements are called alternatives and they are described by a set of numerical characteristics. The partial criteria for estimation of the alternatives are functions of these characteristics. The system uses normalized decision matrix. There are realization of five methods for multicriterial estimation and choice, all of them use this decision matrix. There are possibilities for combined use of some of the methods.

Two algorithms for choice of a subset of alternatives are realized — the first one is the Pareto algorithm and the second one is the conjunctive satisfying method. Also two order algorithms are realized. They are simple additive weighting method (SAW) and method of maximin. Another method for checking the nondominance is realized. The user chooses only a part of all alternatives and the system checks their nondominance, comparing them with all alternatives. The result is only a part of the nondominated set. Results from other methods can be used for choosing alternatives for nondominance checking.

The combined usage of methods offers to the user: firstly to select a subset of alternatives, and, secondly, to order the selected alternatives using an appropriate method. The obtained results have a corresponding combination of properties.

2 System features and computational properties

The system has a diary of experiments, thus initial data, intermedia data and final results can be recorded on disk. The data in the diary can be viewed on the screen, can be printed or can be used for further computation (for example for combination of methods).

The system uses the program language BASIC, which is useful when the functions of partial criteria are assigned during the dialogue, since the interpretative properties of BASIC are used. Partial criteria functions can be any BASIC allowed functions of the characteristics. In the case, where it is necessary to assign more complex criteria functions, it is possible to use special user written programs.

Many computational experiments have been made with the interactive system. Some data for the working time (in minutes) of the realized methods, are given in the table. These data correspond to problems with 100, 150, 200, 250, 300 alternatives, but the number of characteristics and criteria is 5. The computations are realized on IBM PC/XT compatible computer.

Problem dimensions Methods	$100 \times 5 \times 5$	$150 \times 5 \times 5$	$200 \times 5 \times 5$	$250 \times 5 \times 5$	$300 \times 5 \times 5$
Estimation	10,5	15	23	31	42
Normalization	5	5,5	8	10	12
Pareto	10	15	29	40	51
Conjunctive satisfying	1,5	2	4	5,5	6
Simple additive weighted (SAW)	3,5	7	13	18	22
Maxmin	3,5	7,5	12,5	19	23
Combination of methods					
Pareto — SAW	2	4	5,5	7	8
Pareto — maxmin	2	4	6	7	8,5
Conjunctive — SAW	2,5	4	6	7	8,5
Conjunctive — maxmin	2,5	4	6	7	8

Table 1: Some experimental data — working time (in minutes)

The time results given in the table include reading and writing operations on disk, and the necessary time for working with the keyboard.

Data from the diary are used in the experiments with combination of methods. The shown results are needed for ordering the choosed subset only.

When the problem dimensions are fixed the time needed for applying SAW, maximin and conjunctive satisfying does not depend on the concrete problem. It is not the same with Pareto method and with the nondominance checking. When the number of alternatives increases, the time needed for SAW and maximin increases mainly, because of the work of the program that order the alternatives.

The shown times are acceptable for the application, discussed here (see below).

3 Stability with respect to the weighting coefficients

Many MCDM methods for finite sets use weighting coefficients. The final result of the method depends on the choosed vector l^0 of these coefficients. But very often there are different ways to choose such vector, on the other hand the exact determination of an unique vector l^0 may be difficult. Therefore, the answer of the following question is of some interest: what are the maximal admissible changes in the vector l^0 that keep the obtained result unchanged.

Let $l \in L$, $l = [l_1, l_2, \ldots, l_n]$ be a vector of weighting coefficients, let us assume, that the problem is solved when $l = l^0$, and let $L_{ad} \subseteq L$ be the subset with the following property: for each $l \in L_{ad}$ the obtained result is the same as when $l = l^0$. Of course $l^0 \in L_{ad}$. We assume that the set L_{ad} can be presented by the following system of linear inequalities: $g_k(l) \geq 0$, $k = 1, 2, \ldots, p$. The method of simple additive weighting can be used as an example. Following this method we attach a weighted average value to each alternative. These average values order the alternatives. When the values of the partial criteria are constants, the set of all weights keeping the same order between alternatives can be described by a system of linear inequalities between the corresponding average values. It is clear that we can obtain an adequate system of linear inequalities when simple additive weighting is used or interpreted in other ways as well as when some other MCDM methods are used.

Also, the set L_{ad} is described by the system $g_k(l) \geq 0$, $k = 1, 2, \ldots, p$. Then $g_k(l^0) \geq 0$, $k = 1, 2, \ldots, p$. But we shall suppose, that $g_k(l^0) > 0$, $k = 1, 2, \ldots, p$.

Let $t > 0$, consider the set L_0^t of vectors l, $l = [l_1, l_2, \ldots, l_n]$, where

$$L_0^t = \{ l / |l_i^0 - l_i| \leq t, \ \forall i \}.$$

The question under consideration is: what is the maximal t, for which the inequalities $g_k(l) \geq 0$, $k = 1, 2, \ldots, p$ hold for each $l \in L_0^t$. We can consider L_0^t as a hypercube with center in l^0 and edges, that are parallel to the coordinate axes. The sense of the question above is: what is the maximal hypercube of the described type that is admissible. For each point of this hypercube the obtained result is the same as the result obtained for l^0.

The inequality $g_k(l) \geq 0$, (k is fixed) can be rewritten as

$$\sum_{i=1}^{n} a_i^k \cdot l_i + d^k \geq 0.$$

Here, a_i^k and d^k are real numbers. Let for $l = l^0$

$$\sum_{i=1}^{n} a_i^k \cdot l_i^0 + d^k > 0.$$

The vector l, corresponding to an arbitrary vertex of L_0^t can be presented by the following n numbers:

$$l_1^0 \pm t, l_2^0 \pm t, \ldots, l_n^0 \pm t.$$

Each choice of the sign plus or minus before t in all these numbers determines a vertex of L_0^t. If all vertexes of L_0^t are admissible, then each interior point of L_0^t as admissible too, i.e. the corresponding weighted sum of the vectors of the vertexes is admissible with respect to the inequality $g_k(l) \geq 0$.

Let I, $|I| = n$ be an index set. Having in mind the inequality $g_k(l) \geq 0$, we shall use the following partition of I:

$$I_1^k \cap I_2^k = \emptyset, \qquad I_1^k \cap I_3^k = \emptyset, \qquad I_2^k \cap I_3^k = \emptyset, \qquad I_1 \cup I_2 \cup I_3 = I.$$

This partition is obtained as follows:

$$i \in I_1^k, \qquad \text{if } a_i^k > 0$$
$$i \in I_2^k, \qquad \text{if } a_i^k < 0$$
$$i \in I_3^k, \qquad \text{if } a_i^k = 0$$

Let $d^k > 0$. Then the inequality $g(l_k^0) > 0$ can be presented as

$$\sum_{i \in I_1^k} a_i^k \cdot l_i^0 + d^k > - \sum_{i \in I_2^k} a_i^k \cdot l_i^0.$$

Here each number of this inequality is positive. (If $d_i^k < 0$, we can shift d_i^k on the right side.)

Now we consider such vertex of the hypercube L_0^t, whose corresponding vector l^m has the following components:

$$l_i^m = \begin{cases} l_i^0 - t, & i \in I_1^k \\ l_i^0 + t, & i \in I_2^k \\ l_i^0 \pm t, \text{ (an arbitrary sign)}, & i \in I_3^k \end{cases}$$

If t is sufficiently small, the inequality:

$$\sum_{i \in I_1^k} a_i^k (l_i^0 - t) + d^k > - \sum_{i \in I_2^k} a_i^k (l_i^0 + t) \tag{1}$$

is true. We can determine the maximal t, denoted by $t_{\max}^k$, for which the vertex in the point l^m is admissible yet:

$$\sum_{i \in I_1^k} a_i^k (l_i^0 - t_{\max}^k) + d^k = - \sum_{i \in I_2^k} a_i^k (l_i^0 + t_{\max}^k)$$

i.e.

$$t^k_{\max} = \left(\sum_{i \in I} a^k_i \cdot l^0_i + d_k\right) : \left(\sum_{i \in I^k_1} a^k_i - \sum_{i \in I^k_2} a^k_i\right).$$

Let $L^{k\,\max}_0$ denotes the hypercube L^t_0, when $t = t^k_{\max}$. It is clear, that inequality (1) is true, when $0 < t < t^k_{\max}$, i.e. the corresponding points of $L^{k\,\max}_0$ are admissible.

On the other hand, the inequality

$$\sum_{i \in I^k_1} a^k_i (l^0_i - t^k_{\max}) + d^k \geq - \sum_{i \in I^k_2} a^k_i (l^0_i + t^k_{\max})$$

is a strict one, when some (or all) signs minus before $t^k_{\max}$ in the left side are changed by plus, or when some (or all) signs plus before $t^k_{\max}$ in the right side are changed by minus. This means that all other vertexes of $L^{k\,\max}_0$ are admissible, too.

Moreover, the inequality

$$\sum_{i \in I^k_1} a^k_i (l^0_i - t_1) + d^k < - \sum_{i \in I^k_2} a^k_i (l^0_i + t_1)$$

is true, for $t_1 > t^k_{\max}$; i.e. the corresponding vertex is not admissible. Now we can determine t_{MAX}:

$$t_{\mathrm{MAX}} = \min_k \cdot t^k_{\max}.$$

We denote by $L^{\max}_0$ the hypercube L^t_0 for $t = t_{\mathrm{MAX}}$. It is clear that $L^{\max}_0$ is a set, admissible with respect to all $g_k(l) \geq 0$, $k = 1, 2, \ldots, p$, and $L^{\max}_0$ is the maximal admissible set of the type under consideration, i.e. when

$$|l^0_i - l_i| \leq t_{\mathrm{MAX}}$$

the result, obtained at $l = l^0$, remains unchanged.

A modification of this approach is possible when different bounds are used for different l_i.

The conditions for the vector l to belong to $L^{\max}_0$ are more strong than the analogous conditions for belonging to the maximal admissible hypersphere. But the checking of the first conditions satisfying is more easy. There is no need to use any special mathematical programming software for finding the maximal admissible hypercube $L^{\max}_0$. It is possible to realize a very simple algorithm, that can process a big amount of data (problems with big dimensions). The proposed method can be used for comparing different results obtained from one method (with different initial data) as well as obtained from different methods.

4 Real applications of the system

The interactive system is used in the Bulgarian Ministry of planning and economics to realize multicriterial analysis of projects, scientific research themes and technologies. The purpose of this analysis is to develop those directions, that are most important, most progressive. The objects (alternatives) that are analyzed with the help of multicriterial analysis, are described with numerical characteristics. These characteristics contain different indicators of technical, economical, ecological type and indicators, reflecting the labour conditions in the productions of a certain article or technology.

The criteria, which are the basis for estimation are:

- technical level and quality of the project or technologies;

- term for covering the development and introduction expenses;

- term for introduction;

- effectiveness of the export of the articles produced;

- degree of satisfying the customer's demand;

- relative finance part of the company, which makes the implementation;

- ecological indicators;

- labour conditions in the production of an article or technology.

These criteria are described as functions of the characteristics.

As a result of using this system an order of alternatives is obtained. This order becomes an object for additional analysis and decision making.

5 Conclusion

There are different possibilities for further development of the described system. One way is to include usage of more sophisticated program tools or approaches as well as to allow including of this system in other program systems. Another way is to include usage of more sophisticated theoretical results, allowing more deep analysis of different problems.

The authors are grateful to their colleague Boyan Metev for the helpful discussion.

References

Hwang, C.L. and Kwangsun, Y. (1981). Multiple Attribute Decision Making Methods and Applications. LNEMS, Berlin etc., Springer-Verlag, Vol. 186.

Li, H.L. (1987). Solving Discrete Multicriteria Decision Problems Based on Logic — Based Decision Support Systems. *Decision Support Systems*, Vol. 3, No. 2.

Popchev, I., Metev, B., Markova, L. (1985). Interactive System for Multicriterial Estimation and Choice. Bulgarian Academy of Sciences, Sofia, (in Bulgarian).

Organizational Aspects of Decision Support Systems Integration

Ivan Stanchev

Institute for Systems Analysis and Management
53, G. Dimitrov Blvd., 1000 Sofia, Bulgaria

Abstract

The main design problems of an integrated DSS (i.e., a complete DSS, consisting of separate DSS-modules, tied together), are presented and discussed. Some differences between the existing models of integration, regarding the methodological and organisational side of DSS projects, are outlined, and their applicability (especially for PC-based products in distributed DSS projects in distributed DSS multi-user environments) is discussed.

1   Introduction

The study of the characteristic features of the process of Decision Support Systems (DSS) building and implementation and of the problems concerning their effective use in the reality of decision maker's practical activities necessitates the search of answers to the following principle questions:

- Is it possible and to what an extent is it really possible to use in DSS designing ready parts representing modules of previously developed systems or of systems offered at the market of software products as "ready-made clothes" for the needs of decision making process support?

- Is it necessary when building and implementing DSS in a concrete organizational environment to analyze and to keep in mind the approach, style and methods that are traditionally used by the decision maker?

The standpoints of the specialists and the theoretical studies give different answers to these questions. The existing widespread opinion about the unique nature of each DSS presupposes a negative answer to the first question. At the same time, the great expenses connected with the application of the "zero based approach" in DSS building make analysts and programmers look for "ready-made software products" interpreting some procedures and models in the process of decision making. On the other hand, this tendency leads to the disregard of the specific, connected with the concrete organizational culture, peculiarities of the process of decision making which on its part reduces very much the real efficiency of DSS use.

The attempts to solve this discrepancies presume the application of a new approach in DSS building and implementation which is based on the principles and methods of situation analysis in the organizational theory and is evolutionary by nature (Stanchev, 1989).

As a consequence of the application of this approach however there arises the problem for the successive integration of the already created or borrowed and adapted modules with new ones in the process of the extension of the scope and content of the DSS built. This problem is often evaded, the efforts of the system analysts and designers being usually directed towards the separate solving of partial tasks in the management system on the basis of the classical optimizational or stochastic models. By using simulation techniques as well as sophisticated software tools for dialogue with the end user, they actually offer their customers user's friendly systems but in a number of cases these software products are only labelled as DSS without exercising the basic functions of such a system already defined by the authors of the DSS conception (Sprague and Carlson, 1982).

On the other hand, the specialists having scientific interests in the field of decision theory, most of them being mathematicians, try hard mainly to improve the exact mathematical methods stipulating that the problems of integration are of technical nature and that they are within the competence of software engineering, i.e. that they are problems of the systems' programmers.

All this results in the existing nowadays situation which may be characterized by the availability of quite a small number of complex DSS integrating the solving of the basic for the economic organizations tasks. The survey made in (Hopple, 1988) is eloquent testimony to the above assertion.

2 Cases of integration

From organizational point of view we should draw a line between two main trends analyzing the situations under which integration is realized:

- investigation and modelling of the decision making process;

- choice and development of DSS modules.

The first trend is connected with the existing organizational technology of the decision making process and the degree of its centralization.

In the presense of formalized technology and strongly centralized system of decision making it is usually the normative approach in models' development that is applied. This approach prescribes a strictly defined behaviour on behalf of the decision maker and presumes absolute rationality and optimal choice. It also presumes that the decisions are more or less of routine nature and even in the cases of uncertainty and risk it is assumed that the models built by using stochastic methods give enough grounds for determining the best decision.

The normative approach may be traditionally connected with the classical methods of operational research and their development, while the attempts to integrate the models with the procedures for data processing are connected with the conception about Management Information Systems (MIS) building developed in the 1960's.

In a decentralized system of management and decision making involving non-formal procedures and possibilities for application of multicriteria and expert evaluations in the interpretation of the decision maker's behaviour the descriptive approach is applied. This approach presumes restricted rationality and satisficing choice. It is presumed as well that the decisions are of non-trivial nature and that the problem situations arise "ad-hoc" in a complex and conflict organizational environment.

It is the very realization of the fact that a considerable number of the decisions made in the process of management in the real economic practice belong to this group that has brought about the creation and dissemination of the DSS conception.

The problems concerning the transition from normative to descriptive approach in the investigation and modelling of the decision making process with a view to the methodology and development of DSS are elaborated in (Stanchev, 1988). In the logical analysis made a particular attention is paid to the question related to the use of the technology of Expert Systems (ES) development for the purpose of integration in DSS. The survey of the activities carried out during the pre-design stage of DSS building (Stanchev, 1989) gives one a clear notion about the role of descriptive and normative models in the interpretation of the "key decisions" in the process of the decision making procedures' description.

Here great attention should be paid to the second trend treating the analysis of the situations in which the integration in DSS is realized. This trend is connected first of all with the selected approach for realization of the design stage (Stanchev, 1989) and especially of the activities giving priority to the development of one or another module depending on the existing restrictions and the exactly determined operational objectives of the project.

Generally the approaches may be formulated as follows:

- designing of new modules which would be later integrated in a common system for decision support;

- integration of the existing modules or parts of ready-made program systems in a common system for decision support.

Each of these two approaches has its advantages and faults. When the first approach is applied the existing restrictions may be taken into account already during the process of designing, but they would require a greater expenditure of resources (time and labour). When the second approach is applied it is necessary to develop an additional software mechanism for the realization of the integration but resources would be saved and favorable conditions would be provided for the further extension and improvement of the system.

The latter argument is may be of greatest significance bearing in mind the evolutionary nature of the process of DSS buiding and implementation.

The restrictions representing original criteria in the choice of an approach should therefore be treated in two aspects — technological and organizational.

The technological restrictions are connected with the selected operational system, the programming language, the working mode (single-user's — multi-user's mode), the characteristics of the hardware used, etc.

Not less important are the organizational restrictions. Together with the operational purposes of the project they are essentially connected with the content of the process of decision making itself, on the one hand, and on the other hand, with the terms and financing of the project.

The technological restrictions and their overcoming in the process of integration are treated from a conceptual point of view in (Nitchev, 1989). On this basis during the last two years the development of the software mechanism for linking separate modules in a common DSS began by making use of the product DESQview of the firm QUARTER-DECK.

The observance of the organizational restrictions gives rise to many variants when determining the approach for realization of the design stage and this necessitates the search for adequate to the real situations integrational models.

3   Models of integration

The binding of the extreme situations along the two main trends of the analysis in a grid table affords the opportunity to formulate four basic models of integration in DSS (Buxton and Becker, 1986).

The Tool Box Model

Each module in this model has its own, exactly determined and previously known purpose. Figuratively speaking, the modules are arranged in "shelves" as in the tool warehouse of an engineering enterprise. The DSS user uses a given module according to the concrete tasks and the sequence in which is solving them. After finishing his work with a given module he may move to another one either immediately after using the module or after a certain period of time. His behaviour is determined by the formally described technology of the process of management. Actually the integration is realized only through the actions of the DSS user. When compatibility is lacking in relation to the input-output data, the movement from one module to another is secured through transformation and processing of the data by the user. Since the modules have been borrowed from different systems or have been independently developed in the different periods of the DSS building, in the general case such a compatibility does not exist. This is why, in order to facilitate the work of the DSS user tools are developed such as I have already mentioned (see Nitchev, 1989). In this model the extension of the systems does not raise problems.

The Linear Model

In this model, regardless of the independent purpose of the separate modules, and because of the compatibility between them, this compatibility being built in the process of design, the transitions are directly realized, usually by using menu techniques. The content of the separate menus and the logic of linking are determined by the initially formalized process of decision making and management. The behaviour of the DSS user is considerably restricted, in fact it is predetermined within the possible branchings envisaged in the DSS architecture.

The movement from module to module determines the linear route and wherever branchings are possible usually the user may be assisted by the system at request with "help" functions.

The inclusion of new modules in this model is considerably more difficult especially if changes should be made in the automated transition provided by the separate menus.

The Market Place Model

In the "market place" model, DSS users move around playing the role of investigator, seeking wisdom or changing the "goods" in the stalls surrounding the market place. There are different types of stalls: Information, Parameters, Achieve, Models, Simulation, Calculation, Evaluation, etc. The principle idea is that the tour around the market is not guided in any way; DSS users learn from making their own observations and decisions. This allows for great freedom in the behaviour of the system's user but presupposes the presence of special knowledge both about the operation of the system and about the possibilities and restrictions in applying the different models.

The inclusion of new modules in the system gives rise to fewer problems than in the linear model since the modules are especially designed for it and at the same time are relatively independent of the already existing ones. However, it also requires considerable expenditure of time and labour. On the other hand, since this model is based on the descriptive approach in the interpretation of the process of decision making, it is more easily perceived by the user.

The requirement for additional knowledge and skills is often compensated by including a highly qualified "assistant" who works with the system when elaborating and making decisions.

In his model as in the linear one, the integration is based on the compatibility of the modules but the determining factor for their linking is the user's behaviour.

The Guide Model

This model combines the advantages of the previous two models affording at the same time better possibilities for use of the already developed or borrowed modules. Since it is based on the descriptive approach, the behaviour of the DSS user is considerably more independent than that of the Tool Box Model user, but in order to reinforce the operation of the integration mechanism of the modules with a different degree of compatibility an advisory system is included in it. This system is developed on the basis of ES technology. In it knowledge of the logical sequence in working with the separate modules and the necessary transformations of the input-output data at the transitions and knowledge of the guiding and recommended information about the possibilities and restrictions of the separate modules is integrated. The system makes possible the use of hypertext conception in linking this information, thus enriching considerably the environment in which the DSS user works (Lewandowski, 1989). A more detailed description of the components and the functions of the developed for the purposes of the DSS integration system is given in Viktor Nichev's paper prepared for this Conference.

The inclusion of new modules in the DSS as well as the modification and the extension of the knowledge base allows actually unlimited changes and extensions of the system in the model. This is of great importance for the management of the economic activities because at present the development of the economic organizations is characterized by the exceptional dynamics of the changes in the normative base which are reflected in the technology of management and the models of decision making.

4 Conclusion

The study of the organizational aspects of DSS integration is not prompted only by purely scientifical interests in the methodology of DSS building and implementation. It has a considerable practical value oriented towards real evaluation of the experience accumulated so far and towards search for new possibilities for improvement of the entire activity related to the support of the decision making process.

The achievement of a high level integration in a given DSS, however not at the expense of its "user-friendliness", represents a basic factor for the effective use of the system.

The solving of this dilemma is of great importance in the transition to the multi-user mode of operation, a necessity prompted by the general tendency for decentralization of the decision making process. In this sense, the development of the integration models is actively stimulated by a number of new investigations related to the development of DSS for negotiations and elaboration of group decisions.

On the other hand, the mutual enrichment of the design techniques of DSS and ES, a fact which until recently has been a subject only of scientific discussions but is now proved by practical developments, represents an uninterrupted process which opens new vistas for integration problems solving.

All research and applied developments would acquire however new value only if committed to the context of the organizational environment for the purposes of which they are made.

One should never forget that behind each DSS there stand the real users who have their own style and methods of management and decision making, their own organizational culture and their own traditional scepticism with a view to the new computer technologies application in management.

References

Buxton, W. and Becker, R. (1986). Human-computer interaction: selected theories, technologies, techniques & tools. Proceedings of SIGGRAPH'86.

Hopple, G.W. (1988). The state of the art in decision support systems. Qed Inf. Sciences, Inc., Wellesley, Mass.

Lewandowski, A. (1989). Hypertext concepts in GDSS design. Abstracts of the 10th European Conference on operational research, Belgrad, June 1989.

Nitchev, V. (1989). Some aspects of the integration between DSS and KBS. Proceedings of the International Workshop held in Albena, Bulgaria, October 1987. Springer.

Sprague, R.H. and Carlson, E.D. (1982). Building effective decision support systems. Prentice-Hall International, London.

Stanchev, I. (1988). DSS-ES integration problems. Proceedings of the International Workshop held in Yalta, USSR, October-November 1988.

Stanchev, I. (1989). Software engineering principles in the building of decision support systems. Proceedings of the International Workshop held in Albena, Bulgaria, October 1987. Springer.

Part 5

Applications of Multiple Criteria Decision Support

Part A

Solving Multiobjective Diet Optimization Problem under Uncertainty

Piotr Czyżak
*Center of Education
and Development in Agriculture
61-659 Poznań, Poland*

Roman Słowiński
*Technical University of Poznań
Institute of Computing Science
60-965 Poznań, Poland*

Abstract

The diet optimization problem considered in this paper concerns feeding farm animals. The nature of this problem requires taking into account multiple objectives on the one hand, and uncertainty following from imprecision of data on the other hand. Since the uncertainty has an epistemological character, it is natural to express imprecise data in terms of tolerance intervals with a most possible value (or subinterval) and decreasing possibility for other values within the interval. This corresponds exactly to the definition of fuzzy numbers. In consequence, the feeding problem is formulated as a multiobjective linear programming problem with fuzzy coefficients. In order to solve it, the interactive method FLIP proposed by Słowiński is applied. A large part of the paper is devoted to solving a real feeding problem with the FLIP software on a micro.

1 Introduction

We deal with an agricultural decision problem which concerns feeding farm animals. A classical version of this problem is known under the name of diet optimization problem and was originally formulated in terms of linear programming. Evaluation of a diet for a farm animal needs, however, taking into account multiple criteria which are in general conflicting. This leeds to a multiobjective linear programming problem. Moreover, the data used in the model cannot be considerd as deterministic. Indeed, the coefficients of the MOLP (multiobjective linear programming) problem corresponding to the chemical composition of fodders, the lower and upper bounds to be imposed on some components of the diet, as well as the costs of buying or producing a unit of a given fodder are neither certain nor precise. The imprecision follows from unpredictable variation of the chemical composition, approximate requirements concerning components of the diet and fluctuation of costs connected with such uncontrollable factors as climate, soil conditions and the market. It turned out to be very difficult to estimate data used in the model. The uncertainty following from the imprecision has an epistemological character because of high subjectivity in the estimation. In this situation, the experts accepted expressing data in terms of tolerance intervals with a most possible value (or subinterval) and decreasing possibility for other values within the interval. This corresponds exactly to the definition of fuzzy numbers, i.e. normal convex continuous fuzzy subsets of the real line. So, in this case, the modelling of uncertainty using fuzzy numbers seems quite natural. In consequence, the feeding problem is formulated as a MOLP problem with fuzzy coefficients. In order to solve it, we shall apply the interactive method FLIP proposed by (Słowiński, 1986).

In section 2, we formulate the multiobjective diet optimization problem under uncertainty. The idea of FLIP is recalled in section 3. In the last section, we solve a real feeding problem using FLIP software on a micro.

2 Problem formulation

The feeding problem has been formulated in terms of a MOLP problem by (Czyżak, 1989). The objective is to prescribe a qualitative and quantitative composition of a daily diet that gives the "best" results (e.g. an increse of weight) at the "lowest" cost. Because of the uncertainty raised above, some cost coefficients in the objective functions, as well as some coefficients on the both sides of the constraints are fuzzy numbers.

A solution is defined by vector $\underline{x} = [x_1, \ldots, x_n]$, where x_j denotes an amount of fodder j in the daily diet $(j = 1, \ldots, n)$ and n is a number of all kinds of fodders at farmer's disposal.

The region of variation of $\underline{x}$ is bounded by two groups of constraints: qualitative and quantitative.

Qualitative constraints ensure a chemical composition of the diet adapted to the animal's needs; they define lower and upper bounds on the content of proteins, amino acids, calcium, vitamins etc.:

$$\tilde{b}_d^L \leq \sum_{j \in B_d} \tilde{a}_{ij} x_j \leq \tilde{b}_d^U \qquad i = 1, \ldots, m_1 \tag{1}$$

where $d \in \{1, \ldots, D\}$, D is the total number of components, $B_d \subseteq \{1, \ldots, n\}$ is a subset of fodders containing component d, $\tilde{a}_{ij}$ is an amount of component d in fodder j, $\tilde{b}_d^L$ and $\tilde{b}_d^U$ are lower and upper bounds on the content of component d in the daily diet, respectively.

There are two types of **quantitative constraints**. The first type of quantitative constraints limits the mass fractions of particular fodders in the diet:

$$x_j - \tilde{a}_{i,n+1}^j \sum_{j=1}^n x_j \leq 0 \qquad i = m_1 + 1, \ldots, m_2 \tag{2}$$

where $\tilde{a}_{i,n+1}^j$ is a maximum mass fraction of fodder j in the diet, $j \in \{1, \ldots, n\}$. The second type of quantitative constraints imposes lower and upper bounds on the total mass of the daily dose:

$$b_{\min} \leq \sum_{j=1}^n x_j \leq b_{\max} \tag{3}$$

where $b_{\min}$ and $b_{\max}$ are the respective bounds.

In order to evaluate a daily diet we use three criteria:

- **cost**

$$\sum_{j \in B_c} \tilde{c}_j^1 x_j + \sum_{j \in B_c'} \tilde{c}_j^2 x_j \tag{4}$$

where $B_c \subseteq \{1, \ldots, n\}$ is a subset of fodders which have to be bought, $\tilde{c}_j^1$ is a price of a unit of fodder j, $B_c' \subseteq \{1, \ldots, n\}$ is a subset of home made fodders (produced at the farm), $\tilde{c}_j^2$ is a cost of a unit of fodder j, $B_c \cap B_c' = \emptyset$, $B_c \cup B_c' = \{1, \ldots, n\}$,

- **amino acid content**

$$\sum_{j \in B_A} \tilde{c}_j^3 x_j \tag{5}$$

where $B_A \subseteq \{1, \ldots, n\}$ is a subset of fodders containing amino acids (methionine and cystine), $\tilde{c}_j^3$ is a content of amino acids in a unit of fodder j,

- **fibre content**

$$\sum_{j \in B_W} \tilde{c}_j^4 x_j \tag{6}$$

where $B_W \subseteq \{1, \ldots, n\}$ is a subset of fodders containing fibres, $\tilde{c}_j^4$ is a content of fibres in a unit of fodder j.

The cost and the fibre content should be minimized while the amino acid content should be maximized.

Formally, the feeding problem is a MOLP problem which consists in finding vector x which satisfies constraints (1)–(3) and yields a best compromise between objectives (4)–(6). The imprecision of data makes all coefficients with a tilde ($\tilde{}$) uncertain.

Generally speaking, we have to solve the following MOLP problem with fuzzy coefficients:

$$\text{MAX} \begin{bmatrix} \tilde{\underline{c}}_1 \underline{x} \\ \ldots \\ \tilde{\underline{c}}_k \underline{x} \end{bmatrix} \quad \text{s.t.} \quad \begin{array}{ll} \tilde{\underline{a}}_i \underline{x} \leq \tilde{b}_i & i = 1, \ldots, m \\ x_j \geq 0 & j = 1, \ldots, n \end{array} \tag{7}$$

where $\tilde{\underline{c}}_l$ is a row vector of cost coefficients of objective l ($l = 1, \ldots, k$), $\tilde{\underline{a}}_i$ is the i-th row of the matrix of coefficients and $\tilde{b}_i$ is a right-hand-side coefficient of the i-th constraint ($i = 1, \ldots, m$).

3 A sketch of FLIP

The FLIP method proposed for solving problem (7) consists of three main steps:

A — formulation of problem (7) and definition of fuzzy coefficients and fuzzy aspiration levels on objectives.

B — transformation of the fuzzy problem into a deterministic multiobjective mathematical programming problem.

C — application of an interactive method for solving the deterministic problem; if a best compromise solutions has been obtained then stop, otherwise return to step A or B for revision.

As we can observe, this is a usual way for solving multiobjective mathematical programming problem under uncertainty.

FLIP (Słowiński, 1986) is intended to solve problem (7) where all uncertain coefficients are supposed to be given as fuzzy numbers, i.e. normal convex continuous fuzzy subsets of the real line.

The method uses an L–R representation of fuzzy numbers. An L–R type fuzzy number is denoted by $\tilde{m} = (m, \alpha, \beta)_{LR}$ and its membership function is defined as:

$$\mu_m(x) = \begin{cases} L((m-x)/\alpha) & \text{if } x \leq m \\ R((x-m)/\beta) & \text{if } x \geq m \end{cases}$$

where m is the "middle" value, α and β are non-negative left and right "spreads" of $\tilde{m}$, respectively, and L, R are symmetric bell-shaped reference functions which are decreasing in $(-\infty, +\infty)$ and $L(0) = R(0) = 1$, $L(1) = R(1) = 0$.

Taking into account that fuzzy aspiration levels $\tilde{g}_1, \ldots, \tilde{g}_k$ are defined on all objectives, one can easily see that the main question to be answered is the comparison of the left-hand- and right-hand-sides of the objectives and constraints which are fuzzy numbers for a given $\underline{x}$.

In order to compare fuzzy numbers $\tilde{m} = (m, \alpha, \beta)_{LR}$ and $\tilde{n} = (n, \gamma, \delta)_{L'R'}$, FLIP uses two indices: σ and π, which express in a different way the degree of possibility that the first number is greater than the second one.

$$\begin{aligned} \sigma(\tilde{n} > \tilde{m}) &= F(m-n), & \text{where } F = (\delta R'^{-1} + \alpha L^{-1})^{-1} \\ \sigma(\tilde{m} > \tilde{n}) &= G(n-m), & \text{where } G = (\gamma L'^{-1} + \beta R^{-1})^{-1} \\ \pi(\tilde{n} >_\eta \tilde{m}) &= n + \delta R'^{-1}(\eta) - m - \beta R^{-1}(\eta) \\ \pi(\tilde{m} >_\eta \tilde{n}) &= m - \alpha L'^{-1}(\eta) - n - \gamma L'^{-1} \end{aligned}$$

where $0 \leq \eta \leq 1$ is a level of comparison. The situation is illustrated in Fig. 1.

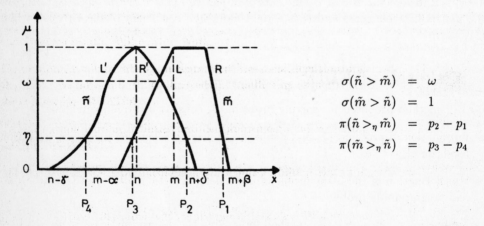

Figure 1: Comparison of fuzzy numbers $\tilde{n}$ and $\tilde{m}$.

If $L = R'$, $R = L'$ and $\eta = 0$, as we assume here for the sake of clarity, the above comparison indices are simplified:

$$
\begin{aligned}
\sigma(\tilde{n} > \tilde{m}) &= L((m - n)/(\alpha + \delta)), \\
\sigma(\tilde{m} > \tilde{n}) &= R((n - m)/(\beta + \gamma)), \\
\pi(\tilde{n} >_\eta \tilde{m}) &= n + \delta - m - \beta \\
\pi(\tilde{m} >_\eta \tilde{n}) &= m - \alpha - n + \gamma
\end{aligned}
$$

It is supposed that $\tilde{n} \geq \tilde{m}$ at level τ, η and θ

$$
\text{if} \quad \sigma(\tilde{n} > \tilde{m}) \geq \tau \quad \text{and} \quad \pi(\tilde{n} >_\eta \tilde{m}) \geq \theta
$$

where τ and θ are safety coefficients, called "optimistic" and "pessimistic", respectively, $\tau \in [0,1]$, $\theta \in (-\infty, +\infty)$.

In step B, using the comparison principle for fuzzy goals and objectives, and fuzzy rigth-hand- and left-hand-sides of the constraints, one arrives to an associate deterministic problem. Assuming that

$$
\begin{aligned}
\underline{\tilde{a}}_i &= (\underline{a}_i, \alpha_i, \underline{\beta}_i)_{LR}, & \tilde{b}_i &= (b_i, 0, \delta_i)_{LL} & i &= 1, \ldots, m \\
\underline{\tilde{c}}_l &= (\underline{c}_l, \varepsilon_l, \underline{\gamma}_l)_{LR}, & \tilde{g}_l &= (g_l, 0, \nu_l)_{LL} & l &= 1, \ldots, k
\end{aligned}
$$

and that τ_i, θ_i, η_i ($i = 1, \ldots, m$) are given, the deterministic problem equivalent to problem (7) is the following :

$$
\text{MAX} \begin{bmatrix} L((\underline{c}_1\underline{x} - g_1)/(\varepsilon_1\underline{x} + \nu_1)) \\ \cdots \\ L((\underline{c}_k\underline{x} - g_k)/(\varepsilon_k\underline{x} + \nu_k)) \end{bmatrix} \tag{8}
$$

$$
\begin{aligned}
\text{s.t.} \quad & \underline{a}_i\underline{x} - b_i \leq L^{-1}(\tau_i)(\alpha_i\underline{x} + \delta_i) & i &= 1, \ldots, m & (9) \\
& b_i - \underline{a}_i\underline{x} + \delta_i L^{-1}(\eta_i) - \underline{\beta}_i\underline{x}R^{-1}(\eta_i) \geq \theta_i & i &= 1, \ldots, m & (10) \\
& x_j \geq 0 & j &= 1, \ldots, n & (11)
\end{aligned}
$$

The objective functions of (8) are equal to $\sigma(\underline{\tilde{c}}_l\underline{x} > \tilde{g}_l)$ ($l = 1, \ldots, k$), constraints (9) are equivalent to $\sigma(\underline{\tilde{a}}_i\underline{x} < \tilde{b}_i) \geq \tau_i$ ($i = 1, \ldots, m$), and constraints (10), to $\pi(\underline{\tilde{a}}_i\underline{x} <_{\eta_i} \tilde{b}_i) \geq \theta_i$ ($i = 1, \ldots, m$).

If L in (8) is linear, i.e. $L(y) = 1 - y$, then problem (8)–(11) is transformed into multicriteria linear fractional programming problem:

$$
\text{MIN} \begin{bmatrix} f_1 = 1 - (\underline{c}_1\underline{x} - g_1)/(\varepsilon_1\underline{x} + \nu_1) \\ \cdots \\ f_k = 1 - (\underline{c}_k\underline{x} - g_k)/(\varepsilon_k\underline{x} + \nu_k) \end{bmatrix} \quad \text{s.t.} \quad (9)–(11) \tag{12}
$$

In step C, the interactive method of (Choo and Atkins, 1980), has been used to solve problem (12).

4 Solving an illustrative diet optimisation problem

Let us take a real-life diet optimization problem considered in (Czyżak and Słowiński, 1989). It concerns feeding a gilt using 8 kinds of fodders: turnip leafs, grass, steamed potatoes, lucerne, T–1 mixture, unpeeled barley, corn, molasses. The corresponding set of constraints (1)–(3) is composed of 12 fuzzy linear conditions involving 8 variables.

After entering the data, the next stage in problem formulation is defining aspiration levels for different criteria. Let us take fuzzy aspiration levels:

$$\text{for } z_1 \quad - \quad \tilde{g}_1 \quad = \quad (100, 0, 40),$$
$$\text{for } z_2 \quad - \quad \tilde{g}_2 \quad = \quad (15, 1, 0),$$
$$\text{for } z_3 \quad - \quad \tilde{g}_3 \quad = \quad (200, 0, 30),$$

The aspiration level for z_2 results from demand for amino acids, and the aspiration level for z_3 is the upper bound on the quantity of fibres that can be digested by the animal during one day.

The next step of the method is defining coefficients τ_i, η_i and θ_i. To begin with, let us assume $\tau_i = 0.6$ and $\eta_i = 0$ for all i. Let us assume that $\theta = \theta_1 = \theta_2 = 0$. It is equivalent to the requirement that there is no risk of violation of fuzzy constraints at level 0.

Then, the fuzzy problem is transformed into the deterministic one. The following stage consists in examining the efficient border of the transformed deterministic problem in view of looking for the best compromise solution. Let us denote the l-th solution examined in the j-th iteration by l_j. Let S be the number of compromise solutions that decision maker wants to examine in a given iteration; it is, obviously, a multiple of the number of criteria.

Iteration 1.

Let $S = 18$. Table 1 contains middle values of the solutions obtained. We have got a wide range of criteria values. Preliminary analysis of the solutions enables us to point out solutions that are not attractive because of too high cost of the diet ($1_1, 2_1, 3_1, 5_1, 6_1, 8_1, 9_1,$ $11_1, 12_1, 14_1, 17_1$) and those for which the content of amino acids or fibres differs too much from the aspiration levels ($4_1, 10_1, 13_1, 15_1, 16_1, 18_1$). Thus, we have got solution 7_1 which becomes a starting point for the next iteration.

Iteration 2.

Taking $S = 12$, we obtain 11 solutions (Tab. 2) and one of generated problems is contradictory (no feasible solution).

For all solutions obtained, the value of the cost criterion is within the range of the fuzzy aspiration level. In dropping out some nonattractive solutions, a decisive role is played by the amino acid content criterion. For solutions $5_2, 8_2, 11_2$, the content of amino acids is relatively close to the aspiration level (Fig. 2 — upper left, right and down left windows).

	1_1	2_1	3_1	4_1	5_1	6_1	7_1	8_1	9_1
z_1	282	282	282	184	348	348	141	414	300
z_2	24	24	24	18	29	19	13	35	11
z_3	318	318	318	396	404	178	367	497	123

	10_1	11_1	12_1	13_1	14_1	15_1	16_1	17_1	18_1
z_1	115	480	202	97	547	148	94	613	139
z_2	8	40	7	4.7	45	4	1.8	50	4
z_3	320	578	123	273	655	124	162	729	124

Table 1.

	1_2	2_2	4_2	5_2	6_2	7_2	8_2	9_2	10_2	11_2	12_2
z_1	146	141	121	150	150	100	159	159	95	169	139
z_2	13.5	13	9.2	14.3	9.6	5.6	16	5.1	3	17	4
z_3	367	367	330	384	156	292	401	125	206	425	124

Table 2.

In the course of iterations 3 to 7, we continue examination of the neighbourhood of solution 5_2. We try to get a diet which would cost about 170 units and would be the most digestible possible.

Iteration 7.

Let us take solution $4_6 = (165, 13, 243)$ as the starting point. For $S = 12$, we have 12 solutions listed in Tab. 3.

	1_7	2_7	3_7	4_7	5_7	6_7	7_7	8_7	9_7	10_7	11_7	12_7
z_1	165	165	165	159	170	170	152	174	174	146	178	178
z_2	13	13	13	12.7	14	12	11.5	14	11	10	14.7	10.4
z_3	242	242	242	231	232	174	220	224	155	209	210	146

Table 3.

Three of them have interesting values of amino acid and fibre content criteria. That are solutions 5_7, 8_7 and 11_7. Somewhat better values of both criteria have been obtained for solution 8_7. So, in spite of a high cost, we can accept this solution.

To get full evaluation of solution 8_7, let us analyse also the state of fuzzy constraints. In the problem there are only two. The first constraint, corresponding to the demand of oats, has been satisfied with some surplus. The second constraint ensuring appropriate

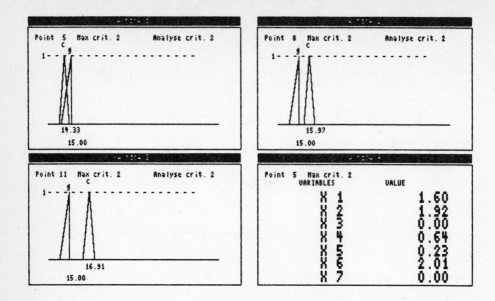

Figure 2: Amino acid content criterion for solutions 5_2, 8_2 and 11_2.

amount of proteins in the diet is shown in Fig. 3. As we can see, a large part of the fuzzy left-hand-side of the constraint is below the fuzzy right-hand-side. Therefore, we have a relatively big risk of violation of this constraint.

For reduction of this risk we return to the level of defining safety coefficients τ, η and θ. So, let us assume $\tau_i = 0.8$, $\eta_i = 0$ and $\theta_i = 0$ for all i.

Again, in the course of iterations $1'$ to $7'$, we have got a series of solutions which are not much different from those obtained earlier.

Let us analyse solutions obtained in iteration $7'$ only.

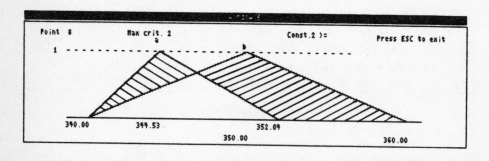

Figure 3: Fuzzy constraint for solution 8_7.

Iteration 7'.

As a starting point we take solution $4_{6'} = (165, 13, 242)$. For $S = 12$, we obtain solutions listed in Tab. 4.

	$1_{7'}$	$2_{7'}$	$3_{7'}$	$4_{7'}$	$5_{7'}$	$6_{7'}$	$7_{7'}$	$8_{7'}$	$9_{7'}$	$10_{7'}$	$11_{7'}$	$12_{7'}$
z_1	165	165	165	159	170	170	152	174	174	147	178	178
z_2	13	13	13	12.6	14	12	11.5	14	11	10	14.6	10.3
z_3	242	242	242	231	232	175	220	221	156	209	210	147

Table 4.

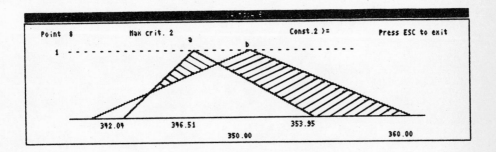

Figure 4: Fuzzy constraint for solution $8_{7'}$.

Fig. 4 shows the state of the second fuzzy constraint of solution $8_{7'}$. As we can see, the risk of violation of this constraint is much smaller than in the case of solution 8_7.

Finally, we can accept solution $8_{7'}$ as the best compromise. Thus we have got the diet which consist of:

0.91	units of turnip leafs,
0.20	units of lucerne,
0.25	units of T–1 mixture,
3.17	units of unpeeled barley.

The total mass of the daily dose is equal to 4.53 units.

References

Choo, E.U. and Atkins, D.R. (1980). An interactive algorithm for multicriteria programming. *Computers & Operations Res.* 7, pp. 81–87.

Czyżak, P. (1989). Multicriteria Agricultural Problem Solving under Uncertainty. *Foundations of Control Engineering*, 14, 2, pp. 61-80.

Czyżak, P. and Słowiński, R. (1989). Multiobjective Diet Optimization Problem under Fuzziness. In Verdegay, J.L., Delgado, M., (eds.), The Interface between Artificial Intelligence and Operations Research in Fuzzy Environment, Verlag TUV, Rheinland, Köln, pp. 85-103.

Słowiński, R. (1986). A multicriteria fuzzy linear programming method for water supply system development planning. *Fuzzy Sets and Systems*, 19, pp. 217-237.

Multicriteria Analysis of R&D Projects

B. Danev, K. Kolev
Bulgarian Industrial Association
134 Rakovski str.,
1000 Sofia, Bulgaria
G. Slavov
Atom Engineering
80 Assen str.,
1000 Sofia, Bulgaria

1 Introduction

The multicriteria analysis technique is applied for the development of strategic R&D projects. The main strategic directions for the national electronics industry are determined on the basis of a technology-commodity structure matrix. In the framework of these directions, R&D projects for financial support are nominated. The finite set of R&D projects in every direction is analyzed with respect to a great number of criteria with economic, social and technological natures.

Some modifications of post-optimal analysis are used for determination of the acceptable changes in the characteristics (parameters) of some fixed projects. The object of this analysis is to find (under constraints of limited resources) the appropriate values of characteristics, which would improve the position in the final ranking of certain projects.

2 Needs for multicriteria analysis of R&D projects in electronics

The competitiveness of manufactures on the electronic market mainly depends on the technological level of the producer, which defines the market success of the commercialized products. The project's choice is not unique. The selection has to fulfill contradictory requirements by the decision maker.

It is accepted that applying innovation projects in practice and its commercialization is concerned not only with investment decisions.

The needs for multicriterial analysis of R&D projects in electronics are mainly defined by the following factors:

- Dynamics in electronics development;
- Diversification of product structure;

- Exponentially decreasing life-cycle;
- Shortage of resources;
- Overlapping of product, technology and organizational structures.

3 Strategies in electronics development

The strategies for electronics development combine several major directions. Four basic strategies are applied:

- **Internationalization of the development.** It is realized through joining the efforts of resources of more countries for mutual interest projects.

- **Market "niche" orientation.** It is characteristic of small countries, oriented towards a narrow — specialized and specific product structure.

- **Following the development of leading companies.** Typical of this strategy is the use of existing technologies with market success, which are further developed. It involves two stages. Firstly diffusion of technology and knowledge and purchase of licenses; secondly R&D activities for enriching the product.

- **Development on local branch base.** An example of such a strategy is Finland, one of the leading producers of electronic products with application in the timber, woodworking and cellulose industry.

- **Mixed strategy.** The most possible approach is the use of all four strategies, giving priority to one of them.

The key point of the application of each of these strategies, as well as the mixed strategy, is related to the scientific R&D activity, which shapes the product's structure of the electronics complex and its competitiveness. The final project choice is to be based on several mixed strategies for the purpose of minimizing the risk of failing of any of them.

4 Electronics product-technological structure for R&D projects evaluation

A matrix of product-technological structure is given as a basic element of the system-informational technology for working out strategic R&D programmes. Table 1 represents simplified product-technological matrix of engrossed technology and product structure.

PRODUCT–TECHNOLOGICAL STRUCTURE OF ELECTRONICS FOR R&D PROJECTS EVALUATION

product str. technol. str.	houshold electronics	medical electronics	computers and peripherals	tools and instruments	informational equipment
materials element base technolog. equipment hardware software	local/import				

Table 1

The technology structure is described vertically in sequence, and horizontally are given separate product groups, subject to commercialization, within the scope of activities of the complex.

The sub-elements of the technological structure (some materials, elementary basis, etc.) can also be subjects of market realization.

The product-technology matrix can be detailed along the vertical, as well as along the horizontal. The matrix, specified up to a certain level of detailization, is of interest from the system analysis point of view. Thus, for instance, the materials can be split into supper clear substances, superclear materials, lacquer cover, chemicals, quartzplates, crystals and others. Respectively, the home appliances can be split into TV sets, video-recorders, audioequipment, microwave ovens, etc.

The product-technology matrix can be used in various other sections, as the matrix elements have other meaning and are filled with other data. E.g. the matrix elements can express the existence of own R&D activities. Another section is the distance between the respective product-technology element and the world level, a third section is the expression of the organizational structures.

The following matrix structure types are applied:

TYPES OF MATRIX STRUCTURES:

- for existence of local R&D projects;
- for choice organizational structure;
- for evaluation of technological infrastructure;
- for evaluation of the dependence on import;
- for redistribution of expenditures and efforts;
- for evaluation of the disadvantages of the technological relation of R&D with the final product.

The development of similar matrixes is a significant part of the technology for strategic programmes development in the stage of separate strategies analysis.

5 Expenditures for R&D projects — structure and problems

After defining the scope of scientific R&D activities (SRDA) arises the problem of distributing the funds for each of the tasks, which guarantee a technology-production chain. It must be clear what part of the total expenditures for the scientific and research activity (SRA) and for introduction and development activity (IDA) require all separate elements. SRA is connected, all above, with innovation problems. A small part of them reach technological maturity, so that they can be realized.

The SRDA funds must be distributed in accordance with the requirements of the technological structure. Fig. 1 shows an example of a **technological (vertical) structure**.

Analogically to the technology-product matrix, the detailization of the technology chain can be significantly extended, which guarantees the following of the SRDA process all along up to the final product by reading also the time-chart for the preparation of a research product.

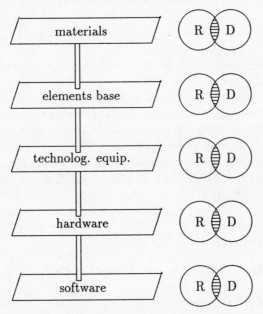

Figure 1: Technological (vertical) structure

Each technological level is connected also with a respective **horizontal structure** according to the ratio and quantity of SRDA, along which the expenditures for SRDA of a certain programme are to be distributed.

When a big programme of strategic importance is being executed, the resources can be distributed also according to the organizational structure. It is expedient to execute programmes, like, for instance, computerized joint production, with the common efforts and resources of several countries. The separate trends of the programme are executed at the levels of countries, branches, enterprises (laboratories, institutes). A model of distribution is shown in Fig. 2.

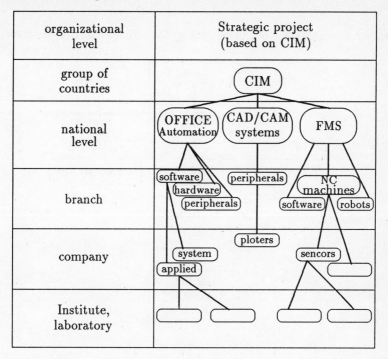

Figure 2: Organizational structure for the realization
of R&D projects

6 Generation of alternative SRDA projects

The alternate projects for SRDA can be divided into four groups:

- product-oriented. The decomposition of the SRDA, the creation of the whole technological chain of SRDA and licenses are oriented towards achievement of a final product's production. Various alternatives are possible, according to the redistribution of the task along the vertical and horizontal structures of SRDA.

- technology-oriented. The developments for SRDA are oriented towards the aim of creating definite technologies. Various technological alternatives for the achievement of a particular goal are generated. To each alternative corresponds a different goal of SRDA.

- innovation-oriented. The developments here are related with innovative solutions, unknown to the world practice. Such alternatives have strongly revealed risky character, but contain potentials for commercialization.

- organization-oriented. The alternatives are generated with respect with the execution organizations, the respective time of achieving the final result and the branches of its accomplishment.

The basic structural scheme of the technology for project selection are shown in Fig. 3.

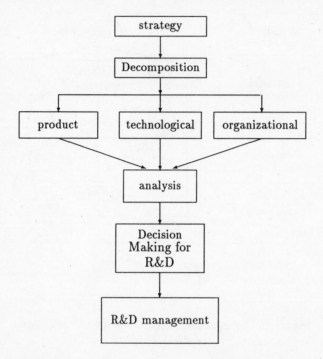

Figure 3: Technology for choise of R&D projects

7 Multicriteria evaluation of R&D projects

In accordance with the chosen strategy for development a set of alternatives for SRDA can be generated. The evaluation and choice of a suitable alternative is a task, connected with the carrying out of a multicriteria analysis (MA).

The technology of multicriteria evaluation and decision making for choosing a certain alternative comprises a number of steps (see fig. 4).

The separate elements are of various information nature. Some of them are individual computing procedures, others are man-machine procedures.

The generation of a sufficient number of alternatives is a necessary condition in the search for an "optimum" solution. In case the alternatives do not satisfy the preliminary conditions, the technology requires an iterative return to the beginning and generation of a full enough set of alternatives. The preliminary conditions are also defined by the decision makers. In the cases of R&D project on a license basis, these can be the industrial areas, the existence of commercial conditions and others. When working out an individual

R&D project, these are the terms of execution, expenditures for SRDA, pay-back period, sensitivity, etc.

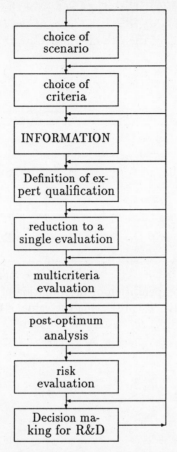

Figure 4: Multicriteria evaluation of R&D projects

The criteria can be quantitative — technological and technical parameters, economic indicators, etc., as well as quantitative — technological level, prospectiveness, ecology-friend-liness, etc. The qualitative evaluations can be of the "yes-no", "poor-good-very good-excellent" type or other, as well as various combinations of them or preference relations.

8   Sensitivity analysis

Investigation of the sensitivity of the final ranking to changes in the values of the characteristics or the weights is an important requirement to the analysis. When there is a bad final estimation for a particular alternative an additional analysis of the reasons has to be made to find which criterions cause the unsatisfactory ranking and according to which ones the investigated alternative is relatively invariant.

The analysis of the sensitivity includes determination of possibilities of mutual compensation of variation of any of the characteristics or weights of different criteria. The task is to define the necessary variation d_{ik}, $k = l, p$, of the k-the characteristics that is able to compensate he variation d_{il}, $l = l, p$, $l \neq k$, of the l-th characteristic in order to preserve the same final ranking of the i-th alternative R&D project (fig. 5, fig. 6).

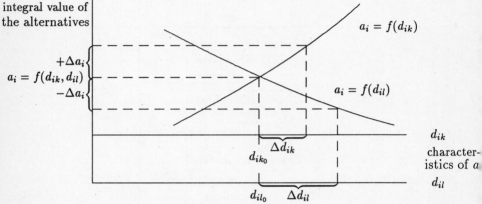

Figure 5: Mutual compensation of the variation of characteristics d_{ik} by the characteristics d_{il} preserving the value of the alternative a_i

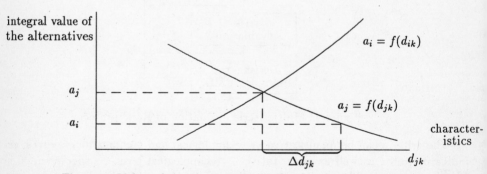

Figure 6: Value of the characteristics d_{jk} that leads to $a_j \geq a_i$

9 Applications of the technology for multicriteria analysis

The proposed technology is successfully used for choice of strategic R&D projects in electronics (on the base of CIM). The following directions for CIM development are considered:

DIRECTIONS FOR R&D DEVELOPMENT

1.   INNOVATIONAL:
1.1.   Local R&D projects.
1.2.   Know-how and licenses.
1.3.   Adaptation of imported products.
1.4.   Complex import.
1.5.   Mixed.

2.   TECHNOLOGICAL:
2.1.   Classical technology (low level of automatization)
2.2.   Middle level of automatization.
2.3.   Light level of automatization.
2.4.   Principally new technology.

3.   ORGANIZATIONAL:
3.1.   Pilot prototype.
3.2.   Successive realization.
3.3.   Small company.
3.4.   Large company.
3.5.   Incorporation of companies.

4.   FUNCTIONAL:
4.1.   Computer-aided design (CAD).
4.2.   Production planning (CAPL).
4.3.   Process and technology planning (CAP-CAT).
4.4.   Computer-aided manufacturing (CAM).
4.5.   Control and diagnostics (CACD).
4.6.   Strategic planning and control (CASP/C).
4.7.   Communication (CAC).
4.8.   Distributed data base (CADBD).

Based on these trends are chosen five scenario.

- optimistic I;

- optimistic II;

- optimistic III;

- realistic;

- pessimistic.

The ranking of the separate versions (alternatives) is shown in fig. 7^1.

---

[1]in brackets are indicated the chosen components of the trends for development and choice of R&D projects, forming the separate versions (alternatives). Thus, for example, 1.4. indicates an innovation R&D project, realized by means of a complex import; 2.2. means, that the project is at an average technological level and so on.

DIRECTIONS FOR R&D DEVELOPMENT

RANKING OF SCENARIO

1. Optimistic I   [1.4, 2.2, 3.3, 4.1]
2. Realistic   [1.3, 2.4, 3.2, 4.4]
3. Optimistic II   [1.4, 2.3, 3.4, 4.2]
4. Optimistic III   [1.4, 2.2, 3.4, 4.4]
5. Pessimistic   [1.2, 2.3, 3.2. 4,3]

Figure 7

Project development means finding, selection and application of the necessary volume and structure of resources for project execution. With calculation of the development effects, there is also the consideration of the probability and associated risk of repayment of invested assets into the development. In this sense the following steps are encouraged:

- evaluation of the development objectives of the R&D project subject to financial means as the restrictive factor;

- evaluation of the results of the achieved goals with consideration of risk;

- assessment of necessary financial resources;

- coordination of the structure, volume and the movement of assets and sources of financing.

References

Danev, B., Popchev, I., Slavov, G. (1987). Real-Life Applications of Multiple Criteria Decision Making Technology. In: Methodology and Software for Interactive Decision Support (Proceedings...), Albena, Bulgaria. Lecture Notes in Economics and Mathematical Systems, Springer Verlag, Berlin.

Danev, B., Slavov, G., Metev, B. (1986). Multicriterial Comparative Analysis of Discrete Alternatives. In: Toward Interactive and Intelligent DSS (Proceedings...), Kioto, Japan. Lecture Notes in Economics and Mathematical Systems, vol. 273, Springer Verlag, Berlin.

Georgiev, R., Danev, B. (1986). Multicriteria Evaluation of Technological Interrelations between Industrial and Agricultural Sectors of the Bulgarian Economy. 7-th World Congress of the Int. Economic Association, New Delhi, India.

Goicoechea, A., Hansen, D., Duckstein, L. (1982). Multiobjective Decision Analysis with Engineering and Business Applications. John Wiley and Sons, N.Y.

Graphical Decision Support Applied to Decisions Changing the Use of Agricultural Land

Ron Janssen, Marjan van Herwijnen

1 Introduction

Due to a combination of increasing productivity and stagnating demand, agricultural production in the Netherlands exceeds demand. This offers opportunities to use agricultural land for recreation, forestry, nature development, etc. The policy question is raised in what order regions should be withdrawn from agricultural production and to what extent.

Although knowledge on multicriteria methods is available within the Dutch Physical Planning Agency — an extensive research program on the use of Multiple Criteria Decision Methods (MCDM) in physical planning was carried out between 1975 and 1980 (see Voogd, 1983) — the number of actual applications within the agency is limited. In our opinion, this is caused by

1. complexity of methods,
2. inadequate presentation of results,
3. difficulties for the policy makers to work directly with the methods.

To meet these problems

1. a multicriteria method is chosen that can be explained and applied graphically,
2. maps are used to present the results,
3. the approach is embedded in a decision support system.

This paper is organised as follows. The next section deals with the appraisal matrix used as a basis for both questions. In section 3 a ranking procedure is applied whereas section 4 focuses on map representations of results. Finally in section 5 a linear programming approach is applied to determine the optimal land use combination. Section 6 offers some concluding remarks.

2 The appraisal table

The data for the analysis are retrieved from the Geographical Information System (ARC-INFO) of the Dutch Physical Planning Agency. The data matrix describes 118 regions on 24 criteria.

In the Dutch context there are two main policy options:

- The use of land can be changed from agriculture into recreation, forestry or nature conservation.

- Agricultural land use can be combined with recreation, landscape and nature management.

Since there is no competition between the potential uses within the two main options, overall utility indices are constructed for each option. The suitability of a region for, e.g., change of land use depends on the utility of the region for recreation, forestry or nature conservation as well as on its utility for agriculture. The demand score in Figure 1 shows the potential of the region for combined land use. The opportunity score reflects the potential of the agricultural sector in the region for agriculture if land use is combined. A region with a labour surplus and low income, for example, will have good opportunities for nature and landscape management by the farmers. A high opportunity score for a region usually reflects a low agricultural quality of that region.

Weighted summation is used to calculate the utility indices from the data table. The weights are obtained through interviews with experts within the agency. The weights are determined twice: firstly through direct estimation, and secondly using the Saaty approach. The experts are confident about their weights but are not always consistent. In one case the weights obtained through direct estimation differed considerably from the weights derived through the Saaty procedure (Saaty, 1980). On the whole, however, the experts seemed to be most confident about the weights derived through direct estimation. It seemed that the experts preferred to weight every criterion against all other criteria simultaneously rather, then to weight them in pairs.

To calculate the indices the scores are standardised between 0 and 100, multiplied by their weights and summed. The results for the first 40 regions are shown in Figure 1. The highest bar in Figure 1 reflects the best score. Region Salland Twente, for example, combines fairly high opportunities with maximum demands. Regions with maximum opportunities for both combined land use and for change of land use are not found within the first 40 regions.

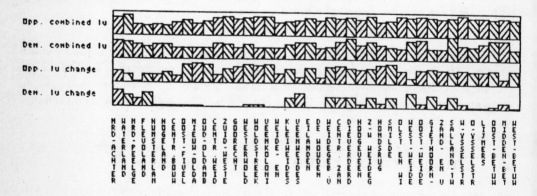

Figure 1: The evaluation table for region 1 to 40.

3   Ranking 118 agricultural regions for change of land use

The opportunities and demands for change of land use as listed in the evaluation table (Figure 1), are shown again in Figure 2. The demands scores (vertical axis) represent the benefits that can be obtained from through forestry nature development and recreation; the opportunities scores (horizontal axis) reflect the costs to agriculture. The ideal region for this policy combines maximum demands (highest benefits) with maximum opportunities (lowest costs). This ideal region would have scored (100,100) and would be found in the top right corner of the diagram. It is clear from Figure 2 that this ideal region does not exist.

The regions are ranked on the basis of their distance from the nonexistent ideal region: the region closest to the ideal region ranks as number 1, the next closest as number 2, etc. This multicriteria method is known as the Ideal Point Method. Various measures are available to determine the distance of the alternatives to the ideal point (Steuer, 1986). In this case, the distance is measured as the weighted sum of the horizontal and the vertical distance from the ideal region.

The line in this diagram intersects the opportunities and demands axis at the same distance from the ideal region. This reflects the equal weight given to nature and agriculture. All points on this line have the same position in the ranking. The regions can now be ranked visually by moving the line from top right to bottom left. The first to cross the line and therefore the most suitable region is region 41 (the Oost Veluwe). It is clear that this region is closely followed by region 96 (West Zeeuws Vlaanderen), and region 100 (the Biesbosch). Note also that the points in this diagram are fairly evenly distributed.

The correlation coefficient shown at the top of Figure 2 shows to what extent opportunities and demands for combined land use coincide or conflict. A value close to one indicates minimal conflict between opportunities and demands: regions with high demands offer good opportunities. A value close to minus one shows extreme conflict: regions with high demands offer no opportunities and **vice versa**.

The negative value of the correlation coefficient (-0.196) indicates that the ranking will be sensitive to changes in weights. In Figure 3 the weight assigned to nature is four times the weight given to agriculture. The distance of the intersection with the opportunities axis is now four times the distance of the intersection with the demands axis. This implies that a region with high demands will rank high even if the opportunities are limited. Region 64 ('t Gein), a region with maximum demands but fairly low opportunities, is now the first to cross the line closely followed by region 41 (the Oost Veluwe). Next, map presentations are used to show the influence of these weight changes on the spatial pattern of the rankings.

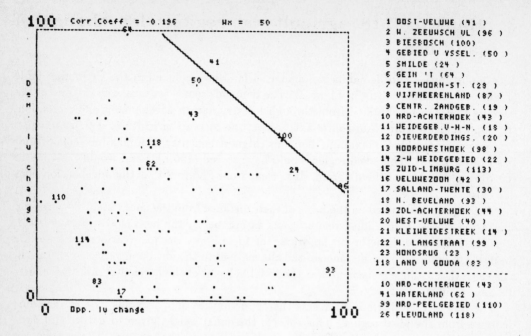

Figure 2: Opportunities and demands for change of land use.
(weight nature = weight agriculture)

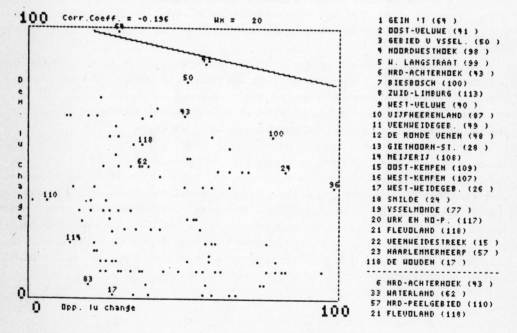

Figure 3: Opportunities and demands for change of land use.
(weight nature = 4× weight agriculture)

4 Map representations

Each weight combination results in a list of 118 regions with the most suitable region at the top, the least suitable region at the bottom and all other regions, according to their suitability, in between. This offers precise information on the position of each region in the ranking but offers no insight in the spatial pattern of the ranking. Therefore the rankings are also shown on maps. The loss of detailed information on these maps is compensated for by insight in the relation between position on the map and position in the ranking.

Map 1 shows the ranking corresponding to Figure 3. On this map the weight assigned to nature is four times the weight assigned to agriculture. The complete ranking is replaced by six rank classes: the best 20 regions in the first group, etc. Map 1 shows that regions in one class are generally close to one another and even form bigger groups of adjacent regions. The influence of the weights on the spatial pattern of the ranking can be analyzed using the following three maps:

Change of land use.

Map 1: weight nature $= 4\times$ weight agriculture;

Map 2: weight nature $=$ weight agriculture;

Map 3: weight agriculture $= 4\times$ weight nature.

The number of regions in each class is equal on all three maps. The change of weights results in a shift of the 20 regions over the map while keeping the number in each group constant. Maps 1–3 show that a shift in the weight assigned to nature from 0.20 in Map 1 to 0.80 in Map 3 results in a shift of the position on the map of a large number out of the 20 highest ranked (black coloured) regions, in such a way that these regions move from the centre (Map 1), through the east (Map 2) to the north of the country (Map 3). Note that the regions in the east of the country rank within the best 20 regions if equal weights are given to nature and agriculture and between 20 and 40 if the weight of nature is either increased or decreased. This indicates a balance between opportunities and demands in these regions.

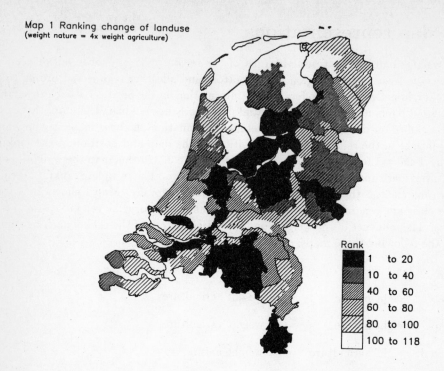

Map 1 Ranking change of landuse
(weight nature = 4x weight agriculture)

Rank

1	to 20
10	to 40
40	to 60
60	to 80
80	to 100
100	to 118

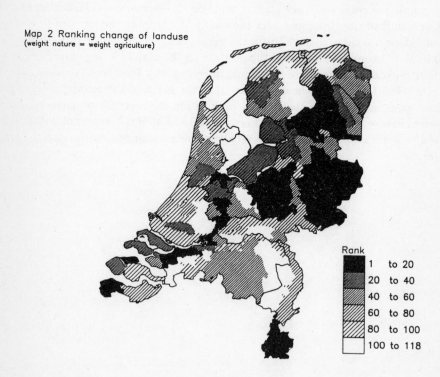

Map 2 Ranking change of landuse
(weight nature = weight agriculture)

Rank

1	to 20
20	to 40
40	to 60
60	to 80
80	to 100
100	to 118

5   The optimal land use combination: an integrated approach

In the previous section, the regions were ranked according to their suitability for either combined land use or change of land use. No trade-off was made between these two options. In this section both options will be dealt with simultaneously. Another difference from the approach in the previous section is that for each region the area allocated to each type of land use is calculated, and that the solution is made subject to constraints such as the available budget for a policy option. The aim of the approach is to calculate the optimal feasible combination of land uses.

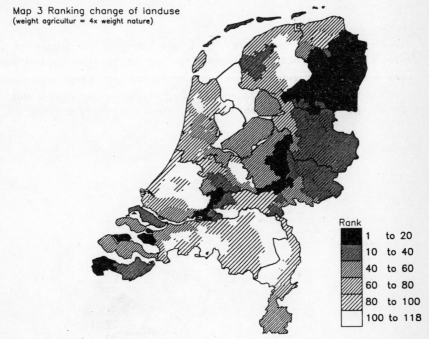

Map 3 Ranking change of landuse
(weight agricultur = 4x weight nature)

Rank
1 to 20
10 to 40
40 to 60
60 to 80
80 to 100
100 to 118

The objective function

For each region a decision needs to be made about the percentage of the region to be allocated to: change of land use; combined land use; and agriculture. Since there are 118 regions this results in $118 \times 3 = 354$ decision variables. The utilities per region for each type of land use are derived from the utility scores calculated in section 2. Total utility is calculated as the sum of utilities of all regions. Optimization of the utility function is subject to constraints per region and constraints on totals for all regions, such as the total budget available. The second type of constraints results in the problem of the optimal allocation of policy effort over all regions. This type of constraint creates the necessity to use a linear programming approach.

Optimization

A linear programming routine is used to find the percentages for the three types of land use in all regions that:

- maximises total utility and
- meets all the constraints.

The resulting percentages for combined land use and change of land use are shown on Map 4. The percentage agriculture is calculated by subtracting these percentages from 100%. In the Oostelijk Weidegebied, for example, 0% is allocated to change of land use, 38% to combined land use and 62% to agriculture. In the optimal solution the constraints set to the maximum area of change of land use and combined land use are both met exactly. This implies that 200.000 ha of agricultural land was reallocated. Total budget spent equals DFL 5 billion. This means that the available budget is not a limiting factor in this solution.

Weights

To reach the solution presented in Map 4, equal weights are assigned to nature and agriculture. The influence of these weights on the percentages allocated to the three types of land use is shown in Figure 4. This figure shows that the percentage combined land use remains constant as long as the weight of agriculture is between 0 and 0.74. This percentage sharply declines in favour of agriculture if the weight assigned to agriculture exceeds 0.74.

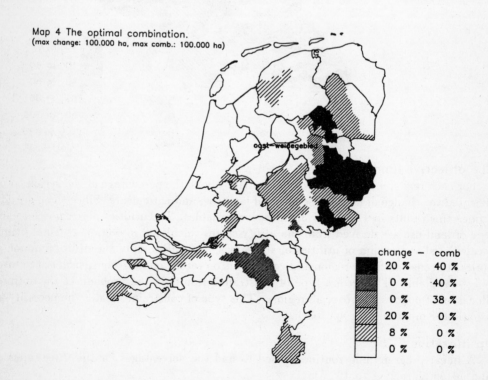

Map 4 The optimal combination.
(max change: 100.000 ha, max comb.: 100.000 ha)

change	—	comb
20 %		40 %
0 %		40 %
0 %		38 %
20 %		0 %
8 %		0 %
0 %		0 %

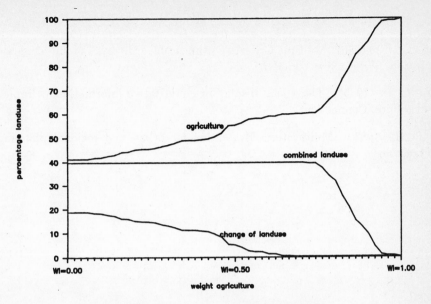

Figure 4: Sensitivity of land use to priorities,
(weight nature = 1 – weight agriculture)

6 Concluding remarks

A graphical version of the ideal point method is used to rank 118 regions according to their suitability for combined land use and change in land use. A diagram proves useful to present all scores in one figure and to explain the principle of the method and the concept of weights. A linear programming approach is used to determine the optimal land use combination. Map representations prove to be useful in this application. The loss of detailed information is compensated for by a better overview of the results. Data available in a GIS are by their nature useful to support decisions with a spatial dimension. Multicriteria methods in combination with adequate map presentations of the results allow for an optimal use of these data.

The procedure described is available as a decision support system. This allows people involved in the decision process to change the definition of the indices, the weights and the constraints according to their own opinions, and hence promotes the use of the procedure (see also Herwijnen and Janssen, 1988).

References

Herwijnen, M. van and Janssen, R. (1988). DEFINITE, A support system for decisions on a finite set of alternatives. Proceedings of the VIIIth International Conference on MCDM, Manchester.

Janssen, R. and Rietveld, P. (1985). Multicriteria Evaluation of landreallotment plans: A case study. *Environment and Planning*, Volume 17, pp. 1653–1668.

Saaty, T. L. (1980). The analytical hierarchy proces. McGraw Hill, New York.

Steuer, R. E. (1986). Multiple Criteria Optimization: Theory, Computation and Application. Wiley, New York.

Tufte, E. R. (1985). The visual display of quantitative information. Graphics Press, Cheshire, Connecticut.

Voogd, H. (1983). Multicriteria Evaluation for urban and regional planning. Pion, London.

Integrated Decision Support System for Oil Refinery

Chuandong Liu, Zhongtuo Wang

Institute of Systems Engineering

Dalian University of Technology

116024, Dalian, P.R. China

Abstract

This paper describes a newly developed integrated decision support system for oil refinery, the focus of which is on the strategic planning. For the upper level of this refinery enterprise, the decision support is more critical in the problem finding and structuring process rather than problem solving. It is not unusual the decision makers have only decision intentions under the environment impacts. The main task of decision support is not only to identify the current problem, but also to perceive future trends and search the problem need to be anticipated. In this system, a new conceptional framework is suggested, including the following components: identification of intention of DM, formulation and analysis of scenario, problem definition, problem solving, optimization and evaluation. After a step-by-step procedure of man-machine interaction, the decision problem is gradually formulated and solved.

The system integration takes part over different time span and space distribution. It offers not only the support at the strategic level, but also at management and operational levels on conventional DM.

1 Introduction

Decision support system (DSS) as a powerful computer-based tool, is used by decision maker in connection with his(her) problem-solving and decision making duties. Decision making within organizations is achieved through a process approach. As pointing out by Weber and Konsynski (1987), the majority of current DSS have concentrated on managing solutions rather than on managing the full range of problem-solving that produce those solutions. To prove more effective support, especially for high level decision maker, the DSS must be developed on the focus of supporting the whole process of problem-solving. Firstly, critical issues must be identified and problems must be structured. DSS need to help decision maker identify those issues which when resolved, will contribute significantly to managerial or organizational effectiveness. Identification of a critical problem can be a more significant achievement than solve it. Moreover, the top level manager confronted with a complicated and changing environment, can create only decision intentions. How to transform it into a clear decision problem is also a crucial task. Once when a problem has been defined, how to organize the relevant methods and tool with the application orientation is also an important step.

In this paper, an Integrated Production Decision Support System (IPDSS) for refinery is developed and dedicated to high level decision aid in a changing environment. In following sections, a brief description of a new system frame is given. Then the problem-generation (problem structuring) system module is proposed in order to transform the decision intention into clear problem. A problem-solving system module is also built to organize the decision-analysis process. Finally a special knowledge-based system module for lubricating oil production scheduling is developed. The system is implemented on an enhanced microcomputer and works satisfactorily.

2   Brief description of IPDSS

The Integrated Production Decision Support System (IPDSS) is developed for strategic planning, managerial planning and scheduling at different levels to support the decision maker(s) to solving a great variety of decision problems. Instead of offering a result, the system helps the decision maker(s) create some new idea and deepen his(their) insights through the whole process of decision analysis.

The decision problems in a refinery have following features:

- Large time and space span;

- Too many influencing factors;

- Success or failure of decision making has significant influences on the profits of the refinery;

- With ever increasing contingent decision activities.

The main tasks of production decision of a refinery include the following activities:

- Create long-term strategic plan (for 5 to 10 years);

- Create annual, seasonal and monthly production plan and plan for inventories;

- Create operational schedule;

- Decision making for future perspectives;

- Decision making for some emergent events.

The ordinary data-based and model-based DSS may tackle some conventional planning (annual, monthly etc.) work effectively. Even in the multiple-objective case, the existing algorithms and software may offer powerful support to create production plan. But for some contingent events, or for some opportunity-seeking case, the problems are not so well structured, and even the goals are also not so clear, the DSS cannot aid the top leaders easily to select some actions.

In order to overcome these shortcomings, a new framework for integrated production DSS is proposed. Fig. 1 and Fig. 2 show the frame and structure of the IPDSS, in which

PGS is the problem-generation system; PSS is the problem-solving system; MLP Generation System is a model generating system of multiple-objective linear programming, this system can be used to generate a basic model of multiple-objective LP when the constraints of crude oil supply, inventory and products are given; MLP Solution System is a general-purpose solver of multiple-objective LP based on Nonobjective submerged interactive algorithm (Wang Yanzhang and Wang Zhongtuo, 1989).

The functions of IPDSS are:

- Effective decision support to conventional decision problems.

In the production and sale environment, the conventional decision problems include the annual, seasonal, monthly production planning, inventory planning and adjustment, operational scheduling. IPDSS offers an integrated environment of decision support for these activities.

- Intentional decision support to unconventional decision problems.

Unconventional decision problems include the long-range strategic analysis of the whole enterprise, decision around the changes of crude oil supply and products demand, some emergency events. For these problems, IPDSS offers supports through the whole process of problem-solving, e.g., identification of decision intentions, formulation of decision processes, analysis of alternatives and creating a solution (if possible) and/or explain how and why it can be formulated or not. This system has the following features:

- Integration of different knowledge and methods, tools with the orientation to application.

- Intelligence of problem-generation and problem-solving.

- Man-machine interaction in the whole process of system operation.

- A consistent computer supporting environment.

3 Problem-generation (problem-structuring) system

The aim of development of problem-generation system (PGS) is to find a way of computer-aided support to intentional decision. Intention means a purpose, an imaginary, it cannot structure a problem, at least in the first stage. Especially at the high decision level, the decision makers are confronted with some issues which are not so clear. They can only create a vague intention and an approximate goal. In other words, there is only a fuzzy "decision intention", not a definite decision problem.

It is not unusual in the area of real world decision making that the decision maker(s) has only such an intention. For example, for a large refinery the international market has a demand of several kinds of oil products at this time, but after a short period, there appears a demand of other kinds of oil products. Therefore the decision maker — the top manager of the enterprise, has an attempt to get decision support from the DSS, e.g., facing the market condition, what is the policy that the enterprise must adopt. This is just an intention of decision, because a clear problem has not yet been formulated. The existing model-based and/or information-based DSS cannot directly create a definite answer and therefore cannot offer effective support. In this case, the decision maker(s) must structure the problem himself, or discuss with decision analyst. After several round of discussions and adjustments, to transform the decision intention into a clear decision problem.

The computer-aided support of decision process, in fact, is to emulate the mental process of the human brain to complete the above transformation. The first step in this process, is to analyze the scope of the issues concerned, to identify the influencing factors and their relations, to recognize the strength of these influences and compare the problem-situation with previous cases in his(her) experience. By using of the common-sense reasoning (which is one of characteristic method of human reasoning), decision maker gradually transforms his intention into a decision problem. This is the second step of the whole process. We may call the first step as "association step" and the second as "commonsense reasoning step".

Suppose I — space of decision intention, P — space of decision problem, S — space of solution. The problem-solving process may be classified into two kinds. In the first kind, the problem $p \in P$ is given directly and the problem-solving corresponds to create a mapping g:

$$g : P \to S$$

In the another kind, $p \in P$ cannot be given directly. Only $i \in I$ is known. The problem solving corresponds to create a mapping h:

$$h : I \to S$$

But in real cases, h cannot be created. If we can construct the mapping relation f between I and P:

$$f : I \to P$$

then we have:

$$h = g \star f$$

and f is just the problem-generation process.

The construction of f is as follows. Firstly, we construct:

$$f1 : I \to A$$

A is space spanned by m "factors" (such as time, space, attribute, etc.). Another mapping $f3$ may also be created:

$$f3 : E \to P$$

in which E is space of "elements" which are concerned by a given problem. According to experiences, $f1$ and $f3$ may be created without too much difficulties. The most crucial task is to create $f2$:

$$f2 : A \to E$$

so as

$$f = f1 \star f2 \star f3$$

usually, $f3$ is fuzzy mapping. For every specific decision problem, $f1$, $f2$, $f3$ have their own forms.

Fig. 3 describes the process mentioned above and therefore describes the operation mechanism of PGS.

Once when the PGS is started, the system firstly identifies the intention of decision maker. According to the decision intention, system retrieves the appropriate knowledge in knowledge-base SAsKB and create the scenario to the decision maker. The information related to the aspects and scope of the issue, the possible goals and indexes, etc., may lead the decision maker heuristically to create a primitive thinking process. This corresponds to the first step. At this step, through the man-machine interaction, the decision maker may clarify his intention, and describe it in detail. After receiving a series of heuristic information, decision maker may step by step analyze the scenario by the help of the knowledge, taking from the knowledge-base SAbKB. There may be some reasoning processes. Finally, a decision problem is created and displayed to the decision maker on the screen.

A real case of such a process is as follows. According to the open policy of China, a refinery may import some crude oil from Indonesia and export all the products to southeast Asia. Once when the market conditions are known, the decision maker may have a preliminary attempt to import a given amount of crude oil for processing. This initiation may influence the production of the whole refinery in several aspects. In the time span, is the annual or monthly plan may be influenced due to this additional input or not? Are there any changes in objectives previously defined and also some constraints in the real production conditions? Once when these questions are answered, a new decision problem may be structured consequently. Fig. 4 shows the structure of PGS; Fig. 5 shows the flow chart of the system operation (Liu, 1989).

4   Problem-solving system in IPDSS

Kotteman (1986) considered the managerial problems as the iterative implementation of the following three tasks:

- Problem/opportunity recognition;

- Meta-decision-making;

- Specific-decision-making.

The problem/opportunity recognition starts a decision-making process (in it's narrow sense). The decision-making process include selection of appropriate decision methods and tools corresponding to the specific decision problem, gathering of information, etc., and then by the help of them, to create, evaluate and select alternatives. The process of "decision-making of decision-making" is the meta-decision-making. Most of the DSS developed in past years, are dedicated to specific domain of decision, so we may call them specific DSS. The structure of the system, interconnections of modules and the operating mode are of "hard-wired" fashion. But at the higher level of organization, these are a large varieties of problems of decision-making. We cannot separately build a large number of specific DSS for every problem. Especially, the problem area of the user are rapidly enlarging and specific DSS have their limited application domains. They must be modified according to the changes of the decision problem, even the change may be very small. Obviously the hard-wired structure is not suitable for high level decision making. A new structure in which the meta-decision-making can be carried on is necessary. In other words, only the frame of DSS with flexible structure can fulfill the requirement of meta-decision-making. This is another sense of integration.

The problem-solving system of IPDSS, namely PSS, is designed for this purpose. The functional structure of DSS is shown in Fig. 6.

The task realized by PSS is: according to the type of basic decision analysis and the framework of problem description, the relevant knowledge, modules and procedures are organized synergetically with application orientation. Hence a problem-solving process is formulated and the integration thus completed. The problem-solving process is realized by inference machine, which utilizes the problem-solving knowledge (control knowledge), calling appropriate modules and procedures, to generated s specific problem-solving process. The inference machine is realized by the inference network.

5   A hybrid expert system module for lubricating oil production scheduling

In the system IPDSS, there is a special module of computer-aided scheduling of lubricating oil production. This is a multi-products, multi-operating-unit, multi-processing production. The arrangement of operating units and oil tanks must fulfill the technological requirements with minimum shifting loss. The system is under the constraints, both external (e.g. transportation) and internal (technological requirements, tank condition and capabilities of operating units). It must provide an order and working time arrangement of each unit and each tank, and also the kind of products.

This is a dynamic resource allocation problem. There exist not only quantitative, but also qualitative constraints (e.g. technological requirements of shifting of products). Moreover, the real-time requirement is also very crucial. In normal condition, the scheduling system must provide a feasible arrangement as soon as possible. When the external and internal constraints are changing significantly, the system must adjust even rearrange the production on time.

The quantitative approach such as mathematical programming, network planning, etc. cannot solve the operating optimization problem effectively. In the real life, the schedule is arranged by the experienced scheduling personnel, who can create a feasible arrangement in a very short period. Therefore, the possible way of solving the operating optimization problem is to build a computer aided system based on the experiences of scheduling personnel. The expert system approach may be adopted. But the existing experiences of scheduling personnel are not enough to form a complete set of domain knowledge. A hybrid system, combining the experience of scheduling personnel and methods of optimization is a more effective tool.

A rule-based production system as hybrid expert system has been built for the production scheduling of lubricating oil. The whole system consists of DB, DBMS, knowledge base, inference machine and user's interface. Knowledge base is composed with three sub-knowledge-base each corresponding to one production process. The tree-search method is used. Experiences of scheduling personnel are collected and deduced into several criteria, combined with some ideas of system optimization, constitute the knowledge base. The optimization idea is also implemented in the form of inference machine.

The preliminary results show that, to build a hybrid expert system for the scheduling problem, which cannot be effectively solved solely by quantitative or qualitative approach, is a feasible and good solution.

Fig. 7 and Fig. 8 show the structure and working process of this scheduling module.

References

Bonczek, R.H., Holsapple, C.W. and Whinston, A.B. (1981). Foundations of Decision Support Systems. Academic Press, New York.

Kottemann, J.E. (1986). Some requirements and decision aspects for the next generation of decision support systems. Proceedings of the Nineteenth Annual Hawall International Conference on System Sciences.

Liu Chuandong (1989). Integrated Production Decision Support System for Refinery. Doctor Dissertation of Dalian University of Technology, (in Chinese).

Scott Morton, M.S. (1971). Management decision support: computer based support for decision making. Division of Research, Harvard University, Cambridge, Mass.

Sen, A. and Biswas, G. (1985). Decision support systems: An expert systems approach. *Decision Support Systems* 1, pp. 197–204, Elsevier Science Publishers B.V. (North-Holland).

Simon, H.A. (1960). The New Science of Management Decision. N.Y., HARPER and RAW.

Sol, H.G. (1987). Paradoxes around DSS. Decision Support Systems: Theory and Application. Springer-Verlag, Berlin, Heidelberg.

Sprague, R.H., Jr. (1980). A framework for the development of decision support systems. *MIS Quarterly*, 4(4), pp. 1–26.

Sprague, R.H. and Carlson, E.D. (1983). Building Effective Decision Support Systems. Crolier Computer Science Library.

Wang Yanzhang and Wang Zhongtuo (1989). Non-Objective-Submerged Interactive Algorithm for Multi-Objective Linear Programming. *Jour. of Systems Engineering*, No. 1, pp. 27–36, (in Chinese).

Wang Zhongtuo (1988). DSS for Integrated Development Study — A Case Study of Shanxi. Vol. 1, (in Chinese).

Weber, E.S. and Konsynski, B.R. (1987). Problem management: neglected elements in DSS. Proceedings of the Twentieth Annual Hawaii International Conference on System Sciences.

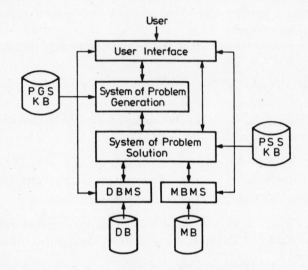

Figure 1: Advanced frame for DSS

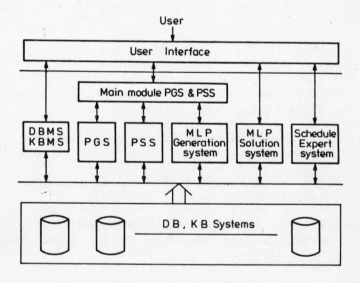

Figure 2: Construction of IPDSS

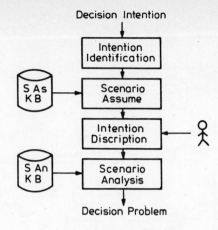

Figure 3: Operation mechanism of PGS

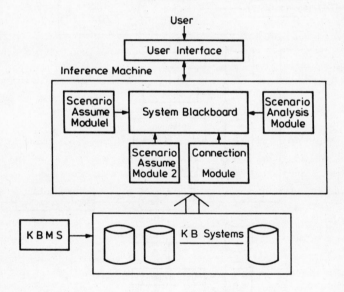

Figure 4: Construction of PGS

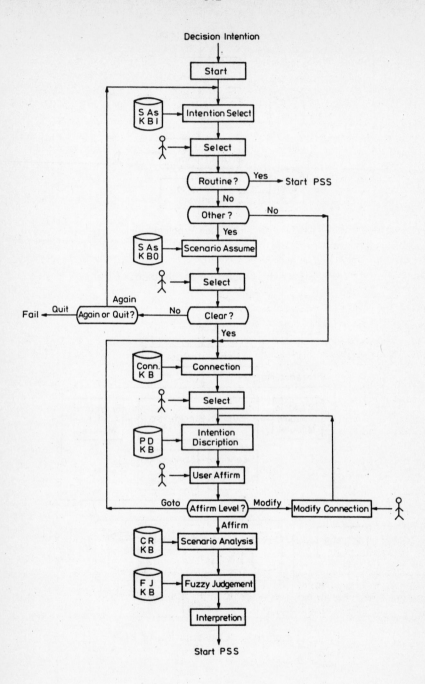

Figure 5: Principle of PGS

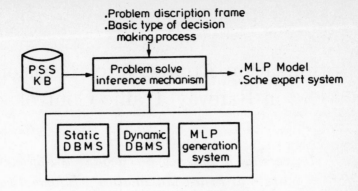

Figure 6: Construction of PSS

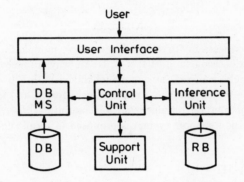

Figure 7: Construction of schedule extern system

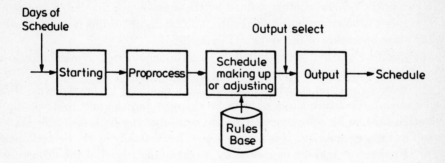

Figure 8: Process of making up schedule

An Optimization Approach for Decision Support in Railway Traffic Control

Antonio Sforza

Universita' di Salerno — Facolta' di Ingegneria
Istituto di Fisica Matematica e Informatica
84084 Fisciano (Salerno) Italy

Abstract

This work describes a multicriteria optimization module for insertion in a prototype version of a decision support system for railway traffic control. The problem is formulated through a mixed integer model solved with a branch and bound algorithm. Both the model and the algorithm were tested and gave very promising results in terms of solution obtained and of computer time. Finally the general pattern of the decision support system is proposed in terms of structured analysis.

1 Introduction

The management of a public transportation system involves many problems and therefore requires the formulation of many optimization models: network design, flow pattern, scheduling.

The solution of these models requires computer times depending on the periodicity of the problems. Anyway, it does not necessarily have to be a real time solution.

However, in the general context defined by these problems, the daily management of the system raises problems requiring a real time solution, depending on perturbations on the steady state operation of the system (Florio, 1986).

Recently, some contributions appeared in literature about railway regulation and control (Benoit and Wajsbrot, 1989; Bienfait and Franckert, 1989; Casalino et al., 1989).

In particular, when the scheduled time-table is modified by breakdowns, delays or peaks of demand, departure times need to be changed and the new route of the trains in the station area to be determined. This problem may rise both for single stations or for a complex railway junction. It is usually solved heuristically by the central operations controller. However, it may be expressed by a scheduling model of the departure time, solved with exact or approximate algorithms.

This work describes a multicriteria optimization module for insertion in a prototype version of a decision support system for railway traffic control (Atzeni, Bielli and Cini, 1986). The problem is formulated through a mixed integer model solved with a branch and bound algorithm (Murty, 1976). Both the model and the algorithm were tested and gave very promising results in terms of solution obtained and of computer time. Finally the general pattern of the decision support system is proposed in terms of structured analysis.

2   Railway traffic control

A railway station is constituted by a set of lines, which can also represent a complex network. However, some subsets of lines can be identified.

The traffic of a railway station is determined by the trains in-coming to and out-coming from the station area. Each train can use some paths to go through this area. Each path is constituted by some branches. Each branch can be common to more paths. For this reason two paths sharing at least one branch cannot be used simultaneously. They will be said to be incompatible. Two paths without a common branch will be said compatible.

Station traffic control consist in the determination of the departure times of trains, with the incompatibility constraints, according to the arrival times of the trains. This is an important task when some disruption modifies the scheduled timetable. To this aim some parameters should to be defined.

For sake of simplicity we will assume that there is only one train for each path in an observation time interval.

If two paths (i) and (j) are incompatible, we can say that (i) interdicts (j) and viceversa. The interdiction time $a(ij)$ of a path (i) on a path (j) is the time during which (i) interdicts (j), starting from the instant when a train enters path (i). During this time the train associated to path (j) waits before entering the path.

Moreover, the set of paths of a railway station and related incompatibilities can be described by the matrix of interdiction times, $A = \{a(ij)\}$.

According to this definition some temporal parameters can be defined:

$p(i)$ = instant of arrival of the train on path (i);

$t(i)$ = instant of access of the train on path (i);

$r(i)$ = delay time at traffic signal = $t(i) - p(i)$;

$d(i)$ = instant of release of the path (i);

R = total delay, equal to the sum of the delays of all trains in a fixed observation time interval;

H = total engagement of the station area, equal to the time during the which the station area is engaged by the trains arriving in a fixed observation time interval.

3   Traffic optimization in a railway station

The solution of the traffic control problem in a railway station requires a mathematical model describing the interaction of trains in a fixed observation time interval, during which some trains arrive sequentially to the station.

A scheduling policy has to be determined, such that the trains go through the station area, respecting incompatibilities, with one or more optimization criteria for the system efficiency parameters.

3.1 A mathematical model

The first optimization criterion is the minimization of total delay, expressed by the weighted sum of train delays:

$$R = \sum_{i=1,\ldots,n} c(i)r(i)$$

where n is the number of trains arrived at the station in the observation interval and $c(i)$ is the weight of the train arriving on path (i).

The second optimization criterion is the minimization of the weighted sum of the squares of train delays:

$$RS = \sum_{i=1,\ldots,n} c(i)r^2(i)$$

This objective function allows to obtain a better distribution of delays among trains.

The third criterion is the minimization of the total engagement of the station area, expressed by parameter H as above defined.

The main constraints of the model take into account the incompatibilities between paths, expressed by matrix A.

For a pair of trains associated to a pair of paths (i) and (j), the incompatibility constraint can be expressed by the following relations:

$$t(i) - t(j) - a(ij) \geq b(ij)(-\infty)$$
$$t(j) - t(i) - a(ij) \geq (1 - b(ij))(-\infty)$$

where $t(i)$ and $t(j)$ are the instants of access on the paths and $b(ij)$ is a boolean variable defined as follows:

$$b(ij) = \begin{cases} 1 & \text{if } (i) \text{ has priority over } (j) \\ 0 & \text{if } (j) \text{ has priority over } (i) \end{cases}$$

Moreover a set of constraints expressing the relation between $t(i)$ and $p(i)$ is required:

$$t(i) \geq p(i), \qquad i = 1, \ldots, n$$

Finally, an upper bound constraint can be imposed to the delay of each train (path).

$$r(i) \leq M(i), \qquad i = 1, \ldots, n$$

If n is the number of trains arriving to the station in the fixed observation time interval, we obtain a mixed integer mathematical programming model with n continuous variables, $n(n-1)/2$ integer variables and $2n + n(n-1)$ constraints.

3.2   A branch and bound algorithm

The proposed model can be solved through a classical branch and bound algorithm consistent with the adopted set of variables. However, it can be solved efficiently with a branch and bound algorithm which assumes delays as variables.

Both the model and the algorithms were tested on small (but realistic) size problems ($n = 6, 9, 12$).

The algorithm allows to obtain very rapidly a "good" solution to the problem, as expressed in fig. 1, which shows the values of two objective functions: R, total delay, and H, total engagement of the station. Assuming R as the main criterion, it decreases during the algorithm, while H remains substantially unchanged.

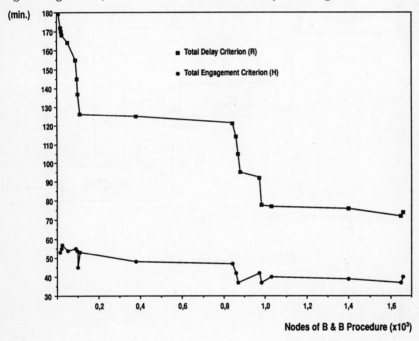

Figure 1: Objective function values for criteria R and H

4   A decision support system scheme

The tests performed gave very promising results in terms of solution obtained and computer time, thus supporting the idea of using the proposed optimization module in a decision support system for the central operations controller of a railway station.

Moreover, this module could be integrated with a knowledge-based approach oriented to choose between the many solutions produced by the same optimization module (Rich, 1983; Dolk and Konsysky, 1984; Waterman, 1986; Lagana', Mancini e Maraschini, 1986; Kusiak and Heragu, 1989).

In terms of DSS the traffic control problem of a railway system can be expressed with the activity diagrams obtained from a structured analysis of the problem.

Fig. 2 reports in diagram A0 the general process, formed by Analysis, Decision Support and Decision. In fig. 3 diagram A1 describes the Analysis activity. In fig. 4 diagram A2 describes the Decision Support activity.

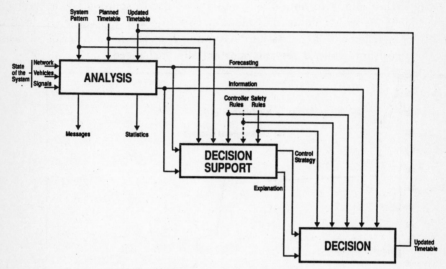

A0: *Analysis, Decision Support and Decision for Traffic Control*

Figure 2: Diagram A0

5 Conclusions

This paper supports the possibility to adopt an optimization module to approach the solution of a railway traffic control problem.

It could be inserted in a decision support system for the central operations controller of a railway station. Moreover it could be integrated with a knowledge-based approach oriented to solve the choice among the many solutions produced by the same optimization module.

Some semplifying hypotheses in the problem definition could be removed in order to obtain a more realistic model of the phenomenon.

The algorithm could be improved, adopting efficient dominance tests between the sets of solutions (Fischetti e Toth, 1987). The computation time is very small (few seconds on a PC) for a problem with 12 variables and so it allows a real time response to the railway traffic control problem.

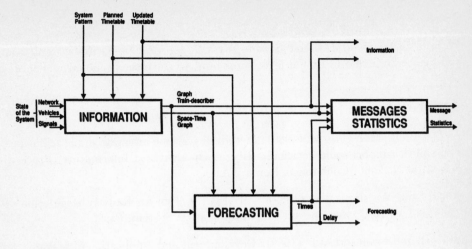

A1: *Analysis*

Figure 3: Diagram A1

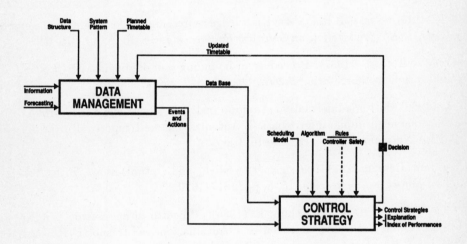

A2: *Decision Support*

Figure 4: Diagram A2

Acknowledgements

The author is grateful to Mr. Paolo de Vito Piscicelli for his cooperation in implementing and testing the Branch and Bound algorithms built to solve the proposed model.

References

Atzeni, P., Bielli, M. e Cini, M. (1986). Metodi di gestione integrata di modelli e dati nei sistemi di supporto alle decisioni. Ricerca Operativa ed Informatica. Proceedings of AIRO National Conference, Roma, FAE.

Benoit, C. and Wajsbrot, J.P. (1989). TRAFIC: A Tool for Railway Regulation. Preprints of VI IFAC Symposium on Transportation System, Paris.

Bienfait, B. and Franckert, J.P. (1989). Development and Application of a Traffic Automatic Management System (TAMSY). Preprints of VI IFAC Symposium on Transportation System, Paris.

Casalino, C., Di Febbraro, A., Ferrara, A. and Minciardi, R. (1989). Discrete-event simulation and control strategies for underground railways. Preprints of VI IFAC Symposium on Transportation System, Paris.

Dolk, D.R. and Konsysky, B.R. (1984). Knowledge representation for model management systems. *IEEE Transaction on Software Engineering*, SE–10, 6, pp. 619–628.

Fischetti, M. e Toth, P. (1987). Procedure di bounding e di dominanza per problemi di ottimizzazione combinatoria. *Ricerca Operativa*, 7, pp. 41–58.

Florio, L. (1986). Sistema informativo in tempo reale per la gestione e il controllo della circolazione negli impianti ferroviari. L'Automazione nei trasporti. Proceedings of ANIPLA National Conference, Trieste, Italy.

Kusiak, A. and Heragu, S.S. (1989). Expert Systems and Optimization. *IEEE Transaction on Software Engineering*, 15, 8, pp. 1017–1020.

Lagana', A., Mancini, D. e Maraschini, F. (1986). Progetto di un sistema esperto per l'ottimizzazione del traffico ferroviario. L'Automazione nei trasporti. Proceedings of ANIPLA National Conference, Trieste, Italy.

Murty, K. (1976). Linear and Combinatorial programming. Wiley.

Rich, E. (1983). Artificial Intelligence. Mc Graw-Hill.

Waterman, D.A. (1986). A guide to expert systems. Addison-Wesley.

Pan-Objective Ecological Programming (POEP) — Application of Mathematical Programming to Ecological Research

Rusong Wang   Bangjie Yang
Yonglong Lu   Zhaoying Chen

Research Center for Eco-Environmental Sciences
Academia Sinica
19 Zhongguancun Road, Beijing, 100080, P.R. China

Abstract

POEP is a multiple criteria decision supporting method which aims at regulating the function of ill-structured system under a varying environment other than getting an optimal solution within a well defined set of parameters. It is a searching or learning process for improving the system relationship F within the ecological niche N along an optimization path. Its potential use is shown in a case study of Tianjin City.

The essence of traditional mathematical programming is to turn complex reality into a simpler mathematical framework and to optimize it according to some fixed rules. It is in fact a projection of system parameters to optimum results. Though it is a good method for well-defined physical system, it is not always suitable for human involved system, i.e., the social, economic and ecological system, for the information is usually so rough, vague, incomplete and varied that the optimum results can't be easily accepted. Table 1 shows the differences between physical system and human involved system study. Here we are going to develop a new programming method to manage these ill-structured systems, which is called Pan-Objective Ecological Programming (POEP).

1 The characteristics of POEP

POEP is an ecological decision supporting method aimed at regulating the function of an artificial ecosystem by use of ecological principles and MCDS techniques. Its main characteristics are as follows:

Programming = Planning + Programming

Here the "programming" has both the meaning of practical planning and mathematical programming. The reason why mathematical programming and practical planning rarely

	Physical System	Human Ecosystem
basic theory	physics	ecology
target	physical matter	ecological relation
dynamics	known	unknown
content	dynamics of matter	relationship between man and envir.
reasoning	cause-effect chain	interacting network
emphasis	mechanical force	man's role
number of relationships	finite	infinite
inner structure	white box	black box, ill-structure
parameter	predictable, fixed	uncertain, varied
succession	entropy increase	entropy decrease
outer envir.	identifiable	uncertain
goal	single, compatible	multiple, conflict
evaluate criterion	objective	subjective
controled by	outer force	inner force
method	hard	soft and hard
research process	optimizing	learning
final objective	optimum control	reasonable regulation

Table 1: The differences between physical system and human ecosystem optimization

combined closely is that many parameters are often based on some unrealistic presumptions. Even if the presumptions are true, the parameters have changed before the research is over. Therefore, the results are often not satisfied by the decision-makers. Although most of the decision-makers make their decision not through optimizing but by means of simple trial and error method, the result chosen out from a big heap of schemes is often more feasible than that from a strict mathematical programming. We take advantage of both practical "planning" and mathematical "programming" to set up a group programming process joined by decision-makers, researchers and experts to embody human thinking into the MCDS.

Programming system functions according to the eco-principles

The basic idea of ecological programming is using the high efficiency and harmonious relationship principles in ecological cybernetics to regulate and improve function of the system.

The ecology here means the relationships between human activities and their environments including adaptation of mankind to the varying environments by raising the efficiency of resouces utilization and reducing the environmental impacts, and reformation of environment to suit man's demands through expanding man's ecological niche.

The aims of the programming are not to obtain the optimum value of one or more indices of the system, but a reasonable regulation of the system relationships to make the whole process sustainable.

We pay more attention to the changes of those variables which have reached or will reach their thresholds in the process of optimization, and their relationships with other components and outer systems. These relationships determine the function and behavior of the whole system. While the absolute values of base variables are unimportant for decision-makers, as long as they are far from the upper and lower limits, their changes will produce little effects on the system dynamics.

From multiple objective to pan-objective

According to the principles of ecological cybernetics, we expand the multi-objective to pan-objective which has following three meanings:

(1) The objectives of the programming are extensive.

In POEP each of the structure variables, the relationship matrixes and the control vectors is possibly an objective at different stages of the programming. The optimization rules and indices may be varied through man-computer dialogue whenever necessary. The multi-objectives of the traditional programming are at most a vector, while the objectives in the ecological programming are a network which consists of the whole system relationships.

(2) The target of the programming is extensive.

The mathematical programming is usually suitable for those systems with definite and complete parameters. But POEP allows the data rough, incomplete and indefinite.

In the programming, we don't expect to predetermine all of the parameters, but treat them as variables, and leave full room to the programmers and decision-makers in order to get rid of the data indefiniteness. In order to manage the roughness of the data, it is needed to input only initial data which are required to have the relatively same level of statistical error among the data rather than their accuracy, because we are only interested in their relationships rather than their exact states. As for the incompleteness of the data, what we are going to do is not to control the whole system but to learn the dynamics which is caused by some main relationships (not all) among the system components. So it is enough for POEP to have some main data about the system.

(3) The programming results are diversified.

The outputs of the computer are not one or several optimal values, but a series of regulation strategies which not only come out at the final stage, but also at each step of POEP. Furthermore, the solution got from each iteration is always feasible but often not sole.

2   The mathematical description of POEP

PEOP is an ecological thinking and strategy searching process which aims at functional identification. Its ultimate goal is not to get an optimum panacea for a target system, but to ascertain the system's dynamics and the possible directions of improving it. The mathematical description of POEP can be expressed simply as follows:

$$\text{Opt.}\quad F$$

$$\text{s.t.}\quad F(x) \in N$$

where $X(T) = \{x_j(t)\}$, $j = 1, 2, \ldots, n$, is a structure vector of a target system. It is projected by the system relationship F into a new ecological niche vector of $Y(t) = F(x, t)$, within a certain realistic ecological niche of

$$N(t) = \{\, \underline{n}_i(t), \bar{n}_i(t) \,\}, \qquad i = 1, 2, \ldots, m$$

Here the $\bar{n}_i(t)$ and $\underline{n}_i(t)$ are the upper and lower boundary of i-th ecological factor n_i respectively.

While F has the meanings of both ecological and mathematical function. From the ecological point of view, it has three functional meanings: the resource utilization relationships, the mutual promoting and restraining relationships among components and the relationships with outer environment and future opportunity. From the mathematical point of view, it contains three kinds of ecological characteristic matrixes: the efficiency matrix $E = \{e_{ij}\}$, the correlation matrix $C = \{c_{ij}\}$ and the vitality matrix $V = \{v_{ij}\}$, each of them is projected from X, but we can't usually find their explicit descriptions of projection. It is only through the procedure of POEP that we can continuously ascertain the system function F and steer it to a satisfied direction of high efficiency, harmonious relationship and robust vitality.

The basic idea of POEP is a combination of common optimization methods or hard methods and qualitative, fuzzy methods or soft methods in the whole decision process.

3   The procedure of POEP

We take the ecological strategy analysis of Tianjin Urban industrial development as an example to explain the procedure (Fig.1).

Identification

Tianjin urban ecosystem is a high material-consuming ecosystem whose major production is industry. Its main problems are the inefficient utilization of resources, serious environmental pollution and unreasonable production structure and space distribution. The essence of the problems is the contradiction between economic development and environmental burden. Therefore, the emphasis is put on the resource consumption and environmental pollution.

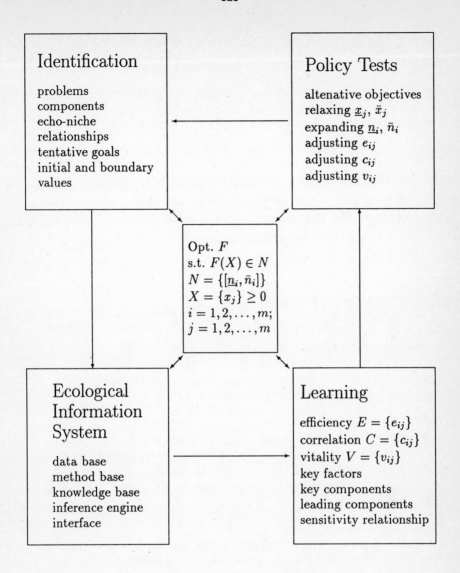

Figure 1: The process of Pan-Objective Ecological Programming

Heuristic structure

The industrial system and subsystems are divided into many interrelated components according to sector, trade, management system, etc.

The state variables x_j, the relationship variables e_{ij} (the status of j-th state variable in the use of i-th ecological niche factor) and the control variable n_i (the i-th ecological niche factor) are selected to measure the structure and function of the system.

Relationship setting

As most of the data of industrial development come from statistics which are usually associated with linear connection, we project the x_j with linear operator of multiplication into a new eco-vector. Our task is to

$$\text{Opt.} \quad F = \{f_{ij}\}$$

$$\text{s.t.} \quad \underline{n}_i \leq \sum_{j=1}^{n} f_{ij} x_j \leq \bar{n}_i$$

$$\underline{x}_j \leq x_j \leq \bar{x}_j$$

$$i = 1, 2, \ldots, m$$

$$j = 1, 2, \ldots, n$$

Iteration

- Choosing goals for each iteration.
  At each step of optimization one or several ecological factors from the ecological niche are chosen to be single or multiple objectives according to the decision-makers' intents. As this kind of optimization is only a searching process which serves to probe the integrated countermeasures, the optimum result of each iteration has no much significance in practice.

- Determining initial and boundary values.
  The world is limited. For any ecological factor, too much or too little of the quantity is harmful to the whole system. So we have to predetermine the upper and lower limits for every factor of the system. We take the practical situation as an initial state of the system. These boundary and initial values ensure the feasibility of the final result in each iteration.

- Multiple objective programming.
  Having selected the present goals and initial values, we begin with the tentative optimization using ordinary techniques of MOP. And a tentative solution S^k will be obtained from the k-th iteration based on the k-th parameters of E^k, N^k, X_0^k and optimizing rule f^k

$$S^k = f^k(E^k, N^k, X_0^k)$$

The final goal is not to get the optimum solution, but to trace the system dynamics, and to find he inefficiency, inharmony and risk of the system.

• Learning from each iteration

From each iteration we can get three kinds of ecological characteristic matrixes: efficiency matrix $E = \{e_{ij}\}$ shows the resource utilization efficiency or environmental impact intensity of different components; correlation matrix $C = \{c_{ij}\}$ shows the eco-niche occupating proportions of each component in the whole system, and the vitality matrix $V = \{v_{ij}\}$ shows the opportunity and risk of relaxing limiting factors, i.e. the effects of improving e_{ij}, n_j, for j-th limiting factor.

Relationship regulation

The ordinary iteration of optimization is only a start of the regulation process. A series of result can be obtained from further analysis.

• Key factor analysis

The optimal solution S^k of each iteration is inevitably on the edge of the ecological niche. There must be one or several ecological niche factors which limit further optimization of the objective values, e.g., n_1, n_2, in Fig. 2. We call them limiting factors, and put them in order according to limiting roles. Then we will have the following countermeasures:

If the decision-makers are satisfied with the present goals and the relationships, the parameters needn't be adjusted further, we may switch to other goals to start new iteration.

Otherwise we'll try to search a feasible way of either improving e_{ij} or expanding n_l (suppose factor l is the first limiting factor). At this time we should first check the rationality and accuracy of e_{ij}, $\underline{n}_l$ and $\bar{n}_l$, then collect additional data for searching the strategy of improving those inner and outer relationships connected with the l-th eco-niche factor, which is done by going into other sub-procedure of optimizing e_{il} and n_l. From this sub-optimization we can get improved initial values of $E^{k'}$ and $N^{k'}$ for $(k+1)$-th iteration:

$$E^{k+1} = E^{k'}$$
$$N^{k+1} = N^{k'}$$

The some new limiting factors will appear or the old one is still the limiting factor. We will repeat the above procedure together with decision-makers to expand eco-niche and reduce inner expenditure.

• Key components analysis

There are some key components in the system which have great effects on improving the present goal. We call them key components and suppose the first key component be X_k.

After rechecking the rationality and accuracy of e_{ik}, $\underline{x}_k$ and $\bar{x}^k$, and supplementing relevant data, we will negotiate with decision-makers to search the possibility of improving e_{ik} and changing $\underline{x}_k$, $\bar{x}_k$, and then turn to another sub-programming to identify

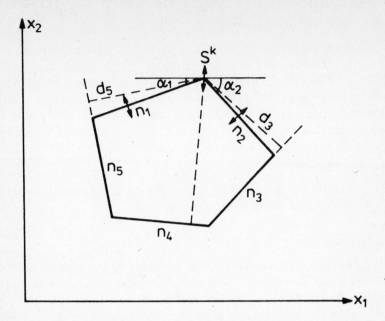

Figure 2: The optima S^k is not on the vertex or edge in each iteration of POEP, and the present goal is to search the opportunity of moving n_1, n_2, S^k and to make full use of d_i.

the cost-benefit of their changes. The e_{lk} which is connected with both limiting factor and key component should be given a special consideration, because a slight change of e_{lk} will exert a great influence on the system goals. So we call it sensitive variable.

To sum up, the basic technique of POEP is to ascertain the key relation as detail as possible and neglect the less important relations.

• **Correlation analysis**

A correlation matrix $C = \{c_{ij}\}$ outputs from each iteration in which each row stands for a component such as an industrial sector, while each column an ecological factor. The sum of the figures in each column is 100%. We can compare the contribution or burden proportions among different components in each column, and find out leading component (one with highest benefit) and burden component (one with heaviest burden) for each eco-factor. In each row we can compare the contribution and burden proportions of the same component, find its advantage and disadvantage. According to the benefit-cost ratio of each component calculated from the correlation matrix, we can order all components and find the best and worse one. People usually tend to reach a conclusion that the best one should be encouraged and worse one discouraged. But in practice we often have to develop the later and limit the former. After adding some social and ecological costs and benefits to them and recalculating them according to the varying situations, we can get some new interesting conclusions.

From the C matrix we can also get some derived qualitative matrixes according to different goals and preferences of decision-makers.

• Opportunity and risk analysis

There are two kinds of vitality matrix V_1 and V_2 which can be got from analysis of the system dynamics.

V_1 is the outer risk-opportunity matrix. Each v_{ij} of V_1 stands for the risk (intensity of limiting factors, e.g. in Fig. 2 $V_{61} = \alpha_1$, $V_{62} = \alpha_2$, the smaller the α_i is, the stronger the limiting role is) or opportunity (the distance from the threshold of each non-limiting factor, e.g. in Fig. 2, $V_{63} = d_3$, $V_{64} = d_4$, $V_{65} = d_5$, the bigger the d_i is, the larger the opportunity is) of j-th ecological factor if n_i is taken as the objective. We can search the strategy of reforming eco-niche by use of V_1.

V_2 is the inner opportunity and risk matrix, the v_{ij} of which stands for the contribution or impact of improving e_{ij} on i-th ecological factor. Through V_2 we can search the strategy of taping inner potentials.

4 Policy test

Learning from the different kinds of ecological characteristic matrixes, the decision-makers can do policy test, e.g., to alter objectives, expand eco-nich space, adjust boundaries of X and improve e_{ij}, c_{ij} and v_{ij} so as to find a satisfied path towards sustainable development by themselves.

Then the e_{ij}, c_{ij} and v_{ij} are adjusted to a level that the limiting intensities are not so high, the surplus eco-factors are reasonably used and the decision-makers are satisfied with the results, the essential goals could be considered to be realized and the iterations can be tentatively ceased.

5 Discussion

Traditional multiple objective programming is to do the compromising work among the different objectives and find a sole optimal solution. But in POEP, the optimal value is not at the vertex or edge of the polyhedron enclosed by all objectives within it. The exact position depends on the opinion of decision makers. POEP can't point out which position is absolutely best but only provide a learning tool to decision-makers to let them simultaneously regulate their system in practice.

The whole procedure of POEP is an intelligence-aided decision support process. The experts knowledge and various data are fed and renewed in the Ecological Information System in each iteration.

In the study of Tianjin industrial development, the method and results were well accepted by the local decision makers and awarded the National Prize of Science and Technology.

References

Sharpe, R. (1982). Optimizing Urban Futures. *Environment and planning* B, 9, pp. 209–220.

Simon, H.A. (1982). The Sciences of the Artificial. The MIT Press, second edition.

Wang, R. (1988). Towards High Efficiency and Harmonions Relationship, Principles and Methodology of Urban Ecological Regulation. Hunan Educational Press, Changsha, 276p.

Wang, R. and Ma, S. (1985). Probing the Urban Ecological Programming. In D. Xu (ed.): Study on Chinese Ecological-Economic Problems, Zhejiang People's Press, pp. 97–108.

Zeleny, M. (1982). Multiple Criteria Decision Making. Mcgraw-Hill Book Company.

Part 6

Decision Support for Negotiations

Simulating Political Negotiations Using NEGOPLAN: The Meech Lake Accord

Michal Iglewski
Department d'Informatique
Université du Quebec à Hull
Hull, Quebec J8X 3X7 Canada

Wojtek Michalowski
Decision Analysis Laboratory
School of Business
Carleton University
Ottawa, Ontario K1S 5B6 Canada

1   Introduction

This paper presents a methodology for structuring and supporting complex, hierarchical decision processes. The proposed approach can be classified within the "intelligent decision system" category (Holtzman, 1989), and it is applicable to the analysis of different forms of decision making activities. The primary focus of this paper is the negotiation process.

The proposed method of modelling and supporting the negotiation process is based on the following assumptions:

- There are only two negotiating parties (in case of many opponents, and aggregated adversary (Kersten et al., 1989) is created.

- The negotiation process is seen through the eyes of one side only; this side is the source of all the information about the negotiation and about the opponent.

- The problem of negotiation is complex, but it can be decomposed into smaller subproblems.

- The negotiating side creates a model of an opponent.

The dynamic and sequential nature of the negotiation process means that a decision is first made, then communicated or implemented. This leads to a response from the opponent, which is turn requires a new decision, and so on, The negotiating problem changes as the negotiation itself proceeds, partly because of the negotiation process, and partly due to the availability of new information. These changes have to be recorded and analyzed before another decision is made. From this short description, one may conclude that a negotiating side, in addition to the traditional challenges of determining a negotiation problem representation and a feasible decision, is faced with determining responses to the opponents actions.

The paper is organised as follows. The next section introduces the problem to be modelled, namely negotiations on the implementation of the Meech Lake Accord (MLA). In Section 3 a modelling framework is outlined, and the general principles of rule-based formalism are presented. In Section 4 this framework is applied to model negotiations aimed at the ratification of MLA by all Canadian provinces. The paper ends with conclusions regarding the applicability of this framework for modelling political negotiation.

2   The Meech Lake Accord

The 1982 Constitution Act which gave Canada rather than Great Britain control over the founding document was signed by all Canadian provinces except predominantly French-speaking Quebec. At this time, the province of Quebec was under the Parti Quebecois government, and was isolated at the end of the negotiations to bring the constitution to Canada, and to add a Charter of Rights and Freedoms. In 1987 the federal government and the Canadian provinces brokered an accord to change the constitution, so that is can also be signed by the province of Quebec. The agreement reached in 1987 is popularly known as the Meech Lake Accord (Government of Canada, 1987). The major issue agreed to by the signing parties is a recognition of Quebec as a "distinct society", and therefore, the requirement that the constitution will be interpreted in a manner consistent with this fact. The MLA therefore, contains the amending formula of the constitution itself, and as such requires the unanimous approval of the provincial legislatures. So far New Brunswick and Manitoba have expressed opposition to MLA and have yet to approve it, while Newfoundland is threatening to withdraw its approval if the accord is not amended. In 1989, the prime minister of Canada organised a meeting with Canada's then provincial premiers to discuss approval of MLA, so that it can be ratified by June 23, 1990. This meeting reveled a resistance to MLA and divisions between the provinces. The federal government which believes that failure of MLA will lead to the alienation of Quebec and ultimately to the segregation of Canada, has started complex negotiations to save the accord. In this paper we demonstrate how these negotiations between the prime minister of Canada and the provincial premiers can be modelled, simulated and supported. A system called NEGOPLAN (Kersten et al., 1988; Matwin et al., 1989) is used as a modelling and simulation vehicle. It is an intelligent negotiation support system written in Arity Prolog and implemented on a microcomputer.

NEGOPLAN allows the side being supported to organise knowledge about a negotiation problem. In the MLA negotiations, the side to be supported is the Prime Minister's Office (PMO). The opponents, contracted to an aggregated adversary, are the premiers of the ten Canadian provinces. It seems reasonable to assume that the PMO has sufficient knowledge about the negotiating situation to anticipate the reactions of the provincial premiers to political decisions made by the federal government, and aimed at the ratification of MLA.

3 Modelling framework

A comprehensive presentation of a modelling framework based on rules representation is given in (Kersten and Szpakowicz, 1989). In general, such a framework is based on the assumption that a negotiation problem is decomposable into smaller subproblems whose decomposition can be described in the language of a goal/subgoals hierarchy, where a goal/subgoal is expressed as a predicate $\alpha_i(\beta_{1i}, \ldots, \beta_{ni})$ (Hogger, 1984). A predicate may be assigned one of the three values: *true*, *false* and *any*. A given value is assigned through a valuation function φ (Rescher, 1969) such that $\varphi(\alpha_i) = v$, where $v \in V = \{true, false, any\}$, (equivalently, $\alpha_i ::= v$). The value *any* corresponds to the situation when a predicate may be either *true* or *false* without influencing the values of its consequents.

A purpose of negotiations is modelled as the root of a decomposition hierarchy, and is represented as a *principal goal* having the property that no other goal cannot be inferred from it. In other words, a subgoal which is not an antecedent of any other subgoal is a principal goal. A subgoal which is an antecedent only (it represents a non/decomposable subproblem) is called a *fact*.

Predicate α_i represents a subgoal and is the consequent of antecedents $[\alpha_{i1}, \ldots, \alpha_{imi}]$, if there is a well-formed formula r_i such that:

$$\alpha_i \Longleftarrow r_i([\alpha_{ij}] \; j \in J_i)$$

where "$\Longleftarrow$" is the connective *if... then...*, the permissible connectives in r_i are: *and*, *or* and *not*, and J_i is the index set of antecedents of α_i.

The above formula defines a *rule*. Deviating from this formula, repetition of the rules is used instead of the connective *or* (e.g. $\alpha_1 \Longleftarrow \alpha_2$ *or* α_3 is replaced by $\alpha_1 \Longleftarrow \alpha_2$, $\alpha_1 \Longleftarrow \alpha_3$). The rule-based model of a negotiation problem is a collection of rules which forms a knowledge base. The model itself allows for the deductive thought inherent in logic models (Leblanc and Wisdom, 1976). A desirable feature of such a model is the possibility of representing it in the form of an and/or tree (further referred to as a *goal tree*) (Charniak and McDermott, 1985). A solution of a rule-based model is a set of facts and their truth valuations such that a principal goal has valuation *true*. Any such solution can be obtained with arbitrary valuation of facts, or through chaining the rules. Use of rule-based representation for negotiation problems allows for flexibility in modeling, by taking into account quantitative as well as qualitative information, and allowing for the organisation of knowledge about a problem in simple and clear way.

A rule-based framework has other interesting features. One of them is the possibility to select an action (described by a solution of the model) following information which is not included in the knowledge base. This external information can be taken into account using *response rules*, namely rules which infer the truth value of a predicate using valuations of other predicates not necessarily included in an initial description of a problem.

In negotiations, a final decision is seldom made which resolves a problem as initially stated. Usually, one makes a decision, observes the reactions of the parties involved, perform necessary corrections in problem perception and representation, makes new decision, etc. The observed reactions yield new information which may require changing the initial representation of a negotiation problem. These anticipated reactions are taken into account in a rule-based model by the introduction of *restructure rules* which modify the definitions of rules used in the problem representation. As a result of application of the restructure rules, a new problem decomposition, i.e. new goal tree, is obtained. When a new solution of a rule-based model cannot be inferred through the application of the response rules only, NEGOPLAN consults the restructure rules. Forward chaining (Charniak and McDermott, 1985) of these rules introduces modifications to a goal tree. These modifications depend on the actual positions of both negotiating sides, and on the negotiation phase. The process of solving a goal tree, followed by the application of the response rules, and if necessary of the restructure rules, continues until a desirable solution of a negotiation problem is found.

4 Simulation of political negotiations

An initial goal tree of MLA negotiations represents a situation which took place two years ago, when the accord was signed in 1987 (time = time(0)). Modelling of the negotiation process starts in 1989 (time = time(2)), when persuasion of undecided or opposed provinces starts in order to have the accord ratified before the due date of June 23, 1990. The goal tree created from NEGOPLAN's knowledge base contains information available or anticipated by PMO (the side being supported), and the premiers of Canadian provinces play the role of an aggregated adversary. A knowledge base at time (2) has the following set of rules:

```
quebec_sign    ⇐ ratification.
quebec_sign    ⇐ wait_and_see.
ratification   ⇐ meech_lake & time(2).
```

The corresponding goal tree is presented on Figure 1.

A predicate wait_and_see described an option for PMO to do nothing (maintaining the *status quo*). A possible solution of the goal tree at moment time (2) is presented on Figure 2.

An interpretation of this solution is as follows: all the provinces signed MLA, so it should be ratified (observe *true* valuation of meech_lake predicate in "our position" window).

In the meantime, the political situation has changed:

- Manitoba, New Brunswick, and Newfoundland changed governments and demand the amendments in form of a parallel accord or withdrew their support for MLA.

- the government of Quebec passed the controversial law (Bill 178) requiring French only on all commercial signs in the province;

- the government of Alberta wants senate reform, and is using support for MLA as leverage;

- the government of Nova Scotia wants a guarantee for minority rights similar to the rights of French Canadians specified in MLA.

337

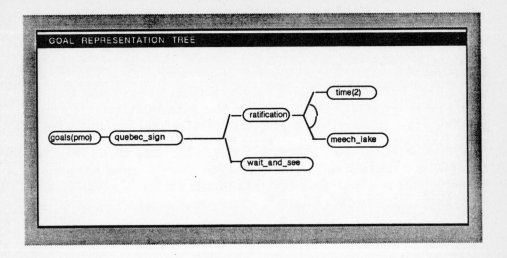

Figure 1: Goal tree at moment time (2)

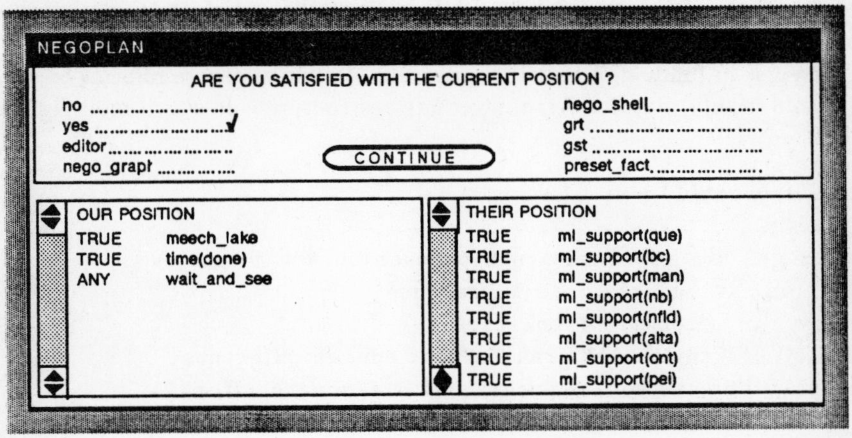

Figure 2: Accepted solution

These changes of political climate are modelled in NEGOPLAN using response rules. A response rule representing the changes outlined above is the following:

```
pmo:time(2) ::= true
==>
prov:ml_support(man) ::= false & prov:ml_support(nb) ::= false &
prov:ml_support(nfld) ::= false & prov:disc_parallel(alta) ::= true &
prov:sing_law(que) ::= true & prov:disc_parallel(nb) ::= true &
prov:disc_parallel(ns) ::= true & prov:disc_parallel(que) ::= false.
```

Introduction of the "sign law" by the Quebec government triggered a strong reaction in Manitoba, which now wants amendments to MLA in the form of a parallel accord. A corresponding response rule is a follows:

```
pmo:time(2) ::= true & prov:sign_law(que) ::= true
==>
prov:spirit_of_compromise(man) ::= false &
prov:ml_support(man) ::= false &
prov:disc_parallel(man) ::= true.
```

The new political climate requires redefinition of the initial assumptions regarding ratification of MLA. The PMO may consider some forms of persuasion which can be of political (changes in funding of social programs or stalling of senate reform) or economic (cuts in federal grants) nature. An appropriate restructure rule which modifies the goal tree is given below:

```
prov:ml_support(X) ::= false
==> modify (
quebec_sign  ⇐  ratification & persuasion # wait_and_see,
persuasion  ⇐  concessions # pressure,
pressure  ⇐  economic # political,
economic  ⇐  cut_health_grants # cut_education_grants,
political  ⇐  cut_social_programs # not senate_reform).
```

where # denotes *or*.

We shall not describe here the consecutive phases of a negotiation process as generated by NEGOPLAN. The general idea is to give PMO the possibility of selecting actions (concessions and pressures) leading to the ratification of MLA. A goal tree created at each stage of a process has many solutions, and the PMO's role is to select a desirable one. One of the last actions leading to the modification of a goal tree is senate reform (change from a senate nominated by a prime minister to a senate nominated/elected by the provinces). Such a bargaining issue requires rule, a solution of a modified goal tree is presented on Figure 3.

The solution presented in Figure 3 results in ratification of MLA. This solution was selected to illustrate a particular path leading to achievement of a principal goal which is the signing of a constitution by Quebec. However, it is necessary to stress that there are other solutions of a goal tree which if accepted define different sets of actions.

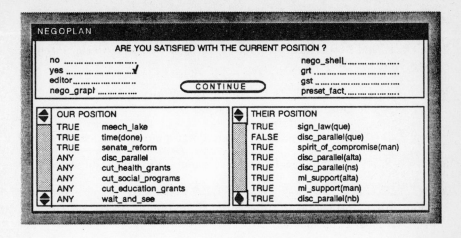

Figure 3: Accepted solution

Conclusions

This paper discusses a particular modelling framework for negotiations support, and illustrates its applicability with an example of political negotiations characterised by an outcome which is difficult to predict. The framework itself is applicable to any negotiating situation where the assumptions outlined in the paper hold. For example, it was applied in modelling management/union bargaining (Matwin et al., 1989), in modelling negotiations with a hostage-taker (Kersten and Michalowski, 1989; Michalowski et al., 1988), and in modelling financial decision making (Szpakowicz et al., 1990).

Negotiations require flexibility in modelling and decision support. We believe that a rule-based framework provides such flexibility, thus accommodating changes in problem understanding and in problem perception. A clear distinction between the knowledge base (rules), and the metaknowledge base (response and restructure rules), allows for the modification of a problem representation according to negotiation dynamics.

Political negotiations require above all systematic organisation of knowledge about a situation, about opponent(s), and about possible actions. NEGOPLAN provides a convenient framework for such an organisation by:

- requiring the representation of a negotiation problem as a set of rules of action;

- controlling the inference of these actions in systematic manner;

- making consecutive modifications of the problem context-dependent.

During actual political negotiations NEGOPLAN can be used either as a simulation tool at a preparatory stage, or as a tool to analyse the validity of a proposal (solution) in terms of concessions or pressures.

References

Charniak, E. and McDermott, D. (1985). Introduction to Artificial Intelligence. Reading, Addison Wesley.

Government of Canada, (1987). A Guide to the Meech Lake Constitutional Accord. Ottawa, The Queens Printer of Canada.

Hogger, C.J. (1984). Introduction to Logic Programming. London, Academic Press.

Holtzman, S. (1989). Intelligent Decision Systems. Reading, Addison Wesley.

Kersten, G.E. and Michalowski, W. (1989). A Cooperative Expert System for Negotiation with a Hostage-taker. *International Journal of Expert Systems: Research and Applications*, 2, pp. 359-381 .

Kersten, G.E., Michalowski, W., Cray, D. and Lee, I. (1989). An Analytic Basis for Decision Support in Negotiations. School of Business, Carleton University, WP 89–08.

Kersten, G.E., Michalowski, W., Matwin, S. and Szpakowicz, S. (1988). Representing the Negotiation Process with a Rule-based Formalism. *Theory and Decision*, 25, pp. 225–257.

Kersten, G.E. and Szpakowicz, S. Rule-based Formalism and Preference Representation: An Extension of NEGOPLAN. *European Journal of Operational Research* (forthcoming).

Leblanc, H. and Wisdom, W.A. (1976). Deductive Logic. Boston, Allyn and Bacon.

Matwin, S., Szpakowicz, S., Koperczak, Z., Kersten, G.E. and Michalowski, W. (1989). NEGOPLAN: An Expert System Shell for Negotiation Support. *IEEE Expert*, 4, pp. 50–65.

Michalowski, W., Kersten, G.E., Koperczak, Z., Matwin, S. and Szpakowicz, S. (1988). Negotiation with a Terrorist: Can an Expert System Help? In M. Singh et al. (eds): Managerial Decision Support Systems, New York, North Holland, pp. 193–200.

Rescher, N. (1969). Many-valued Logic. New York, McGraw-Hill.

Szpakowicz, S., Kersten, G.E. and Koperczak, Z. (1990). Knowledge-based Decision Support, Preferences, and Financial Planning. Proceedings of the Conference on Artificial Intelligence Applications, pp. 222-228.

Negotiation and Autonomous Agents for Decision Support*

Gregory E. Kersten
Decision Analysis Laboratory
School of Business
Carleton University Ottawa
Ontario, Canada, K1S 5B6

Stan Szpakowicz, Zbig Koperczak
Department of Computer Science
University of Ottawa
Ontario, Canada, K1N 6N5

1   Introduction

Negotiation is a powerful technique of decision making and conflict resolution. It can be applied to individual decision making in dynamic environments. The decision-maker is an autonomous agent that conducts negotiations in a generalized, metaphorical sense. We consider one such agent, a robot which conducts an exploratory mission in an unknown, changing world. The use of the negotiation metaphor in decision support is not unique in the literature but it is an extension of the use in expert systems (Hotaran, 1987) and distributed artificial intelligence (Davis and Smith, 1981).

The behaviour of the robot is modelled with NEGOPLAN, an expert system shell for negotiation support. The first prototype of NEGOPLAN has been described elsewhere (Kersten et al., 1988; Matwin et al., 1989). To simulate the robot's decision process, the system was extended so that it now models the environment and its changes. Although the same system is used to model the agent and its environment, the agent does not know the future states of the environment. Therefore, its decisions are based on its past experiences.

This paper is based on our experiments with the NEGOPLAN system and the modelling of autonomous decision making (Szpakowicz et al., 1989; Kersten et al., 1990). Here, we outline the approach and its applicability to modelling individual decision making. We conclude with another metaphor: the use of autonomous agents as intelligent decision support systems.

The level and the quality of support increases if the system can make complex decisions independently, that is, if the system can actually simulate the whole decision-making process together with the analysis of its consequences, the determining of the subsequent decisions and the revision of the decision model. The system's ability to make decisions

---

*Sections 3 and 4 of this paper are based on the article "Modelling Autonomous Agents in Changing Environments", which is a chapter by the same authors in C. Y. Ho and G. W. Zobrist (eds.), "Progress in Robotics and Intelligent Systems", to be published by Ablex, Norwood, NJ.

This work was partially supported by the National Science and Engineering Research Council of Canada.

is postulated in "intelligent decision systems" (Holtzman, 1989; Schorr and Rappaport, 1989) and in the artificial intelligence research on decision making and rationality (Pollock, 1990).

2 The NEGOPLAN approach

The decision-theoretic paradigm of NEGOPLAN can be summed up in three issues in decision-making:

1. development of a representation of the decision problem,

2. determination of a procedure which transforms the representation into decision alternatives,

3. choice of a decision alternative.

These issues permeate most of the research on decision making and support. Decisions often lead to other decisions, so decision outcomes affect the problem representation. An additional issue can be identified in negotiations and in other ongoing decision processes. It is:

4. determination of a procedure which builds and modifies the problem representation.

Modelling with NEGOPLAN makes it possible to take into account all four issues.

NEGOPLAN is a rule-based system which helps solve solution complex and initially ill-structured decision problems (Szpakowicz et al., 1987). It was used to model processes with two participants, where the structure of the problem at any moment can be derived from the previous structure and the previous decisions. The system was used to model negotiations between two agents, for example police and a hostage taker (Michalowski et al., 1988), union and management (Matwin et al., 1989), or two large corporations in contract negotiation (Kersten et al., 1989).

The negotiation metaphor is a view of individual decision-making as generalized negotiation, where one of the partners is inactive or unable to make autonomous decisions. This metaphor, and the expressiveness of the rule-based formalism enabled us to apply extended NEGOPLAN to the modelling and simulation of individual complex decision processes (Kersten et al., 1990a; Szpakowicz et al., 1989). To verify the usefulness of the enhanced tool, two experiments were conducted: one in financial decision-making (Koperczak et al., 1990), and one in simulating autonomous decision-making of a robot (Kersten et al., 1990b).

In NEGOPLAN decision problems are assumed to be hierarchically decomposable: the representation of the decision problem has a hierarchical structure. The structure of the representation may change when there are changes in the perception of the problem, or in the state of the environment or the opponent.

We assume that the agent's methods of reasoning do not change, in that there exists a fixed way in which the problem representation is analyzed and a decision derived from it. Usually there is more than one alternative decision. In autonomous decision-making, the procedure contains an "evaluator" or a selection mechanism. Thus, we can say that the procedure and the representation together represent the agent at time at any point of time.

The representation is consistent if at least one feasible decision alternative can be inferred from it. By applying the procedure to the problem representation a local decision is obtained. This decision is made in the environment which is in a given state. A decision may also aim at changing the condition of the agent rather than the environment; for example, such would be a decision to repair the robot's malfunctioning element. The agent does not know the exact representation of the environment but only "senses" its states. This helps model the uncertainty of the agent when faced with the unknown.

The agent knows the initial representation of the decision problem and the selected aspects of the current state of the environment. However, making rational decisions requires the agent's ability to modify or restructure the problem according to own changes and changes in the environment. A procedure which modifies or transforms the problem representation is an important mechanism of NEGOPLAN. If the agent were a closed system, the information on the last representation, the choice mechanism, and the transformation procedure would be sufficient to determine the new representation. The agent's dependence on the state of the environment requires makes its current state necessary in determining the new problem representation.

The possibility of modifying the problem representation means that local decisions can be evaluated not only from the point of view of what are the direct outcomes, but also from the point of view of the agent's future opportunities. These opportunities are included in future representations. Changes in the current representation result directly from the outcomes of a decision, and the decision influences future representations of both the problem and the environment. This relationship between the present decision and the future opportunities is consistent with our understanding of rationality which cannot be considered only locally.

3 The negotiation metaphor

NEGOPLAN was originally aimed at the support of negotiators. For the purpose of the present considerations, the environment is viewed as the negotiator's opponent, and the actors other than the negotiator and the opponent are modelled as neutral entities. The extension of NEGOPLAN to individual decision-making is possible because of the flexibility of the rule-based method, but first of all it stems from the rôle that conflict plays in individual decision-making (Levi, 1987). Whenever there is a choice, there also may be a conflict, and negotiation is an exemplary method of conflict reduction. Moreover, decision-making through negotiation has features which makes this method suitable when problems are complex, dynamic, and dependent on the states of the environment. Specifically:

- Decision-making through negotiation focuses on the integration of decisions with their outcomes. Although the outcomes cannot influence a decision which has been made, they certainly can influence future decisions. This relationship is restricted to decisions but it covers the agent's understanding of the problem, its perspectives, and so forth. From the modelling viewpoint this means integration of the model of a decision problem with the models of the opponent and the environment.

- Decision-making through negotiation is a process. Actions or decisions do not end with the evaluation of their outcomes. They are made so that other actions or decisions can be made. In negotiation, the process has an arbitrary final state (a compromise reached) but it is not defined in terms of a number of steps. Rather, it is defined through a particular type of equilibrium in the world consisting of the agent, the opponent and the environment. Note that even the equilibrium need not be well defined, and that its (imprecise?) definition can evolve during negotiation.

The adoption of the negotiation metaphor for individual decision-making can be further justified by the following observations.

- The integration of the agent's decisions with the environment is a natural extension of the interplay between the negotiating parties.

- The environment is not uniform, so one can distinguish elements which react to the agent's decisions and actions from elements which are independent. The distinction is typical of negotiation: the elements which react represent the opponent, other elements represent the "outer world".

- Negotiation is a goal-oriented process in which partial decisions are made to obtain compromise proposals and counter-proposals. Similarly, the robot's mission is a process with local decisions which get the robot closer to (or farther from) the mission's overall goals.

- A common property of negotiation and the decision processes considered here is that the underlying models change when new information becomes available. The agent's viewpoints, perspectives, and criteria of choice depend on the context.

- The negotiation process depends on the outcomes of partial decisions. The agent does not prepare a new proposal before the results of its previous proposals have been analyzed. Similarly, the robot's next action depends on the outcomes of its previous actions.

The power and generality of negotiation makes it possible to use the negotiation metaphor in a variety of decision processes. In a metaphorical sense, it is not even necessary to have an opponent: the agent can "negotiate the surface of the planet". In all these cases the focus is on the difficulty and complexity of decisions and their implementations, and on the dynamic aspect of decisions. It is not relevant that the "other side" does not respond to one's actions but that the agent cannot *a priori* determine its future states.

4 The robot and its mission

The robot has a mission to perform on a planet. It may choose points to visit in its effort to achieve the global goal of the mission which is to collect the required number of samples and pictures, and then return to the base. Both samples and pictures have to be taken from different but not predetermined points of the planet. It is assumed for simplicity that the robot's sensory capabilities only enable it to monitor itself and the environment at the beginning and the end of a move. A move consists of changing the location and collecting a sample and a picture, if possible.

The environment where the mission is carried out is unknown. It is being unveiled gradually, while the robot moves on the surface. The grid model of the surface is assumed (Bares, 1989; Elfes, 1989). The grid has integer co-ordinates; the surface is assumed to be locally planar, and the robot never manages to circle the planet around. Each point of the grid is characterized by: temperature, radiation, level of sun-light, and roughness of the surface between the present position and this point.

Conditions on the planet may be prohibitive, that is, the robot may be unable to visit a grid point if it is separated from the present position by an insurmountable obstacle (a "wall"). Also, the robot cannot visit points where the temperature or radiation is excessively high.

The robot has a limited amount of energy for the duration of the mission. The amount of energy is assumed to be the main limitation in fulfilling the mission, and there is no time constraint. Besides the energy constraint, there is a number of limitations that have to taken into account. For example, only one sample and one picture can be taken at one position; a sample or picture is not taken twice from the same position; conditions on the planet may make it impossible for the robot to take a sample; if the sun is exposed, one energy unit is saved; the robot cannot move over a wall. These limitations define conditions on the planet that the robot considers acceptable or unacceptable, situations when a sample or a picture can be taken, and expected energy expenditure. These are taken into account in the robot's decisions and actions and also in the criteria which the robot is using in the decision making.

The mission is divided into three major phases. In the starting phase the robot lands on the planet and start its routine. It moves on the planet's surface, collecting samples and taking pictures; this is the exploring phase. After all samples and pictures have been collected, or all energy has been used up, the robot goes back to the mother-ship (the returning phase). The first action of the robot, preceding the starting phase, is a preliminary (remote) investigation of the planet.

If the robot decides to continue the mission, a number of conditions is generated to represent the robot's state indicators (for example, the amount of energy, number of pictures and samples). Then the robot uses these indicators to choose a decision making criterion from the three options that were encoded (energy, samples or pictures). For example, if the energy level is higher than some limit, the criterion is samples, but if energy is less than sufficient, energy is chosen. This way a specific combination of conditions is chosen.

This combination of conditions is used to modify the current problem representation. The new representation describes a particular instance of the robot which is prepared to begin the mission, has particular goals to achieve, has given limitations and criteria. An arbitrary point on the planet is prepared and the robot "lands" there. The robot can move in one of four directions, or it can stay at the present position. The conditions in four adjacent points are sensed. The robot chooses one point and moves to it. If the robot cannot choose any of these points, it remains in its present position and waits for a change in the conditions. After the move, the grid is refreshed, that is, the conditions in each known or newly unveiled point change according to certain gradients and present values of the parameters.

Each grid point holds information about the conditions, and also binary information about the presence of a sample or picture. It may happen that the point does not contain a sample when it is first looked at, but it is always possible to take a picture. The information about a visited grid point is updated when the robot takes a picture or collects a sample. This allows us to model the situation in which the robot may return to a point where it was previously but it did not take a picture or a sample.

While moving on the planet's surface, the robot is prone to accidents which affect its equipment. Information about an accident is generated from "outside" of the robot, in a similar matter as the information about points of the grids. Each accident changes the state of the robot with the use of the restructure procedure. The robot cannot continue the mission unless the equipment is in working condition. Therefore it attempts to repair itself, and the repair is a decision obtained from the current problem representation. As the repair requires energy, and in an extreme case the robot may not have enough energy to repair the damage. This may cause the robot to be unable to return to the mother ship.

5 Autonomous decision making

The robot's principal goal is to accomplish the mission by meeting several global goals such as "collect the required material" or "return safely". At each step during the mission, the robot will also have specific immediate or local goals. The definition of global goals reflects our model of the robot, in particular its status and its preferences. Local goals are more related to the circumstances, especially the state of the environment at a given moment.

The robot has limited resources and therefore control of its global and local goals, equipment and resources is essential (Bares, 1989). The information on goals and resources is structured, always available to the robot and used to choose between the possible courses of action.

The choice of the visited points is made with the help of a simple reward function which assigns a value to each candidate point. The candidate points are accessible to the robot, other points cannot be visited because of the obstacles (a wall) or high radiation. All visible points are evaluated first, and the candidate points are identified. Next, the point's attributes are used to determine its attractiveness, that is, the presence of a picture and the sample, the condition of the terrain, level of radiation and the temperature are aggregated and the value of the point is determined. The reward function is calculated for each candidate point, and that with the maximal value is chosen.

It may happen that two or three points are equally attractive. Then, a lower level choice model may be invoked. In this model the neighbours of the attractive candidates would be considered. A number of choice methods can be applied here. For instance, we might add up the values of the reward function for the candidate's neighbors and choose the point with a maximal total value.

We see that a number of hierarchically organized methods can help resolve possible conflicts. This hierarchical structure can be seen as borrowed from the behaviour-generating and sensory processing hierarchies of the human brain (Albus, 1981). It invokes a lower-level model which allows a finer analysis only if there is a tie (conflict) in a higher-level model.

The use of choice models may have to be monitored and the models may need to be modied according to the current situation. This is because the robot may use different global evaluation criteria. A criterion may change depending on the state of the mission and the availability of resources. Initially, one of the two criteria is chosen:

1. the criterion is energy efficiency, that is, the robot attempts to minimize energy use if energy is a scarce resource;

2. the aggregate criterion is pictures and samples (with the emphasis on one of these) if there is sufficient energy.

This approach is consistent with (Lumelsky and Stepanov, 1987) where it is said that in an unknown terrain navigation algorithms do not attempt to optimize parameters. We also used additional criteria in the experiments. The criterion changes from energy to pictures if the robot reaches the full capacity of its sample container, or from energy to samples if it has taken all the planned pictures. The change of the criterion introduces changes in the reward function used to the choice of a point. Note that the criteria used in the decision process are context-dependent.

If the energy level falls below another threshold, the robot decides to return. The decision to return drastically changes the representation. Instead of deciding about points on the grid, pictures and samples, the robot has to prepare for the return to the base.

The robot also monitors its equipment. If an accident occurs and a part is broken, the mission is suspended and the robot concentrates on the repair. A criterion which pre-empts all the other criteria is invoked and the robot attempts to repair the broken part.

6 Decision support

The robot is a device which is activated and then makes a number of decisions leading to the achievement of its goals. The goals may be modified or amended during the decision process, and the robot may need to 'create' new goals from a predefined repertoire. In the introduction to this paper we said that two metaphors promote a novel view of decision support.

Decision support systems (DSS) are developed to solve unstructured or semi-structured problems by means of data and models (Scott-Morton, 1971). Without getting into a discussion on the nature of unstructured problems, it is obvious that complex and difficult problems require effort in data collection and analysis, but also in structuring and re-structuring. Two lines of reasoning apply here.

First, during the intelligence and design phases of Simon's model (Simon, 1960), the required support should include the choice of the structuring tools. Application and, very often, adaptation of these tools consists initially in making the model fit the knowledge about the problem. In a dialog between two agents, one chooses a tool, adapts it and determines a model of the problem, the other evaluates the model and proposes modifications. This dialog is a sequential decision process which ends when one of the agents cannot present a better model, or the other agent is satisfied. For complex decisions this is a difficult process in itself, and one may expect a human decision-maker to be relieved from it. We see the need for intelligent negotiating agents that attempt to structure the problem and construct its model. This line of reasoning is an extension of work done in the areas of structured modelling (Geoffrion, 1987) and support for the problem-dependent choice of solution methods (Banerjee and Basu, 1989; Dutta and Basu, 1984).

The second line of reasoning is along Simon's design and choice phases. Two main issues can be identified. The two phases, choice and design, are related: the choice process introduces feedback to the design process. This, in turn, leads to a new dialog which aims at the modifications of the model and data from the point of view of the considered decision alternative. Choosing among alternatives unveils new possibilities or restrictions which are fed back to the design phase. The outcome is an 'enriched' alternative with justification as to its usefulness and validity. Here, support would mean providing the human decision-maker with a few well documented alternatives. Developing a justification is a process during which the environment, as well as the models and solution procedures, change; changes influence the argumentation.

The second issue is the analysis of the chosen decision alternative from the point of view of its implementation and outcomes. We said that decisions lead to new decisions, so that there are two types of decision outcomes: the immediate outcomes and the possibility of making future decisions. Here, support would consist in expanded 'what-if' analysis. It should be intelligent in the sense of relieving the human decision-maker of the burden of analyzing extensive amounts of data, scenarios, and argumentations.

References

Albus, J. S. (1981). Brains, Behavior, and Robotics. Peterborough: BYTE Books.

Banerjee, S. and Basu, A. (1989). Knowledge-based Framework for Selecting Management Science Models. IS Technical Report TR–89–41, College of Business, University of Maryland, College Park, MA.

Bares, J. et al. (1989). AMBLER: An Autonomous Rover for Planetary Exploration. IEEE Computer, Vol. 22, No. 6, pp. 18–28.

Davis, R. and Smith, R. G. (1983). Negotiation as a Metaphor for Distributed Problem Solving. Artificial Intelligence, Vol. 20, pp. 63–109.

Dutta, A. and Basu, A. (1984). An Artificial Approach to Model Management in Decision Support Systems. Computer, Vol. 17, No. 9, pp. 89–97.

Elfes, A. (1989). Using Occupancy Grids for Mobile Robot Perception and Navigation. IEEE Computer, Vol. 22, No. 6, pp. 46–58.

Geoffrion, A. (1987). An Introduction to Structured Modelling. Management Science, Vol. 33, No. 5, pp. 547–588.

Hotaran, A. (1987). Explanation and Negotiation Facilities in INTEXEP. In: I. Plander (ed.), Artificial Intelligence and Information-Control Systems of Robots — 87, Amsterdam: North-Holland, pp. 247–252.

Holtzman, S. (1989). Intelligent Decision Systems. Reading, MA: Addison-Wesley.

Kersten, G. E., Szpakowicz, S. and Koperczak, Z. (1990a). Modelling of Decision Making for Discrete Processes in Dynamic Environments. *Computers and Mathematics with Applications*, (to appear).

Kersten, G. E., Koperczak, Z. and Szpakowicz, S. (1990b). Modelling Autonomous Agents in Changing Environments. In: C. Y. Ho and G. W. Zobrist (eds.), Progress in Robotics and Intelligent Systems. Ablex, Norwood, NJ, (in print).

Kersten, G. E., Michalowski, W. Matwin, S. and Szpakowicz, S. (1988). Representing the Negotiation Process with a Rule-based Formalism. *Theory and Decision*, vol. 25, pp. 225–257.

Koperczak, Z., Kersten, G. E. and Szpakowicz, S. (1990). The Negotiation Metaphor and Decision Support for Financial Modelling. HICSS–23, January 1990.

Levi, I. (1987). Hard Choices. Cambridge, MA: Cambridge Univ. Press.

Lumelsky, V. J. and Stepanov, A. A. (1987). Path Planning Strategies for a Point Mobile Automation Moving Amist Unknown Obstacles of Arbitrary Shape. *Algorithmica*, Vol. 2, pp. 403–430.

Matwin, S., Szpakowicz, S., Koperczak, Z., Kersten, G. E. and Michalowski, W. (1989). NEGOPLAN: An Expert System Shell for Negotiation Support. *IEEE Expert*, Vol. 4, No. 4, pp. 50–62.

Pollock (1990). How to Build a Person. Cambridge, MA: MIT Press.

Schorr, H. and Rappaport, A. (1989). Innovative Applications of Artificial Intelligence. Menlo Park, CA: AAAI Press.

Scott-Morton, M. S. (1971). Management Decision Systems: Computer-Based Support for Decision Making. Division of Research, Harward University, Cambridge.

Simon, H. (1960). The New Science of Management Decision. New York: Harper and Row.

Szpakowicz, S., Matwin, S., Kersten, G. E. and Michalowski, W. (1987). RUNE: An Expert System Shell for Negotiation Support. Proc. 7th International Workshop on Expert Systems and Their Applications, Avignon, May 1987, pp. 711–727.

Szpakowicz, S., Kersten, G. E. and Koperczak, Z. (1990). Knowledge-based Decision Support, Preferences, and Financial Planning. 6th IEEE Conf on AI Applications, March 1990 (to appear).

Some Models and Procedures for Decision Support in Bargaining

Lech Kruś

Systems Research Institute
Polish Academy of Sciences
Newelska 6, 01–447 Warsaw, Poland

Abstract

A multicriteria bargaining problem is formulated in a multidecision space of players. An example of the problem is presented dealing with an allocation of excess resulting from a cooperation. Different phases of the decision support are considered, especially a mediation procedure inspired by Raiffa single test procedure and Fandel, Wierzbicki's limited confidence principle, with application of multicriteria optimization approach.

1 Introduction

During the last few years a growing interests in group decision support systems based on multicriteria optimization approach and aiding negotiations processes can be observed, including among others the papers by Korhonen, Moskowitz, Wallenius, Zionts (1986), Jarke, Jelassi, Shakun (1987), Kersten (1988), DeSanctis, Gallupe (1987), Korhonen and Wallenius (1989). On the other hand there exists the developed theory of bargaining problem started by Nash (1950), continued by Raiffa (1953), Harsanyi, Selten (1972), Kalai, Smorodinsky (1975), Roth (1979), Thomson (1980), Imai (1983) and others. Parallel to the theory an experience is collected from experiments in bargaining and negotiations. It seems be reasonable to construct systems supporting negotiations combining the multicriteria optimization approach, and achievements of the theory and the experience in bargaining. However in this case new theoretical problems arise related to a generalization of the solution concepts and their axiomatization, a construction of interactive processes making easier the decision analysis of the bargaining game and supporting the negotiation. In the classical theory the bargaining problem is defined by a given and known agreement set and by a status quo point in a space of the players utilities. The problem consists in a selection of the nondominated in the set, agreeable to all the players outcome. In practice utility functions of the players are not given explicitly. In the paper by Bronisz, Kruś, Wierzbicki (1989) some results have been obtained for so called multicriteria bargaining problem formulated in multiobjective spaces of the players and some interactive processes supporting the bargaining has been proposed and analyzed. On the base, a decision support system MCBARG has been constructed by Kruś, Bronisz, Łopuch (1990). It is assumed in the system that the bargaining problem is formulated directly in the space of objectives.

In this paper some proposals are given to construct such a system but for wider class of problems formulated in a space of decisions and with application of the achievement function approach and mechanisms elaborated within DIDAS systems family by Wierzbicki (1982), Kreglewski, Paczyński, Granat, Wierzbicki (1988), Rogowski, Sobczyk, Wierzbicki (1988).

Within the conference also a computer presentation of the MCBARG system has been given.

2 Problem formulation

The problem is formulated in the case of n players. Decision variables of the player i ($i = 1, 2, \ldots, n$) are denoted by the vector $z^i = (z_1^i, z_2^i, \ldots, z_{k^i}^i)$, where k^i is the number of the variables. Objectives of the player i are denoted by the vector $x^i = (x_1^i, x_2^i, \ldots, x_{m^i}^i)$, where m^i is the number of the objectives. The vector of decision variables of all the players $z = (z^1, z^2, \ldots, z^n) \in R^K$, $K = \sum_i k^i$, where R^K is the multidecision space (of all the players). The vector of multiobjectives (outcomes) $x = (x^1, x^2, \ldots, x^n) \in R^M$, $M = \sum_i m^i$, where R^M is the multiobjective (outcomes) space .

We assume that a substantive model of the game is given by a set of admissible decisions Z_0 and by an outcome mapping P. The set $Z_0 \subset R^K$ is assumed to be compact, and the mapping $P : Z_0 \to R^M$, to be continuous. In such a case the set of attainable outcomes denoted by Q_0 is compact.

In the objective, outcome space a partial ordering is introduced. It is done in analogical way as in the DIDAS systems methodology (see Rogowski, Sobczyk, Wierzbicki, 1988). Similarly we assume that each player has some number of objectives-criterions that he would like to maximized, or to minimized. The partial ordering is introduced by the following definition of the cone D in the objective space:

$$D = \{\, x \in R^M : \quad x_j^i \geq 0, \ j = 1, 2, \ldots, m'^i,$$
$$x_j^i \leq 0, \ j = m'^i + 1, \ldots, m^i, \ \text{for } i = 1, 2, \ldots, n \,\},$$

where respectively the objectives to be maximized are indexed by $j = 1, 2, \ldots, m'^i$, and to be minimized — by $j = m'^i + 1, \ldots, m^i$.

Pareto optimal (D-efficient) elements $\hat{q}$ of the set Q_0 are defined as the elements that belong to the set:

$$\hat{Q}_0 = \{\, \hat{q} \in Q_0 : Q_0 \cap (\hat{q} + D \setminus \{0\}) = \emptyset \,\}.$$

Weakly Pareto optimal elements $\hat{q}^w$, are defined as the elements that belong to the set:

$$\hat{Q}_0^w = \{\, \hat{q} \in Q_0 : Q_0 \cap (\hat{q} + \text{int } D) = \emptyset \,\}.$$

The problem consists in aiding the players in finding an agreeable and Pareto optimal solution being close to their preferences, in an interactive, learning procedure. In the following we assume the bargaining game case in which the players do not create subcoalitions.

3 Example of the problem

The problem can be illustrated on an example of cooperation of two agricultural farms. Two farmers dealing with production plans of their farms are considered here as players. Decision variables of the farmers include: a structure of crops, arable land utilization, production inputs utilization and others. Let us denote the decision variables vectors by z^1 and z^2 for the first and second farmer. Vectors of criteria include production of particular agricultural products, production inputs. Some of the criteria are maximized, other minimized. We denote the criteria vectors by x^1 and x^2 respectively for the first and second farmer. Each farmer deals with a multicriteria optimization problem which can be described with use of linear model P1 and P2 respectively:

$$P1: \quad A^1 z^1 \leq b^1 \qquad\qquad P2: \quad A^2 z^2 \leq b^2$$

$$x^1 = C^1 z^1 \qquad\qquad\qquad x^2 = C^2 z^2$$

The problems are typical ones that can be solved with an aid of IAC–DIDAS L package elaborated by Rogowski, Sobczyk, Wierzbicki (1988). Let us denote $\hat{x}^1$, and $\hat{x}^2$ the preferred solutions of the players found after interactive sessions with use of the package. The associated decision vectors $\hat{z}^1$, and $\hat{z}^2$ are calculated by the package respectively.

We described above the situation in which the farmers dealt with the production plans independently. Let us assume that they decide to cooperate. In this case they deal with a joint multicriteria optimization problem PJ which can be described as follows:

$$PJ: \quad Az \leq b, \quad x = Cz,$$

where $z = (z^1, z^2)$, $x = (x^1, x^2)$, the matrix A is composed respectively from the A^1 and A^2 and the vector b from b^1 and b^2. In general, in the cooperation case some surplus is obtained in comparison to the independent production activities. It results from scale effects, better utilization of inputs. The following problem arises: how to divide the surplus resulting from the cooperation, taking into account the players preferences. The division should be done unanimously, closely to the players preferences. Let us notice that the preferences of each player are in general different. The surplus is described by all solutions of the problem PJ dominating, in the sense of the cone D, the status quo point $q_0 = (\hat{x}^1, \hat{x}^2)$ resulting from the preferred solutions of the players in no cooperation case. This set is called the agreement set, and in this set we look for the solution of the problem.

4 Phases of decision support

A decision support process in a case of the presented problem can be divided into several phases. It seems be reasonable to consider the following phases:

p1. Definition and edition of the substantive model of the game.

p2. Definition and edition of the multicriteria bargaining problem with use of the model.

p3. Playing the simulation game.

p4. Unilateral decision support with use of the interactive multicriteria optimization.

p5. Multilateral, mediation support.

The first two phases p1 and p2 are rather technical. The p1 phase includes formulation of the model i.e. selection of the decision and objective spaces, formulation of the relation P and the set of admissible decisions Z_0 and if required modification of already existing model. The phase p2 relates to formulation of the decision problems i.e. it includes specification which criteria should be maximized or minimized, assumptions of the reasonable bounds for the criteria and others. Both the phases should be done with an aid of an analyst.

The following phases allow the players to learn the nature of the bargaining problem. Playing the simulation game (phase p3) is the simplest form of such a learning.

The unilateral decision support is oriented to learn a particular player with use of interactive multicriteria optimization procedure. Dealing with this phase some assumptions on the decisions (behavior) of the counterplayers have to be set. Dependently on the assumption different variants of the phase can be considered.

The first variant (p4a) of the unilateral support can be considered under assumption of the full control over the counter players decisions. It gives to the given player an information about his maximal, possible results. It can be done by a maximization of the following achievement function:

$$q^i(x^i, \overline{x}^i, \underline{x}^i) = \min_{1 \leq j \leq m_i} v_j(x_j^i, \overline{x}_j^i, \underline{x}_j^i), \tag{1}$$

subject to the constraints defined by the set Z_0 and the mapping P, with respect to the decision variables vector z^i, where

$$v_j(x_j^i, \overline{x}_j^i, \underline{x}_j^i) = \begin{cases} (x_j^i - \overline{x}_j^i)/|\overline{x}_j^i - \underline{x}_j^i|, & \text{for } 1 \leq j \leq m^{ri}, \\ (\overline{x}_j^i - x_j^i)/|\overline{x}_j^i - \underline{x}_j^i|, & \text{for } m^{ri} + 1 \leq j \leq m^i, \end{cases}$$

$\overline{x}_j^i$ is reference, and $\underline{x}_j^i$ is status quo of the player i.

The maximization done for different reference points gives as a result some characterization of the Pareto frontier, in the sense of the cone D, of the solutions set. Changing the reference point the player has possibility to analyze and to find in an interactive procedure his preferred solution. Of course the selected outcome can not be in general the solution of the bargaining problem. It gives an information about the best solution the player can obtain, according to his preferences, which can aid him in formulation of demands in verbal negotiations. In the analysis a simple form of achievement function has been used, however also other forms (for example the forms considered by Rogowski, Sobczyk, Wierzbicki, 1988) can be applied in an analogical way.

The next p4b phase of the unilateral decision support deals with an interactive review of efficient solutions under simulation of the counter player decisions. It can be done by a maximization of the same achievement function

$$q^i(x^i, \overline{x}^i, \underline{x}^i) = \min v_j(x_j^i, \overline{x}_j^i, \underline{x}_j^i), \tag{2}$$

subject to the constraints defined by the set Z_0 and the mapping P, with respect to the decision variables vector z^i, however in this case the counterplayers decisions z^l, $l = 1, 2, \ldots, n$, $l \neq i$ are assumed in the mapping P given, while in the previous case p4a where free. In this case the player i can also review the set of efficient solutions by changing the reference points. The set of efficient solutions is of course different for different counterplayers decisions, and in general, different than in the previous case.

The third variant of the unilateral support p4c is considered if not directly decisions but rather aspirations of the counter players are assumed. It can be given by a maximization of the following achievement function:

$$q(x, \overline{x}, \underline{x}) = \min_{\substack{1 \leq l \leq n \\ 1 \leq j \leq m_i}} v_j^l(x_j^l, \overline{x}_j^l, \underline{x}_j^l), \tag{3}$$

subject to the constraints defined by the set Z_0 and the mapping P, with respect to the decision variables vector z^i, where

$$v_j^l(x_j^l, \overline{x}_j^l, \underline{x}_j^l) = \begin{cases} (x_j^l - \overline{x}_j^l)/|\overline{x}_j^l - \underline{x}_j^l|, & \text{for } 1 \leq j \leq m'', \\ (\overline{x}_j^l - x_j^l)/|\overline{x}_j^l - \underline{x}_j^l|, & \text{for } m'' + 1 \leq j \leq m^l, \end{cases}$$

are defined for all $l \in [1, n]$.

In comparison to the phase p4a and p4b the function q is defined for whole the vector of criteria x and reference $\overline{x}$ in the space R^M while the q^i function were defined for particular player i, i.e. in the space R^{m^i}.

The above variants of support allow for limited information on the nature of the problem under some assumptions on the behavior of the counterplayers. In the mediation procedure it is assumed that the computerized system is used under multilateral actions of the players, and it allows not only for deeper understanding of the problem but also for creation of an interactive mediation procedure (including multilateral actions of all the players) close to the idea of "single test" procedure proposed by Raiffa (1982). The principles of the mediation support are considered below.

5   The mediation procudure

Dealing with mediation procedures it is useful to consider the problem presented in point 2 directly in the objective spaces of the players. The problem is called as a multicriteria bargaining one and is formulated as follows:

Let us consider given set of players $N = \{1, 2, \ldots, n\}$, each player having m^i number of criteria. The multicriteria bargaining problem is defined by a pair (S, d) where $S \subset R^M$, $M = \sum m^i$, S is an agreement point, $d \in S$ is a disagreement (or status quo) point. Any solution belonging to the agreement set can be obtained under unanimous agreement of all the players, and if there is no such an agreement the result is given by disagreement point. For simplicity we assume in the following that all the criteria are maximized, which can be done without loss of generality, if we use a negative transformation for the minimized criteria.

The formulation is a simple generalization of the classical definition of the bargaining problem given and analyzed by Nash (1950), and after him by Raiffa, Roth, Kalai and Smorodinsky, Thomson, and others. In this classical case, under assumptions of given utilities of all the players and for different axioms describing the players behavior, different solution concepts have been proposed and analyzed. The generalization of the definition is simple, however the solution concepts and their properties do not transfer in straight forward way. In the case considered here, the utilities of the players are not assumed as given explicitly, so the agreement set is considered in the cartesian product of the multiobjective spaces of all the players, and some learning, interactive mechanisms developed within multicriteria optimization has to be applied here to allow the players to express their preferences and to look for the solution in the agreement set. However the solution to be adopted by the players as a compromise outcome and mutually accepted should fulfill some fairness rules.The rules can be described in form of axioms describing the players behaviour — feeling of fairness. The approach developed within axiomatic theory of bargaining applies in looking for appropriate solution concept. Therefore combination of the ideas of multicriteria optimization and the axiomatic theory of bargaining approach seems be reasonable in construction of the mediation procedure.

The mediation procedure consists in creation of an interactive process in which a sequence of single test outcomes is generated and presented to the players. It is constructed on the base of the following preassumptions:

1. The process starts at a disagreement point.

2. The process is progressive.

3. The process should lead to an efficient outcome in the agreement set S.

4. The players having limited confidence to the substantive model of the game and to the future consequences of their moves try to limit possible improvements of the counterplayers.

5. Each player behaves rationally trying to optimize his outcomes in particular rounds according to his preferences.

Comments:
The iterativeness of the process and its progressiveness are close to the Raiffa concepts of the single test negotiation procedure.

The preassumption 4 has been formulated by Fandel (1979) and Fandel, Wierzbicki (1985) as a principle of limited confidence.

Formulation of such an iterative process has been preceded by a theoretical research on the solution concepts that could be utilized in the procedure as the mediation ones. To assure fairness of the solutions, such properties as independence of linear transformations of objectives, symmetry, monotonicity, players rationality have been considered. So called one shot solution has been proposed based on the concept of utopia point related to the players aspirations (see Bronisz, Kruś, Wierzbicki, 1989). The solution is calculated on the base of the players preferences. Properties of the solution has been analyzed. In comparison to other solution analyzed, this one has very important property of resistance on the players manipulations, especially the players can not benefit from changing scales in his particular objectives, nor from making decisions during the process not according to their preferences, nor from proposing some dummy objectives. The solution has been applied in proposition of an iterative process based on the above preassumptions. Uniqueness and convergence of the process has been proved, under typical, not restrictive assumptions on a class of bargaining problems.

Formally the procedure can be described as follows:

Let d^t denote the single test in particular rounds, $d^t \in S$, and $d^0 = d$, $t = 1, 2, \ldots$ is a number of the round. Let $S^t = \{ x : x \in S, \ x \geq d^{t-1} \}$. Each player i has two control parameters by which at each round he can inflow on the course of the process: a reference point $\overline{x}^{i,t} \in R^{m^i}$, and a confidence coefficient $\alpha^{i,t} \in (\delta, 1]$, where δ is a number $\delta > 0$. The reference points are used for expressing the players preferences and testing a set of possible outcomes, while the confidence coefficients allow the player (according to the confidence principle) to limit possible improvements of counterplayers outcomes.

Step 1.   Assume $t = 1$.

Step 2.   Start an interactive scanning with particular players $i = 1, 2, \ldots, n$, for each player independently.

Step 3.   Calculate the ideal point $I^{i,t}$, and present it and the status quo point to the player i.

Step 4.   Ask the player i for his confidence coefficient value $\alpha^{i,t}$.

Step 5.   Ask the player i for his reference point $\overline{x}_j^{i,t}$, $j = 1, 2, \ldots, m^i$.

Step 6.   Calculate corresponding tentative outcome $\hat{x}^{i,t}$ and so called i-nondominated outcome $u^{i,t}$.

Step 7.   Go back to the step 4 and generate through the steps 5, 6 other $\hat{x}^{i,t}$ and $u^{i,t}$ outcomes as long as the player decides to select his preferred reference $\hat{\overline{x}}^{i,t}$ and corresponding outcomes $\hat{\hat{x}}^{i,t}$ and $\hat{u}^{i,t}$ from the collected vectors $\overline{x}^{i,t}$, $\hat{x}^{i,t}$ and $u^{i,t}$ respectively.

Step 8.   Check if all the players have selected their preferred outcomes if no, wait till they pass the interactive scanning steps 2–7.

Step 9.   Calculate the single test outcome of the round d^t, and the corresponding decision variables vector z^t.

Step 10.   Present the outcomes $d^{i,t}$ and corresponding decisions $z^{i,t}$ to the players independently.

Step 11.   Check if the result of the round is an efficient outcome in the set S. If so — stop, the process is finished; otherwise assume the round number $t = t + 1$ and go to the Step 2.

Comments:

In the procedure we deal with a sequence of bargaining problems (S^t, d^{t-1}). In each round the players first independently scan the set of possible outcomes S^t by use of reference points and select preferred tentative outcomes, then on the base of the outcomes and the confidence coefficients assumed by all the players the system calculates the proposed mediation solution of the round.

The vector of tentative outcomes $\hat{x}^{i,t}$ at the step 6 is calculated by maximization of the achievement function $q(x^t, \overline{x}^t, d^{t-1})$ of the form (3) subject to the constraints defined by the mapping P, attainable set Z_0 and inequality $x^t \geq d^{t-1}$. The reference subvector $\overline{x}^{i,t}$ has been given by the player at step 5. The references of the counterplayers are assumed on the basis of their decisions undertaken at previous round, however for analysis can be also assumed by the player i arbitrary. The i-nondominated outcome at the round t is defined by

$$u^{i,t} = \max_{\geq} \{\, x^i \in R^{m^i} : x \in S^t, \ x^i = d^{i,t-1} + a * (\hat{\overline{x}}^t - d^{i,t-1}) \,\},$$

(a is some positive number). It gives an information about possible outcomes of the player i under assumption that counterplayers have outcomes on the levels of status quo. It can be calculated by maximization, for $i = 1, 2, \ldots, n$, of the achievement function $q^i(x^i, \hat{\overline{x}}^i, d^{i,t-1})$ of the form (1) subject to the constraints defined by the mapping P, attainable set Z_0 and inequality $x^t \geq d^{t-1}$. $d^{i,t-1}$ denotes vector of components of the vector d^{t-1} related to particular player i.

The outcome of the round (single test proposal) is calculated at the step 9 by: $d^t = d^{t-1} + \varepsilon^t * [u^t(S^t, d^{t-1}, \hat{\overline{x}}^t) - d^{t-1}]$, where so called RA utopia $u^t(S^t, d^{t-1}, \hat{\overline{x}}) = (\hat{u}^{1t}, \hat{u}^{2t}, \ldots, \hat{u}^{nt})$ is defined as a composition of selected i-nondominated outcomes of the players at the round t. The RA utopia is generally different than the ideal point obtained by independent maximization of particular criteria. It depends on the players preferences. $\varepsilon^t = \min\{\alpha^t_{min}, \alpha^t_{max}\}$, $\alpha^t_{min} = \min\{\alpha^{1t}, \alpha^{2t}, \ldots, \alpha^{nt}\}$ is the joint confidence coefficient, α^t_{max} is the maximal number α such that $d^{t-1} + \alpha * (u^t - d^{t-1})$ belongs to S.

The limited confidence principle (the preassumption 4) can be formally described by:

$$d^t - d^{t-1} \leq \alpha^t_{min}[u^t - d^{t-1}]$$

where α^t_{min} is the joint confidence coefficient. Therefore if the players have more limited confidence they should assume smaller the confidence coefficients. In such a case the improvements of the outcomes are smaller, and the process has more rounds.

6 Final remarks

In the paper an attempt is made to combine multicriteria optimization approach (especially achievement function ideas) and some new theoretical results related to multicriteria bargaining problem in construction interactive procedures supporting negotiations. The decision support system is considered as a tool aiding the players, first in analysis of the bargaining problem allowing learning of the players, and second — supporting the negotiation process by proposing a sequence of players dependent single test outcomes leading to an efficient compromise outcome.

References

Axelrod, R. (1985). The Evolution of Cooperation. Basic Books, New York.

Bronisz, P., Kruś, L. and Łopuch, B. (1987). An Experimental System Supporting Multiobjective Bargaining Problem. Methodological Guide. In A. Lewandowski, A.P. Wierzbicki (eds.): Theory, Software and Testing Examples for Decision Support Systems. WP-87-26, IIASA, Laxenburg, Austria.

Bronisz, P., Kruś, L. and Wierzbicki, A. (1989). Towards Interactive Solutions in Bargaining Problem. In A. Lewandowski, A.P. Wierzbicki (eds.): Aspiration Based Decision Support Systems. *Lectures Notes in Economics and Mathematical Systems*, Vol. 331, Springer Verlag, Berlin.

Dreyfus, S. (1985). Beyond Rationality. In M. Grauer, M. Thompson, A.P. Wierzbicki (eds.): Plural Rationality and Interactive Decision Processes. Proceedings Sopron 1984, Springer-Verlag, Heidelberg.

Fandel, G. (1979). Optimale Entscheidungen in Organizationen. Springer-Verlag, Heidelberg.

Fandel, G. and Wierzbicki, A.P. (1985). A Procedural Selection of Equilibria for Supergames. (private unpublished communication).

Grauer, M., Thompson, M., Wierzbicki, A.P. (eds.) (1985). Plural Rationality and Interactive Decision Processes. Proceedings Sopron 1984, Springer-Verlag, Heidelberg.

Harsanyi, J.C. and Selten, R. (1972). A Generalized Nash Solution for Two-Person Bargaining Games with Incomplete Information. *Management Sciences*, Vol. 18, pp. 80–106.

Imai, H. (1983). Individual Monotonicity and Lexicographical Maxmin Solution. *Econometrica*, Vol. 51, pp. 389–401.

Jarke, M., Jelassi, M.T. and Shakun, M.F. (1987). Mediator: Towards a negotiation support system. *European Journal of Operation Research* 31, pp. 314–334, North-Holland.

Kalai, E. and Smorodinsky, M. (1975). Other Solutions to Nash's Bargaining Problem. *Econometrica*, Vol. 43, pp. 513–518.

Kersten, G.E. (1988). A Procedure for Negotiating Efficient and Non-Efficient Compromises. *Decision Support Systems* 4, pp. 167–177, North-Holland.

Korhonen, P., Moskowitz, H., Wallenius, J., Zionts, S. (1986). An Interactive Approach to Multiple Criteria Optimization with Multiple Decision-Makers. *Naval Research Logistics Quarterly*, Vol. 33, pp. 589–602, John Wiley & Sons.

Korhonen, P. and Wallenius, J. (1989). Supporting Individuals in Group Decision-making. Helsinki School of Economics, Finland, (forthcoming).

Kreglewski, T., Paczyński, J., Granat, J., Wierzbicki, A.P. (1988). IAC-DIDAS-N A Dynamic Interactive Decision Analysis and Support System for Multicriteria Analysis of Nonlinear Models with Nonlinear Model Generator Supporting Model Analysis. IIASA working paper, IIASA, Laxenburg, Austria.

Kruś, L. Bronisz, P., and Łopuch, B. (1990). MCBARG - Enhanced. A System Supporting Multicriteria Bargaining. CP-90-006, IIASA, Laxenburg, Austria.

Luce, R.D. and Raiffa, H. (1957). Games and Decisions: Introduction and Critical Survey. New York: Wiley.

Nash, J.F. (1950). The Bargaining Problem. *Econometrica*, Vol. 18, pp. 155–162.

Raiffa, H. (1953). Arbitration Schemes for Generalized Two-Person Games. *Annals of Mathematics Studies*, No. 28, pp. 361–387, Princeton.

Raiffa, H. (1982). The Art and Science of Negotiations. Harvard Univ. Press, Cambridge.

Rogowski, T., Sobczyk, J. and Wierzbicki, A.P. (1988). IAC-DIDAS-L A Dynamic Interactive Decision Analysis and Support System, Linear Version. WP-88-110, IIASA, Laxenburg, Austria.

Roth, A.E. (1979). Axiomatic Models of Bargaining. *Lecture Notes in Economics and Mathematical Systems*, Vol. 170, Springer-Verlag, Berlin.

Roth, A.E. and Malouf, M.W.K. (1979). Game-Theoretical Models and the Role of Information in Bargaining. *Psychological Review*, Vol. 86, pp. 1163–1170.

DeSanctis, G. and Gallupe, R.B. (1987). A Foundation for the Study of Group Decision Support Systems. *Management Science*, Vol. 33, No. 5, pp. 589–609.

Thomson, W. (1980). Two Characterization of the Raiffa Solution. *Economic Letters*, Vol. 6, pp. 225–231.

Wierzbicki, A.P. (1982). A Mathematical Basis for Satisficing Decision Making. *Mathematical Modelling*, Vol. 3, pp. 391–405.

Wierzbicki, A.P. (1983). Negotiation and Mediation in Conflicts I: The Role of Mathematical Approaches and Methods. WP-83-106, IIASA, Laxenburg. Also in H. Chestnat et al. (eds.): Supplemental Ways to Increase International Stability. Pergamon Press, Oxford, 1983.

Wierzbicki, A.P. (1985). Negotiation and Mediation in Conflicts II: Plural Rationality and Interactive Decision Processes. In M. Grauer, M. Thompson, A.P. Wierzbicki (eds.): Plural Rationality and Interactive Decision Processes. Proceedings Sopron 1984, Springer-Verlag, Heidelberg.

Interactive Group Decision Support

Martin Read
Tony Gear
Decision Dynamics Ltd
Parsons Walk, PO Box 142
Wigan, Lancs, UK

Abstract

The paper describes a communication system known as Teamworker (TW) which enables all members of a decision-making group to be simultaneously on-line during a meeting. One of several early trials of the system is briefly presented. The data supports a contention that modelling paradigms need to be centrally concerned with differences of opinion during on-line group decision processes as this leads to dynamic changes of key aspects such as the alternatives and criteria, as well as individual judgements and assessments.

1   Introduction

There has been considerable progress in the theory of individual decision-making over the last forty years. See for example (Hammond et al., 1980) and (Belton, 1986) for a useful description of the various approaches which have evolved over this period.

By comparison, much less progress has been made in the theory of group decision-making. A major stumbling block has been the inability to develop group based utility or probability functions. In particular Arrow (1951) has shown that a general method of aggregating consistent individual preferences into a single consistent group preference function does not exist. In addition Dalkey (1972) has proved the impossibility of a general group probability function. It appears that attempts to extend individual theory to encompass groups do not provide a fruitful line of enquiry.

Another aspect of the group problem is that individuals typically disagree about any or all components of decision situations. The paper describes an on-line communication system designed to collect judgements and then feedback differences of opinion at each stage of a decision process. The contention is that awareness of differences of opinion can help the group to reach a decision with known compromises at the individual level. Additionally, clear communication and agreement on criteria definitions, measurement scales, reference objects and other anchor points becomes more practicable. Interestingly, this route may relieve the theoretical issues referenced above. For example, Dalkey (1975) has demonstrated that the sum of individual rankings of objects fulfills the analogues of the Arrow conditions for group preference scales, and is thus one example of a consistent group scale.

The philosophy of the present paper is to provide effective means of communication between each group member and a micro-computer. This enables individual judgements to be received and displayed back to the group for debate at each stage in a Delphi type of procedure. An early trial of the approach is described by Gear et al. (1985). In this experiment individual feelings related to group processes were displayed back to the group. The present paper is more concerned with feedback of preferences related to a decision task. In general both task related and/or process related data can be involved in the feedback (Gear, 1988). This means that the group can define and redefine its problem until a stable pattern of mutual understanding is reached in a dynamic and interactive process during which any or all aspects can change.

Presentation to a group of its own differences of opinion can be regarded as a negative process of conflict generation. However, we take the view that conflict can have constructive effects depending upon its management. Wedley et al. (1978) has described procedures based on extensions of the Delphi process to participative decisions, differentiating clearly between communication for decision analysis and decision-making. Keeney et al. (1972) in a description to promote good decision-making has stated, "...a good analysis should illuminate controversy — to find out where basic differences exist, in values and uncertainties, to facilitate compromise, to increase the level of debate and undercut rhetoric...".

To achieve this in practice, the group requires an inobtrusive means of communication with a central processor to enhance its own communication patterns. The detailed system design is described in the next section. This is followed by an example application, and finally some interim results and conclusions.

2 The on-line system

The system, called Teamworker (TW), facilitates communication in a group to support work on three complimentry activities:

a. pooling of information, expertise and opinions

b. comparison and debate of disagreement and differences of opinion

c. redefinition of key aspects of the decision problem.

To accomplish this, each member of the group is provided with a personal handset comprising a key-pad and individual display panel. This enables individual opinions, beliefs, judgements, decisions, feelings and preferences to be input and then transmitted by remote means to a single receiver module. The receiver is linked to a micro-computer so that inputs from the handsets are recorded, analysed and displayed on an output screen as required. The screen size depends on the size of the group. At present the system can handle up to 32 members. The screen is also able to present questions to the group, so providing a degree of structure to, for example, a decision-making meeting. The group leader (or chair) is provided with a unique handset which provides additional capabilities to enable the group leader to select menu options at critical stages, following a group debate.

The system is flexible, as the software can be changed to suit various group processes and objectives. In particular, software has been developed for problem-solving, decision-making, delphi forecasting, risk assessment and market research. The supporting nature of the system is modelled in Figures 1 and 2.

The system has been applied to a large number of real group situations, mainly involving decision-making and market research (Gear, 1988; Davies, 1989). An example of an application is described in the following section.

3   An example application

A group of seven managers was concerned with a decision involving the selection of a brand of car, within a defined price range, to be adopted for the company car fleet. After a discussion, a short-list of six brands was selected. It was further decided to evaluate these brands with respect to criteria.

The decision problem was broken down into three major stages selected from the software menus. These were:

a. scoring of each brand on each of the criteria taken in turn

b. evaluation of the relative importance of the criteria set

c. an overall analysis involving the summed and weighted scores of each of the managers.

At each stage and substage of entering data, the values were fed back to the group, so that differences of opinion could be studied and debated. At some of these substages, a rerun of inputs was selected by the chair after a group discussion.

The scoring of the brands on the criteria was carried out by direct rating using the following scale:

1	:	Very low
2	:	Low
3	:	Medium
4	:	High
5	:	Very high

In the prior discussion, each of the criteria was given a short paragraph of definition, and summarised by a keyword which was then used in the screen displays. The interpretation and meaning of very low and very high scale scores were discussed in relation to each of the criteria before the scoring stage. This meant that comparisons of scores from individuals were valid, and the scores could be related to the criteria weights at the second stage. An example scores screen for one of the criteria, fed back to the group for debate, is shown in Figure 3.

The evaluation of criteria weights was carried out by means of a complete set of pairwise comparisons of the six criteria, using a constant sum (100 points) allocation

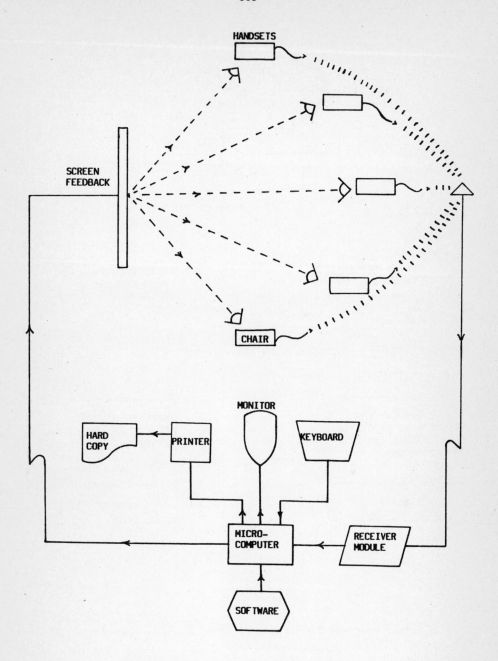

Figure 1: The IT group support system.

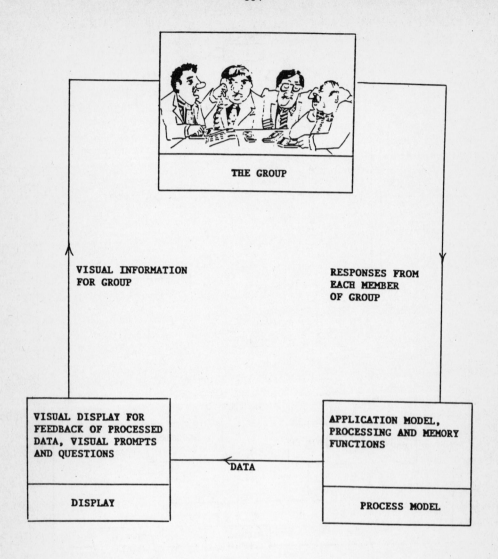

Figure 2: The group feedback model.

Summary table for "performance" criterion

	Scores						
Options	1	2	3	4	5	Ave	St Dev
BMW				2	5	4.7	0.5
Rover			3	4		3.6	0.5
Honda			4	3		3.4	0.5
Peugeot			4	3		3.4	0.5
Citroen	1		4	2		3.1	0.7

Figure 3: Example of scores screen.

method. A Saaty type of ratio scale has also been used in other applications and both approaches have been found to be easy to use. The pairwise comparison questions were posed to provide the relative values of a unit change on the direct scoring scales. An example criteria weights screen, fed back to the group for debate, is shown in Figure 4.

Criteria weights (%)

	Participant								
Criterion	1	2	3	4	5	6	7	Ave	St Dev
Safety	19	23	22	12	19	37	21	22	8
Reliability	28	18	26	14	19	24	20	21	5
Driver Comfort	18	25	17	13	17	8	25	18	6
Performance	17	13	8	26	19	15	14	16	6
Space	11	19	14	9	10	9	12	12	4
Prestige	6	3	13	26	15	7	8	11	8

Figure 4: Example of criteria weights screen.

At the third stage, overall analysis, the weighted and summed scores for each manager were presented back to the group. An example weighted sum screen, fed back to the group for debate, is shown in Figure 5.

4 Interim results

A large number of on-line runs of the type described in the preceeding section have been carried out with groups varying in size from 4 to 30 members. Despite detailed differences from run to run, some interesting and potentially useful general points are emerging. These are summarised below:

    a. Groups of managers who know each other well are frequently surprised, even shocked, by the degree of differences of opinion revealed.

Individual weighted and summed scores

Option	Participant							Ave	St Dev
	1	2	3	4	5	6	7		
BMW	3.6	4.8	3.5	4.7	4.5	4.4	4.1	4.2	0.5
Honda	2.9	4.2	3.9	3.8	3.0	3.0	3.7	3.5	0.5
Peugeot	3.5	3.2	2.8	4.1	3.7	3.5	3.0	3.4	0.4
Rover	3.0	2.4	2.7	3.6	3.9	3.6	4.0	3.3	0.6
Citroen	3.5	2.9	3.1	3.0	3.4	2.5	2.8	3.0	0.3

Figure 5: Example of weighted and summed scores screen.

b. A study of the group process shows considerable reduction of time-wasting or task deviation and a great level of sustained concentration at each input stage.

c. There is often a revealed need to return to criteria definitions when differences of opinion are displayed and debated.

d. Re-runs of pairwise inputs result in improved individual group member consistencies.

e. Analysis of data from many runs leads to the general conclusion that uncertainties resulting from individual member inconsistencies are typically less significant than between member differences of opinion.

The last of these observations can be shown with data from the run described in the last section. In Figure 6, the weights for one of the participants are shown, calculated by using row by row data from the input comparisons. This allows an approximate calculation of the mean and standard deviation of the weights for each of the six criteria, based on inputs, for the given individual member.

Criterion	Row number						Ave	SD
	1	2	3	4	5	6		
Safety	21	23	23	21	20	18	21	2
Reliability	21	19	23	17	17	23	20	3
Driver Comfort	21	28	23	26	25	23	25	2
Performance	14	13	11	14	16	15	14	2
Space	12	10	11	14	13	12	12	1
Prestige	10	6	8	7	8	8	8	1

Figure 6: Criteria weights (%) for participant 7 calculated using
row by row data from the input comparisons.

It is pertinent to compare this uncertainty of individual weights (as measured by the standard deviations in Figure 6) with the group average weights and standard deviation, shown previously in Figure 4. A study of Figures 4 and 6 clearly supports observation (e) above.

5   Conclusions

The On-Line system described in this paper is easy to use and improves group effectiveness by both reducing time-wasting and drawing attention rapidly to key issues. The system can be used to support a wide variety of group based tasks by simply changing software. In particular, it can be used to test and compare various decision-making models in a realistic group context.

Group based decision analysis needs to be centrally concerned with developing procedures for handling differences of opinion at each stage, a behavioural rathar than a mathematical issue. This emphasis on measuring and displaying differences of opinion at each stage of a decision analysis is consistent with developing behavioural paradigms of decision aiding, particulary those concerned with methods of expanding participant habitual domains (HD's), for example (Yu, 1989) and (Zeleny, 1989).

References

Arrow, K. (1951). Social Choice and Individual Values. John Wiley and Sons.

Belton, V. (1986). A Comparative Study of Methods for Multiple Criteria Decision Aiding. Ph.D. Thesis, Emmanuel College, Cambridge.

Dalkey, N. (1972). An Impossibility Theoreom for Group Probability Functions. Rand Corporation, P–4862.

Davies, B. (1989). The Decision In Your Hands. *OR Insight*, Vol. 2, No. 4, pp. 3–5.

Gear, A.E., Marsh, N.R. and Sergent, P. (1985). Semi-Automated Feedback and Team Behaviour. *Human Relations*, Vol. 38, No. 8, pp. 707–721.

Gear, T. and Read, M.J. (1988). On-Line Group Decision Support. Published Proceedings of VIIIth International Conference on Multiple Criteria Decision Making, Springer-Verlag.

Hammond, K.R., McClelland, Gary, H., Murnpower and Jeryl. (1980). Human Judgement and Decision Making, Theories, Methods and Procedures. Praeger Press.

Keeney, R.L. and Raiffa, H. (1972). A Critique of Formal Analysis in Public Decision-Making. In: Drake, N.W., Keeney, R.L. and Morse, P. (eds.), Analysis of Public Systems, MIT Press.

Wedley, W.C., Jung, R.H. and Merchant, G.S. (1978). Problem Solving The Delphi Way. *Journal of General Management*, Vol. 5, pp. 23–36.

Yu, P.L. (1989). Effective Decision Making Using Habitual Domain Analysis. Revised version of the tutorial lecture delivered at ORSA/TIMS Joint National Meeting, Denver, Oct 23–26, 1988.

Zeleny, M. (1989). Stable Patterns from Decision-Producing Networks: New Interfaces of DSS and MCDM. *MCDM WorldScan*, Vol. 3, Nos 2 & 3.

GDSS-X: An Experimental Group Decision Support System for Program Planning

Rudolf Vetschera

University of Vienna

Institut für Betriebswirtschaftslehre

Türkenstraße 23/11

A-1090 Vienna, Austria

1 Introduction

Group decision support systems (GDSS) are a rapidly emerging field of research within the general area of decision support (Gray, 1987; DeSanctis/Gallupe, 1987). Apart from systems that focus on communication processes within the group, several approaches were proposed to support the aggregation of opinions in a group decision situation (e.g. Bui/Jarke, 1986; Lewandowski et al., 1987; Jarke et al., 1987).

This paper describes an experimental group decision support system GDSS-X, which does not only support the aggregation of opinions, but also explicitly incorporates feedbacks that lead to changes in individual evaluations based on preliminary group results.

In section two, we describe the decision process to be supported by GDSS-X. Section three briefly reviews the theoretical models underlying the aggregation and feedback processes. Section four gives an overview of the implementation and section five presents possible extensions to the system. A more complete description of the system is given by Vetschera (1989).

2 Decision Process

2.1 Problem Specification

The system GDSS-X is intended to support group decision making in program planning. Program planning consists in the selection of one or several proposed projects under some constraints restricting their implementation. Examples for such decisions can be found in industry (e.g. the capital budgeting problem) as well as in the public sector.

Program planning becomes a group decision problem when projects can be proposed by or affect different persons (or entities like departments, regional governments etc.). We assume that group members view the planning process as a cooperative effort, although they propose different projects and pursue different goals.

Each group member uses several criteria in his decision process that might differ from those of other members. Decision alternatives are programs, which are obtained by aggregating sets of projects. It is the task of the group to select at least one program for implementation or to provide a ranking of several possible programs.

2.2   Phases

For technical tasks associated with the use of GDSS-X, the group needs an administrator, who may but need not be one of the group members. Figure 1 gives an overview of the entire decision process using GDSS-X, showing the tasks performed by the administrator or automatically by the system on the left side and the tasks performed by group members on the right side.

The solution process for each decision problem is called a 'conference' in GDSS-X. The system allows for several conferences to exist at the same time. Each conference may have different members, but members may also participate in several conferences. The administrator initiates a conference by specifying the members of the conference and the set of criteria that may be used. The main reason for specifying the criteria at this step is a semantic one: while it would be possible that the group members themselves specify the criteria, it is difficult to verify whether two criteria proposed by different group members are identical. This problem is avoided if the group administrator sets up a precisely defined catalogue of criteria, from which the group members can choose.

Not all projects proposed by group members affect all criteria. For example, if members represent different branches of a company located in different regions, projects carried out in one region will not affect environmental quality in another region. Since a program might consist only of projects not affecting a given criterion, the group administrator also has to specify a status quo value for each criterion.

For each criterion, the group administrator also has to define an aggregation technique and can define an upper bound. The aggregation technique is used in obtaining the consequences of a program, given the consequences of projects contained in the program. If for a criterion a bound is specified, the system will generate only programs that do not exceed that bound. For example, in an investment planning problem, the total amount of funds available might be specified as a bound on the financial requirements of programs. For computational reasons, bounds can be specified only for criteria aggregated through summation.

In the next step, the group members define their initial evaluation systems and propose projects. Defining the evaluation system consists in selecting some (or all) of the criteria from the catalogue set up by the administrator and specifying a weight and a partial utility function for each criterion. For projects, group members have to specify a project identification and data on the criteria affected.

As soon as all group members have completed this step, the system automatically begins the first aggregation phase. The system generates all feasible programs as combinations of the projects proposed. A branch-and-bound process is used to take the bounds into account. The system then eliminates all dominated programs and retains only the set of programs efficient with respect to the entire set of criteria. Then the utility functions of group members are aggregated. The aggregated utility function is applied to the set of

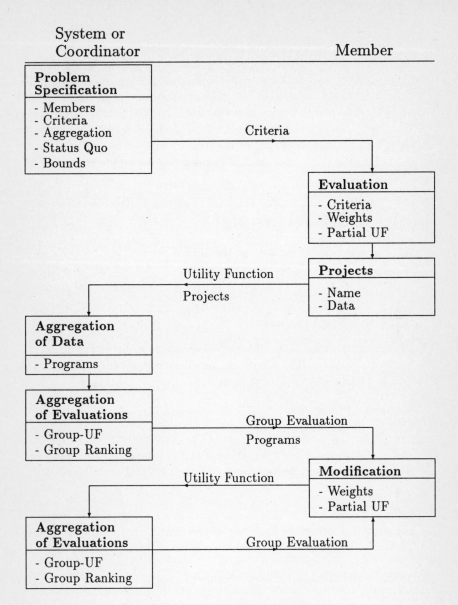

Figure 1: Overview of the decision process

efficient programs, leading to a group ranking of programs. The set of programs and the group ranking are then communicated back to the members.

The group members obtain an individual ranking of programs based on their utility functions as well as the group ranking. An optimal modification model (described in the next section) is then applied to generate suggestions for changes in the individual utility functions that will bring the individual ranking closer to the group ranking. The group members then have the possibility to change their individual utility functions. Using the changed functions, the aggregation module calculates a new group ranking. This iterative process is repeated until consensus is reached or the group decides to terminate the process without reaching consensus.

3   Theoretical Background

In this section, we will briefly discuss the theoretical concepts underlying the GDSS-X system. Since most of the material discussed here is explained elsewhere in detail, the reader is also referred to the literature (Vetschera, 1988; Vetschera, 1990).

3.1   Preference Specification

The feedback-oriented methodology of group decision support is applicable to several decision techniques. In the GDSS-X system, multi-attribute utility functions are used. This choice can be justified by several arguments:

- Multi-attribute utility theory is a well-established framework for multicriteria analysis (Huber, 1974; Fisher, 1979; Evans, 1984).

- User-friendly software for the estimation of utility functions is available on PC's, so the method itself need not be incorporated into the GDSS (e.g. von Nitzsch/Weber, 1986).

- The feedback model for a utility-based decision technique can be solved by linear programming. For other decision techniques integer or nonlinear models are required, which would lead to inacceptable response times.

We denote the multi-attribute utility function of group member m ($m \in \{1, \ldots, M\}$) by

$$U^{(m)}(X) = \sum_{k \in K(m)} w_k u_k(x_k) \qquad (1)$$

where $K(m)$ is the set of criteria considered by member m, X is a vector of attribute values and x_k is the k-th component of X. The weight of criterion k is represented by w_k, its partial utility function by $u_k(.)$.

3.2 Aggregation

Following the work of Keeney (1976) and Dyer/Sarin (1979), a linear scheme is used to aggregate individual utility functions (1). The group utility function thus is given by:

$$U^g(X) = \sum_m \alpha_m \sum U^{(m)}(X) \tag{2}$$

where α_m is a voting power coefficient for member m.

3.3 Feedback

The aim of the individual calculations in the feedback phase is to bring the ranking induced by individual utility functions closer to the ranking generated by the group function. The two rankings are said to be in *c-agreement* if the first c programs in both rankings are identical. In order to achieve such an agreement, several modifications of the individual utility function (1) are possible:

- The partial utility functions $u_k(.)$ can be changed.

- The weights w_k can be changed.

- The group evaluation U^g can be included as an additional attribute.

GDSS-X supports all three types of changes, but is focused on the second and third types. Changes in the the partial utility functions can be performed using an interactive, graphic editor. For the second and third types of change, the system will provide suggestions of new weights (including a weight for the group ranking) that will make the individual ranking identical to the group ranking in the first c alternatives. The following bi-criterion linear programming model (Vetschera, 1990) is used to find solutions in which the change in weights $(\sum \delta_k^+)$ and the weight given to the group evaluation (w_g) are minimized.

$$
\begin{aligned}
&\text{minimize } \sum \delta_k^+ \\
&\text{minimize } w_g \\
&s.t. \\
&\sum_k [w_k(1 - w_g) + \delta_k^+ - \delta_k^-]u_k(x_{n,k}) + w_g u_{n,g} > \\
&\qquad \sum_k [w_k(1 - w_g) + \delta_k^+ - \delta_k^-]u_k(x_{n+1,k}) + w_g u_{n+1,g} \quad n = 1, \ldots, c-1 \\
&\sum_k [w_k(1 - w_g) + \delta_k^+ - \delta_k^-]u_k(x_{c,k}) + w_g u_{c,g} > \\
&\qquad \sum_k [w_k(1 - w_g) + \delta_k^+ - \delta_k^-]u_k(x_{n,k}) + w_g u_{n,g} \quad n = c+1, \ldots, N \\
&\sum_k \delta_k^+ + \sum_k \delta_k^- = 0 \\
&w_k(1 - w_g) + \delta_k^+ - \delta_k^- \geq 0 \qquad\qquad k \in K(m)
\end{aligned}
\tag{3}
$$

The suggestions provided to the user correspond to points on the efficient frontier with respect to the two objectives of the model.

4   Implementation

The system GDSS-X consists of three main programs. One program is used by the group administrator for setting up and maintaining conferences. The second program is used by group members and performs both the data specification and the modification phases. The third program performs all aggregation operations without user intervention. The system operates on a network of personal computers. Each member and the group administrator use dedicated computers, an additional computer is used to run the aggregation program. All programs provide a consistent user interface based on windows and pull-down menus.

All communication between programs is performed through shared data files. This makes the system independent of the network hardware and network operating system. The system is written entirely in TopSpeed Modula-2. It currently consists of 30 modules, containing a total of about 150 k Bytes of source code.

5   Extensions

Two possible developments concern theoretical aspects of GDSS-X. Currently, the system generates all efficient programs for evaluation by the group. This can lead to a large number of alternatives. In future versions of the system, a filtering process (Steuer/Harris, 1980; Abonyi, 1983) will be used to reduce that number.

The other area concerns the generation of proposals for changing weights. Currently, the proposals generated by the system correspond to points on an efficient trade-off curve between changing the weights of criteria the user is interested in and giving weight to the group opinion. For the user, it might also be interesting to generate points which are not minimal in the sense of those objectives, but structurally different from other proposals. If, for example, an efficient point consists in changing the weight of one attribute by a large amount, the user might be more willing to change several attributes by smaller amounts, even if the total change is greater. Such points can be generated by an extension of the HSJ-method (Brill et al., 1982).

Another important topic in a group decision support system is its integration in the communication system used by the group (Lewandowski, 1988). In the long run, a formal method for group decision support should be integrated into an office environment supporting electronic mail, document processing systems and other office automation components.

The current version of the system provides a theoretically founded implementation of a feedback-oriented approach to group decision support. The planned extensions will help to make the system more flexible and thus to correspond more closely to the mainstream of decision support systems, without eroding its theoretical basis.

References

Abonyi, G. (1983): Filtering: An Approach to Generating the Information Base For Collective Choice. *Management Science* 29: 409–418.

Brill, D., Chang, S., and Hopkins, L. (1982): Modeling to Generate Alternatives: The HSJ Approach and an Illustration Using a Problem in Land Use Planning. *Management Science* 28: 221–235.

Bui, T. and Jarke, M. (1986): Communications Design for Co-oP: A Group Decision Support System. *ACM Transactions on Office Information Systems* 4: 81–103.

DeSanctis, G. and Gallupe, R. (1987): A Foundation For the Study of Group Decision Support Systems. *Management Science* 33: 589–609.

Evans, G. (1984): An Overview of Techniques for Solving Multiobjective Mathematical Programs. *Management Science* 30: 1268–1282.

Fischer, G. (1979): Utility Models for Multiple Objective Decisions: Do They Accurately Represent Human Preferences? *Decision Sciences* 10: 451–479.

Gray, P. (1987): Group Decision Support Systems. *Decision Support Systems* 3: 233–242.

Jarke, M., Jelassi, T. and Shakun, M. (1987): MEDIATOR: Towards a Negotiation Support System. *European Journal of Operational Research* 31: 314–334.

Keeney, R. (1976): A Group Preference Axiomatization With Cardinal Utility. *Management Science* 23: 140–145.

Lewandowski, A. (1988): SCDAS - Decision Support System for Group Decision Making: Information Processing Issues. IIASA Working Paper WP-88-48. Laxenburg.

Lewandowski, A., Johnson, S. and Wierzbicki, A. (1987): A Prototype Selection Committee Decision Analysis and Support System, SCDAS: Theoretical Background and Computer Implementation. In: Y. Sawaragi, K. Inoue, H. Nakayama (eds.): Toward Interactive and Intelligent Decision Support Systems. Volume 2, Springer, Berlin: 358–365.

Steuer, R.; Harris, F. (1980): Intra-Set Point Generation and Filtering in Decision and Criterion Space. *Computers and Operations Research* 7: 41–53.

Vetschera, R. (1988): Unterstützung von Gruppenentscheidungen durch minimale Präferenzmodifikationen. In: H. Schellhaas et al. (eds.): Operations Research Proceedings 1987, Springer, Berlin: 217–224.

Vetschera, R. (1989): GDSS-X: An Experimental Group Decision Support System for Program Planning. Forschungsbericht 8901. Ludwig Boltzmann Institut für ökonomische Analysen, Vienna.

Vetschera, R. (1990): Integrating Databases and Preference Evaluations in Group Decision Support - A Feedback-Oriented Approach. *Decision Support Systems* 6: (forthcoming).

von Nitzsch, R. and Weber, M. (1986): Die verläßliche Bestimmung von Nutzenfunktionen. *Zeitschrift für betriebswirtschaftliche Forschung* 38: 844–862.

Negotiations and MCDM: their Interrelationships

Stanley Zionts
School of Management
State University of New York at Buffalo

Abstract

Some very old ideas of negotiations and multiple criteria decision making are considered. In spite of their age, the ideas are still relevant. The relationships between the two areas are developed, as are some related concepts. In both cases, it is desired to develop decision support systems that encourage and support the choice of "good" decisions and "good" results from negotiations.

1 Introduction

In this paper we consider multicriteria decision making and negotiations, explore their similarities, try to draw on those similarities, and look at some old ideas that seem to have relevance for today's models. We explore these ideas, and see where they lead. In part the motivation is that, at least in the field of management science and management in general, we often prefer to talk about new developments and new ideas, as if new were synonymous with superior. The study of history follows from learning from our (and other's) experiences. Why shouldn't we also learn from history? We begin with multicritera models, and then go to negotiations, and discuss the usefulness of these ideas.

2 Multiple criteria decision making

In multiple criteria decision making (MCDM), we normally assume a single decision maker who chooses among a number of alternatives. The alternatives may either comprise a discrete set of alternatives or they may be infinitely many (continuous or discrete). An example of the former kind of problem would be selecting a car to purchase from a set of available alternatives. An example of the latter kind of problem would be the design of a piece of electronic equipment, for which a continuum of parameter values are possible. This would have a continuous set of solutions with mathematical constraints limiting the space of alternatives. In either case the decision maker acts as if he were maximizing a utility or value function of his objectives, in turn, a function of his attributes. An infinite discrete set would be of the first type of problem, except that the number of alternatives would be infinitely many.

One of the basic concepts used in MCDM is that of dominance (or efficiency). One solution dominates another if it is at least as good as the second solution in all respects. See Figure 1 in which we assume that we are maximizing both objectives.

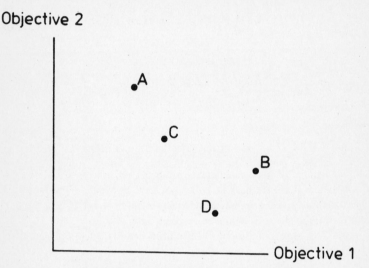

Figure 1: An ilustration of dominance

Point B dominates point D, and a blend of points A and B (roughly 50% of each) dominates point C. Point C is said to be convex dominated. (If the problem is discrete, then solutions can not be blended and convex dominated solutions are not dominated.) If our criteria completely capture the problem, we would only want to consider solutions that are not dominated by other solutions. We call such solutions nondominated or efficient solutions.

In most decision situations, time is an important variable. There is limited time for decision making. Often, the pressure of time can be severe, and the resulting decision may be the best possible in the available time. The decision maker should incorporate the cost of the time to make the decision in the analysis, and deduct the "cost" of the time used from the benefit of the decision, to the extent possible.

Just how is a decision reached? In an ideal environment, decision makers rationally consider all aspects of the problem, think through these aspects, and then come up with an "optimal" solution. In practice, because of the pressures of time as well as incomplete and incorrect information, lack of knowledge, there are all kinds of pressures on people making decisions. Further, there are generally differences of opinion among individuals, and these differences are often translated into concerns and/or conflicts that the decision maker must resolve. As a result, the resulting solutions may not be optimal at all. Further, reflecting some of these difficulties, and simplifying the process, many decisions are made by specifying constraints or aspiration levels, and then either accepting a solution that satisfies them, or choosing among solutions that satisfy the constraints. The aspirations are adjusted, in response to their reasonableness: if no alternatives satisfy them, they are relaxed; if too many alternatives satisfy them, they may be tightened. Simon (1958) calls this procedure satisficing.

Benjamin Franklin's Moral Algebra

In the eighteenth century, Benjamin Franklin developed what he called a moral or prudential algebra: "It was to Dr. (Joseph) Priestly that Franklin imparted the well-known expedient which he called moral or prudential algebra. Priestly asked him in one of his letters how he contrived to make up his mind, when strong and numerous arguments presented themselves for both of two proposed lines of conduct? 'My way is,' replied Franklin, 'to divide half a sheet of paper by a line into two columns; writing over the one pro, and over the other con; then, during three or four days' consideration, I put down under the different heads short hints of the different motives that at different times occur to me, for or against the measure. When I have thus got them all together in one view, I endeavor to estimate the respective weights...[to] find at length where the balance lies. (I)f, after a day or two of farther (sic) consideration, nothing new that is of importance occurs on either side, I come to a determination accordingly.' He added that he derived great help from equations of this kind; which, at least, rendered him less liable to take rash steps." (Parton, 1864) Franklin describes just how he finds the balance, by striking off reasons that balance each other.

Franklin's approach constitutes a way of balancing or trading off objectives against each other by cancelling one or more arguments in favor of a proposition against some number of arguments against the proposition. What is implied in Franklins's moral algebra is an additive utility function. There are no interactive terms.

Kepner and Tregoe's Approach

A well-known approach of Kepner and Tregoe (1965) includes categorizing each objective as a must, a want, or an ignore objective. The must objectives are used as filters for eliminating alternatives; the ignore objectives are sufficiently unimportant that they are ignored. The want objectives are used for making choices among the alternatives that have survived the filter process. Alternatives are compared, according to the objectives, and a solution is taken according to the following seven-step decision making procedure:

1. Establish objectives. They urge specificity and answering the questions what, how much, when, and where.

2. Classify objectives according to importance. They distinguish between the objectives as musts, wants, and ignores.

3. Develop alternatives from which to choose. The authors point out that some alternatives will be available initially, whereas others may have to be carefully and cleverly developed.

4. Evaluate the alternatives against the objectives to make a choice. The must objectives are used as a screen that filters out alternatives. A simple additive scoring system is suggested for completing the evaluation of alternatives.

5. Choose the best alternative as a tentative decision. This involves choosing the alternative with the highest weighted score. The user is advised to choose a "high ranking" solution.

6. Assess the adverse consequences of the tentative decision or decisions. Though not described in this way, this is a sensitivity analysis phase. The authors ask the question, "If we were to do this, then what would happen as a result? What could go wrong?" (ibid., p. 191) They also indicate other specific questions to ask of a solution.

7. Control effects of the final decision by preventing adverse consequences and by follow-up.

That this procedure has been widely used is attested to in the introduction of the Kepner and Tregoe book (ibid., p. 1): "This book needs no introduction to some 15,000 experienced managers who by 1965 had gone through the training programs developed by Drs. Kepner and Tregoe. ...(E)very one of these managers made the same startling discovery that his own private system for handling problems and decisions simply did not work very well and often did not work at all."

Kepner and Tregoe's work is an aspiration level method. It is effectively an implementation of Simon's concept of satisficing, but it uses an additive model for choosing among the better solutions. In their work, Kepner and Tregoe acknowledge Simon's contributions, "As a result of his (Simon's) research, he has independently come up with two of our basic concepts ... . (He) has come very close to what we hold to be the truth." (ibid., p. 252)

In some work (Lotfi et al., 1990) done initially without knowledge of the Kepner and Tregoe work, we use musts, wants, and ignores, not by objective, but for each objective. The must level constitutes a hard constraint on the objective that "must" be satisfied, no matter what. The want level is a level that is desired that can be traded off against other want levels. It is soft in the sense that it may or may not be achieved. The ignore level is one that, once surpassed, makes no difference. For example, in the search for a house, suppose that one of the criteria is proximity to shopping. Suppose that you specify the must level as *at most ten miles*, the want level as preferably *at most five miles*, and the ignore level as *at most two miles*. This means that any houses more than ten miles from shopping will be automatically eliminated. More effort will be given to finding houses that are at five miles or less from shopping, than reducing the distance to less than five miles. If the distance is two miles or less, the distance from shopping ceases to be a factor in the decision. By adjusting these levels, the user knows the closest solution to his want levels, and may choose from these as he wishes. Our approach is eclectic, in that it draws from a number of different approaches. We have a computer program of the procedure that is available for a nominal fee.

Dawes' Work on Linear Models

Robyn Dawes (1988) describes some fascinating research having to do with the predictive ability of linear models. Specifically, it has been found that, on average, linear models determined using regression analysis outperform expert judgment in a wide variety of tasks, ranging from predicting of students performances in academic programs to severity of Hodgkin's disease.

Dawes specifically addressed the question of the choice of the linear model: Did the linear model have to be derived statisticially? Dawes first studied using equal positive weights (unit weights) on a suitably scaled set of data (whereby each attribute had been scaled so that its mean is zero and its variance is one). He found here too that such a linear model outperformed expert judgments.

He did further work allowing the linear models to be completely random: the coefficients were drawn from statistical distributions. Even in this case the linear model outperformed expert judgments! He then made the inference that because both random and unit weights outperformed expert judgment, so then should intuitive weighting. This may be seen as a kind of validation of the Kepner-Tregoe use of additive models.

As interesting and as surprising as Dawes' work may seem, I would like to stress three caveats. First, all of the work that Dawes presents refers to the performance of linear models versus expert judgment, *on average*. That is, on average, a linear model outperforms expert judgment. That does not mean that expert judgment, or even certain experts cannot consistently outperform such linear models.

Secondly, if linear models outperform expert judgment on average, then it is reasonable that nonlinear models (which include linear models as a special case) would be expected to do at least as well as linear models, and also outperform expert judgment. So, there is nothing sacrosanct about linear models; they are simpler and easier to generate than nonlinear models.

The third argument is that there is a clear hierarchy among the linear models. By definition, the statistical regression analysis approach, appropriately used, should be the best approach. The second best approach should be using unit weights, and third should be random weights. (Dawes does acknowledge this.) Bringing in the first point, certainly there is a greater chance when using either unit weights or random weights for expert judgment to outperform a linear model. Though unit weights and random weights are all right on average, there is a rather clear hierarchy. First, if possible, a statistical linear model should be used. Second, if it is not possible, presumably because of a lack of data, then intuitive weighting for scaled data should be used. Finally, I believe unit weights or random weights should not be used. There is knowledge in the intuitive weighting that is not present in either the unit weight or random weight case.

3   Negotiation

Negotiation, as defined by Pruitt (1981), "is a process by which a joint decision is made by two or more parties." It usually involves each party presenting an initial position that they prefer most. Then the parties engage in what Raiffa (1982) defines as a negotiation dance, conceding from the initial point, until they reach a decision or not. Most negotiations progress in such a way that the parties are generally pleased to have the negotiations over once they have reached a decision. Accordingly, they normally do not want to engage in further negotiations on the matter. Though this may seem eminently reasonable, we will see situations in which additional negotiations may be desirable.

There is a concept in negotiations that is closely related to the concept of nondominance in MCDM. It is called Pareto-optimality. A solution is Pareto-optimal if and only if there does not exist another solution for which every party, in comparison to the solution in question, is at least as well off and at least one party is strictly better off. Pareto-optimal solutions are desirable in negotiations. If a solution is not Pareto-optimal, that means that one or more parties can negotiate gains at no cost to the other parties in the negotiations. Pareto-optimal solutions guarantee that all joint gains have been squeezed out, and no additional joint gains remain to be gleaned. An example of a set of solutions is given in Figure 2. The solutions that are possible are the solutions in the region bounded by the broken line O-B-C-E-F-O, and the Pareto-optimal solutions are along the broken line B-C-E-F.

In negotiations, to review the process graphically, each party begins at his initial position (party 1 at point F, and party 2 at point B) and then make concessions. In situations where there are more than two issues involved, there is a tendency for the parties to negotiate along the straight line between B and F, thereby completely missing the Pareto-optimal frontier. Such negotiations are referred to as distributive negotiations, in which the outcomes are zero-sum, and what one party wins, the other loses.

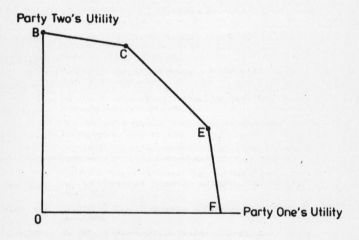

Figure 2: An illustration of Pareto optimality

Howard Raiffa (1982) favors an approach which I call the single negotiating text/win win approach. (See also Fisher and Ury, 1981.) It involves having the parties begin with a solution that is bad for all, such as point O in Figure 2. Then the parties search for joint gains, whereby they move from point O in steps up and to the right toward the Pareto-optimal frontier. The process continues until no further joint gains can be identified. Raiffa favors this process because the parties work jointly in identifying joint gains. Though it is usually difficult for them to accept the initial poor point (e.g., O) as a basis for proceeding, he believes that the process of identifying and agreeing to joint gains is helpful. The parties share in the success of generating and agreeing to joint gains, thereby making agreement on a solution by the parties easier.

An alternative way of representing the Pareto-optimal frontier is to use an Edgeworth box and contract curve. Edgeworth (1881) proposed a model that is useful for representing two-party, two-issue negotiations. For convenience, we assume that one party wants to maximize both objectives, and the other wants to minimize both objectives. We may then construct a graph for the two parties (see Figure 3) using the objectives as axes, so that at the origin (point 2) we have what party two regards as its best possible solution and what party one regards as its worst possible solution. At the appropriate point (point 1), we construct party one's best possible solution, the worst solution for party two. By reference to our example, the two points would be points B and F (corresponding to points 1 and 2, respectively).

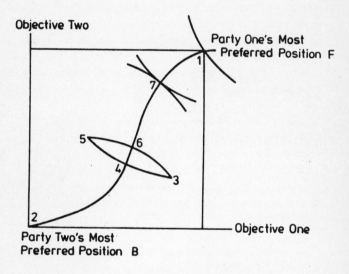

Figure 3: An Edgeworth box

Further, by superimposing curves of constant utility of both parties on the graph, we may construct the set of Pareto-optimal solutions. As a result, we have a construct known as an Edgeworth box. By constructing the locus of points where the curves of constant utility for each party are tangent to each other (special changes being made in the case of degeneracy, e.g., linearity or piecewise linearity), we have what is called the contract curve (the curve from 1 to 7 to 6 to 4 to 2). The contract curve is the locus of Pareto-optimal solutions to the negotiation. Though the Edgeworth box concept can be extended to higher dimensions, it has been almost exclusively used in two-party and two-objective (or issue) situations for obvious reasons. As a motivation as to how the

Edgeworth box works, consider a solution such as 3. Party one's utility at point 3 is on an isoutility curve going from 3 to 4 to 5, and increasing to the upper right. Party two's utility is on an isoutility curve going from 3 to 6 to 5 and increasing to the lower left. From point 3 both parties can improve their utilities, or achieve joint gains, by moving to an interior point of the region 3–4–5–6. The argument may be repeated until a point on the contract curve within the region has been reached. At such a point, the two isoutility curves will be tangent, and no further joint gains are possible. (See point 7, for example.)

How can we assure ourselves of a Pareto-optimal solution, at least from a theoretical perspective? If we know all of the relationships, and further if they involve maximizing a concave function subject to a set of constraints that constitute a convex set, it is possible to find Pareto-optimal solutions. One way to find a Pareto-optimal solution is to use a positive weight for each party, and to maximize the weighted sum of utilities. Different sets of weights generate different solutions, although in the case of linear objectives, more than one set of weights will usually generate the same solution. For two-party negotiations, the Pareto-optimal set is one-dimensional, and it is not difficult to construct, provided that we know the relationships. (We observe the one-dimensional nature of the two-party contract curve in both Figures 2 and 3.)

How can we achieve Pareto-optimal solutions in practice? That is not as easy. Let us assume that somehow or other we know which solutions are Pareto-optimal. We must then convince the parties that they would be better off by restricting their choice to Pareto-optimal solutions. Why must they be convinced? They may not be willing to limit themselves to Pareto-optimal solutions, however, because of concerns that their adversary may gain at their expense by such behavior, in spite of any assurances we may give.

Now, let us consider the more-likely reality in which we do not know which solutions are Pareto-optimal. Were our functions known, then we could at least try to use the procedure identified above, namely maximizing weighted sums of the parties' utilities to identify Pareto-optimal solutions. Different weighted sums give different Pareto-optimal solutions. Unfortunately, the functions are usually not known. In that case, we could, of course, try to use proxy functions or otherwise estimate the utility functions, (e.g., using the procedure of Keeney and Raiffa, 1976) hoping that any resulting solutions were Pareto-optimal.

Another way to identify Pareto-optimal solutions, both in two-party negotiations as well as in larger negotiations, is to determine the contract curve of the Edgeworth box. (With more than two parties, the procedure is complicated. With two parties, the contract curve is one dimensional; with three or more it is higher dimensional. In general, with q parties, the contract function (not necessarily a curve) has $q-1$ dimensions. Accordingly, we describe the procedure for only two parties.)

Jeffrey Teich, a Ph. D. student in the School of Management at the State University of New York at Buffalo, in work on his doctoral dissertation, has developed a way of approximating the contract curve. The idea is as follows: First, have the two parties determine their (reasonable) most desirable solution points. (Because of the gaming aspects of negotiations, they may think it desirable to exaggerate their desired position. Accordingly, having the parties indicate their most desirable solution is nontrivial also!) Such solution points would define a range on each issue. Then, partitioning the range on each issue (between their most desirable solution points) into four equal segments, determine three intermediate levels of each issue. For each level, use the Cartesian product of a corresponding pair of levels as an anchor point to construct a common "budget constraint" to be used by each party. Such a budget constraint is arbitrary initially, in that, for example, the sum of the levels of all issues might be whatever constant is determined by the anchor point.

Then each party is asked to determine his preferred point, subject to the "budget constraint". If the preferred points of the two parties are sufficiently close, then that point is assumed to be on the contract curve. Otherwise, the "budget constraint" prices are adjusted, so that the constraint still passes through the anchor point, using a search procedure in which convergence to a common point is guaranteed, subject to mild assumptions. Once the parties agree on a point on a suitably adjusted "budget constraint", then the process is repeated for each of the other anchor points. Three roughly equally spaced points on the contract curve together with the most preferred points of each party give us five points for fitting an approximate contract curve. (This procedure of fitting points is roughly the same as that used by Keeney and Raiffa (1976), for fitting utility functions.)

Teich has evaluated some assumed linear and nonlinear utility functions using this approach, and is applying it in his dissertation. His procedure for then determining a settlement of the negotiation is to have the parties negotiate along the contract curve to come up with a final agreement. An alternative way of using the contract curve would be to use it on a single negotiating text/win-win basis, by beginning with a suitably poor outcome for both parties, and then have them move toward the contract curve.

4 Implications and conclusions

The structuring of a decision situation is good, and hopefully such structure can help people make better decisions. Additive models are not unreasonable and they are useful in many situations, though they may not be as comprehensive as more elaborate models. Raiffa (1982) makes the point that a simple additive model may be preferable to a more comprehensive one, because of its ease of development and use, and its robustness. The use of a decision function and/or weights can help in the decision process. As one would expect, it will never be possible to have a decision calculus that will ever do more than help in the decision-making process, that is, to ask questions of the decision maker and to point out considerations.

How can we use such structure in negotiations? Though there has been some writing about negotiation support, the actual use of such models has involved only very simple ideas, which have worked well in practice. (See for example, Jelassi and Foroughi, 1989). The approaches used involve tabulating votes for a group and submitting ideas to the group, both usually anonymously.

A simple approach that seems to be of some value in negotiations is to use a simple MCDM procedure to determine what your party would like to do. Then make assumptions about the other parties' objectives and use such a procedure to determine what they would like to do. If this is consistent with their actions, then use this for future rounds of negotiations; otherwise revise your assumptions based on their revealed preferences and redetermine what you think they will do. Continue the procedure as appropriate.

What can we conclude from these deliberations? We should learn from those who have preceded us: old ideas may have merit. Second, simple ideas have merit, and should not be dismissed without further consideration. Finally, some of the new approaches have aspects that are drawn from the old and simple ideas.

References

Dawes, R. M. (1988). Rational Choice in an Uncertain World. New York, Harcourt Brace Jovanovich.

Edgeworth, F. Y. (1881). Mathematical Psychics. Kegan Paul, London.

Fisher, R. and Ury, W. (1981). Getting to Yes. Boston, Houghton Mifflin.

Jelassi, M. T. and Foroughi, A. (1989). Negotiation Support Systems. *Decision Support Systems*, **5**, pp. 1–15.

Keeney, R. L. and Raiffa, H. (1976). Decisions with Multiple Objectives, Preferences and Value Tradeoffs. New York, John Wiley.

Kepner, C. H. and Tregoe, B. B. (1965). The Rational Manager: A Systematic Approach to Problem Solving and Decision Making. New York, McGraw-Hill.

Lotfi, V., Stewart, T. J. and Zionts, S. (1990). An Aspiration-Level Interactive Model for Multiple Criteria Decision Making. Working Paper No. 711, School of Management, State University of New York at Buffalo, Revised May, 1990.

Parton, J. (1864). Life and Times of Benjamin Franklin. Vol. I, New York, Mason Brothers, p. 547.

Pruitt, D. (1981). Negotiation Behavior. New York, Academic Press.

Raiffa, H. (1982). The Art and Science of Negotiation. Cambridge, Harvard University Press.

Simon, H. A. (1958). Administrative Behavior. MacMillan, New York.

List of Participants

Mr. Carlos Antunes
Universidade de Coimbra
Faculdade de Ciencias e Technologia
Departemento de Engenbara Electrotecnia
3000 Coimbra
PORTUGAL

Prof. Ami Arbel
AT&T
100 South Jefferson Road
Whippany, NJ 07981
U.S.A.

Dr. Carlos Bana e Costa
IST/CESUR
Av. Rovisco Pais
1000 Lisbon
PORTUGAL

Prof. Joao Climaco
University of Coimbra
Dept. of Electrical Engineering
Largo Marques de Pombal
3000 Coimbra
PORTUGAL

Mr. Piotr Czyzak
Center for Education
and Development in Agriculture
Ul. Winogrady 61,
61-659 Poznan
POLAND

Mr. Bojil Dobrev
Institute for Information Technologies
Volov Street 2
Sofia
BULGARIA

Dr. Grzegorz Dobrowolski
Institute for Control
and Systems Engineering
Academy of Mining and Metallurgy
Al. Mickiewicza 30
30-059 Krakow
POLAND

Prof. Anthony Gear
Decision Dynamics, Ltd.
Parsons Walk
P.O. Box 142, Wigan
Lancashire WNI IRW
UNITED KINGDOM

Prof. Henryk Gorecki
Institute of Automatic Control
and Systems Engineering
Academy of Mining and Metallurgy
Al. Mickiewicza 30
30-059 Krakow
POLAND

Ms. Merja Halme
Helsinki School of Economics
Runeberginkatu 14-16
00100 Helsinki
FINLAND

Dr. Zsolt Harnos
University of Horticulture
Villanyi u. 31
H-1118 Budapest
HUNGARY

Prof. Tom Hemming
University of Stockholm
Dept. of Business Administration
10691 Stockholm
SWEDEN

Prof. Mordechai Henig
Tel-Aviv University
Recanati School of Business
Administration
Tel-Aviv 69978
ISRAEL

Prof. Marjam Van Herwijnen
Free University
Institute for Environmental Studies
P.O. Box 7161
1007 MC Amsterdam
THE NETHERLANDS

Prof. Raimo Hämäläinen
Helsinki University of Technology
Systems Analysis Laboratory
Otakaari 1 M
02150 Espoo
FINLAND

Prof. Valeri Irikov
Moscow Physics Technological Institute
Dept. Management and Applied Mathematics
Institusky Str. 9
Moscow
U.S.S.R.

Prof. Peri Iz
University of Baltimore
Information & Quantitative Science Dept.
1420 N. Charles Street
Baltimore, Maryland 21201-5779
U.S.A

Dr. Ron Janssen
Free University
Institute for Environmental Studies
P.O. Box 7161
1007 MC Amsterdam
THE NETHERLANDS

Prof. Tawfik Jelassi
INSEA
Boulevard de Constance
77305 Fontainebleau Cedex
FRANCE

Prof. Arno Jäger
Ruhr University Bochum
Dept. of Economics
Nussbaumweg 25,
D-4630 Bochum
F.R.G.

Prof. Birsen Karpak
Youngstown State University
Dept. of Management
Youngstown, Ohio 44555
U.S.A.

Prof. Gregory Kersten
Carleton University
School of Business
Ottawa - Ontario
CANADA K1S 5B6

Mr. Kamen Kolev
Bulgaria Industrial Association
134 Rakovski Street
BG-1000 Sofia
BULGARIA

Prof. Pekka Korhonen
Helsinki School of Economics
Runeberginkatu 14-16
00100 Helsinki
FINLAND

Mr. G. Kotkin
IIASA
(Young Summer Scientist, U.S.S.R.)
2361 Laxenburg
AUSTRIA

Dr. Tomasz Kreglewski
Warsaw University of Technology
Institute of Automatic Control
Ul. Nowowiejska 15/19
00-665 Warsaw
POLAND

Dr. Lech Krus
Institute of Systems Research
Dept. of Large Scale System Theory
Ul. Newelska 6
01-447 Warsaw
POLAND

Mr. Markku Kuula
IIASA
(Young Summer Scientist, FINLAND)
2361 Laxenburg
AUSTRIA

Dr. Murat Köksalan
Middle-East Technical University
Industrial Engineering Dept.
Ankara 06531
TURKEY

Dr. Andrzej and Dr. Anna Lewandowski
IIASA
2361 Laxenburg
AUSTRIA

Prof. Mikalas and Anna Luptacik
Technical University of Vienna
Institute for Econometrics,
Operations Research and System Theory
Argentinierstrasse 8/119
A-1040 Vienna
AUSTRIA

Dr. Marek Makowski
IIASA
2361 Laxenburg
AUSTRIA

Dr. Loreta Markova
Institute for Technology, Cybernetics
and Robotics
Acad. G. Bonchev Str., Bl. 2
1113 Sofia
BULGARIA

Prof. Benedetto Matarazzo
Universita di Catania
Instituto di Matematica
Facolta di Economia e Commercio
Corso Italia 55
95129 Catania
ITALY

Prof. Wojtek Michalowski
Carleton University
School of Business
Ottawa - Ontario
CANADA K1S 5B6

Ms. Kaisa Miettinen
University of Jyväskylä
Seminaarinkatu 15
40100 Jyväskylä 10
FINLAND

Prof. Herbert Moskowitz
Purdue University
School of Management
Krannert Graduate School of
Management
Krannert Bldg.
West Lafayette, Indiana 47907
U.S.A.

Prof. Hirotaka Nakayama
Konan University
Dept. of Applied Mathematics
Faculty of Sciences
Higashinada
Kobe 658
JAPAN

Mr. Victor Nitchev
Institute for Information Technologies
Volov St. 2
Sofia
BULGARIA

Prof. I. Nykowski
Central School of Planning and Statistics
Instytut Ekonometrii
Al. Niepodleglosci 162
02-544 Warszawa
POLAND

Prof. Anna Ostanello
Politecnico di Torino
Dipartimento di Automatica
e Informatica
Corso Duca degli Abruzzi 24
10129 Torino
ITALY

Prof. Vladimir and Natasha Ozernoy
California State University
School of Business and Economics
Hayward, California 94542
U.S.A.

Dr. Jerzy Paczynski
Warsaw University of Technology
Institute of Automatic Control
Ul. Nowowiejska 15/19
00-665 Warsaw
POLAND

Ms. Johanna Pajunen
Helsinki School of Economics
Runeberginkatu 14-16
00100 Helsinki
FINLAND

Dr. Peter Parizek
Institute of Applied Cybernetics
Hanulova 5A
844 16 Bratislava
CZECHOSLOVAKIA

Dr. Aleksei Petrovsky
VNIISI
Laboratory of Decision Support Systems
Prospect 60 Let Octyabria 9
117312 Moscow
U.S.S.R.

Mr. Martin Read
Decision Dynamics, Ltd.
Parsons Walk
P.O. Box 142, Wigan
Lancashire WNI IRW
UNITED KINGDOM

Dr. Sergei Rebrik
VNIISI
Laboratory of Decision Support Systems
Prospect 60 Let Octyabria 9
117312 Moscow
U.S.S.R.

Prof. Asim Roy
Arizona State University
College of Business
Dept. of Decision
and Information Systems
Tempe, Arizona 85287-4206
U.S.A.

Dr. Tomasz Rys
Institute of Automatic Control
and Systems Engineering
Academy of Mining and Metallurgy
Al. Mickiewicza 30
Krakow
POLAND

Mr. Pekka Salminen
University of Jyväskylä
Seminaarinkatu 15
40100 Jyväskylä 10
FINLAND

Mr. Ahti Salo
Helsinki University of Technology
Systems Analysis Laboratory
Otakaari 1 M
02150 Espoo
FINLAND

Prof. Seppo Salo
Helsinki School of Economics
Runeberginkatu 14-16
00100 Helsinki
FINLAND

Prof. Antonio Sforza
Universita di Salerno
Instituto di Fisica Mathematica e Informatics
Facolta di Ingegneria
84084 Fisciano
Salerno
ITALY

Dr. Gennadi Shepelev
VNIISI
Laboratory of Decision Support Systems
Prospect 60 Let Octyabria 9
117312 Moscow
U.S.S.R.

Prof. Bernard Sinclair-Desgagne
INSEA
Boulevard de Constance
77305 Fontainebleau Cedex
FRANCE

Prof. Roman Slowinski
Technical University of Poznan
Institute of Computer Sciences,
Control Engineering and Robotics
Ul. Piotrowo 3a
60-965 Poznan
POLAND

Dr. Czeslaw Smutnicki
Technical University of Wroclaw
Institute of Technical Cybernetics
Ul. Z. Janiszewskiego 11
50-372 Wroclaw
POLAND

Dr. Janusz Sosnowski
Institute of Systems Research
Polish Academy of Sciences
Ul. Newelska 6
01-447 Warsaw
POLAND

Prof. Grazia Speranza
Universita of Udine
Matematica e Informatica
Via Zanon 6
33100 Udine
ITALY

Prof. Jaap Spronk
Erasmus University
P.O. Box 1738
3000 DR Rotterdam
THE NETHERLANDS

Mr. Antonie Stam
IIASA
(Young Summer Scientist, U.S.A.)
2361 Laxenburg
AUSTRIA

Prof. Ivan Stanchev
National Committee for Applied Systems
Analysis and Management
Ekzarkh Iosif 37
BG-1100 Sofia
BULGARIA

Prof. Ralph Steuer
University of Georgia
College of Business Admistration
Brooks Hall
Athens, Georgia 30602
U.S.A.

Ms. Leena Tanner
Helsinki School of Economics
Runeberginkatu 14-16
00100 Helsinki
FINLAND

Prof. Felix Tarasenko
Tomsk State University
36 Lenin Ave.
Tomsk, 634050
U.S.S.R.

Mr. Jeffrey Teich
SUNY at Buffalo
School of Management
Dept. of Management Science
and Systems
Jacobs Management Center
Buffalo, New York 14260
U.S.A.

Prof. Luis Vargas
University of Pittsburgh
Graduate School of Business
314 Mervis Hall
Pittsburgh, PA 15260
U.S.A.

Dr. Rudolf Vetschera
University of Vienna
Institute for Business Management
Türkenstrasse 23/11
A-1090 Vienna
AUSTRIA

Ms. Hannele Wallenius
University of Jyväskylä
Seminaarinkatu 15
40100 Jyväskylä 10
FINLAND

Prof. Jyrki Wallenius
Helsinki School of Economics
Runeberginkatu 14-16
00100 Helsinki
FINLAND

Prof. Rusong Wang
Research Center for Eco-
Environmental Sciences
Academia Sinica
19 Zhongguancun Road
100080 Beijing
P.R. CHINA

Prof. Zhongtuo Wang
Dalian University of Technology
Institute of Systems Engineering
116024 Dalian
P.R. CHINA

Dr. Irena Yordanova
Institute for Technology, Cybernetics
and Robotics
Acad. G. Bonchev Str.,Bl.2
1113 Sofia
BULGARIA

Prof. Po-Lung Yu
University of Kansas
School of Business
Lawrence, Kansas 66045
U.S.A.

Prof. Maciej Zebrowski
Institute of Automatic Control
and Systems Engineering
Academy of Mining and Metallurgy
Al. Mickiewicza 30
Krakow
POLAND

Dr. Hákan Zetterström
Statistics Sweden
S-115 81 Stockholm
SWEDEN

Dr. Wieslaw Ziembla
Institute of Automatic Control
and Systems Engineering
Academy of Mining and Metallurgy
Al. Mickiewicza 30
Krakow
POLAND

Prof. Stanley Zionts
SUNY at Buffalo
School of Management
Dept. of Management Science
and Systems
Jacobs Management Center
Buffalo, New York 14260
U.S.A.

THE INTERNATIONAL INSTITUTE FOR APPLIED SYSTEMS ANALYSIS

is a nongovernmental research institution, bringing together scientists from around the world to work on problems of common concern. Situated in Laxenburg, Austria, IIASA was founded in October 1972 by the academies of science and equivalent organizations of twelve countries. Its founders gave IIASA a unique position outside national, disciplinary, and institutional boundaries so that it might take the broadest possible view in pursuing its objectives:

To promote international cooperation in solving problems arising from social, economic, technological, and environmental change

To create a network of institutions in the national member organization countries and elsewhere for joint scientific research

To develop and formalize systems analysis and the sciences contributing to it, and promote the use of analytical techniques needed to evaluate and address complex problems

To inform policy advisors and decision makers about the potential application of the Institute's work to such problems

The Institute now has national member organizations in the following countries:

Austria
The Austrian Academy of Sciences

Bulgaria
The National Committee for Applied Systems Analysis and Management

Canada
The Canadian Committee for IIASA

Czechoslovakia
The Committee for IIASA of the Czechoslovak Socialist Republic

Finland
The Finnish Committee for IIASA

France
The French Association for the Development of Systems Analysis

German Democratic Republic
The Academy of Sciences of the German Democratic Republic

Federal Republic of Germany
Association for the Advancement of IIASA

Hungary
The Hungarian Committee for Applied Systems Analysis

Italy
The National Research Council

Japan
The Japan Committee for IIASA

Netherlands
The Netherlands Organization for Scientific Research, NWO

Poland
The Polish Academy of Sciences

Sweden
The Swedish Council for Planning and Coordination of Research

Union of Soviet Socialist Republics
The Academy of Sciences of the Union of Soviet Socialist Republics

United States of America
The American Academy of Arts and Sciences

Vol. 261: Th. R. Gulledge, Jr., N. K. Womer, The Economics of Made-to-Order Production. VI, 134 pages. 1986.

Vol. 262: H. U. Buhl, A Neo-Classical Theory of Distribution and Wealth. V, 146 pages. 1986.

Vol. 263: M. Schäfer, Resource Extraction and Market Structure. XI, 154 pages. 1986.

Vol. 264: Models of Economic Dynamics. Proceedings, 1983. Edited by H. F. Sonnenschein. VII, 212 pages. 1986.

Vol. 265: Dynamic Games and Applications in Economics. Edited by T. Başar. IX, 288 pages. 1986.

Vol. 266: Multi-Stage Production Planning and Inventory Control. Edited by S. Axsäter, Ch. Schneeweiss and E. Silver. V, 264 pages. 1986.

Vol. 267: R. Bemelmans, The Capacity Aspect of Inventories. IX, 165 pages. 1986.

Vol. 268: V. Firchau, Information Evaluation in Capital Markets. VII, 103 pages. 1986.

Vol. 269: A. Borglin, H. Keiding, Optimality in Infinite Horizon Economies. VI, 180 pages. 1986.

Vol. 270: Technological Change, Employment and Spatial Dynamics. Proceedings 1985. Edited by P. Nijkamp. VII, 466 pages. 1986.

Vol. 271: C. Hildreth, The Cowles Commission in Chicago, 1939–1955. V, 176 pages. 1986.

Vol. 272: G. Clemenz, Credit Markets with Asymmetric Information. VIII, 212 pages. 1986.

Vol. 273: Large-Scale Modelling and Interactive Decision Analysis. Proceedings, 1985. Edited by G. Fandel, M. Grauer, A. Kurzhanski and A. P. Wierzbicki. VII, 363 pages. 1986.

Vol. 274: W. K. Klein Haneveld, Duality in Stochastic Linear and Dynamic Programming. VII, 295 pages. 1986.

Vol. 275: Competition, Instability, and Nonlinear Cycles. Proceedings, 1985. Edited by W. Semmler. XII, 340 pages. 1986.

Vol. 276: M. R. Baye, D. A. Black, Consumer Behavior, Cost of Living Measures, and the Income Tax. VII, 119 pages. 1986.

Vol. 277: Studies in Austrian Capital Theory, Investment and Time. Edited by M. Faber. VI, 317 pages. 1986.

Vol. 278: W. E. Diewert, The Measurement of the Economic Benefits of Infrastructure Services. V, 202 pages. 1986.

Vol. 279: H.-J. Büttler, G. Frei and B. Schips, Estimation of Disequilibrium Models. VI, 114 pages. 1986.

Vol. 280: H. T. Lau, Combinatorial Heuristic Algorithms with FORTRAN. VII, 126 pages. 1986.

Vol. 281: Ch.-L. Hwang, M.-J. Lin, Group Decision Making under Multiple Criteria. XI, 400 pages. 1987.

Vol. 282: K. Schittkowski, More Test Examples for Nonlinear Programming Codes. V, 261 pages. 1987.

Vol. 283: G. Gabisch, H.-W. Lorenz, Business Cycle Theory. VII, 229 pages. 1987.

Vol. 284: H. Lütkepohl, Forecasting Aggregated Vector ARMA Processes. X, 323 pages. 1987.

Vol. 285: Toward Interactive and Intelligent Decision Support Systems. Volume 1. Proceedings, 1986. Edited by Y. Sawaragi, K. Inoue and H. Nakayama. XII, 445 pages. 1987.

Vol. 286: Toward Interactive and Intelligent Decision Support Systems. Volume 2. Proceedings, 1986. Edited by Y. Sawaragi, K. Inoue and H. Nakayama. XII, 450 pages. 1987.

Vol. 287: Dynamical Systems. Proceedings, 1985. Edited by A. B. Kurzhanski and K. Sigmund. VI, 215 pages. 1987.

Vol. 288: G. D. Rudebusch, The Estimation of Macroeconomic Disequilibrium Models with Regime Classification Information. VII, 128 pages. 1987.

Vol. 289: B. R. Meijboom, Planning in Decentralized Firms. X, 168 pages. 1987.

Vol. 290: D. A. Carlson, A. Haurie, Infinite Horizon Optimal Control. XI, 254 pages. 1987.

Vol. 291: N. Takahashi, Design of Adaptive Organizations. VI, 140 pages. 1987.

Vol. 292: I. Tchijov, L. Tomaszewicz (Eds.), Input-Output Modeling. Proceedings, 1985. VI, 195 pages. 1987.

Vol. 293: D. Batten, J. Casti, B. Johansson (Eds.), Economic Evolution and Structural Adjustment. Proceedings, 1985. VI, 382 pages. 1987.

Vol. 294: J. Jahn, W. Krabs (Eds.), Recent Advances and Historical Development of Vector Optimization. VII, 405 pages. 1987.

Vol. 295: H. Meister, The Purification Problem for Constrained Games with Incomplete Information. X, 127 pages. 1987.

Vol. 296: A. Börsch-Supan, Econometric Analysis of Discrete Choice. VIII, 211 pages. 1987.

Vol. 297: V. Fedorov, H. Läuter (Eds.), Model-Oriented Data Analysis. Proceedings, 1987. VI, 239 pages. 1988.

Vol. 298: S. H. Chew, Q. Zheng, Integral Global Optimization. VII, 179 pages. 1988.

Vol. 299: K. Marti, Descent Directions and Efficient Solutions in Discretely Distributed Stochastic Programs. XIV, 178 pages. 1988.

Vol. 300: U. Derigs, Programming in Networks and Graphs. XI, 315 pages. 1988.

Vol. 301: J. Kacprzyk, M. Roubens (Eds.), Non-Conventional Preference Relations in Decision Making. VII, 155 pages. 1988.

Vol. 302: H. A. Eiselt, G. Pederzoli (Eds.), Advances in Optimization and Control. Proceedings, 1986. VIII, 372 pages. 1988.

Vol. 303: F. X. Diebold, Empirical Modeling of Exchange Rate Dynamics. VII, 143 pages. 1988.

Vol. 304: A. Kurzhanski, K. Neumann, D. Pallaschke (Eds.), Optimization, Parallel Processing and Applications. Proceedings, 1987. VI, 292 pages. 1988.

Vol. 305: G.-J. C. Th. van Schijndel, Dynamic Firm and Investor Behaviour under Progressive Personal Taxation. X, 215 pages. 1988.

Vol. 306: Ch. Klein, A Static Microeconomic Model of Pure Competition. VIII, 139 pages. 1988.

Vol. 307: T. K. Dijkstra (Ed.), On Model Uncertainty and its Statistical Implications. VII, 138 pages. 1988.

Vol. 308: J. R. Daduna, A. Wren (Eds.), Computer-Aided Transit Scheduling. VIII, 339 pages. 1988.

Vol. 309: G. Ricci, K. Velupillai (Eds.), Growth Cycles and Multisectoral Economics: the Goodwin Tradition. III, 126 pages. 1988.

Vol. 310: J. Kacprzyk, M. Fedrizzi (Eds.), Combining Fuzzy Imprecision with Probabilistic Uncertainty in Decision Making. IX, 399 pages. 1988.

Vol. 311: R. Färe, Fundamentals of Production Theory. IX, 163 pages. 1988.

Vol. 312: J. Krishnakumar, Estimation of Simultaneous Equation Models with Error Components Structure. X, 357 pages. 1988.

Vol. 313: W. Jammernegg, Sequential Binary Investment Decisions. VI, 156 pages. 1988.

Vol. 314: R. Tietz, W. Albers, R. Selten (Eds.), Bounded Rational Behavior in Experimental Games and Markets. VI, 368 pages. 1988.

Vol. 315: I. Orishimo, G. J. D. Hewings, P. Nijkamp (Eds.), Information Technology: Social and Spatial Perspectives. Proceedings, 1986. VI, 268 pages. 1988.

Vol. 316: R. L. Basmann, D. J. Slottje, K. Hayes, J. D. Johnson, D. J. Molina, The Generalized Fechner-Thurstone Direct Utility Function and Some of its Uses. VIII, 159 pages. 1988.

Vol. 317: L. Bianco, A. La Bella (Eds.), Freight Transport Planning and Logistics. Proceedings, 1987. X, 568 pages. 1988.

Vol. 318: T. Doup, Simplicial Algorithms on the Simplotope. VIII, 262 pages. 1988.

Vol. 319: D.T. Luc, Theory of Vector Optimization. VIII, 173 pages. 1989.

Vol. 320: D. van der Wijst, Financial Structure in Small Business. VII, 181 pages. 1989.

Vol. 321: M. Di Matteo, R.M. Goodwin, A. Vercelli (Eds.), Technological and Social Factors in Long Term Fluctuations. Proceedings. IX, 442 pages. 1989.

Vol. 322: T. Kollintzas (Ed.), The Rational Expectations Equilibrium Inventory Model. XI, 269 pages. 1989.

Vol. 323: M.B.M. de Koster, Capacity Oriented Analysis and Design of Production Systems. XII, 245 pages. 1989.

Vol. 324: I.M. Bomze, B.M. Pötscher, Game Theoretical Foundations of Evolutionary Stability. VI, 145 pages. 1989.

Vol. 325: P. Ferri, E. Greenberg, The Labor Market and Business Cycle Theories. X, 183 pages. 1989.

Vol. 326: Ch. Sauer, Alternative Theories of Output, Unemployment, and Inflation in Germany: 1960–1985. XIII, 206 pages. 1989.

Vol. 327: M. Tawada, Production Structure and International Trade. V, 132 pages. 1989.

Vol. 328: W. Güth, B. Kalkofen, Unique Solutions for Strategic Games. VII, 200 pages. 1989.

Vol. 329: G. Tillmann, Equity, Incentives, and Taxation. VI, 132 pages. 1989.

Vol. 330: P.M. Kort, Optimal Dynamic Investment Policies of a Value Maximizing Firm. VII, 185 pages. 1989.

Vol. 331: A. Lewandowski, A.P. Wierzbicki (Eds.), Aspiration Based Decision Support Systems. X, 400 pages. 1989.

Vol. 332: T.R. Gulledge, Jr., L.A. Litteral (Eds.), Cost Analysis Applications of Economics and Operations Research. Proceedings. VII, 422 pages. 1989.

Vol. 333: N. Dellaert, Production to Order. VII, 158 pages. 1989.

Vol. 334: H.-W. Lorenz, Nonlinear Dynamical Economics and Chaotic Motion. XI, 248 pages. 1989.

Vol. 335: A.G. Lockett, G. Islei (Eds.), Improving Decision Making in Organisations. Proceedings. IX, 606 pages. 1989.

Vol. 336: T. Puu, Nonlinear Economic Dynamics. VII, 119 pages. 1989.

Vol. 337: A. Lewandowski, I. Stanchev (Eds.), Methodology and Software for Interactive Decision Support. VIII, 309 pages. 1989.

Vol. 338: J.K. Ho, R.P. Sundarraj, DECOMP: an Implementation of Dantzig-Wolfe Decomposition for Linear Programming. VI, 206 pages. 1989.

Vol. 339: J. Terceiro Lomba, Estimation of Dynamic Econometric Models with Errors in Variables. VIII, 116 pages. 1990.

Vol. 340: T. Vasko, R. Ayres, L. Fontvieille (Eds.), Life Cycles and Long Waves. XIV, 293 pages. 1990.

Vol. 341: G.R. Uhlich, Descriptive Theories of Bargaining. IX, 165 pages. 1990.

Vol. 342: K. Okuguchi, F. Szidarovszky, The Theory of Oligopoly with Multi-Product Firms. V, 167 pages. 1990.

Vol. 343: C. Chiarella, The Elements of a Nonlinear Theory of Economic Dynamics. IX, 149 pages. 1990.

Vol. 344: K. Neumann, Stochastic Project Networks. XI, 237 pages. 1990.

Vol. 345: A. Cambini, E. Castagnoli, L. Martein, P. Mazzoleni, S. Schaible (Eds.), Generalized Convexity and Fractional Programming with Economic Applications. Proceedings, 1988. VII, 361 pages. 1990.

Vol. 346: R. von Randow (Ed.), Integer Programming and Related Areas. A Classified Bibliography 1984–1987. XIII, 514 pages. 1990.

Vol. 347: D. Rios Insua, Sensitivity Analysis in Multi-objective Decision Making. XI, 193 pages. 1990.

Vol. 348: H. Störmer, Binary Functions and their Applications. VIII, 151 pages. 1990.

Vol. 349: G.A. Pfann, Dynamic Modelling of Stochastic Demand for Manufacturing Employment. VI, 158 pages. 1990.

Vol. 350: W.-B. Zhang, Economic Dynamics. X, 232 pages. 1990.

Vol. 351: A. Lewandowski, V. Volkovich (Eds.), Multiobjective Problems of Mathematical Programming. Proceedings, 1988. VII, 315 pages. 1991.

Vol. 352: O. van Hilten, Optimal Firm Behaviour in the Context of Technological Progress and a Business Cycle. XII, 229 pages. 1991.

Vol. 353: G. Ricci (Ed.), Decision Processes in Economics. Proceedings, 1989. III, 209 pages. 1991.

Vol. 354: M. Ivaldi, A Structural Analysis of Expectation Formation. XII, 230 pages. 1991.

Vol. 355: M. Salomon, Deterministic Lotsizing Models for Production Planning. VII, 158 pages. 1991.

Vol. 356: P. Korhonen, A. Lewandowski, J. Wallenius (Eds.), Multiple Criteria Decision Support. Proceedings, 1989. XII, 393 pages. 1991.